ELDERS' VERSES

II

THERĪGĀTHĀ

2nd edition

Pali Text Society

ELDERS' VERSES
II
THERĪGĀTHĀ

2nd edition

Translated
with an introduction and notes
by

K.R. Norman

Published by
The Pali Text Society
Bristol
2015

First published	1971
Reprinted	1992
Reprinted	1995
2nd edition	2007
Reprinted	2015

ISBN-10 0-86013-031-2
ISBN-13 9780-86013-031-4

Printed and bound by CPI Group (UK) Ltd, Croydon, CRO 4YY

Contents

Preface to the Second Edition

Elders' Verses II (= EV II) was published in 1971, and the notes were written a year or more before that date. Since then I have learned a little more about MIA, and I have changed my mind about a number of explanations and comments I gave in the notes. There was also a number of misprints which needed correction.

The translation is a revised version of *Poems of Early Buddhist Nuns* (PEBN (1989)), which was a slightly revised version of EV II, designed to appeal to a class of readership for whom the style of English I normally use in my translations was unlikely to prove attractive. I have retained the PEBN style in this revision but I have at the same time made a number of changes in the translation, reflecting suggestions made by reviewers and readers and my own belief that some points in my earlier translation were incorrect or could be improved. I have, in particular, profitted from comments made by a reader in Sri Lanka, who wishes to remain anonymous.

In the notes to the first edition I spent much time trying to improve Müller's text of Thī-a (1893). I now use Pruitt 1998A, unless otherwise specified. Some readers have regretted the fact that I did not give any translation for the frequent quotations I made from Thī-a. That omission has now been met by Pruitt 1998B, where the circumstances in which the therīs uttered their verses can now be seen.

There are changes and additions in the notes, arising in part from the changes in translation, references to publications which have appeared since 1971 (including GD and WD where appropriate), and changes in my views about the way in which things should be explained.

K.R. Norman
Shepreth
June, 2007

PREFACE TO THE FIRST EDITION

All that I wrote in the preface to Elders' Verses I to justify a new translation of Th applies even more to a new translation of Thī. Mrs Rhys Davids' translation of Thī was earlier (1909) than her translation of Th and was based upon a text which the editor confessed was not quite satisfactory (P, p. 120). Pischel relied upon a ms of the unpublished Thī-a, without which, he stated, he would hardly have ventured to publish the text at all. An edition of Thī-a, which the editor claimed (M, p. vii) eliminated some of Pischel's errors, was published by the PTS in 1893, but even that edition, as Stede noted (p. 31), has many discrepancies of readings on nearly every page. Both editions were based upon inadequate mss, and any improvements which can be made to Mrs Rhys Davids' translation stem mainly from the improvements to the text which can be made by reference to the oriental editions of Thī and Thī-a which have appeared in the last sixty years.

In presenting this translation I am happy to acknowledge my debt to Miss I.B. Horner, who not only lent me B[e] of Thī and Thī-a but also read through the whole of the first draft of the translation and notes and made then and subsequently in correspondence many valuable suggestions. I have inserted the initials [IBH] into the notes to show where I owe information to her. Mr L.S. Cousins, lecturer in Comparative Religion in the University of Manchester, has provided me with extracts from the unpublished *ṭīkā* on the Saṃyutta-nikāya, and this is duly shown by the insertion of the initials [LSC]. I am grateful to Dr W.B. Bollée, who kindly lent me K[e] of Thī, and whose suggestions for **252–70** acted as a help and an encouragement.

I have found the publications of two other scholars to be very helpful: Professor Alsdorf's reconstruction of the *āryā* stanzas of Thī (App. II) has relieved me of the task of re-editing those verses myself, and Professor Warder's *Pali Metre* and the dating of the metrical portions of the Pāli canon which it contains have greatly eased my task of attempting to date Thī.

K.R. Norman
Cambridge
June, 1970

BIBLIOGRAPHY

(This bibliography contains only those works which are referred to in the introduction and notes. Where two or more of an author's works are listed, they are distinguished in references by the addition of the year of publication.)

Alsdorf, L., 1936, "Vasudevahiṇḍi: a specimen of archaic Jaina Mahārāṣṭrī", *BSOS* VIII, pp. 319–33

———, 1958, "Itthīpariṇṇā", *IIJ* II, pp. 249–70

———, 1965, *Les études jaina: état présent et taches futures*, Paris

———, 1966, Thera-Therī-gāthā, Appendix II, PTS London

———, 1968, *Die Āryā-Strophen des Pali-Kanons*, Mainz

Andersen, D., 1901, *Pali Reader*, Copenhagen

———, 1907, *Pali Glossary*, Copenhagen

Bailey, Sir Harold W., 1952, "Kusanica", *BSOAS* XIV, pp. 420–34

———, 1954, "Analects Indoscythica II", *JRAS*, pp. 26–34

———, 1979, *Dictionary of Khotan Saka*, Cambridge

Bentley, R. & Trimen, H., 1880, *Medicinal Plants*, Vol. IV, London

Bernhard, F., 1965, Udānavarga, Vol. I, Göttingen

———, 1968, Udānavarga, Vol. II, Göttingen

Bollée, W.B., 1969, Review of Thera-Therī-gāthā, second edition (*IIJ* XI, pp. 146–49)

———, 1970, Kuṇālajātaka, *SBB* 26, London

———, 1973, rev. of EV II, *JAOS* 93, 4, pp. 601–3

———, 1983, *Reverse Index of the Dhammapada, Suttanipāta, Thera- and Therīgāthā pādas*, Reinbek

Brough, J., 1953, *Early Brahmanical system of Gotra and Pravara*, Cambridge

———, 1962, *Gāndhārī Dharmapada*, London

Brown, W. Norman, 1962, *The Vasanta Vilāśa*, New Haven (= American Oriental Series 46)

Buddhadatta Mahathera, A.P., 1957, *Corrections of Geiger's Mahāvaṃsa*, etc., Ceylon

Burrow, T., 1937, *Language of the Kharoṣṭhī Documents from Chinese Turkestan*, Cambridge

———, 1947–48, "Dravidian Studies VII", *BSOAS* XII, pp. 365–96

———, 1955, *Sanskrit Language*, London

———, 1956, "Sanskrit Lubh- 'To disturb' ", *JRAS*, pp. 191–200

———, 1967, Review of CDIAL, Fasc. II–XI, *JRAS*, pp. 39–42

———, 1979, *The Problem of Shwa in Sanskrit*, Oxford

Burrow, T. & Emeneau, M.B., 1961, *Dravidian Etymological Dictionary*, Oxford

———, 1968, *DED: Supplement*, Oxford

Chakravarti, N.P., 1930, *L'Udānavarga sanskrit*, Paris

Chalmers, Lord, 1932, *Buddha's Teachings* (translation of Sn), Harvard

Charpentier, J., 1922, Uttarādhyayanasūtra, Uppsala

Chatterji, S. K. & Sen, S., 1957, *Middle Indo-Aryan Reader*, Calcutta
Childers, R.C., 1874, *A Dictionary of the Pāli Language*, London
Chopra, T.R., 1966, *The Kuśa-Jātaka*, Hamburg
Cone, M., 2001, *A Dictionary of Pāli*, Vol. I, PTS Oxford
Cowell, E.B. & Neil, R.A., 1886, Divyāvadāna, Cambridge
Edgerton, F., 1953A, *Buddhist Hybrid Sanskrit Dictionary*, New Haven
———, 1953B, *Buddhist Hybrid Sanskrit Grammar*, New Haven
Emeneau, M.B. (see also Burrow, T.), 1931, "Confusion in Prakrit between the Sanskrit prepositions *prati* and *pari*", *JAOS* 51, pp. 33–39
Fausbøll, V., 1855, Dhammapada, Copenhagen
———, 1900, Dhammapada (second edition), Copenhagen
Filliozat, J., 1949, "Les Deva d'Asoka: 'Dieux' ou 'Divines majestés' ?", *JA* 237, pp. 225–47
Geiger, W., 1908, Mahāvaṃsa, PTS London
———, 1912, *The Mahāvaṃsa* (translated into English), Colombo
———, 1916, *Pāli Literatur und Sprache*, Strassburg
———, 1943, *Pāli Literature and Language* (= English edition of 1916), Calcutta
———, 1994, *Pāli Grammar* (= revised version of 1943), PTS Oxford
———, 2000, *Pāli Grammar* (= corrected reprint of 1994), PTS Oxford
Gombrich, R.F., 1974, rev. of EV II, *BSOAS* 37, 3, pp. 703–5
Haebler, C., 1964, "Ein verkanntes Kompositum im Pali", *MSS* 16, pp. 21–31
Hara, M., 1996A, "Ānṛṇya", *Langue, style et structure dans le monde indien (Centenaire de Louis Renou)*, Paris, pp. 235–61
———, 1996B, "Bhart?-piṇḍa-niṣkraya — the Hindu concept of loyalty to the kings", *Bulletin of the Deccan College Post-Graduate and Research Institute (Sir William Jones' Bicentenary of Death Commemoration volume)*, Volumes 54–55, 1994–1995, pp. 299–311
Hardy, E., 1902, Netti-pakaraṇa, PTS London
Hare, E.M., 1934–35, *Gradual Sayings* (translation of A), volumes III–IV, PTS London
Hendriksen, H., 1944, *Syntax of the Infinitive Verb-forms of Pāli*, Copenhagen
Hinüber, O. von, 1986, *Das ältere Mittelindisch im Überblick*, Vienna
———, 1994, *Selected Papers*, PTS Oxford
———, 2001, *Das ältere Mittelindisch im Überblick*, second edition, Vienna
Hinüber, O. von, and Norman, K.R., 1994, Dhammapada, PTS Oxford
Horner, Miss I.B., 1938–67, *Book of the Discipline* (translation of Vin), 6 volumes, SBB London
———, 1954–59, *Middle Length Sayings* (translation of M), 3 volumes, PTS London
———, 1963–64, *Milinda's Questions* (translation of Mil), 2 volumes, SBB London
Hultzsch, E., 1925, CII, Volume I (new edition), *Inscriptions of Asoka*, Oxford
Jacobi, H., 1879, *The Kalpasūtra of Bhadrabāhu*, Leipzig
———, 1884, *Jaina Sūtras* (Part I), SBE XXII, Oxford
———, 1886, *Ausgewählte Erzählungen in Māhārāṣṭrī*, Leipzig
———, 1895, *Jaina Sūtras* (Part II), SBE XLV, Oxford

Jones, J.J., 1949–56, *The Mahāvastu* (translated into English), 3 volumes, SBB London

Jong, J.W. de, 1972, rev. of EV I, *IIJ* XIII, pp. 297–301

Kern, H., 1916A, "Toevoegselen I", *VKAWA* 16,4, pp. 1–179

———, 1916B, "Toevoegselen II", *VKAWA* 16,5, pp. 1–140

——— 1928, *Verspreide Geschriften*, 15 volumes, The Hague

Konow, S., 1901, Karpūramañjarī, Harvard

Kuiper, F.B.J., 1948, *Proto-Munda words in Sanskrit*, Amsterdam

Lamotte, É., 1958, *Histoire du Bouddhisme indien*, Volume I, Louvain

La Vallée Poussin, L. de, 1923–31, *L'Abhidharmakośa de Vasubandhu*, 6 volumes, Paris

Lehot, M., 1933, Harṣa : Ratnāvalī, Paris

Leumann, E., 1883, Das Aupapātika Sūtra, Leipzig

Lévi, S., 1932, Mahākarmavibhaṅga et Karmavibhaṅgopadeśa, Paris

Lüders, H., 1940, *Philologica Indica*, Göttingen

———, 1954, *Beobachtungen über die Sprache des buddhistischen Urkanons*, Berlin

Macdonnell, A.A., 1927, *A Sanskrit Grammar for Students* (third edition), Oxford

Macdonnell, A.A. & Keith, A.B., 1912, *Vedic Index of Names and Subjects*, 2 volumes, London

Malalasekera, G.P., 1937–38, *Dictionary of Pali Proper Names*, 2 volumes, London

Mayrhofer, M., 1956–80, *Kurzgefasstes etymologisches Wörterbuch des Altindischen*, Heidelberg

Meile, P., 1949, "*Misa devehi* chez Asoka", *JA* 237, pp. 193–223

Mehendale, M., 1955–56A, Review of Lüders 1954, *BDCRI* 17, pp. 53–75

———, 1955–56B, "Some remarks on the language of the original Buddhist canon", *BDCRI* 17, pp. 157–71

Minayeff, J., 1886, "Anāgatavaṃsa", *JPTS* 1886, pp. 33–53

Monier-Williams, Sir Monier, 1899, *Sanskrit-English Dictionary*, new edition, Oxford

Moore, J.H., 1908, "Metrical Analysis of the Pāli Itivuttaka", *JAOS* 28, pp. 317–30

Morris, Rev. R., 1884, "Notes and queries", *JPTS* 1884, pp. 69–108

———, 1886, "Notes and queries", *JPTS* 1886, pp. 94–160

———, 1891–93, "Notes and queries", *JPTS* 1891–93, pp. 1–75

Müller, E., 1893, Paramatthadīpanī, PTS London

Ñāṇamoli, Bhikkhu, 1956, *Path of Purification* (translation of Vism), Colombo

———, 1960, *Minor Readings and Illustrator* (translation of Khp and Khp-a), PTS London

———, 1994, *A Pali-English Glossary of Buddhist Technical Terms*, Kandy

Neil, R.A. (see Cowell, E.)

Neumann, K.E., 1899, *Lieder der Mönche und Nonnen*, Berlin

Norman, H.C., 1906–14, Dhammapada-aṭṭhakathā, 4 volumes, PTS London

Norman, K.R. (see also Rhys Davids, Mrs C.A.F.), 1958A, "Samprasāraṇa in MIA", *JRAS*, pp. 44–50 (= *CP* I, pp. 1–8)

———, 1958B, "Some absolutive forms in Ardha-Māgadhī", *IIJ* II, pp. 311–15 (= *CP* I, pp. 9–14)

———, 1962, "Middle Indo-Aryan Studies III", (*JOI*(B) XI, pp. 322–27 (= *CP* I, pp. 15–20)
———, 1964, Review of W. Norman Brown 1962, *JRAS*, p. 67
———, 1966, Thera-Therī-gāthā, Appendix I, PTS London
———, 1967, "Notes on the Aśokan Rock Edicts", *IIJ* X, pp. 160–70 (= *CP* I, pp. 47–58)
———, 1969, *Elders' Verses* I (Theragāthā), PTS London (see 2007B below)
———, 1970, "Some aspcts of the phonology of the Prakrit underlying the Aśokan inscriptions", *BSOAS* XXXIII, pp. 132–43 (= *CP* I, pp. 93–107)
———, 1971A, *Elders' Verses* II (Therīgāthā), PTS London
———, 1971B, "Notes on the GDhp", *Ind. Ling.* 32, pp. 213–20 (= *CP* I, pp. 113–21)
———, 1972, "Middle Indo-Aryan Studies IX: The blind turtle and the hole in the yoke", *JOI*(B), XXI, pp. 331–35 (= *CP* I, pp. 156–60)
———, 1980, review of Bailey 1979, *Modern Asian Studies* 14, pp. 700–3
———, 1981, review of Bollée 1977, *WZKS* XXV, pp. 195–203 (= *CP* VI, pp. 171–8)
———, 1987, "Pāli Lexicographical Studies IV", *JPTS* XI, pp. 33–49 (= *CP* III, pp. 157–72)
———, 1988, "An aspect of external sandhi in Pāli", *Buddhist Studies* (Bukkyō Kenkyū), XVII, pp. 89–95 (= *CP* III, pp. 219–24)
———, 1989, "Pāli Lexicographical Studies VI", *JPTS* XIII, pp. 219–27 (= *CP* IV, pp. 72–79)
———, 1990–2007, *Collected Papers* I–VIII, PTS Oxford & Lancaster
———, 1992, *The Group of Discourses* (Sutta-nipāta), Part II, PTS Oxford
———, 1993, "External sandhi in Pāli", *JPTS* XIX, pp. 203–13 (= *CP* V, pp. 169–79)
———, 1994A, "Mistaken ideas about nibbāna", *Buddhist Forum* III, pp. 211–25 (= *CP* VI, pp. 9–30)
———, 1994B, "Pāli Lexicographical Studies XII", *JPTS* XX, pp. 211–30 (= *CP* VI, pp. 47–67)
———, 1997A, *Poems of Early Buddhist Monks* (Theragāthā), PTS Oxford
———, 1997B, *The Word of the Doctrine* (Dhammapada), PTS Oxford
———, 1999, "The Elders' Verses" (review article), *Acta Orientalia*, 60, pp. 191–205
———, 2000, "Pāli *anaṇa* — 'free from debt'", *Harānandalaharī* (Festschrift for Minoru Hara), Reinbek, pp. 161–74 (= *CP* VIII, pp. 80–95)
———, 2001A, *Collected Papers* VII, PTS Oxford
———, 2001B, *The Group of Discourses* (Sutta-nipāta), second edition, PTS Oxford
———, 2007A, *Collected Papers* VIII, PTS Lancaster
———, 2007B, *Elders' Verses* I, 2nd ed. PTS, Lancaster
Nyanatiloka, 1950, *Buddhist Dictionary*, Colombo
Oldenberg, H. (see also Rhys Davids, T.W.), 1883, Theragāthā, PTS London
Phūlchandjī Mahārāj, 1953–54, *Suttāgame*, 2 volumes, Gurgaon
Pischel, R., 1883, Therīgāthā, PTS London
———, 1900, *Grammatik der Prakrit-Sprachen*, Strassburg
———, 1957, *Comparative Grammar of the Prakrit Languages* (= English translation of 1900), Benares

Pruitt, W., 1998A, Therīgāthā-aṭṭhakathā, PTS Oxford

——— 1998B, *The Commentary on the Verses of the Therīs* (= trsl of 1998A), PTS Oxford

Rhys Davids, Mrs C.A.F., 1909, *Psalms of the Sisters* (translation of Thī), PTS London

———, 1913, *Psalms of the Brethren* (translation of Th), PTS London

———, 1917–22, *Kindred Sayings* (translation of S), volumes I and II, PTS London

———, 1920–21, Visuddhimagga, 2 volumes, PTS London

Rhys Davids, Mrs C.A.F., & Norman, K.R., 1989, *Poems of Early Buddhist Nuns*, PTS Oxford

Rhys Davids, T.W., 1890, *The Questions of King Milinda* (translation of Mil), 2 volumes, SBE XXXV, XXXVI, Oxford

———, 1899–1921, *Dialogues of the Buddha* (translation of D), 3 volumes, SBB London

Rhys Davids, T.W. and Oldenberg, H., 1881–85, *Vinaya Texts*, 3 volumes, SBE XIII, XVII, XX, Oxford

Schubring, W., 1910, Ācārāṅgasūtra, Leipzig

Schwarzschild, L.A., 1961, "The indeclinable *je* in Middle Indo-Aryan", *Bhāratīya Vidyā*, XX–XXII, pp. 211–17 (= 1991, pp. 104–10)

———, 1991, *Collected Articles of L.A. Schwarzschild on Indo-Aryan* 1953–1979, Australian National University, Canberra

Sen, S. (see also Chatterji, S.K.), 1953, *Historical Syntax of Middle Indo-Aryan*, Calcutta

Senart, E., 1882–97, Mahāvastu, 3 volumes, Paris

Sheth, H.D.T., 1963, Pāia-sadda-mahaṇṇavo, second edition, Benares

Simon, R., 1890, "Der Śloka im Pali", *ZDMG* 44, pp. 83–97

Smith, H., 1949, Saddanīti, Volume IV, Lund

Speyer, J.S., 1886, *Sanskrit Syntax*, Leyden

———, 1906–9, Avadāna-śataka, 2 volumes, St Petersburg

Stede, W., 1924–27, "The Pādas of Thera- and Therī-gāthā", *JPTS* 1924–27, pp. 31–226

Trenckner, V., 1880, Milindapañha, London

Trimen, H. (see Bentley, R.)

Turner, Sir Ralph L., 1966, *A Comparative Dictionary of the Indo-Aryan languages*, London

———, 1970, "Early shortening of geminates with compensatory lengthening in Indo-Aryan", *BSOAS* XXXIII, pp. 171–78

Waldschmidt, E., 1970, "Buddha frees the disc of the moon", *BSOAS* XXXIII, pp. 171–78

Warder, A. K., 1967, *Pali Metre*, PTS London

Wayman, A., 1969, Review of R.E. Emmerick: *Book of Zambasta* (*JAS* XXIX, pp. 151–52)

Windisch, E., 1895, *Māra und Buddha*, Leipzig

Winternitz, M., 1933, *History of Indian Literature*, Volume II, Calcutta

Woodward, F.L., 1924–30, *Kindred Sayings* (translation of S), volumes III–V, PTS London

———, 1929–37, Sārattha-ppakāsinī, 3 volumes, PTS London

———, 1932–36, *Gradual Sayings* (translation of A), volumes I–II, V, PTS London

———, 1940–59, Paramattha-dīpanī Theragāthā-aṭṭhakathā, 3 volumes, PTS London

Wright, J.C., 1999, "Old Wives' Tales in Therīgāthā: A Review Article", *BSOAS* 62, pp. 519-28

Yamanaka, Yukio, 1997, " 'Tamokkhando padālito' as a stock phrase in the Theragāthā and the Therīgāthā", *Buddhist Studies* (*Bukkyō Kenkyū*), Vol. XXVI, March 1997, pp. 195–216 (in Japanese)

ABBREVIATIONS

Editions of Therīgāthā:

P	Pischel, 1883
B^e	Chaṭṭhasaṅgāyana, third edition, Rangoon, 1961
C^e	Text of Thī included in Paramatthadīpanī, ed. Bihalpola Siri Dewarakkhita Thera, Colombo, 1918 (Simon Hewavitarne Bequest Series)
K^e	Cambodian edition, Phnom Penh, 1958
N^e	Text of Thī included in Nālandā Devanāgarī Pāli Series, Khuddaka-nikāya Vol. II, 1959
S^e	Second Siamese edition, Bangkok, 1926–28
O	Oldenberg, 1883
App. I	First appendix to second edition of O, 1966
App. II	Second appendix to second edition of O, 1966

Editions of Therīgāthā-aṭṭhakathā:

M	Paramatthadīpanī (= E. Müller 1893)
WP	Therīgāthā-aṭṭhakathā (Paramatthadīpanī VI) (= W. Pruitt 1998A)
B^e	Chaṭṭhasaṅgāyana edition, Rangoon, 1959
C^e	Paramatthadīpanī, ed. Bihalpola Siri Dewarakkhita Thera, Colombo, 1918 (Simon Hewavitarne Bequest Series)
Thī-a	text as given in WP

Texts:

Abh	Abhidhāna-ppadīpikā (= W. Subhūti 1883)
Divy	Divyāvadāna (= E.B. Cowell and R.A. Neil 1886)
Erz	Ausgewählte Erzählungen in Māhārāṣṭrī (= H. Jacobi 1886)
GDhp	Gāndhārī Dharmapada (= J. Brough 1962)
Kalp	Kalpasūtra (= H. Jacobi 1879)

Manu	Mānava-dharma-śāstra
MBh	Mahā-bhārata
Mhv	Mahāvaṃsa (= W. Geiger 1908)
Mil	Milindapañha (= V. Trenckner 1880)
Mvu	Mahāvastu (= E. Senart 1882–97)
Nett	Netti-pakaraṇa (= E. Hardy 1902)
Ova	Ovavāiya-sutta (= E. Leumann 1883)
Sadd	Saddaniti (= H. Smith 1949)
Sutt	Suttāgame (= Phūlchandjī Mahārāj 1953–54)
Sūyag	Sūyagaḍaṃga (= Sutt, Vol. I, pp. 101–82)
Th	Theragāthā
Thī	Therīgāthā
Utt	Uttarādhyayanasūtra (= J. Charpentier 1922)
Udāna-v	Udānavarga (= F. Bernhard 1965, 1968)
Vism	Visuddhimagga (= Mrs C.A.F. Rhys Davids 1920–21)

The abbreviations for the titles of canonical and commentarial Pali texts are those adopted for CPD

Translations:

BD	*Book of the Discipline* (= Miss I.B. Horner 1938–67)
Breth.	*Psalms of the Brethren* (= Mrs C.A.F. Rhys Davids 1913)
Dial.	*Dialogues of the Buddha* (= T.W. Rhys Davids 1899–1921)
EV I	*Elders' Verses* I, 2nd ed. (= K.R. Norman 2007)
EV II	*Elders' Verses* II (= K.R. Norman 1971)
GD	*Group of Discourses*, 2nd ed. (= K.R. Norman 2001)
GS	*Gradual Sayings* (= E.M. Hare & F.L. Woodward 1932–36)
KS	*Kindred Sayings* (= Mrs C.A.F. Rhys Davids & F.L. Woodward 1917–30)
MLS	*Middle Length Sayings* (= Miss I.B. Horner 1954–59)
MQ	*Milinda's Questions* (= Miss I.B. Horner 1963–64)
PEBN	*Poems of Early Buddhist Nuns* (= Mrs C.A.F. Rhys Davids & K.R. Norman 1989)
Pruitt	*The Commentary on the Verses of the Therīs* (= W. Pruitt 1998B)
Sist.	*Psalms of the Sisters* (= Mrs C.A.F. Rhys Davids 1909)
VT	*Vinaya Texts* (T.W. Rhys Davids & H. Oldenberg 1881–85)
WD	*Word of the Doctrine* (= K.R. Norman 1997B)

Periodicals and Series:

BDCRI	*Bulletin of the Deccan College Research Institute*, Poona
BSO(A)S	*Bulletin of the School of Oriental (and African) Studies*, London
CII	*Corpus Inscriptionum Indicarum*
IIJ	*Indo-Iranian Journal*, The Hague
Ind. Ling.	*Indian Linguistics,* Calcutta
JA	*Journal asiatique*, Paris
JAOS	*Journal of the American Oriental Society,* New Haven
JAS	*Journal of Asian Studies*, New York
JOI(B)	*Journal of the Oriental Institute*, Baroda
JPTS	*Journal of the Pali Text Society*, London
JRAS	*Journal of the Royal Asiatic Society,* London
MSS	*Münchener Studien zur Sprachwissenschaft*, Munich
PTS	Pali Text Society
SBB	Sacred Books of the Buddhists, PTS Oxford
SBE	Sacred Books of the East, Oxford
VG	*Verspreide Geschriften* (= H. Kern 1928)
VKAWA	*Verhandlingen der Koninklijke Akademie van Wetenschappen Amsterdam*
ZDMG	*Zeitschrift der Deutschen Morgenlandischen Gesellschaft*, Leipzig/Wiesbaden

Dictionaries, etc.:

AR	*Abhidhāna-rājendra*, Ratlam 1913–25
BHSD	*Buddhist Hybrid Sanskrit Dictionary* (= F. Edgerton 1953A)
BHSG	*Buddhist Hybrid Sanskrit Grammar* (= F. Edgerton 1953B)
CDIAL	*Comparative Dictionary of the Indo-Aryan Lnguages* (= Sir Ralph L. Turner 1966)
CPD	*A Critical Pāli Dictionary*, Copenhagen, 1924–
DED(S)	*Dravidian Etymological Dictionary* (Supplement) (= T. Burrow and M.B. Emeneau 1961, 1968)
DPPN	*Dictionary of Pali Proper Names* (= G.P. Malalasekera 1938)
EWA	*Etymologisches Wörterbuch des Altindischen* (= M. Mayrhofer 1956–80)
MIAR	*Middle Indo-Aryan Reader* (= S.K. Chatterji and S. Sen 1957)

MW	*Sanskrit–English Dictionary* (= Sir Monier Monier-Williams 1899)
NPED	*New Pali–English Dictionary* (= M. Cone 2001)
PED	*Pali–English Dictionary*, PTS, 1925
PM	*Pali Metre* (= A.K. Warder 1967)
PSM	*Pāia-sadda-mahaṇṇavo* (= H.D.T. Sheth 1963)
PTC	*Pali Tipiṭaka Concordance*, PTS, 1952–93
VI	*Vedic Index* (= A.A. Macdonnell and A.B. Keith 1912)

General:

(X)-a	the aṭṭhakathā upon (X)
AMg	Ardha-Māgadhī
BHS	Buddhist Hybrid Sanskrit
CP	*Collected Papers* (= K.R. Norman 1990–2007)
cty	commentary
E^{e}	PTS edition
m.c.	metri causa
MIA	Middle Indo-Aryan
n.	footnote
(X)-pṭ	the ṭīkā upon (X)
Pkt	Prakrit
Skt	Sanskrit
(X)-ṭ	the ṭīkā upon (X)
v.l.	variant reading
⟨ ⟩	add enclosed reading
[ ]	delete enclosed reading
˘	read as short metrically
< – > and ^	read as long metrically
[IBH]	information obtained from Miss I.B. Horner
[LSC]	information obtained from Mr L.S. Cousins

numbers in heavy type refer to verses of Thī

(§) without any further reference refers to paragraphs of the Introduction.

INTRODUCTION

I. THE AUTHORS OF THERĪGĀTHĀ

§ 1. Dhammapāla begins his cty on Thī by giving a brief account of the circumstances in which the first bhikkhunīs left the world and obtained ordination into the Order. At the end of this introduction he states (Thī-a 4) *tā hi udānâdi-vasena tattha tattha bhāsitā gāthā pacchā saṅgīti-kārakehi ekajhaṃ katvā eka-nipātâdi-vasena saṅgītiṃ āropiṃsu. imā theriyā gāthā nāmā ti*. As in the case of Th, however, it is clear that many of the verses were not uttered by the therīs in the first place, if at all (cf. EV I § 1).

§ 2. Dhammapāla recognises this, and in his cty designates the speaker, e.g. the Buddha is said to have uttered verses **1–6 8–10 14 16 19–20 35–36 51 82–84 163–68 337 362–64**; **33** is ascribed to Abhaya, **54–55** to a devatā, **57 60 139 183 190 197 230** to Māra: of Paṭācārā's 30 followers' verses **117–118** are ascribed to Paṭācārā herself; the same is said of **127–30** in the verses uttered by her 500 followers; **207 210–12** are ascribed to Vaḍḍha; of Uppalavaṇṇā's verses **224–26** are ascribed to Gaṅgātīriya's wife; **238–39 245 250–51** are ascribed to a brahman, **271–73 286–87** to Rohiṇī's father, **291–92 294 296 299 301 303 305–6 308** to Upaka; of Sundarī's verses **312–13 316 319 323** are ascribed to Sujāta, **314–15 317–18 325 327 329** to Vāsiṭṭhī, Sundarī's mother, and **326** to a charioteer; of Subhā Jīvakambavanikā's verses **370–79 381–83** are ascribed to the dhuttaka who accosted her; **403** is ascribed to Bodhī. The authorship of other verses too can be ascribed elsewhere, e.g. 209, despite the cty, must have been uttered by Vaḍḍha (cf. EV I § 12), while **289–90** must be ascribed to Rohiṇī's father, and **397**cd–**98** to the dhuttaka.

§ 3. In two of these cases, viz. Muttā (**2**) and Nandā (**19–20**), the rubric actually states that the verses were uttered by the Buddha to the therīs in question. It is difficult to understand why only these two examples were singled out, since it is clear from the form of many of the verses that Dhammapāla is correct in his ascriptions. It is strange that Dhammapāla makes no reference of the discrepancy between the rubrics and his own version of the circumstances in which the verses were uttered. It would seem that the rubrics were known to him, for he comments on the rubric to verses **23–24**: *apaññātā ti pāḷiyaṃ vuttā*.

§4. We find in the cty, as in Th-a (cf. EV I §2), references to the fact that the verses became the therī's because she repeated them, e.g. *tam eva gātham abhāsi. tenâyaṃ gāthā tassā theriyā gāthā ahosi* of **1** (Thī-a 7), and *imā gāthā abhāsi. ten' etā theriyā gāthā nāma jātā* of **163–68** (Thī-a 159). In a number of other cases we are told that the therī repeated the verse(s) but no stress is laid upon the fact that this made the verses hers, e.g. *sā tam eva gātham abhāsi* of **2**, *sā therī tam eva gātham udānesi* of **3**; the same is applied of **4** by *ādi-nayaṃ heṭṭhā vutta-nayen' eva veditabbaṃ*; **5–10** are so similar that they are dealt with together by Dhammapāla, who states that the therīs' stories are all the same as Tissā's (**4**), except for Dhīra (**7**) who had no *obhāsa-gātha* from the Buddha and therefore declaimed her own verse (*therī aññaṃ viya katvā attānaṃ dasseti* (Thī-a 13)). The reason for this difference of story may simply be that verse **7**, unlike **1–6 8–10**, contains no vocative form, although it does contain an imperative. Similar statements about repeating verses are made about other therīs, e.g. *tam eva gātham abhāsi* of **16**, *tā yeva gāthā abhāsi* of **19–20**, *Abhaya-therena tā gāthā bhāsitā, tā eva paccudāharantī* of **33**, *tā eva gāthā parivattitvā abhāsi* of **35–36**, *ovāda-gāthāhi saddhiṃ imā gāthā abhāsiṃsu* of **117–18**, *ovāda-gāthāhi saddhiṃ imā gāthā visuṃ visuṃ abhāsiṃsu* of **127–30**; in **178** Uttarā states that **175–77** are Paṭācārā's words; *Gaṅgātīriya-ttherassa mātuyā gāthā va vuttā paccanubhāsantī* is said of **224–26**; *pitarā attanā vacana-paṭivacana-vasena vutta-gāthā udāna-vasena bhāsantī* of **271–73**, *upakena attanā ca kathita-gāthāyo udāna-vasena ekajjhaṃ katvā* of **291–92 294 296 299 301 303 305–6 308**, *pitarā vutta-gāthaṃ ādiṃ katvā udāna-vasena imā gāthā paccuda-bhāsi* of **312–13 316 319 323**, *attano tena dhutta-purisena vutta-gāthā udāna-vasena imā gāthā paccudabhāsi* of **370–79 381–83**.

§5. As in the case of Th, there are verses which appear to have been added later to introduce or conclude a narrative story. Dhammapāla recognises this, and ascribes these verse to the *saṅgīti-kārā* (**365 366 400–2 404**). Pischel (p. 121) claims that a number of other verses, e.g. **309–11 448–49 460–61 479–82 494 514–22**, also shows signs of being later additions. He also states (p. 122) that **119–20 121**ab **320–22 324 465**ab **485**ab were not in the original collection of verses. I would not accept that all these verses are to be ascribed to the *saṅgīti-kāra*. I think, however, that a plausible case could be made out for assuming that **399** is a later addition. The cty is silent about all these.

§6. In EV I §4 I pointed out that I thought Winternitz had gone too far in his assertion (p. 101, f.n. 1) that the monks who ascribed verses to Ānanda and the other theras knew as little about them as the compilers of the Anukramaṇīs knew of the compilers of the Ṛgvedic hymns. With regard to the composers of the verses of Thī, however, I must, to some extent, agree with Mrs Rhys Davids' statement (Sist., p. xvii) that the identity of the authors had, for the preservers of the verses, something of a Shakespearian or Homeric indefiniteness. As will be noted below (§23), there is no need to doubt the existence of a number of therīs about whom we read elsewhere in the canon, but it must be confessed that some of the others are shadowy figures, about whom the cty tells us little or nothing.

§7. There are, however, several verses which give an unmistakable reference to their author, either by naming her or by making a pun upon her name:

(a) Therikā's name is included in **1**; Muttā's name is quoted in **2** and Puṇṇā's in **3** as well as puns upon their names; the two Tissās' name occurs in **4** and **5**; the two Dhīrās' name is found in **6** and **7**, as well as a pun on the name in **7**; Mittā's name occurs in **8** and Bhadrā's in **9**, as well as references to their names; Upasamā's name occurs in **10**; Muttā's name occurs in **11** with a pun upon it; Nandā's name is found in **19**, Abhayā's in **35**, Ubbirī's in **51**; Sukkā's name occurs in **54** and **56** with a pun on the name in **56**; Bhaddā Kāpilānī's name occurs in

65, Nandā's in **82**, Bhaddā's in **109** and **111**, Khemā's in **139**, Anopāmā's in **152–53**, Guttā's in **163**, Kisāgotamī's in **223**, Puṇṇikā's in **238**, Rohiṇī's in **272** and **286**, Cāpā's in **292 296 308 311**, Sundarī's in **327 333** and **335**, Subhā's in **362** and **365**, the second Subhā's in **366**, Isidāsī's in **401 403–4 414–16** and **425**, and Sumedhā's in **448 460 465 480–82 485** and **514–15**.

(b) In **119** Paṭācārā's followers' verses refer to *Paṭācārāya sāsanaṃ*; in **204–6** and **208** Vaḍḍha's mother's verses refer to Vaḍḍha by name.

(c) In **2** we find *muccassu yogehi* in Muttā's verse; in **3** *pūrassu dhammehi* in Puṇṇā's verse; in **7** *dhīrehi dhammehi* in Dhīrā's verse; in **8** *mittaratā bhava* in Mittā's verse; in **9** *bhadraratā bhava* in Bhadrā's verse; in **11** *sumuttā sādhu mutta mhi* in Muttā's verse; in **25** *Kāsijana-pado* in Aḍḍhakāsī's verses; in **50** *disvā adantaṃ damitaṃ* in Dantikā's verses; in **56** *sukkehi dhammehi* in Sukkā's verses.

(d) In **16** we find *vuḍḍhike* in Sumanā vuḍḍhapabbajitā's verse.

II. The Arrangement of the Verses

§8. As in Th, the verses are arranged in nipātas according to the number of verses in each utterance, single verses in the eka-nipāta, pairs of verses in the duka-nipāta, and so on. Again as in Th, the numbers attached to the vīsati- and later nipātas seem to be intended merely as guides to the number of verses contained in them, for the vīsati-nipāta contains five groups, of 19, 20, 21 and 28 verses, the tiṃsa-nipāta one group of 34 verses, the cattālīsa-nipāta one group of 48 verses, and the mahā-nipāta one group of 75 verses.

§9. Since there is doubt about the number of verses in the *vīsati-* and later nipātas, it is impossible to be certain whether P is correct in taking **287–88** as two verses, or whether they should be divided into three as in B[e]. There are other places in Thī too where alternative verse divisions would be possible, but it is clear from the *uddāna* (P p. 174 f.n.) that Thī has at some time existed in a rather different form, since the discrepancies between that verse and the present state of affairs are too great to be resolved by mere variation of verse division.

§ 10. The problem is probably insoluble in our present state of knowledge, but certain comments may be made upon P's observations (pp. 120–21). There seems to be no objection to regarding Muttā (**2**) and Muttā (**11**), and Nandā (**19–20**) and Nandā (**82–86**) as separate individuals. The cty gives a different descent and story for the two Muttās, and actually draws attention to the similarities and differences in the stories of the two Nandās. Furthermore the problem of Paṭācārā's 500 followers can be avoided by assuming that *pañcasatā* does not mean '500' but is a name given to the second Paṭācārā to distinguish her from the first (see the note on **127–32**). This then gives 102 therīs, against 101 in the *uddāna* verse.

§ 11. We might assume that if we have one therī too many, and 28 verses in excess of the total given in the *uddāna* verse, the problem could be solved by deducing that one utterance of 28 verses has been added to Thī since the verse was composed. There is one utterance of 28 verses, that of Subhā kammāradhītā (**338–65**), although the number of verses in her utterance depends on decisions about verse division (§ 8). Subhā's verses, however, conclude with **365** which the cty, almost certainly correctly, ascribes to the *saṅgītikārā* (§ 5). In EV I § 11 I quoted Dhammapāla's statement that certain verses were added to Th at the Third Council, and we may assume that the saṅgītikārā had made their additions by the time of the same Council. It seems most unlikely that the *uddāna* was added before the Third Council, and it was probably much later, perhaps as late as the time when the canon was first committed to writing. It seems certain, therefore, that Subhā's verses are older than the *uddāna* verse, and cannot account for the excess of therīs and verses.

§ 12. Within the nipātas there is no clear order of arangement, except in the *vīsati-nipāta*, where the groups are arranged in ascending order of magnitude. Since the nipātas contain fewer groups than those in Th, there is less room for variation of order, and queries about the reasons for the precise order of arrangement do not arise so frequently. In the *eka-nipāta* there are only eighteen utterances, in the *duka-nipāta* ten, in the *tika-nipāta* eight, in the *pañca-nipāta* twelve, in the *cha-nipāta* eight, and in the *satta-nipāta* three, while there is one each in the *catu-*, *aṭṭha-*, *nava-*, *ekādasa-*, *dvādasa-*, and *soḷasa-nipātas*.

§ 13. Certain patterns are, however, apparent in some nipātas:
(a) Some verses are linked together by subject, or refrain, or by a "catch-word", e.g. **2** and **3** have a similar syntactical structure, and both contain puns upon their author's names; **4** and **5** have a similar pāda in common; **8** and **9** are almost identical in structure; **27–28** and **29–30** have pādas in common; **35–36** and **37–38** have a verse in common; **37–38** and 39**–41** (in different nipātas) have more than a verse in common; **39–41** and **42–44** have two pādas in common; **57–59** and **60–62** have their last verse in common; **12–16** and **117–21** have their second pāda-yuga in common; **127–32** and **133–38** have the theme of *putta-soka* in common; **182–88** and **189–95** have several pādas and their last verse in common; **271–90** and **291–311** have the jingle in **290** and **291** in common.

(b) Other verses are linked because of some relationship, real or fanciful, between the speakers, e.g. **4** and **5** are both by therīs names Tissā; **6** and **7** are both by therīs named Dhīrā (if P is correct in reading Dhīrā in both verses); **17** by Dhammā is followed by **18** by Saṅgha; **33–34** are by Abhayamātā and **35–36** by Abhyattherī; **37–38** and **39–41** (in different nipātas) are both by therīs named Sāmā; **42–44** and **45–47** are both by therīs named Uttamā; **82–86** are by Nandā and **87–91** by Nanduttarā; **112–16** are by Paṭācārā and **117–21** are by her 30 followers; **182–88** are by Cālā and **189–95** are by her sister Upacālā.

III. The compilation of Therīgāthā

§ 14. It is thus possible to deduce that the *saṅgītikārā* compiled Thī in much the same way as they compiled Th (EV I § 9). Verses were recited as they were remembered, no distinction being made between "verses by ..." and "verses to ...". Further verses were remembered by the prompting of name, subject or other association. There is, however, one important difference between Th and Thī. The latter contains only one set of verses which were uttered piecemeal at different times, viz. those by Uppalavaṇṇā (**224–35**), and proportionately far more of the narrative type of composition (cf. EV I § 4), where the different speakers' words are quoted verbatim, e.g. Māra and Selā (**57–59**), Māra and Somā (**60–62**), Māra and Khemā (**139–44**), Cālā and Māra (**182–88**), Upacālā and Māra (**189–95**), Sīsûpacālā and Māra (**196–203**), Vaḍḍha and his mother (**204–12**), Māra and Uppalavaṇṇā (**230–35**), Puṇṇā and a brahman (**236–51**), Rohiṇī and her father (**271–90**), Cāpā and her husband (**291–311**), Sundarī, her father, mother and charioteer (**312–37**), Subhā and a dhuttaka (**366–99**). The number of poems of this type accounts for the proportionately larger quantities of verses in Thī which were not uttered by therīs in the first place (cf. § 1).

§ 15. Although it is quite likely that some of these utterances were in fact made by the therīs, this is probably not true of all. So we may feel certain that Selā, Somā Khemā, Cālā, upacālā, Sīsûpacālā, and Uppalavaṇṇā did recite Māra's verses when they were relating their psychological experiences to their companions, in a typical "He said to me, and then I said to him" way, but the same may well not be true of Sundarī's story (**312–37**) which seems more likely to have been recited about her, rather than by her.

§ 16.In one case, at least, it can be seen conclusively that we are dealing with a narrative story, in which presumably authentic utterances have been put together to form a continuous narrative, for Winternitz (p. 104, f.n. 2) pointed out that Vaḍḍha's verses (Th 335–39) seem to have been arbitrarily divided from his mother's (**204–12**), in such a way that some of Vaḍḍha's verses are in Thī (**207 210–12**). In view of this, we shall probably not be wrong if we assume that Sumedhā's long poem (**448–522**), told in the third person with dialogue inserted, was from the first a literary production, and was never spoken as a whole by the therī.

§ 17. We may note that the *saṅgītikārā* did not seem to be disturbed by the fact that verses which had clearly been uttered by Vaḍḍha were nevertheless not included in Th. Similarly Dhammapāla himself preserves a verse which he ascribes to Kisā-Gotamī (Thī-a 175), but he makes no comment upon its omission from Thī. In his introductory story to Paṭācārā's verses (**112–16**) he ascribes to her a verse which greatly resembles **219**, ascribed to Kisā-Gotamī, again without comment. Nor does he make any reference to the fact that the verses which certain therīs state they heard Paṭācārā recite (**117–18 175–77**) are not included in Paṭācārā's verses. This leads to the more general question of the omission from Thī of verses which are elsewhere ascribed to therīs, e.g. those in the *bhikkhunī-saṃyutta* (cf. § 20).

§ 18. Winternitz considered (p. 101, f.n. 2) that the fact that the same verses occur again literally in different places is evidence of careless redaction. It is true that **38**cdef is identical with **41**, that **59** recurs again at **62 188 195 203 235**, and that if pādas of verses are compared the situation is even more striking. I have, however, pointed out (EV I § 5) that there is no need to suspect the redactors, since the inclusion of a therī's verse in Thī only implies that tradition records that she recited the verse on some occasion, not that she was the original composer of it. Hence there is no reason to doubt the ascription of **63**cd **64**ab to Bhaddā Kāpilānī although at M II 144 it is stated that the Bhagavat uttered the verse to Brahmâyu.

§ 19. Mrs Rhys Davids has translated (Sist., pp. 180–91) the verses of the *Bhikkhunī-saṃyutta* (= S I 128–35), and pointed out that some of these verses are not in Thī, others found there in a slightly different form, and still others are ascribed to different therīs, e.g. Cālā's verses (**183–85**) are uttered by Sīsûpacālā, Upacālā's (**191–92**) by Cālā, and Sīsûpacālā's (**197–98 200–1**) by Upacālā. The confusion which exists in the case of these three sisters perhaps helps us to understand the circumstances which led to the variation in tradition about the other therīs' verses too. We may deduce that the verses were remembered as being important, i.e. canonical, but the tradition about the authors and the circumstances of their utterance was less fixed. The ten groups of verses in the *Bhikhunī-saṃyutta* were presumably remembered together because of the Māra incident connected with each of them. At some stage of the tradition, perhaps at the Third Council, prose narratives were added to the verses in Saṃyutta to make them more intelligible, the bhikkhunīs' names being supplied from tradition. At some stage, rubrics were also supplied for Saṃyutta; this was probably later than the prose narratives, perhaps at the time of committing the canon to writing, since the names in the narratives frequently differ from those in the rubrics and *uddāna* verses.

§20. At the same time the same thing was being done for the verses in Thī, but because the tradition about names and circumstances was somewhat vague the precise identity of which of Sāriputta's sisters uttered which verses was confused, and different ascriptions were made in Thī and Saṃyutta. It is clear from these differences that the redactions of Thī and Saṃyutta were made separately, and no attempt was made to use one text as a check upon the other, even when it was a question of establishing the exact form of an utterance. We find, therefore, that the verses ascribed to Selā in Thī (**57–58**) are given to Āḷavikā in Saṃyutta (although Dhammapāla says that Ālavikā was Selā's alternative name (Thī-a 62)), and an entirely different group of verses, not occuring in Thī, ascribed to Selā. Similarly, the verses ascribed to Gotamī, Vijayā and Vajirā do not appear in Thī.

§21. At the time of compilation various verses were added to the *saṅgītakārā*, when they felt that explanation or additional information was required by the listener. We can recognise the incongruity of **366**, since it is in a different metre from **367–99**, but it is not so immediately apparent that **400–2 404** are later additions. Not only are they in the same metre as **403 405–47**, but that metre is the Āryā. We know that the use of this metre in Pāli ceased from quite an early date, although it is impossible to say precisely when. It is, however, noteworthy that at the time of the inclusion of Th 43 in the Canon, i.e. presumably not later than the Third Council, the compilers' understanding of *Gaṇacchandas* metres was such that they did not recognise that that verse is in fact two old Āryā stanzas. It is, therefore, debatable whether at the same council there were those capable of writing Āryā verses.

IV. The date of Therīgāthā

§22. Thī can be dated relatively on several grounds: traditional, historical, doctrinal, metrical and linguistic. The answers gained by these various methods may well be contradictory, for the last three tell of the composition of the verse(s), while tradition and history tell only of the recitation by the therī concerned.

§23. Tradition, as recorded in the cty, tells us that some of the therīs whose verses are included in Thī were spoken to, and admitted to the Order by, the Buddha, e.g. Dhammadinnā (**12**), Paṭācārā (**112–16**), Khemā (**139–44**), Mahāpajāpatī (**157–62**), Uppalavaṇṇā (**224–35**). Other therīs were converted by these, e.g. Uttamā (**42–44**), 30 therīs (**117–21**), Candā (**122–26**), 500 therīs (**127–32**) and Uttarā (**175–81**) by Paṭācārā; Therikā (**1**), Muttā (**2**), Puṇṇā (**3**), Tissā (**4**), Cittā (**27–28**), Mittā (**31–32**), Dantikā (**48–50**), Bhaddā Kāpilānī (**63–66**), Guttā (**163–68**), Subhā kammāra-dhītā (**338–65**), Subhā Jīvakambava-nikā (**366–99**) by Mahāpajāpatī; Sukkā (**54–56**) and Vaḍḍhesī (**67–71**) by Dhammadinnā; Vijayā (**169–74**) by Khemā; Subhā kammāra-dhītā (**338–65**), mentions Uppalavaṇṇā by name in verse **363**. Other therīs are said to have been spoken to by followers of the Buddha who were alive during his lifetime, e.g. Sāmā (**37–38**) heard Ānanda preach, Vimalā (**72–76**) was rebuked by Mahāmoggallāna, and Nanduttarā (**87–91**) was defeated in argument by the same thera. Other therīs are said to have been related to theras who were alive during or soon after the Buddha's lifetime, e.g. Sumaṅgala's mother (**23–24**), Abhaya's mother (**33–34**), Sāriputta's sisters Cālā (**182–88**), Upacālā (**189–95**) and Sīsûpacālā (**196–203**) and Vimala-kondañña's mother Ambapālī (**252–70**). Some of the therīs are named in other canonical texts, e.g. Dhammadinnā (**16**), Bhaddā Kāpilānī (**63–66**), Sakulā (**97–101**), Soṇā (**102–6**), Bhaddā Kuṇḍalakesā (**107–11**), Paṭācārā (**112–16**), Khemā (**139–44**), Mahāpajāpatī (**157–62**), Kisā-gotamī (**213–23**), and Uppalavaṇṇā (**224–35**) are all at A I 25 assigned pre-eminence in some attribute or other by the Buddha.

§24. Some therīs can be dated by the references to historic personages or happenings in their verses or in the tradition about them, e.g. there is a reference to King Pasenadi in Sumanā's story (**16**), and references to King Bimbisāra in the stories about Abhaya's mother (**33–34**), Somā (**60–62**), and Khemā (**139–44**). Similarly, the mention of the city of Pāṭaliputta in **400** must mean that this verse was composed after the foundation of that city, when it had become famous enough to warrant its name being included in a poem. Since, however, we know that Pāṭaliputta was already well known in Candragupta's time, I am unable to accept the suggestion made by Nakamura (quoted by de Jong in his review of EV I) that this verse must be post-Aśokan. Even so, the dating of the verse does not help us with the dating of the poem as a whole, since **400** is one of the verses alleged to have been added by the *saṅgīti-kārā* (§ 5). If we exclude those therīs whose story is merely said to be similar to another therī's, there are only four, viz. Muttā (**11**), Dhammā (**17**), Isidāsī (**400–47**) and Sumedhā (**448–522**), whose stories give us no traditional or quasi-historical information whatsoever, and the information we receive about the others tells us that the majority of the therīs were alive during, or soon after, the Buddha's lifetime.

§ 25. Winternitz claimed (p. 111) that the story of Isidāsī (**400–47**) seemed to belong to a (later) period of decay, when as a matter of course a girl only became a nun in consequence of some misfortune, or a monk could discard his robe in order to marry and then return to the monastic life after a fortnight. It is hard to believe that such phenomena can be dated precisely. The long lists of sexual aberrations recounted in the Vinaya make it seem quite probable that even during the Buddha's lifetime there could be back-sliding bhikkhus who very soon saw the error of their ways, while in connection with a religion whose main teaching was the *dukkha* of the world around us, the equation of *dukkha* and personal misfortune is hardly a mark of lateness. Mrs Rhys Davids was perhaps nearer the mark when she pointed out (Sist., p. xviii) as a mark of lateness the fact that although several therīs are reputed to have remembered their previous existences only Isīdāsī (**400–47**) and Sumedhā (**448–522**) actually recount these remiscences to their contemporaries. Mrs Rhys Davids was, however, going too far when she said that Sumedhā's harangues are sermons preached *from a Bible*.

Verses **488–92** are certainly quotations, but it is not possible to say from what, nor can we date them. Aversion to *kāma* is found in both Buddhism and Jainism and is likely to be older than both. Mnemonic verses listing illustrations for sermons on *kāma* may also be older than Buddhism. Even if this is not so, there is no need to surmise that these verses are anything other than a metrical summary of the type of sermon recounted in M I 130 364 foll., and they may well be contemporary with the Buddha. It would not be surprising if many of the utterances made by the Buddha in his 40 years of preaching were re-echoed by his followers. The same is true of similies employed by Sumedhā to illustrate the endlessness of *saṃsāra* (**496–501**). These could be older than Buddhism, and need not be later than the Buddha's lifetime. The view that the mention of the former Buddha Koṇāgamana in Sumedhā's poem (**518**) also implies lateness, since it refers to a time when the cult of former Buddhas was well enough established for authors to include mention of them in their literary works, ignores the fact that the cult is certainly pre-Aśokan since we have an Aśokan inscription recording the fact that Aśoka enlarged a stūpa which had been built to Konākamana.

§ 26. I have pointed out in EV I § 14(c) some of the difficulties which arise when trying to date a text on metrical grounds. In some ways the problems of dating Thī are even greater than those of dating Th, since the number of *Śloka* verses is far fewer, and the statistical analysis is correspondingly more suspect. Furthermore, five of the larger groups of verses in Thī are in metres (āryā, vatālīya and rathoddhatā) which are not particularly common elsewhere in the canon. Consequently, although it is possible to say that verses in these metres in Thī seem to be earlier or later than verses in other texts, there is not enough material available to be able to place the Thī verses exactly in their place in the development of the particular metre and thus to give a reasonably clear date to them. Professor Warder concluded that Thī covered a long period of development, some portions being old and others being as late as Mauryan times (PM, §§ 142(ii) 193 225 264 303–4).

§ 27. Attempts to date Thī on linguistic grounds also present difficulties, because of the danger of conscious or unconscious archaising, although the identification of an archaism is largely a matter of subjective judgement. Professor Warder speaks of deliberate archaisms in Thī (PM, p. 10, f.n. 2), and quotes *kātuye* (**418**), *etase* (**291**), *chaḍḍūna* (**469**) and *apakiritūna* (**447**) as examples. Of *kātuye* he says "apparently an old gloss incorporated in the text before the 1st century A.D.". Since there is no old infinitive in *-uye*, which is rather < *-u*(*ṃ*) followed by the particle *ye*, arguments based upon it must necessarily fall. Warder himself points out that his theory of "archaism" should be treated with reserve, since the existence of absolutives in *-tūna*(*ṃ*) in Māhārāṣṭrī suggests that these forms in Pāli (and *abhivādetūnaṃ* in the Aśokan inscription at Bairat) are dialectal borrowings rather than conscious attempts to make rather late texts look old. Certain forms in Thī, however, show Māgadhan features, e.g. the confusion between *-iya*, *-ika*, and *-ita* in **201**, etc., probably going back to Eastern forms in *-iya*, and we can be fairly certain that these verses ante-date the "translation" into Pāli which Professor Warder dates in the third century B.C. (PM, § 13). The Eastern masculine plural forms in *-āni* (**13**, etc.) and the feminine form *tīṇi* (**518**), if genuine, and the confusions arising from old masculine singular forms in *-e* (**2**, etc.) must all date from the same period.

§ 28. We may therefore conclude that all the evidence supports the view that the verses collected together in Thī were uttered over a period of about 300 years, from the end of the 6th century to the end of the third century B.C.

V. The Commentary

§ 29. To each therī's verse(s) Dhammapāla prefixes a narrative story which usually includes the life-history of the therī and an account of the circumstances in which the utterance was made, although sometimes only a truncated story is given, and a comparison is made with other stories already told, e.g. the stories of Cālā (**182–88**), Upacālā (**189–95**), and Sīsûpacālā (**196–203**) are all told in the introduction to Cālā's verses; Tissā (**5**), Dhīrā (**6**), Dhīrā (**7**), Mittā (**8**), Bhadrā (**9**), and Upasamā (**10**) are all said to have stories similar to Tissā's (**4**) except for Dhīrā (**7**): *vatthu eka-sadisaṃ eva ... ṭhapetvā sattamiṃ* (Thī-a 12). Where detailed stories are given we may suppose that they are on the whole based upon tradition, but in some cases the stories are so sketchy that we may not be wrong in thinking that Dhammapāla or his predecessors extracted the story from the verse(s), e.g. Muttā's story (**11**) can be deduced from her verse, with the exception of the information that her husband was a brahman named Oghāṭaka, which could be a mere invention. No information of any value is given in the story prefixed to the verses of Paṭācārā's 30 followers (**117–21**), nor in that given for her 500 followers (**127–32**). Sometimes the stories do not seem to be in agreement with the information which maybe deduced from the verses, e.g. Nanduttarā's verses (**87–91**) mention details of a life of pleasure which finds no place in her story (see Sist., p. 57 note 3); Bhaddā Kuṇḍalakesā's verses (**107–11**) refer to geographical details at variance with the story (see Sist., p. 67 note 3); Kisāgotamī's verses (**213–23**) fit better with the story given for Paṭācārā (**112–16**).

§30. Dhammapāla sometimes gives information about the source of the story he tells, e.g. of Khemā (**139–44**); he points out that the *aṭṭhakathā* and Apadāna differ about the way in which she gained arahantship. In the stories attached to the verses of 34 therīs Dhammapāla includes the portions of the Apadāna referring to them, from which it can clearly be seen that the traditions about some of the therīs had already been formed by the date of the composition of that text. Although this may well be very late, it can hardly be later than the date given for the commission of the canon to writing in the 1st century B.C. (Warder, PM §4), i.e. not more than 200 years later than the latest composition in Thī (see §29 above), or the Third Council at which Thī was probably recited.

§31. It is certain that Dhammapāla had access to traditional material which was not available to, or not used by the composers of the rubrics, for in three places he differs from them. The rubrics say that three therīs were unknown, viz. the reciters of **1**, **23–24** and **67–71**. Dhammapāla says the author of **1** was called Therikā. He may well have extracted this from the verse itself, but he is quite clear about it, explaining *taṃ thirasantasarīratāya Therikā ti vohariṃsu* (Thī-a 5). Furthermore he writes (Thī-a 300) *Subhūti-ādayo therā, theriyo Therikâdayo*. He seems to be explaining the rubric when he states (Thī-a 7) *aññatarā therī aññātā ti nāmagottâdivasena apākaṭā*. About the author of **23–24** he states *yasmā pan' assā nāmaṃ gottaṃ na pākaṭam, tasmā aññatarā bhikkhunī apaññātā ti pāḷiyaṃ vuttā*. However, he begins his cty *Samuttike ti ādikā Sumaṅgalamātuyā theriyā gāthā*, and ends *Sumaṅgalamātuyā theriyā gāthāvaṇnanā samattā*. There is no obvious reason, except for the tradition which he quotes (*puttaṃ labhitvā tassa Sumaṅgalo ti nāmaṃ ahosi, tato paṭṭhāya Sumaṅgalamātā ti paññāyitthā*), for associating this therī with Sumaṅgala, except for the possible similarity of verse style (cf. Th 43). Since *Sumuttike* is vocative, one might have expected the tradition to have extracted Sumuttikā as the therī's name. (B^e does in fact include *Sumaṅgalamātā* in the rubric, which I assume to be a transference from the cty.) Dhammapāla begins his cty on **67–71** with the words *paṇṇavysati vassānī ti ādikā aññatarāya samattā*, omitting the word *apaññātā* in both places. In the story (Thī-a 75), however, he states *Devadahanagare Mahāpajāpatīgotamīdhātī hutvā Vaḍḍhesī nāma, gottato pana apaññātā ahosi*, clearly referrring to the rubric.

§32. There are other differences of tradition revealed in the cty, about which Dhammapāla says nothing. Thus he states about Subhā kammāra-dhītā (**338–65**) that she was admitted to the Order by Mahāpajāpatī (*Mahāpajāpatī-gotamiyā santike pabbajitvā* (Thī-a 237) without reference to the fact that the therīs own verses (**363**) refer to the fact that she was instructed by Uppalavaṇṇā. Similarly Pischel has pointed out (p. 187, n. 1) that in the story about Paṭācārā the cty states that the verse was delivered to a group of bhikkhus, with reference to Dācucīri. Most surprising of all, however, is the way in which some of the sections from Apadāna which Dhammapāla quotes are assigned to other therīs in that text. He makes no comment on this. It seems unlikely that by the time of Dhammapāla the text of Apadāna differed in any way from that which we have at present, although the Apadāna extract given for Muttā (**11**) does not exist in our copies. It is more likely that the tradition had been completely confused by the way in which the therīs were sometimes addressed by their *gotta* name, sometimes by their personal name and sometimes by a geographical name, nick-name or some other appellation.

§33. In two cases at least it can be postulated with a fair degree of certainty that Dhammapāla or his predecessors invented the story because of a misunderstanding of the verse or the rubric. It is most unlikely, despite the cty, that 500 bereaved mothers would all come to Paṭācārā together for comforting. The verses (**127–32**) have singular nouns and verbs, and show no signs of having been deliverd to more than one person. A word meaning "follower of Paṭācārā" would not be expected to have the form *Paṭācārā*. It is far more likely that we are dealing here with a second Paṭācārā, distinguished from her namesake by the adjective *pañcasatā* (whatever its meaning). The existence of two Paṭācārās might well help to explain the apparent mixture of two stories in the history of Paṭācārā (**112–16**) to which Mrs Rhys Davids (Sist., p. xxl) has drawn attention. If by chance the second Paṭācārā was a member of the Gotama *gotta* it would explain why Paṭācārā's story seems far more appropriate to Kisāgotamī's verses, and why the verse which Dhammapāla ascribes to Paṭācārā (Thī-a 110) bears such a close resemblance to one of Kisā-gotamī's (**219**).

§34. In a similar way the inclusion of the name Vāseṭṭhī in **313 316** has led Dhammapāla to identify this Vāseṭṭhī with the author of **133–38**. He therefore has to explain away the discrepancy between the one child which tradition gave to Vāseṭṭhī, and the mention of seven children in **313**. This confusion arose becasue Dhammapāla did not realise that Vāsiṭṭha is only a *gotta* name.

§35. Mrs Rhys Davids has already paid tribute to the indispensibility of the cty (Sist., pp. xvi–xvii). Pischel stated (p. 120) that Dhammapāla had already a corrupt text before him, which he sometimes wholly misunderstood, but in fact the cty is much more helpful than might be guessed by anyone reading only P's extracts (pp. 175–216) or M's edition. C^e^ and B^e^ of Thī-a show that many correct explanations have been obscured by wrong readings in M, e.g. *udaka-sabba-* (= *udaka-sappa-*) and *vuccati* (= *ruccati*) in the cty on **23**; *saddhena* (= *saddena*) in **24**; *saddhāyikā* (= *sādhayikā*) in **43**; *abhinandantī* (= *bhindantī*) in **44**; *upanetvā* (= *uppatitivā*) in **248**; *mattha-lomehi* (= *meṇḍaka-lomehi*) in **253**; *kaṇha-gandhaka-* (= *kaṇha-khandaka-*) in **255**; *paṭisedhikā* (= *pariseditā*) in **258**; *vatthala-* (= *vaṭṭula-*) and *purima-kappa-kataṃ* (= *supari-kamma-kataṃ*) in **259**; *-jalanāya* (= *jālatāya*) in **262**; *kalāpiyo* (= *kalasiyo*) in **265**; *khīra-* (= *cira-*) in **266**; *-matta* (= *maṭṭa*) in **268**; *dinnaṃ yeva* (= *dinnen' eva*) in **273**; *padinna* (= *paritt'assādā*) in **358**; *samanaṃ* (= *sammataṃ*) in **380**; *te puna* (= *voḍhūna*) in **441**; *sunava-madhu* (= *suvāna-vamathu*) in **478**.

§36. It is clear from C^e^ and B^e^ of Thī-a, where most of these wrong readings are corrected, that occasionally the cty is commenting upon a reading which differs from P's text, e.g. *iminā saddena saddhi viharāmi* in the cty on **24** shows clearly that we should read the onomatopoeic *cicciṭi cicciṭī ti* with B^e^ C^e^. On the other hand there is evidence that Dhammapāla did indeed have an already corrupt text before him, e.g. he comments on *dhī tav' atthu jane jammi* in **106**, which as P says (p. 184) is quite out of place in this context; *khādamānā* in **312** and *khāditvā* in **313** must be mistakes for causative forms, but the cty explains them as simple verbs; it seems impossible to fit *maṃ* into **392**, but the cty comments on the word in this form. It is clear from the alternative readings which Dhammapāla quotes, and the alternative explanations he gives, e.g. in the cty on **23** and **255**, that by his time there existed different readings and interpretations of difficult verses.

§37. It is possible to point to a number of cases where Dhammapāla did not understand the meaning of a word or phrase he was commenting on, e.g. *purakkhatā* (**199**), *jana-māraka-majjha-gatā* (**217**), *ubho* (**217**), *su* (**258** foll.), *bandhati* (**294**), *khāditāni* (**314**), *mama tuyhaṃ ca* (**315**), *tayā* (**383**), *vaṭṭo* (**439 441**). Mrs Rhys Davids has pointed out (Sist., p. xviii) that Dhammapāla's knowledge of North Indian geography is occasionally suspect, e.g. Bhaddā Kuṇḍala-kesā's verses have a reference to Gijjhakūṭa (**108**), but the introductory story in the cty is set in Sāvatthi; Kāla renounce the world by the R. Nerañjarā (**309**) but the cty states that he met the Buddha at Sāvatthi. Nevertheless, on the whole Dhammapāla comments accurately upon Thī.

§38. In quoting from Thī-a I have drawn attention to the most important of the probable or certain errors in text, lemmata or explanation in M, and I have quoted B^e and C^e where they differ appreciably from M. It must, however, be suspected that B^e and C^e, or the traditions behind them, have been subjected to a certain amount of simplification, whereby certain problems which appear in M have been solved by omitting them, e.g. M glosses *na vaccham̩* in **414** as *na cemhiyam̩* (?) and in **425** as *na pakkhiyam̩*, and it is probable that these readings in fact conceal the real meaning of the phrase. B^e and C^e, however, gloss *na vasissam̩* in both contexts. Similarly M glosses *marituye* in **426** as *maritum̩ ce* (which must be a mistake for *ve*, i.e. an emphatic particle), but B^e and C^e omit *ce/ve*, although they agree with M in glossing the comparable *kātuye* in **418** as *kātum̩ ayye*.

VI. The text of Therīgāthā

§39. This translation is based upon Pischel's edition of Thī, with certain emendations which are discussed in the notes. I have listed the more important of these at the end of this work, under the heading "Some alternative readings for Therīgāthā". As a general rule I have tried to recover and translate the text which Dhammapāla commented on, if this seemed to be metrical and to make sense, or any *v.l.* which Dhammapāla quoted. *Vv.ll* in the MSS I usually assume to be late, if Dhammapāla does not comment on them, although Mr Cousins' experience with SṬ shows that tradition could sometimes preserve a reading that was older and better than that commented on by Buddhaghosa [LSC].

§40. Pischel himself explained (p. 120) that the materials available to him were nevertheless not sufficient for consituting a quite satisfactory text. He sometimes introduced readings against his MSS which can now be seen to be incorrect. They should consequently be removed from the text of Thī, e.g. *avasāye* (**12**), *uttam'aṅga-bhu* (**253**), *khāhinti* (**509**). Some readings which P stated were no doubt wrong, although he left them in his text, are probably correct, e.g. *khalu tāya* (**50**), *purakkhato* (**199**), although the cty's explanation of the latter is wrong (§37). P sometimes refers to the correct reading in his notes although he does not adopt it in his text, e.g. *akampiyaṃ* (**201**).

§41. Pischel added that without the help of the cty he would hardly have ventured to publish the text at all. As has been mentioned (§35), P's quotations from the cty are in need of much correction. Although M's edition is a great improvement, his practice of putting the "correct" (i.e. P's) reading into the text of Thī (p. vii), despite his MSS, is indefensible. Occasionally his choice of reading is inexplicable, e.g. he reads *kāla-* in **252**, despite his MS of Thī-a, the lemma, P's text and the metre.

§42. Many Western scholars have contributed to the establishment of a better text of Thī since P's edition appeared, and I gladly acknowledge my debt to them, in particular to Professors Alsdorf, Kern and Warder, and to Drs Bollée and Stede. The oriental editions of Thī which have appeared since P's edition also contain many improved readings, and where I have adopted a reading from B^e K^e or S^e of Thī-a, or extracted it from the lemmata or the explanations given in the cty, I state the source as such, even if the same reading was earlier suggested by a Western scholar.

§43. I have occasionally felt unable to accept any of the readings of the editions, or any of the emendations which have been suggested by others, and have consequently made suggestions of my own which are unsupported by any MS, edition or other scholar. I have naturally discussed all such occurrences at length in the notes. There is need of a new critical edition of Thī, for despite the many excellences of the Chaṭṭhasaṅgāyana edition (= B^e) suspicions cannot but be aroused by the frequency with which a hyper-metrical *Śloka* pāda appears in B^e in a regular eight-syllable form. The text of that edition gives the impression of having been subjected to a considerable amount of normalisation, which naturally greatly reduces its value. I have, however, shunned the task of producing a critical edition myself, since I felt that it would unduly delay the appearance of this translation. I hope that the material I have collected from other sources will be of some value to anyone who undertakes this task in the future.

§44. In deciding between alternative readings I have been greatly helped, as in the translation of Th (cf. EV I §20), by the metre. Thī owingdiffers from Th in that it contains five lengthy groups of verses in metres which are governed by rules of prosody which are stricter than those for the *Śloka*. It is possible therefore to apply metrical tests to passages which for other reasons seem corrupt, and to utilise the same metrical considerations to propose corrections or emendations to the text. In the case of the verses in Āryā (**213–23 400–47 448–522**), Rathoddhatā (**252–70**), and Vaitālīya (**267–99**) metres, it has therefore been possible to accept or propose readings which have a very good chance of being correct. We must, however, be alert to the fact that there is no certainty that the compilers of the Pāli canon did always conform to the classical standards of prosody. It seems clear enough that certain openings and cadences were employed in *Śloka* verses which would normally be acceptable in classical literature (see §62), and although most of these variations are probably due to defects in the oral and written tradition during the subsequent centuries, or, as de Jong suggested in his review of EV I and I tried to show in the case of Th ((see EV I 9), to translation errors which arose when the early canon was translated into Pāli, we must probably accept that fact that some verses were defective even when composed.

VII. The Translation of Therīgāthā

§45. I gave in EV I §32 my reasons for preferring a prose translation of Th, and the same considerations hold true for Thī. I have again produced a literal, almost word-for-word, translation because this seemed to me to be the best way in which to convey my understanding of the Pāli. I have again, as in EV I, left some words untranslated where it seemed to me that any English equivalent could only be misleading, and I have retained the non-technical translation of a number of words which in later Buddhist literature have a specifically Buddhist technical meaning. Such words are less frequent in Thī than in Th.

§46. I have once again expanded the notes by including extracts from Dhammapāla's cty, references to errors and omissions in PED, PTC and CPD, and discussions of metrical and phonological points, in the hope that the result will go some way towards serving as a commentary upon the text.

VIII. THE METRES OF THERĪGĀTHĀ

§47. The following metres are found in Thī:
Triṣṭubh: 231
Vaitālīya: 367–99
Rathoddhatā: 252–70
Gaṇacchandas: 23–24 214–17 219–23 242 400–15 417–43 445–71 473–86 493–94 496–522
Śloka: 1–11 13–22 25–43 45–50 52–53 55–110 112–212 224–29 232–42 244–51 271–326 329–66 488–92

Mixed metres:
Triṣṭubh/Jagatī: 230
Triṣṭubh/Śloka: 12 44 54 327–28
Gaṇacchandas/Śloka: 213 218 416 444 472 487 495
Vaitālīya/Śloka: 51
Vaitālīya/Gaṇacchandas: 111

§48. The following analyses are based upon the readings in P, except for the *gaṇa* analysis of the *Gaṇacchandas* stanzas which is based upon Alsdorf's re-edition of the *Āryā* stanzas in Thī (App. II, pp. 238–50). An asterisk (*) signifies that an alternative reading is suggested in the notes; the inclusion of a pāda number in parentheses in the lists of metrical and orthographical variants indicates that the variant listed is found in the alternative reading, not in P. Resolved syllables are ignored in these analyses, but lists of such syllables are added in the case of

Vaitālīya, *Rathoddhatā*, *Triṣṭubh* and *Śloka* pādas. The question of *svarabhakti* vowels is discussed at the end of the introduction (§ 75).

§ 49. Triṣṭubh pādas:

(a) Openings:

– – ⏑ ⟨–⟩	12c*
– – – –	44c*
– – ⏑ –	54a 230b 231cd 327b 328b
⏑ – ⏑ –	230c 231ab
⏑ – – –	230d
– ⏑ ⏑ –	327a* 328a*

(b) Breaks:

, – ⏑ ⏑	12c 54a 230bd 231bd
⏑ – –	44c (with cæsura at third and eighth)
, ⏑ ⏑ –	230c
– – ⏑ ,	231a*
– , ⏑ ⏑	231c 327a 328a
, [⏑] ⏑ ⏑ ⏑	327b* 328b*

(c) Cadences:

– ⏑ – ⏓	12c 44c 54a 230bcd 231abcd 327ab 328ab

(d) **Redundant syllables.** There are redundant syllables in the following pādas: 327b* 328b* (or read *gĕha-* or *gaha-* and assume resolution of the fifth syllable).

§ 50. *Jagatī* pāda:

(a) Opening:

⏑ – ⏑ –	230a

(b) Break:

–, ⏑ ⏑	230a

(c) Cadence:

– ⏑ – ⏑ –	230a

§ 51. *Vaitālīya* pādas:

(a) Openings:

(i) Odd pādas:

[– ⏑]– – ⏑ ⏑	51a*
– – ⏑ ⟨⏑⟩	111a*

– – ⏑ ⏑	367a 369c 376c 380a 381a 386a 387c 389a 390a 392c 2=394a 396a 399a
⏑ ⏑ – ⏑ ⏑	367c 368ac 370a 371a 374a 375c 376a 381c 382c 383ac 384a 394c
– ⏑ ⏑ –	369a 370c 380c 385a 389c 397c
⏑ ⏑ ⏑ ⏑ –	371c
⏑ ⏑ ⏑ ⏑ ⏑ ⏑	372a
– – – ⏑	372c*
– ⏑ ⏑ ⏑	373a* 390c* 398a*
⏑ ⏑ – ⏑ –	373c*
– ⏑ ⏑ ⏑ ⏑	374c 377ac 382a 388c 395a 397a 399c
⏑ – ⏑ ⏑ ⏑	375a 378a (syncopated form of ⏑ ⏑ – ⏑ ⏑)
⏑ ⏑ – ⏑ ⏑ ⏑	378c*
– ⏑ – ⏑ ⏑	379a* 393c*
– – ⏑ –	379c* 388a* 391a*
– – –	384c
⏑ ⏑ – –	385c 386c
– [–] ⏑ – ⏑	387a*
⏑ – –	391c
⏑ – ⏑ –	392a (syncopated form of ⏑ ⏑ – –)
⏑ – ⏑ ⏑ –	393a*
– ⏑ – ⏑ –	395c*
– ⏑ – –	396c*
– – – –	398c*

(ii) Even pādas:

– – – ⏑ ⏑	51b 367b 368bd 369d 375d 380d 381d 382d 384bd 385b 387b 388d 389bd 390b 393d 395b 397b 398b
– – – ⏑ –	111b*
⏑ ⏑ – – ⏑ ⏑	367d 369b 372bd 373d 376b 377bd 382b 383d 385d 386bd 388b 390b 394bd 395d 396b 397d
– – – –	370b
– ⏑ ⏑ – ⏑ –	370d* 371d* 378d* 393b*
⏑ ⏑ ⏑ ⏑ – ⏑ ⏑	371b 374b 375b
– ⏑ ⏑ – ⏑ ⏑	373b 378b 381b 396d

–⏑⏑⏑⏑⟨⏑⏑⟩	374d*
⏑⏑–––⏑	376d*
⏑––⏑⏑	379b 391b*
⏑–⏑––⏑⏑	379d
⏑⏑⏑––⏑⏑	380b*
–⏑⏑––⏑	383b*
––––⏑	387d*
–⏑–⏑⏑	391d* 392d* 399d*
–⏑––⏑⏑	392b*
⏑⏑⏑–⏑⏑	398d* 399b*

(b) Cadences:

⏑⏑–⏑⏓	111a*b* 372c* 381a*d* 388b*
–––⏑⏓	372d* 399a*
–⏑⏑⏑–	375c* 383c* 397b*
⏑⏑––⏑–	379a*
––⏑⏑⏑	384d*
–[⏑]⏑–⏑–	391b*
–⏑––⏑	392b*c*
–⏑–⏑⏓	the remainder

(c)(i) **Syncopation**. There are syncopated openings in the following pādas: 373(a) 375a 378a 391(c) 392a.

(ii) **Redundant syllables.** There are redundant syllables in the following pādas: 51a* 387a8 391b*.

(iii) **Omitted syllables.** Syllables are omitted in the following pādas: 111a* 374d*.

(iv) **Resolution.** A long syllable is resolved in the following pāda: 379a.

§52. *Rathoddhatā* pādas:

(a) Openings:

–⏑–⏑⏑⏑	252ad 253acd 254abcd 255acd 256abcd 257acd 258abcd 259abcd 260d 261bcd 262d 263abd 264d 265abd 266ad 267ad 268acd 269acd 270abcd
–⏑––⏑⏑	252b* 253b* 261a*
–⏑–⏑–⏑	252c* 262a* 264a*

— ˘ — ˘ —	255b 260b 262bc 264b 266b 267b 268b 269b (= — ˘ — ˘ ˘ ˘)
— — — — ˘ ˘	257b*
— ˘ ˘ ˘ ˘ ˘	260a* 266c*
— ˘ — ˘ — —	260c*
— ˘ — ˘ ˘ —	263c* 264c* 267c*
— — — ˘ —	265c* (= — — — ˘ ˘ ˘)

(b) Cadences:

— ˘ ˘ ˘ —	252a* 260a*
˘ ˘ — ˘ —	253a* 255c* 256c* 259c* 260c*
˘ ˘ [˘] — ˘ —	255b*
— ˘ — ˘ ˘	256b* 257a* 258b*c* 260b* 262b* 263b* 264b* 265b* 266b* 267b* 268b*c* 269b*
— ˘ — ˘ [˘ —]	259b*
— ˘ — [— ˘] ˘ —	263c*
— — — ˘ —	265c*
— ˘ — — —	266a*
— ˘ — ˘ —	the remainder

(c) (i) **Resolution.** There is resolution of a long syllable in the following pāda: 263a.

(ii) **Redundant syllables.** There are redundant syllables in the following pādas: 255b* 259b* 263c*.

(iii) **Coalesced syllables.** A long syllable in place of two shorts occurs in the following pādas: 255b 260b 262bc 263b 264b 265c 266b 267b 268b 269b.

§53. *Gaṇacchandas* stanzas:

The following varieties of the *Gaṇacchandas* stanza are found in Thī:

(a) Old *Āryā*: 23–24

(b) *Āryā*: 111cd
213–23 (except for 213abc 218ab (*Śloka*) and 216 (*Gīti*))
243
400–47 (except for 416a* 444a (*Śloka*))
448–522 (except for 472a 487c 488–92 495abc* (*Śloka*) and 505 (*Gīti*))

(c) *Gīti*: 216 505

§54. Old *Āryā*.

(a) Alsdorf (App. II, p. 234 f.n.) and Warder (PM §47) identify the metre of 23–24 as old *Āryā* (which Warder calls *Gīti*, presumably meaning old *Gīti*). the following reconstructed version of these verses is put forward merely as a basis for analysis. The *gaṇa* analysis thus obtained approximates closely to that obtained by Asldorf for old *Āryā* stanzas in AMg (1958, pp. 252–53).

(b) 23ab *sûmuttikā sumuttîkā | sādhû muttika mhi musalassa*
cd *ahirikŏ mĕ chattakaṃ vā pi | ukkhalikaṃ mĕ deḍḍubhaṃ vāti*
c (alternative reading) *ahitikŏ me vāto vāti |*
24ab *rāgañ ca aham dosañ ca | cicciṭi cicciṭī ti viharāmi*
cd *sā rukkha-mūlam upagamma | ahŏ su⟨k⟩khan ti sukhatŏ jhāyāmi*

(c)

pādas	1	2	3	4	5	6	7	8
23ab	– –	⏑ – ⏑	– –	–, –	– –	⏑ – ⏑	⏑ ⏑ –	⏑
cd	⏑ ⏑ ⏑ ⏑	⏑ – ⏑	– –	⏑, –	⏑ ⏑ –	⏑ – ⏑	– –	⏑
(c)	⏑ ⏑ ⏑ ⏑	– –	– –	⏑,				
24ab	– –	⏑ ⏑ –	– –	⏑, –	⏑ ⏑ –	⏑ – ⏑	⏑ ⏑ –	⏑
cd	– –	⏑ – ⏑	⏑ ⏑ –	⏑, ⏑ ⏑	– –	⏑, ⏑ ⏑ ⏑	– –	⏑

§55. *Āryā* and *Gīti*.

The following analyses of *Āryā* and *Gīti* stanzas are based upon Alsdorf's re-edited text, except for 111cd which Alsdorf did not recognise as *Āryā*. They will consequently differ from Warder's analyses (PM §§206–12), which are based upon P's text, as emended (in an unspecified way) by Warder. It is sometimes possible to understand how Warder would wish to emend (see the notes on 401, 420), but occasionally his statements are hard to understand, e.g. he says (PM §212) that ⏑ – does not occur in the first *gaṇa* in Thī 400–522 (but see the note on 243), and that ⏑ occurs in the sixth *gaṇa* of the first pāda-yuga somewhere in Thī 448–522 (where?).

In these analyses I omit 410b 441b 461b, which are too corrupt to analyse with certainty. They are discussed in the notes.

§ 56 (a) Thī 111cd (P's text)

gaṇa	1	2	3	4	5	6	7	8
– –	111				111		111	
– ⏑ ⏑			111					
⏑ – ⏑				111		111		
⏑								111
– ⏑		111*						

(b) Thī 213–23 (Alsdorf's text omitting śloka pādas)

First pāda-yuga:

gaṇa	1	2	3	4	5	6	7	8
– –	215 216 219 221 222	214 216 219 220	215 216 217 221 222 223	214 215 216	219 220 221 222 223		214 215 217 221	
– ⏑ ⏑	220			223	216		216	
⏑ ⏑ –	214 217 223	215 217	214 219 220	217 220 222	214 217		219 220 222 223	
⏑ – ⏑		221 222 223		219 221		214 215 216 217 219 220 221 222 223		
⏑ ⏑ ⏑ ⏑					215			
⏑								215 217 219 221
			–					214 216 220 222 223

Second pāda-yuga:

gaṇa	9	10	11	12	13	14	15	16
– –	215 216 218 219 220 222 223	214 222	215 216 218 219 220 223	214 215 216 218 219 222	213 216 218 219 220 222 223		213 214 215 216 218 220	
– ⏑ ⏑		221 223			221		223	
⏑ ⏑ –	214 217	217 218	214 217 221 222	213	214 217		217 219 221	
⏑ – ⏑		215 216 219 220		217 220 223		216		
⏑ ⏑ ⏑ ⏑	221			221	215			
⏑						213 214 215 217 218 219 220 221 222 223		213 214 215 217 220
–								216 218 219 221 222 223

(c) Thī 243 (Alsdorf's text)

First pāda-yuga:

gaṇa	1	2	3	4	5	6	7	8
– –			243	243	243		243	
⏑ – ⏑		243				243		
–								243
⏑ –	243*							

Second pāda-yuga:

gaṇa	9	10	11	12	13	14	15	16
– –	243		243	243			243	
⏑ ⏑ –					243			
⏑ – ⏑		243						
⏑						243		243

(d) Thī 400–47 (Alsdorf's text, omitting 410b 441b and śloka pādas)

First pāda-yuga:

gaṇa	1	2	3	4	5	6	7	8
– –	402 403 405 407 408 409 410 411 413 414 415 419 422 425 426 428 429 433 434 436 437 438 440 441 442 447	406 413 423 428 439 443 446 447	400 401 402 403 404 406 408□410 411 412 417 418 420 421 422 423 424 426 427 430 431 432 434 435 436 437 438 440 442 445	402 407 409 417 420 424 427 428 429 431 438 440 442 444 445 447	400 401 404 405 406 407 408 411 413 414 415 422 424 425 426 427 431 432 433 434 435 437 438 439 442 445		400 401 402 405 411 412 414 415 416 417 423 425 426 428 430 431 432 436 437 438 440 442 443 444 445 447	
– ⏑ ⏑	404 417 421 423 439 443 446	402 407 427	407 409 419 429	400 404 405 432 443 446	402 418 423 428 430 444 446		404 409 418 421 422 429 435	
⏑ ⏑ –	400 401 406 412 418 420 424 427 430 431 432 435 445	409 418 424 425 429 430 432 433 445	405 413 414 415 425 428 433 439 441 443 446 447	401 403 406 408 413 415 416 418 421 422 423 425 436	403 409 412 416 417 419 420 421 429 436 440 443 447		403 406 407 408 413 419 420 424 427 433 434 439 446	
⏑ – ⏑		401 403 404 405 408 410 411 412 414 415 417 419 420 421 426 431 434 435 436 437 438 440 441 442		411 412 419 426 430 433 434 435 437 439		401 402 403 404 405 406 407 408 409 411 412 413 414 415 416 417 418 419 421 422 423 424 425 426		

gaṇa	1	2	3	4	5	6	7	8
⏑ – ⏑						427 428 429 430 431 432 433 434 435 436 437 438 439 440 442 443 444 445 446 447		
⏑ ⏑ ⏑ ⏑		400 422		414		400 420		
⏑								405 407 414 417 420 421 422 426 432 437 444 446 447
–								400 401 402 403 404 406 408 409 411 412 413 415 416 418 419 423 424 425 427 428 429 430 431 433 434 435 436 438 439 440 442 443 445

Second pāda-yuga:

gaṇa	9	10	11	12	13	14	15	16
– –	401 403 405 406 409 410 412 413 415 416 418 420* 424 426 429 430 431 432 433 436* 437 438 440 441 444 445	418 422 433 434 437 439 440 441 446	400 401 402 403 405 407 408 410 412 414 416 417 418 419 420 421 422 423 425 426 428 432 434 435 436 440 443 444 445 446 447	400 407 408 415 416 418 428 429 431 432 433 434 444 446	402 403 405 406 408 409 410 412 413 414 416–29 431 433 435–42 444–47		401 402 406 408 411 413 414 415 416 417 418 419 420 421 423 425 426 427 430 431 434 435 440 445 447	
– ⏑ ⏑	400 417 419 421 422 427 434 435 442 447	417 427 428 432	404 409 411 430 438	409 410 413 414 422 425 430 435 436 438 447	401		404 424 429 433 436 438	
⏑ ⏑ –	402 404 407 408 411 414 423 425 439 443 446	400 403 430 431 438	406 413 415 424 427 429 431 433 437 439 441 442	404 406 411 412 417 424 426 445	400 404 407 411 415 430 432 434 443		400 403 405 407 409 410 412 422 428 432 437 439 441 442 443 444 446	
⏑ – ⏑		405 406 407 408 410 411		401 402 403 405 419 420				

gaṇa	9	10	11	12	13	14	15	16
⏑ – ⏑		412 413 414 415 416 419 420 421 423 424 425 426 429 435 436 442 443 445 447		421 423 427 437 439 440 441 442				
⏑ ⏑ ⏑ ⏑		401 402 404 409 444		443				
⏑ –	428*							
⏑						400–47		405 408 410 411 412 415 416 422 423 424 430 431 434 443 445 447
–								400–4 406 407 409 413 414 417–21 425–29 432 433 435–42 444 446

(e) Thī 448–522 (Alsdorf's text, omitting 461b and śloka pādas)

First pāda-yuga:

gaṇa	1	2	3	4	5	6	7	8
– –	448 450–56 459–62 464 466 468–71 475–79 483–86 494 496 506–9 514–16 520–22	449 453 459 464 467 474 477 483 484 486 496–98 502 509 518 521	450–53 455 456 459 460 462 465 467–71 473 474 477 481 482 484–87 494 499 500–8 510 511 513–17 519 520 522	448 460 465 471 472 474 477 480 484–86 494 496 507 514 517 518 521	448 449 451–53 459 462–64 466–70 472 474 475 478–84 486 493 497 498 502 504 505 506 511 513 515–21		451–56 458–60 468–70 472 473 476 478 479 484 486 487 493 494 501–4 507–10 512 517 518 520–22	
– ⏑ ⏑	449 458 463 474 481 482 487 493 517	450 456 499 505 512 519	461 463 475 493	457 466 503–6 508 511 515	450 454 455 457 458 477 487 496 499 500 501 503 507 508 512		457 463 466 471 474 477 481 482 496 499 513	
⏑ ⏑ –	457 465 497 500 501 503–5 511 519	448 451 457 461 475 476 481 520	448 449 454 457 458 464 466 476 478–80 483 496–98 509 512 518 521	452 464 468 469 475 476 483 493 497 499 500 510 513	456 460 465 471 473 476 485 494 509 510 514 522		448–50 462 464 465 467 475 480 483 485 497 498 500 505 506 514–16 519	
⏑ – ⏑		452 454 458 462 463 466 468–71 473 478 482 487		449–51 453–56 458 459 462 463 467 470 473		448–52 454–60 462–64 466–75		

gaṇa	1	2	3	4	5	6	7	8
˘ – ˘		493 494 500 501 503 504 506–8 510 511 513 515–17 522		478 479 481 482 487 498 501 502 509 516 520 522		477–87 493 494 496–512 514–17 519–22		
˘ ˘ ˘ ˘	467 473 480 498 499 502 512 513 518	455 460 465 479 480 485 514		512 519		453 465 (476) 513 518	511	
˘ ˘ ˘	510*							
˘								448 455 456 458 462 464 473 476 478 483 484 487 493 494 496 497 499 501–3 510 512 517 518 521 522
–								449–54 457 459 460 463 465–72 474 475 477 479–82 485 486 498 500 504–9 511 513–16 519 520

Second pāda-yuga:

gaṇa	9	10	11	12	13	14	15	16
– –	448 449 451–53 457 459 462–65 468 470 471□□ 474–78 480 481 483–86 494 496 498 501 503–7 509 513 515 517 519 522	450 461 465 469 474 478 486 496 511 516 518	448 450 453 455–58 460–62 464 466 467 471–74 476–78 480–83 485 494 497 500 501 506 507 509 512 514 515 519 521	450 456 457 459 461 463 464 472 473 476 477 479 484 485 487 493 494 498 509 511 514 520–22	448 450 451 454–56 459 462–65 467–75 478 480–83 485 487 493–500 502 503 (504) 505 507 508 511 516 518 519 522		449 452 453 455 457–60 462–65 468 470–72 474–77 479–81 483 485 486 500 502 507–11 513 516–22	
– ˘ ˘	450 460 472 473 508 520 521	448 454 456 458 460 473 480 481 485 495 501 502 508 515 522	452 465 468 470 475 502 513	469 478 483 495 515 516 519	453 513		451 461 469 473 478 487 495–97 (504) 515	
˘ ˘ –	454 455 458 461 466 469 479 493 497 499 500 502 510–12 514 516 518	449 452 453 476 493 499 509 510 512 521	449 451 454 459 463 469 479 484 486 493 495 496 498 499 503–5 508 510 511 516–18 520 522	452 458 462 465 466 470 480 504 506 510 513 517	449 452 457 458 460 461 466 476 477 479 484 486 501 506 509 510 512 514 515 517 520 521		448 450 454 456 466 467 482 484 493 494 498 499 501 503 505 506 512 514	
˘ – ˘			451 455 457 459 462–64 466 468 470		448 451 453–55 467 468 471 474		(505)	

gaṇa	9	10	11	12	13	14	15	16
		477 482–84 494 497 498 503–5 507 513 514 517 520		481 482 486 496 497 499 500–2 505 507 508 518				
⏑⏑⏑⏑	456 467 482 495	467 471 472 475 479 500 506 519		449 460 475 503 512				
⏑□□							448–87 493–503 (504) 506–522	448 449 453 455–58 460 463 464 467 468 470 471 476 477 480 481 485 494 498 499 502 503 506–8 513 516 518 519 522
–								450–52 454 459 461 462 465 466 469 472–75 478 479 482–84 486 487 493 495–97 500 501 504 505 509–12 514 515 517 520 521

(f) Totals (of both pāda-yugas):

gaṇas	1,9	2,10	3,11	4,12	5,13	6,14	7,15	8,16
— —	145	51	157	83	165		142	
— ⏑ ⏑	34	30	21	34	27		37	
⏑ ⏑ —	57	36	75	50	61		75	
⏑ — ⏑		113		78		120		
⏑ ⏑ ⏑ ⏑	14	22		10	2	7	1	
⏑						128		98
—								157
⏑ —	2							
⏑ ⏑ ⏑	1							
— ⏑		1						

§ 57. (a) The following pāda-yugas are *vipulā* (i.e. the cæsura is not after the third *gaṇa*, but the fourth *gaṇa* is then ⏑ ⏕ ⏑) :

411ab 412ab 414ab 419ab 420cd 433ab 434ab 449cd 451ab 454ab 458ab 462ab 478ab 487ab 497cd 501ab 505cd 509ab 516ab 522ab

(b) The following pādaoyugas are *vipulā*, but the fourth *gaṇa* is not ⏑ ⏓ ⏓ ⏑ :

418ab 464ab 470cd 483ab 500ab

(c) P's text has the wrong division between pāda-yugas in the following stanzas:

215 218 400 410 418 419 423 436 445 452 466 472 480 499

(d) There are defective *gaṇas* in the following pāda-yugas:

111cd 243ab 428cd 510ab

§ 58. *Śloka* stanzas

(a) Prior pādas:

(i) Eka-nipāta (1–18):

Openings	Cadences							
	⏑ – – ⏓ (*pathyā*)	⏑ ⏑ ⏑ ⏓	– ⏑ ⏑ ⏓	–, – – ⏓	– ⏑ – ⏓	⏑ ⏑ – ⏓	– – ⏑ ⏓	⏑ – ⏑ ⏓
⏓ – ⏑ –	1a 6c 7c 8a 9a 10c 11c 15a	11e			6a* 18a			13a
⏓ ⏑ – –	1c 2c 3c 14a 16c 17ac					12a		
⏓ – – –	2a 3a 4a 5ac 7a 11a 13c 14c 15c 16a 17e 18ce							
⏓ ⏑ – ⏑	4c							
⏓ – – ⏑								
⏓ – ⏑ ⏑	8c 9c							
⏓ ⏑ ⏑ –	10a							
⏓ ⏑ ⏑ ⏑								

(ii) Duka-nipāta (19–38):

Openings	Cadences							
	⏑ – – ⏓ (*pathyā*)	⏑ ⏑ ⏑ ⏓	– ⏑ ⏑ ⏓	–, – – ⏓	– ⏑ – ⏓	⏑ ⏑ – ⏓	– – ⏑ ⏓	⏑ – ⏑ ⏓
⏓ – ⏑ –	36ac 38ce	27a	22a	19c		31e	31a	29a
⏓ ⏑ – –	20a 21ac 26a 27c 29c 30a 32ac 33c 34c 35c							
⏓ – – –	22c 28a 30ce 37c 38a	20c	26e	28c*	37(a)			
⏓ ⏑ – ⏑	19a 31c 35a	25a						
⏓ – – ⏑	25c 33a							
⏓ – ⏑ ⏑	34a							
⏓ ⏑ ⏑ –	26c*							
⏓ ⏑ ⏑ ⏑								

(iii) Tika-nipāta (39–62)

Openings	Cadences							
	⏑ – – ⏓ (pathyā)	⏑ ⏑ ⏑ ⏓	– ⏑ ⏑ ⏓	–, – – ⏓	– ⏑ – ⏓	⏑ ⏑ – ⏓	– – ⏑ ⏓	⏑ – ⏑ ⏓
⏓ – ⏑ –	41ac 43a 56c 60a 61c	57a	50a	48a 55c	49c			
⏓ ⏑ – –	39c 41e 45ac 46a 53a 58a			46c 61a				
⏓ – – –	40a 42c 43c 44a 47ac 48c 50c 51e 53c 56a			40c*	42(a)			59c 62c
⏓ ⏑ – ⏑	39a 57a							55a
⏓ – – ⏑	49a 51c 52c 54c 58c 60c							
⏓ – ⏑ ⏑	59a 62a							
⏓ ⏑ ⏑ –								
⏓ ⏑ ⏑ ⏑	52a*							
⏓ – – – –	44e							

(iv) Catukka-nipāta (63–66):

Openings	Cadences							
	⏑ – – ⏓ *(pathyā)*	⏑ ⏑ ⏑ ⏓	– ⏑ ⏑ ⏓	–, – – ⏓	– ⏑ – ⏓	⏑ ⏑ – ⏓	– – ⏑ ⏓	⏑ – ⏑ ⏓
⏓ – ⏑ –	64c 65c					63c 65a		
⏓ ⏑ – –	66c							
⏓ – – –	63a 64a 66a							

(v) Pañca-nipāta (67–126):

Openings	Cadences							
	⏑ – – ⏓ (*pathyā*)	⏑ ⏑ ⏑ ⏓	– ⏑ ⏑ ⏓	–, – – ⏓	– ⏑ – ⏓	⏑ ⏑ – ⏓	– – ⏑ ⏓	⏑ – ⏑ ⏓
⏓ – ⏑ –	69a 71a 74a 77a 78a 82a 83a 84c 91a 92a 105c 114c	89a	121c	70c 79c 82c 88c 96c 104c 108a 109a 121a				118a
⏓ ⏑ – –	75a 81a 86ac 89c 95a 99a 102a 105a 113a 117c 120ce 122a	109c*	107a	81c		124c		100c
⏓ – – –	68ac 69c 70a 72a 73ac 75c 76ac 77c 78c 80a 83c 84a 85ac 87ac 90ac 93c 97a 99c 101c 102c 103c 104a 106a 110c 112c 113c 114ac 115ac 116ac 118ac 119c 121e 122c 123a 125c	107c 110a	71e		95c			
⏓ ⏑ – ⏑	67a 72c 91c 97c 100a 106c 108c 112a 117a 120a 124a 125a							
⏓ – – ⏑	74c 79a 80c 93a 94a 96a 101a 103a 119a 123c 126a				98a*			
⏓ – ⏑ ⏑	88a 94c 118e 119e							
⏓ ⏑ ⏑ –			71c*	92c*				
⏓ ⏑ ⏑ ⏑								
⏓ ⏑ – – –	67c							
⏓ – – – –	126c*		□□					

(vi) Cha-nipāta (127–74):

Openings	Cadences							
	⏑ – – ⏓ (pathyā)	⏑ ⏑ ⏑ ⏓	– ⏑ ⏑ ⏓	–, – – ⏓	– ⏑ – ⏓	⏑ ⏑ – ⏓	– – ⏑ ⏓	⏑ – ⏑ ⏓
⏓ – ⏑ –	128a 129ac 130ce 133c 139c 144a 148a 149a 151a 164ac 166a 167c 171a	135a 145a	139a 160a	161a 163a 168c			130a	
⏓ ⏑ – –	127ac 132a 133a 134ac 140a 141a 146c 151c 152a 154c 156c 158ac 173ac					152c		
⏓ – – –	132c 135c 137a 138ac 143c 144c 146a 150ac 154a 155c 156a 157c 159ac 160c 161c 165a 167a 168a 169c 171c	137c			169(a)		147c	142c
⏓ ⏑ – ⏑	140c 153a 157a 170a 172c							
⏓ – – ⏑	131c 136ac 141c 143a 148c 153c 155a 162a 166c 170c 172a							
⏓ – ⏑ ⏑	128c 142a 145c 149c 163c 165c							
⏓ ⏑ ⏑ –				147a*		174a*		
⏓ ⏑ ⏑ ⏑	131a* 162c*							
⏓ – – – –	174c							

(vii) Satta-nipāta (175–95) :

Openings	Cadences							
	⏑ – – ⏓ (*pathyā*)	⏑ ⏑ ⏑ ⏓	– ⏑ ⏑ ⏓	–, – – ⏓	– ⏑ – ⏓	⏑ ⏑ – ⏓	– – ⏑ ⏓	⏑ – ⏑ ⏓
⏓ – ⏑ –	177a 182a	190c	181a 189a	184a				
⏓ ⏑ – –	175c 179c 180a 182c 183ac 186c 189c 190a 193c							
⏓ – – –	176c 178c 181c 184c 187c 194c							188c 195c
⏓ ⏑ – ⏑	175a 177c 179a 185a 191c 192a							
⏓ – – ⏑	178a 180c 185c 186a 187a 192c 193a 194a							
⏓ – ⏑ ⏑	188a 191a 195a							
⏓ ⏑ ⏑ –	176a*							

(viii) Aṭṭha-nipāta (196–203):

Openings	Cadences							
	⏑ – – ⏓ (*pathyā*)	⏑ ⏑ ⏑ ⏓	– ⏑ ⏑ ⏓	–, – – ⏓	– ⏑ – ⏓	⏑ ⏑ – ⏓	– – ⏑ ⏓	⏑ – ⏑ ⏓
⏓ – ⏑ –		201a		199c				
⏓ ⏑ – –	196ac 197a 198a					197e		
⏓ – – –	200a 202c			201c				199a 203c
⏓ – – ⏑	200c 202a							
⏓ – ⏑ ⏑	197c 198c 203a							

(ix) Nava-nipāta (204–12):

Openings	Cadences							
	⏑ – – ⏓ (*pathyā*)	⏑ ⏑ ⏑ ⏓	– ⏑ ⏑ ⏓	–, – – ⏓	– ⏑ – ⏓	⏑ ⏑ – ⏓	– – ⏑ ⏓	⏑ – ⏑ ⏓
⏓ – ⏑ –	208a 210c 212a		205a 207a			206a		207c
⏓ ⏑ – –	204a 205c 211c 212c							
⏓ – – –	209ac							
⏓ – – ⏑	210a 211a					206c		
⏓ – ⏑ ⏑								204c
⏓ ⏑ ⏑ ⏑	208c*							

(x) Ekādasa-nipāta (213–23) :

Openings	Cadences							
	⏑ – – ⏓ (*pathyā*)	⏑ ⏑ ⏑ ⏓	– ⏑ ⏑ ⏓	–, – – ⏓	– ⏑ – ⏓	⏑ ⏑ – ⏓	– – ⏑ ⏓	⏑ – ⏑ ⏓
⏓ – ⏑ –	213a					213c		
⏓ ⏑ ⏑ –						218a		

(xi) Dvādasa-nipāta (224–35) :

Openings	Cadences							
	⏑ – – ⏓ (*pathyā*)	⏑ ⏑ ⏑ ⏓	– ⏑ ⏑ ⏓	–, – – ⏓	– ⏑ – ⏓	⏑ ⏑ – ⏓	– – ⏑ ⏓	⏑ – ⏑ ⏓
⏓ – ⏑ –	227ac		225a 226c	228c 229c 233c				
⏓ ⏑ – –	225c 234a							
⏓ – – –	224a 226a							235c
⏓ ⏑ – ⏑	229a					232c		
⏓ – – ⏑	224c 232a 234c							
⏓ – ⏑ ⏑	233(a) 235a							
⏓ ⏑ ⏑ –			228a*					

(xii) Soḷasa-nipāta (236–51) :

Openings	Cadences							
	⏑ – – ⏓ (*pathyā*)	⏑ ⏑ ⏑ ⏓	– ⏑ ⏑ ⏓	–, – – ⏓	– ⏑ – ⏓	⏑ ⏑ – ⏓	– – ⏑ ⏓	⏑ – ⏑ ⏓
⏓ – ⏑ –	239c 240c 241c 242ce 245c 246a 247ac 249c 250c			242a 249a 244c 250a				
⏓ ⏑ – –	236a 237c						239a	
⏓ – – –	236c 248a 251c							
⏓ ⏑ – ⏑	237a 240a 244a 251a							
⏓ – – ⏑	238ac 241a 245a 246c 248c							

(xiii) Vīsati-nipāta (271–365) : 319c 325a 340ae

Openings	Cadences							
	⏑ – – ⏓ (*pathyā*)	⏑ ⏑ ⏑ ⏓	– ⏑ ⏑ ⏓	–, – – ⏓	– ⏑ – ⏓	⏑ ⏑ – ⏓	– – ⏑ ⏓	⏑ – ⏑ ⏓
⏓ – ⏑ –	271ac 288e 289c 292c 294c 297a 302a 307c 308e 309c 311c 312ac 313c 326ac 328e 350a	299a 341e 356a	273a 285a 287c 288a 289a 300a 305a 314(a) 319c 325a 340ae 346c 357a 363a 364a	280c 284a 301a 305c 309a 329c 330c 335a 337c 349a 360a	273c 287e 356c	281a*	297a 280a	295c
⏓ ⏑ – –	276ac 278a 282c 285c 291a 296c 304a 306c 307a 308c 310c 311a 313a 316c 317c 318c 321c 322a 330a 332ac 334c 335c 337e 340c 342a 344ac 360c	275a	304c			277a		
⏓ – – –	272a 274c 278c 279c 281c 284c 286c 287a 290c 294a 303a 306e 308a 311e 322c 323ce 324ce 325c 331ac 333c 336a 337a 338c 339ac 341ac 342c 345a 346a 348a 350c 351a 353a 354c 357c 358a 359ac 365a	338a 358c	352a	283a*	282a 292a	275c 277c		318(a)

⏓ ⏑ – ⏑	283c 290a 293c 295a 298a 301c 302c 314c 316a 317a 319a 320c 323a 333a 336c 343a 347a 364c			334a*				
⏓ – – ⏑	274a 288a 293a 296a 297c 298c 300c 303c 310a 315ac 321a 327c 328c 329a 343c 347c 349c 351c 353c 355c 361ac 362ac							
⏓ – ⏑ ⏑	286a 291c 306a 324a 329e 345c 352c		365c*					
⏓ ⏑ ⏑ –	272c* 299c* 320a*							
⏓ ⏑ ⏑ ⏑	355a*							
⏓ ⏑ – ⏑ –			354a*					
⏓ – – – ⏑	363c*							

(xiv) Tiṃsa-nipāta (366–99) :

Open-ings	Cadences							
	⏑ – – ⏓ (*pathyā*)	⏑ ⏑ ⏑ ⏓	– ⏑ ⏑ ⏓	–, – – ⏓	– ⏑ – ⏓	⏑ ⏑ – ⏓	– – ⏑ ⏓	⏑ – ⏑ ⏓
⏓ ⏑ – –	366c							
⏓ ⏑ – ⏑	366a							

(xv) Cattālīsa-nipāta (400–47) :

Openings	Cadences							
	⏑ – – ⏓ (*pathyā*)	⏑ ⏑ ⏑ ⏓	– ⏑ ⏑ ⏓	–, – – ⏓	– ⏑ – ⏓	⏑ ⏑ – ⏓	– – ⏑ ⏓	⏑ – ⏑ ⏓
⏓ – ⏑ –					444a			
⏓ ⏑ – –						416a		

(xvi) Mahā-nipāta (448–522) :

Openings	Cadences							
	⏑ – – ⏓ (*pathyā*)	⏑ ⏑ ⏑ ⏓	– ⏑ ⏑ ⏓	–, – – ⏓	– ⏑ – ⏓	⏑ ⏑ – ⏓	– – ⏑ ⏓	⏑ – ⏑ ⏓
⏓ – ⏑ –	487c 488c 489c 490a	491c	490c*					
⏓ ⏑ – –	488a 491a							
⏓ – – –	489a 495(a)							
⏓ ⏑ – ⏑				472a				
⏓ – ⏑ ⏑	492(a)							
⏓ ⏑ ⏑ ⏑							492c*	

(b) Posterior pāda openings (all with the cadence ⏑ – ⏑ ⏓ except where marked (‡)).

(i) Eka-nipāta (1–18):

⏓ ⏑ – –	1d 4d 7b 10b 11bd 13d 14d 15d 16d 17bf 18f
⏓ – – –	1b 2bd 3d 4b 5b 6d 7d 8d 9d 10d 12d 13b 16b 18b
⏓ ⏑ – ⏑	5d 11f 12b
⏓ – – ⏑	3b 6b 8b 9b 18d
⏓ – ⏑ ⏑	14b* 15b 17d

(ii) Duka-nipāta (19–38):

⏓ ⏑ – –	19b 20d 22b 30d 31bf 33d 34d 35bd
⏓ – – –	21bd 25bd 26df 27b 28d 30f 32b 33b 34b 36d 38bf
⏓ ⏑ – ⏑	22d 27d 28b 29bd 30b 36b 38d
⏓ – – ⏑	19d 26b 37b
⏓ – ⏑ ⏑	20b 31d 32d 37d

(iii) Tika-nipāta (39–62):

⏓ ⏑ – –	46b 48b 49bd 52bd 56b 57bd
⏓ – – –	39d 41df 43b 44f 45bd 47b 48d 50b 54(b)d 56d 59b 60d 61d 62b
⏓ ⏑ – ⏑	41b 47d 50d
⏓ – – ⏑	39b 40d 42b 44b 46d 51df 53b 58b
⏓ – ⏑ ⏑	40b 42d 43d 53d 55bd 59d 60b 61b 62d
⏓ ⏑ ⏑ –	58d*
⏓ ⏑ ⏑ ⏑	44d*

(iv) Catukka-nipāta (63–66):

⏓ ⏑ – –	66d
⏓ – – –	63d 64bd 65bd
⏓ ⏑ – ⏑	63b
⏓ – – ⏑	66b

(v) Pañca-nipāta (67–126):

⏓ – ⏑ –	74b* 91b* 106b* 118f* 119f*
⏓ ⏑ – –	68b 70bd 75d 76d 77b 78b 79b 80d 81bd 82b 84d 86d 87d 88d 89bd 90d 92d 93b 98b 100d 101bd 104b 105d 107b 108b 109b‡110d 113d 114d 118d 119d 120d 122d 123bd 124b 125d
⏓ – – –	68d 69b 71df 73b‡ 74d 75b 76b 79d 83b 88b 92(b) 93d 95d 96d 97b 99bd 103d 107d 109d 110b 111(b) 112d 114f 115b 116b 177bd 118b 119b 120f 121f
⏓ ⏑ – ⏑	71b 78d 80b 85b‡ 87b 90b 98d 100b 102d 104d 106d 108d 113b 114b 115d 120b 122b 124d
⏓ – – ⏑	67b 72b 73d 82d 83d 85d 86b 91d 94b 95b 96b 97d 102b 105b 116d 121bd 125b‡ 126bd
⏓ – ⏑ ⏑	67d 69d 72d 77d 84b 94d 103b 112b

(vi) Cha-nipāta (127–74):

⏓ – ⏑ –	165b*
⏓ ⏑ – –	127d 130d 131bd 133b 134d 136d 139d 140d 145b 148d 151b 152bd 154bd 155b 157b 158b 160b 165d 166b 168d 171d 173b
⏓ – – –	128d 129b 130b 137d 138bd 142b 143d 146b 147bd 150d 151d 153b 156d 161d 162d 163b 167d 173d 174d
⏓ ⏑ – ⏑	127b 128b 133d 135b 137b 140b 144d 149d 150b 155d 156b 159b 160d 166d 170d 171b 172d
⏓ – – ⏑	129d 132b 134b 136b 141b 144b 148b 149b 153d 158d 163d 164d 167b 168b 169b 170b 172b 174b
⏓ – ⏑ ⏑	130f 132d 135d 139b 142d 143b 145d 146d 157d 161b 162b 164b 169d
⏓ ⏑ ⏑ –	141d* 159d*

(vii) Satta-nipāta (175–95):

⏓ ⏑ – –	176d 177d 178d 179d 182b 187b 189b 190d 191b 194b
⏓ – – –	175bd 176b 178b 180b 184d 187d 188b 190b 191d 194d 195b
⏓ ⏑ – ⏑	179b 183b 184b 192d
⏓ – – ⏑	177b 180d 181bd 182d 185bd 192b
⏓ – ⏑ ⏑	183d 186bd 188d 189d 193bd 195d

(viii) Aṭṭha-nipāta (196–203):

⏓ ⏑ – –	197b 198b 202b
⏓ – – –	199b 200(b)d 202d 203b
⏓ ⏑ – ⏑	196b 197f 201bd
⏓ – – ⏑	197d 198d
⏓ – ⏑ ⏑	196d 203d
⏓ ⏑ ⏑ ⏑	199d*

(ix) Nava-nipāta (204–12):

⏓ ⏑ – –	204d 207bd 208bd 209b 211b 212d
⏓ – – –	205b 209d 211d
⏓ ⏑ – ⏑	205d
⏓ – – ⏑	206b 210b
⏓ – ⏑ ⏑	204b 206d 210d 212b

(x) Ekādasa-nipāta (213–23):

⏓ ⏑ – –	218b
⏓ – – –	213b

(xi) Dvādasa-nipāta (224–35):

⏓ ⏑ – –	224d 227b 229bd 233b
⏓ – – –	224b 226(d) 228bd 232d 233d 235b
⏓ ⏑ – ⏑	227d
⏓ – – ⏑	225b 226b 232b 234b
⏓ – ⏑ ⏑	235d
⏓ ⏑ ⏑ –	225d* 234d*

(xii) Soḷasa-nipāta (236–51):

⏓ – ⏑ –	251b*
⏓ ⏑ – –	239bd 240d 242f 245b 246b 251d
⏓ – – –	238d 240(b) 241b 242d 244d 245d 246d 248d 249bd 250b
⏓ ⏑ – ⏑	238b 242b 247b
⏓ – – ⏑	236d 237d 241d 248b
⏓ – ⏑ ⏑	236b 237b 244b 247d

(xiii) Vīsati-nipāta (271–365):

⏓ – ⏑ –	286d* 311b*
⏓ ⏑ – –	272b 273b 275b 279b 280b 281b 282b 284b 287df 290bd 292d 294bd 295bd 298d 300bd 302d 303bd 304d 305bd 307bd 308bd 312b 313b 314d 318d 319d 320b‡d 325d 326d 327d 328df 329df 330b 332d 333b 334b‡ 336d 337df 338b‡ 340d 344d 349bd 351bd 352b 353d 355d 356b 358b 359b 360b 361bd 362d 364bd 365b
⏓ – – –	277b 286b 287b 288bdf 289bd 291d 297d 299d 301bd 306bdf 309b 311f 317d 318b‡ 322d 323df 324bdf 325b 326b 327e 329b 331bd 332b‡ 336b 339d‡ 341bd 346b 347bd 348bd 350b 352d 354b 355b 357d 360d 362b 363bd 365d
⏓ ⏑ – ⏑	272d 273d 275d 276d 277d 278d 279d 280d 281d 282d 283d 284d 285d 293d 297b 298b 314b 315b 317b 319b 330d 334d 335b 340bf 343bd 344b 345bd 354d 358d

⏓ — — ⏑	271d 274bd 278b 283b 292b 293b 296b‡d 299b 304b 308b‡ 309d 313d 315d‡ 316bd 322b 335d 337b 341f 342bd 350d 353b 357b 359d
⏓ — ⏑ ⏑	271b 276b 285b 291b 302b 310bd 312bd 321bd 333d 338d 339b 346d 356d
⏓ ⏑ ⏑ ⏑	311d*

(xiv) Tiṃsa-nipāta (366–99):

⏓ — — —	366bd

(xv) Mahā-nipāta (448–522):

⏓ — ⏑ —	495b*
⏓ ⏑ — —	488d 489bd 490b 491d
⏓ — — —	491b 492bd
⏓ — — ⏑	488b 490d

§59. The posterior pādas which do not have the cadence ⏑ — ⏑ ⏓ are, as in the case of Th (see EV I §34), probably to be regarded as *Anuṣṭubh* verses, following the scansion of *Anuṣṭubh* verses in early Skt literature, where variations from the later fixed form are found. The fact that these verses in Thī may be regarded as showing an old variation does not imply anything about their date of composition since an element of conscious archaizing cannot be discounted. Some of the cadences are undoubtely due to faulty readings, and many can be regularised without much difficulty, but it seemed worthwhile to list all those occurring in P.

(a) with long fifth syllable (— — ⏑ ⏓):
85b *vicinantiyā yoniso* (? scan *-iyă*)
91d *pāpuṇiṃ cetaso* (? read *pāpuṇi*[*ṃ*])
251b *saccaṃ brāhmaṇo* (? read *sacca*[*ṃ*])
332b *Sāvatthiṃ gantave* (? read *Sāvatthu*[*ṃ*])
489d *dukkha-pphalā* (? read *du*[*k*]*kha-*)

In addition, in a number of pādas the word *brāhmaṇa* occurs in the cadence so that the fifth syllable becomes long unless the combination *br-* is held not to make position. This is discussed below (§74(a)).

(b) with short sixth syllable (⏑ ⏑ ⏑ ⏓):

109b *pañjali ahaṃ* (? read *pañjalî*)

318b 320b 334b *nirupadhiṃ* (? read *-ûpadhiṃ*)

338b *dhammam asuniṃ* (? read *a⟨s⟩suṇiṃ*)

339d *yeva pihaye* (? read *pîhaye*)

342d *ariya-dhanaṃ* (? read *ariya⟨ṃ⟩* or *ariya-⟨d⟩dhammaṃ*)

(c) with long seventh (⏑ — — ⏓):

125b *Paṭācārā* (Cᵉ reads *Paṭācărā*)

296b 308b *bhāsasi taṃ Cāpe* (Bᵉ reads *tvaṃ ca me*)

315d *paritappāmi* (Bᵉ reads *-ayiṃ*)

(d) with long fifth and short sixth syllables (— ⏑ ⏑ ⏓):

73b *bālâlapanaṃ* (some editions read *bāla-lāpanaṃ*, but we should perhaps read *balollāpanaṃ*, with long fifth (- (a))

§60. **Resolution.** There are resolved syllables in the following pādas:

First syllable: 2d 19c 49a 59d 62d 82c 110c 129b 139a 142d 144c 183d 188d 195d 203d 204b 210c 235d 236a 239c 240c 242e 245c 271abcd 272a 274b 305b 338a 352a 353a

Sixth syllable: 11c 65a 77a 118e 199e 161a 212a 213c 236c 239a 280c 305c 324(c) 341c 488c 492c

Other syllables (some of these examples are doubtful, and should probably be regarded as hyper-metric pādas, or explained in some other way):

Second syllable: 323d 324d

Fourth syllable: 44(b) 52b 131b 305b 342c

Seventh syllable: 109(c) 213a 228c 233c 326a.

§61. **Redundant syllables.** There are redundant syllables in the following pādas:

Nine-syllable pādas: 44c 67c 92b 126c 174c 200b 226d 240b 314a 318a 324c 354a 363c

Some of the pādas listed as showing resolution of syllables other than the first or sixth are probably rather to be regarded as hyper-metric.

Some of these hyper-metric pādas arise from faulty readings. Others can be normalised by contraction (e.g. 92b), or by elision (e.g. 240b). As noted in EV I §37), the inclusion of a name sometimes produces a hyper-metric pāda (e.g. 363c).

IX. Metrical licence

§62. Many verses in Thī, as printed in P, scan only because of certain changes which have been introduced into them *metri causa*. Such changes usually involve the writing of a long vowel as short, or vice versa, but other forms of metrical licence are employed too. Many more verses can be regularised if the necessary changes are made *m.c.* The following lists give examples of the changes that have been made, and suggest pādas where similar changes could be made to improve the metre. The variants listed for the *Gaṇacchandas* stanzas are those needed to convert P into Alsdorf's text (App. II, pp. 238–50), except where otherwise indicated. Other, sometimes better, variants for the *Gaṇacchandas* stanzas are sometimes suggested in the notes. Occasionally a change made *m.c.* has the effect of producing an alteration of vocabulary or morphology. As in the case of Th (see EV I §39), the point must be made that the fact that the metre of a verse can be improved is no evidence that it shuld be so improved, nor that any resultant lexical variation was intended. So although Alsdorf suggests reading *hañce* for *sace* in 243a and *täto* for *tato* in 436c to obtain the scansion – – in the first *gaṇa* of an *Āryā* stanza, it must be noted that defective *gaṇas* are found elsewhere in Thī (e.g. 428c 510a), and moreover alternative corrections, e.g. *sa⟨c⟩ce* and *ta⟨t⟩to*, not involving a change of vocabulary or form, can be suggested. The fact that the metre requires *jhānajjhăyana*-in 401c does not help us to decide whether this is the equivalent of *jhān'ajjhayana*- or *jhāna-jjhāyana*- in meaning. The possibility must always be faced that writers in Pāli did not feel bound to follow the stricter rules of Skt literature. This seems to be particularly so in the case of the openings of *Śloka* pādas. There are several examples in Thī of the opening ⏓ ⏑ ⏑ – in prior pādas and ⏓ – ⏑ – in posterior pādas, but without more information about the acceptability of such openings it would be unwise to correct the text, although in most cases it would be simple to do so.

§63. **The restoration of doubled consonants.**

(a) Examples are found in the following pādas:

106a *kkhandhā* (Śl)

498d 499d *ppahonti* (Gaṇa: we must in fact read *pahonti*)

(b) The metre is improved if consonants are restored in the following pādas:

6a *pha⟨s⟩sehi* (Śl)
111a *pa⟨s⟩savī* (Vait)
159d *anibbisam* (Śl)
256c 259c *⟨p⟩palambitā* (or read *valihî*) (Rath)
338b *a⟨s⟩suṇiṃ* (Śl)
381d *⟨p⟩pavaddhati* (or read *-ratî*) (Vait)
418d *vi⟨d⟩dessate* (Gaṇa)
459d *yāva⟨j⟩jīvaṃ* (Gaṇa)

(c) The following restoration is required to correct a scribal or printing error:

67d *ci⟨t⟩tassa* (Śl)

§64. **The unhistoric doubling of consonants.**

(a) Examples of this are found in the following pādas:

31a *pañcaddasī* (Śl)
151b *mahaddhane* (Śl)
210b *samavassari* (Śl)
279a 280a *dhammaddharā* (Śl)
489d *dukkhapphalā* (Śl)
490a *rukkhapphal-* (Śl)
500b *yuga-cchiddaṃ* (Gaṇa)

Some of these changes may not be genuine changes *m.c.*, since they can be explained in other ways: *dhammaddharā* is probably merely a variant of *dhammaṃ-dhara*, i.e. a compound with the first element in the accusative case; *mahaddhane* is a variant of *mahā-dhane*; *yuga-cchiddaṃ* is in accordance with the rule in Skt that *-ch-* is doubled after a short vowel (in fact *yuga-chiddaṃ* is required *m.c.*).

(b) There are several pādas where the metre becomes more regular if doubling of this kind is postulated:

24d 508b *su⟨k⟩khaṃ* (Gaṇa)
44d 174a *-su⟨k⟩kha-* (or *pītî-*) (Śl)
165b *-⟨d⟩diṭṭhiṃ* (Śl)
218a *upavi⟨j⟩jaññā* (Śl)
243a *sa⟨c⟩ce* (Gaṇa)

342d *ariya⟨d⟩dhanaṃ* (Śl)
375c 383c *pita⟨t⟩taro* (or *piyätaro*) (Vait)
379(b) *su⟨p⟩phullaṃ* (Vait)
391b *vi⟨s⟩saṭṭhe* (Vait)
406c 435b *bahu⟨t⟩ta-* (Gaṇa)
420c 436c *ta⟨t⟩to* (Gaṇa)
426a *vi⟨s⟩sajjito* (Gaṇa)
428c *ni⟨s⟩sinnāya* (Gaṇa)
452b *sad⟨dh⟩ā* (Gaṇa)
484a *ni⟨s⟩saṭṭhaṃ* (Gaṇa)
486c *a⟨t⟩tito* (Gaṇa)
487d *a⟨t⟩tittā* (Gaṇa)
510a *a⟨p⟩parimitañ* (or *aparî-*) (Gaṇa)
516b *pabba⟨j⟩ji* (or *pabbäji*) (Gaṇa)

§ 65. **The simplification of consonant groups.**

(a) Examples of this are found in the following pādas:

84d *dakkhisaṃ* (or is this an aorist?) (Śl)
351d 490b *dukhā* (Śl)

(b) The metre is improved if groups are simplified in the following pādas:

12(b) *phu[ṭ]ṭhā* (Śl)
37a 42a 169a 519b *-[k]khattuṃ* (Gaṇa and Śl)
44c *pa[l]laṅke* (or *palla[ṅ]ke*) (Triṣṭ)
214d 220b 270b 419b 489b 492a 506d *du[k]kha-* (Gaṇa, Rath, and Śl)
266a *suma[ṭ]ṭhaṃ* (Rath)
384d *ma[g]gāyasi* (Vait)
388a *a[k]kuṭṭha-* (Vait)
406d *ta[s]sa* (Gaṇa)
407a 417b *sa[s]sura-* (Gaṇa)
428b *pa[ñ]ñāpayiṃ* (Gaṇa)
437b *ni[l]lacchesi* (Gaṇa)
439b 440d *ni[l]lacchito* (Gaṇa)
439c 441c *aka[l]lo* (Gaṇa)
451d 461a 484d *du[k]khitā* (Gaṇa)
457c 477c *appossu[k]kā* (Gaṇa)

467d *di[y]yati* (Gaṇa)
470c *u[c]cāra-* (Gaṇa)
475b *tira[c]chāna-* (Gaṇa)
476b *kili[s]samānassa* (Gaṇa)
493b *a[t]tano* (Gaṇa)
495c 498a *anamata[g]ge* (Gaṇa)
500b *-[c]chiddaṃ* (Gaṇa)
510c *-yu[t]to* (Gaṇa)
515d *-da[s]sā* (Gaṇa)
519c *upapa[j]jimhā* (Gaṇa)

§66. The metre can frequently be improved by the restoration of one or more syllables:

(a) *Triṣṭubh* pāda:
12c *kāmesu* ⟨*cā*⟩ (or ⟨*vā*⟩)

(b) *Vaitālīya* pādas:
111a *ca*⟨*ta*⟩ (read *vata*)
373a *v*⟨*iy*⟩*āḷa-* (or *vāḷâ-*)
374d *vasan*⟨*avar*⟩*ehi*
391a *avind*⟨*iy*⟩*e*

(c) *Gaṇacchandas* pādas:
215c *aṭṭhaṅgikaṃ* ⟨*ca*⟩
215d *cattāri* ⟨*pi*⟩
217a *gal*⟨*ak*⟩*e*
218c *pantha*⟨*mhi*⟩ (for *panthe*)
222a ⟨*sam-*⟩*bhāvito*
223d ⟨*a*⟩*bhaṇī*
400d ⟨*hi*⟩*guṇavatiyo* (or *guṇavatîyo*)
405d *manāpā* ⟨*ca*⟩
408b *parijano* ⟨*vā*⟩
409a *annena* ⟨*ca*⟩
410a *u*⟨*pa*⟩*ṭṭhahitvā*
410b ⟨*pati-*⟩*gharaṃ*
411a *pasād*⟨*han*⟩*aṃ*
421b *paṭiccha*⟨*ra*⟩*ti*
422b *dantaṃ* ⟨*ca*⟩

433d *aphassayi⟨sa⟩ṃ* (or *aphassayi* ⟨*'ha*⟩*ṃ*)
436d 438d *okkami⟨sa⟩ṃ* (or *okkami* ⟨*'ha*⟩*ṃ*)
441b *dhārayāmi* ⟨*'ham*⟩
452c *kāyena* ⟨*ca*⟩
456b *d⟨u⟩ve*
460(c) *āharisâ⟨mi⟩*
476a ⟨*ghātā*⟩ *nirayesu*
479b *yassa* ⟨*sā*⟩
480c *pāsādaṃ* ⟨*ca*⟩ (or *pid⟨a⟩hitvā*)
494d *rodante* ⟨*sā*⟩
498b ⟨*mahā-*⟩*mahiṃ*
510b ⟨*su-*⟩*bahūni*
511b *jara-*⟨*maraṇaṃ*⟩
512b *asokaṃ* ⟨*ca*⟩
516a *vissajjitā* ⟨*ca*⟩

(d) *Śloka* pādas:
67c ⟨n'⟩ accharā-saṃghāta-mattaṃ
109c ⟨maṃ⟩ avaca

§67. **Removal of syllables.** Hyper-metric pādas can often be corrected by shortening or denasalising vowels and then assuming resolution of a long syllable, but the metre can sometimes be improved by the removal of one or more syllables:

(a) *Vaitālīya* pādas:
51a [*amma*]
379d *s*[*ak*]*es*[*u*]
387a *yass*[*ā*]
391b *pari*[*pa*]*kkate*

(b) *Rathoddhatā* pādas:
255b [*a*]*laṅkataṃ*
259b [*pure*]

(c) *Gaṇacchandas* pādas:
214b [*pa*]*vaḍḍhati*
214d 418b [*pi*]
218c *vijāyitvā*[*na*]
219c *bhātā* [*ca*]

221a 408c 413b [*taṃ*]
221b *khā*[*di*]*tāni*
221c -*kul*[*ik*]*ā*
223d [*su-*]*vimutta-*
243d [*tvaṃ*]
401b 496d 519b [*ca*]
401d *bahussutā*[*yo*]
404c [*idaṃ*]
406d *adā*[*si*]
410a *kāle*[*na*]
412c -*putta*[*ka*]*ṃ*
414c [*saha*]
424b 425b [*me*]
428a *disvān*[*a*]
435a *Era*[*ka*]*kacche*
445b 494c *disvā*[*na*]
446d *tassā*[*haṃ*]
449a -*kath*[*ik*]*ā*
450a [*a*]*haṃ*
450c [*aṅga*]
454a [*amma*]
454c [*ye*]
461b [*sabbaso*]
462a 463d *putta*[*ka*]
465d [*c' eva*]
466a [*iva*]
467c -*kulala*[*yam*]-
473b -*satā*[*ni*]
483d[*su-*]*dullabhā*
486b [*āsi*]
494a *apāpuṇitvā*[*na 'yam*]
498d [*eva*]
499a -[*ṃ sākhā*]-
504d [*kupitā*]
505d [*kāmā*]
510c [-*su*]

512b *-mara[ṇa]-*
515a *uṭṭhāy[a]*

(d) *Śloka* pādas:

200b *pa[ri]dīpito*
240b *ajānantass[a]*
314a *-satā[ni]*
318a [*haṃ*] (or *brāhmaṇ[a]*)

§68. **The shortening of nasalised vowels.** In a number of words a nasalised vowel is to be scanned as short. This is shown in P by the omission of the *anusvāra*, although this is, of course, no guide to the actual pronunciation of a short nasalised vowel.

(a) (i) Examples of the loss of *-ṃ-* internally:

240b *ajānato* (Śl)
256b 257c 259b 260b 263b 264b 265b 267b 268b 269b *sobhate* (Rath)
269c *valīmatā* (Rath)

(ii) The metre is improved if *-ṃ-* is omitted in:

44c *palla[ṅ]ke* (or *pa[l]laṅke*) Triṣṭ)
219a *kāla[ṅ]katā* (Gaṇa)
260c *kha[ṇ]ḍiyā* (Rath)
265c *ri-[n]dī* (Rath)
392bc *vatta[n]ti* (Vait)
451d *haññа[n]te* (Gaṇa)
461c *ghaṭa[n]ti* (Gaṇa)
469b *nhāya[n]tî* (or *nhāya[n]te*) (Gaṇa)
475d (*dīy*)*a[n]te* (Gaṇa)
486c *āla[ṅ]kato* (Gaṇo)
507b *daha[n]ti* (Gaṇa)

(b) (i) Examples of the loss of final *-ṃ*:

14b *jāti* (*-ṃ* omitted incorrectly) (Śl)
138d *sokāna* (Śl)
161d *buddhāna* (Śl)
191b *hattha-padāna* (Śl)
238d *kamma* (Śl)
278c *sukkāna* (Śl)

378a *sudhota-raja* (Vait)
418c *kātu* (-*ṃ* omitted incorrectly) (Gaṇa)
421c 447c *dāsi* (Gaṇa)
426c *maritu* (-*ṃ* omitted incorrectly) (Gaṇa)
441a *naṅgala* (Gaṇa)
473d *c' eva* (Gaṇa)

(ii) The metre is improved if -*ṃ* is omitted in:

91d *pāpuṇi*[*ṃ*] (Śl)
231a *sahassāna*[*ṃ*] (Triṣṭ)
251b *sacca*[*ṃ*] (Śl)
253b -*pūra*[*ṃ*] (Rath)
261a -*kānanasmi* [*ṃ*] (Rath)
283a *sa*[*ṃ*] (Śl)
332b *Sāvatthi*[*ṃ*] (Śl)
372c 415d *tuyha*[*ṃ*] (Vait and Gaṇa)
378d -*maṇḍita*[*ṃ*] (Vait)
379a *uppala*[*ṃ*] (Vait)
379c *tuva*[*ṃ*] (Vait)
393b *cittika*[*ṃ*] (Vait)
405b 408a *mayha*[*ṃ*] (Gaṇa)
410b -*ghara*[*ṃ*] (Gaṇa)
415a 474b 479a *eva*[*ṃ*] (Gaṇa)
428b *āsana*[*ṃ*] (Gaṇa)
434b *phala*[*ṃ*]- (Gaṇa)
437a *sattâha*[*ṃ*]- (Gaṇa)
451c -*ratta*[*ṃ*] (Gaṇa)
460d -*vasa*[*ṃ*] (Gaṇa)
466c *abhisaṃviseyya*[*ṃ*] (Gaṇa)
473b *pateyyu*[*ṃ*] (Gaṇa)
478b *abhinikkhamissa*[*ṃ*] (Gaṇa)
481a *tahi*[*ṃ*] (Gaṇa)
495a *bālāna*[*ṃ*] (Śl)
495b *punappuna*[*ṃ*] (Śl)
496d 497d *aṭṭhīna*[*ṃ*] (Gaṇa)
500c *sira*[*ṃ*] (Gaṇa)
501a *rūpa*[*ṃ*] (Gaṇa)

515d *pabbajitu*[*ṃ*] (Gaṇa)

(iii) The metre is improved if *-m* is read for *-ṃ* before vowels in:

28c *khambhesim* (Śl)

40c *saṃvegam* (Śl)

44c *sattâham* (Triṣṭ)

223a *aham* (Gaṇa)

257b *-âhesum* (Rath)

324c *brāhmaṇim* (Śl)

334a *Sundarim* (Śl)

398c *gaṇhissam* (Vait)

§69. **Lengthening of vowels.** The metre is frequently corrected by lengthening or nasalising a vowel which is normally short, e.g.

(a) *Rathoddhatā* pāda:

269c *valīmatā*

(b) *Vaitālīya* pāda:

374d *'nūpame*

(c) *Śloka* pādas:

1a *therīke*

35d 189a *satīmatī*

79b 123d *cāri*

88a *bahū-*

152d 153b *Anopamā*

292d *puno*

§70. The metre can be corrected in many pādas by lengthening or nasalising vowels:

(a) *Rathoddhatā* pādas:

252ac 260a *-sâdisā*

253a *surabhî-*

255b *venîhi*

255c *khalita*⟨*ṃ*⟩ (for *khalati*)

256c 259c *valihî* (or read ⟨*p*⟩*palambitā*)

260a *pattalî-*

266a *sû-maṭṭhaṃ* (or *saṃ-*)

266c *valîhi*

(b) *Triṣṭubh* pādas:

327a 328a *hatthî-*

(c) *Vaitālīya* pādas:

111a *passavî*

111b *ayaṃ* (i.e. -m > -ṃ)

372c *ratî*

373a *vāḷâ-* (or *v⟨iy⟩āḷa-*)

375c 383c *piyâtaro* (or *piya⟨t⟩taro*)

381a *tûriyā-*

381d *-ratî* (or *⟨p⟩pavaḍḍhati*)

384d *maggâyasi*

388b *satî*

390c *tantîhi*

391d 392d *kimhî*

397b *khamāpayî*

398a *āhaniyâ* (or *āsādiya*)

398d *nû*

399b *agamî*

399d *cakkhû*

(d) *Gaṇacchandas* pādas:

23a *sûmuttike*

23a *sumuttîkā*

23b *sādhû*

111c *Bhaddāyâ*

214b *vaḍḍhatî*

215a *vijāneyyâ*

216a 520d *itthî-*

216c *sâpattikaṃ*

217a *apakantantî*

219b *patî*

219d *ḍayhantî*

220c 496a *assû*

220d 457d 477d *jātî*

222d *apekkhî*

223c *Kîsā-*

243a *nadîyo*

243d *tenâ*
400d *guṇavatîyo* (or ⟨*hi*⟩ *guṇavatiyo*)
403c *valîkaṃ*
406a *Sāketâto*
406c *seṭṭhî*
407a *sassûyā*
408a *sāmikassâ*
408b *bhaginîyo*
410b *samupâgamāmi*
414d 416b 425d *sahâ-*
415a *avacâ*
418c *kātu*⟨*ṃ*⟩ *ye*
419a *pitû*
420c 436c *tâto*
420d *vindathâ*
423c 441b *câ*
423d *punâ* (or *puno*)
424a 425a 430a 432a *bhaṇatî*
424c *idhâ* (or *idha*⟨*ṃ*⟩)
424c *kîrati*
424d *kîrihiti*
426d *maritu*⟨*ṃ*⟩ *ye*
427b *āgacchî*
432c *labhassû*
432d *sacchikarî*
435d *asevî*
437b *-kapî*
441b *dhārayāmî*
442b *vīthîyā*
444b *vaḍḍhîya*
447b *apakîritūna*
448b *-mahisîya*
455a *upapattî*
460(c) *āharisâ*⟨*mi*⟩
461c *ghaṭatî*
462c 463b 479b 481b 482b 494b 514c 515a *Anîkaratta-*

466b *sâvana-*
468a *nibbiyhatî*
469b *nhāyantî* (or *nhāyante*)
472b *saṃkhâtaṃ*
473a *-sattî-*
475b *tiracchāna⟨ṃ⟩*
477c *ghaṭantî*
482 *manasîkarotî*
482b *āruhî*
482b *āruhî*
482d *katañjalî*
484c *ahosî*
485c *abhinandî*
487d *vâ*
493d *tassâ*
497d *Vîpulena* (or *Vepulena*)
499d *pitû-*
502c *kumbhîla-*
504b *parîḷāhā*
508a 521a *hetû*
508b *jahî*
508d *vihaññâsi*
510a *aparîmitañ* (or *a⟨p⟩pari-*)
511c *-vyādhî-*
511d *jātîyo*
512a *ajaraṃ* (i.e. *m* < *ṃ*)
512b *-padaṃ* (i.e. *m* < *ṃ*)
513a *bahūnî*
516b *pabbâji* (or *pabba⟨j⟩ji*)
518c *tīṇî*
520a *mahiddhîkā*
520b *mânussakamhi*

(e) *Śloka* pādas:

26c *punâ* (or *puno*)
44d *pītî-* (or *su⟨k⟩kha-*)
52a 131a *abbuhî*

58d 141d 234d *aratî*
71c 228a *iddhî*
73b *-lâpanaṃ*
74b *-pâkāsikam*
91b 286d *câ*
92c *vicarî* (or *vicâri*)
98a *putta⟨ṃ⟩*
106b *titthantî*
109b *pañjalî*
118f *karothâ*
119f *akamsî* (or *akamsu⟨ṃ⟩*)
147a *râmitvā*
159d *saṃsarî*
162c *vyādhî-*
174a *pītî-* (or *su⟨k⟩khena*)
176a *ghaṭâtha* (or *ghaṭetha*)
199d *jātî-*
208c *aṇû*
225d *sabhâriyā*
251b *amhî*
272c *Rohiṇî*
281a *satîmanto*
294c *atthî*
299c *āhârimena*
311b *katvāna⟨ṃ⟩* (or *karitvā*)
311d *pabbajî* (or *pabbâji*)
318b 320b 334b *nirûpadhiṃ*
320a *addasâ*
339d *pîhaye*
342d *ariya⟨ṃ⟩* (or *ariya-⟨d⟩dhanaṃ*)
355a *duggatî-*
365a *namassatî*
416a *hiṃsatî*
490c *vañcanîyā*
492c *gacchâtha*
495c *pitû*

§71. **Shortening of vowels.** The metre is sometimes corrected by shortening a vowel which is naturally long, e.g.

49d 482b *āruhi* (Śl and Gaṇa)
65a *Kapilānī* (Śl)
87d *oruhāmi* (Śl)
94a 116d 204b 224c 270a *ahu* (Rath and Śl)
114d v' *ajāniyaṃ* (Śl)
183d *momuhā* (Śl)
375d 383d *kinnari-* (Vait)
377b *māla-* (Vait)
404c *abravi* (Gaṇa)

§72. The metre can be corrected in a number of places by shortening vowels:

(a) *Triṣṭubh* pādas:
327–28b *gĕha-* (or *gaha-* or *ghara-*)

(b) *Rathoddhatā* pādas:
252b *vellit'aggă*
252c *sāṇa-*
262a *-kampurĭ* (or read *kambu-r-iva*)
263c 264c 267c *yathă*
264a *-muddikă-*
265c *lambantĕ* (or *-anti*)

(c) *Vaitālīya* pādas:
111b *ăyam*
370–71d *ramāmasĕ* (or *-masi*)
372d *ogăhissasi*
373 *asahāyikă*
376d 393c 396c *tĕ*
378c *abhirŭha*
379a *udakatŏ*
380b *-pŭramhi*
383b *-pamhĕ*
387d *sŏ* (or *sa*)
391a *uddhaṭĕ*
392b *tĕhi*

393a *yathă*
395c *pĭḷikoḷikă*
399a *să*

(d) *Gaṇacchandas* pādas:

23c *ahirikŏ*
23cd 222a 223b *mĕ*
24d *ahŏ*
24d *sukhatŏ*
214b 412d *tathă*
221b *khăditāni*
221c *-kul[ik]ă*
223c *Gotamĭ*
401a 404c *Isidāsĭ*
401c *-ajjhăyana-*
405c *ekă-*
408c *ĕka-*
410(c) *dhovantĭ* (or *dhovitvă*)
414b 416b 431a *-ăhaṃ*
414d *ekăgăre* (or read *ekaghare*)
421c 447c *dāsĭva*
424d *tĕ*
429c *santappayitvă*
433a *abhivādayitvă*
434b *ăyam*
435d *ăsevī*
444b *vaḍḍhîyă*
448b *mahĕsīyă* (or *mahisīya*)
448d *păsādikā*
449b *-sāsanĕ*
453a *desentĕ* (or *-enti*)
457a 458d *anujānătha*
463a 520c *-mahĕsī* (or *mahisī*)
467a *tăham*
467c *-kulăla-*
470c read *-passăva-*
472c *yonisŏ*

473a *divasĕ-divase*
473a *tĭsattī-*
478d *tālă-*
479c *pĭ taruṇă-*
493c *anubaddhĕ*
500d *pubbĕ* (or *pubba-*)
508c *puthulomŏ*
508d *dilitvă*
511b *jară-*
515b *tassă*
517d *yathă*
520b *ahumhă*

(e) *Śloka* pādas:
73b *bālă-*
85b *vicinantiyă*
233a *vasībhūtâhaṃ*

§73. **Conversion of vowels into semivowels.** In a number of pādas a final *-i* or *-u* is changed into the corresponding semivowel before a vowel.

(a) Examples are found in the following pādas:
226a 485d *kāmesv* (Gaṇa and Śl)
248a *pamuty* (Śl)
499d *-pitusv* (Gaṇa)

(b) The metre is improved if vowels are converted in the following pādas:
326a *hotv* (Śl)
514c *anunenty* (Gaṇa)

X. ORTHOGRAPHY AND PHONOLOGY

§74. **Consonant groups not making position.** In general the language of Thī follows the usual rule that a naturally short vowel is scanned as long if it is followed by a consonant group. Simon, however, pointed out (pp. 95–95) that certain groups appear not to make position, i.e. a short vowel before them is still to be scanned as short. The evidence for this depends upon the occurrence of the vowels in question in positions where a short vowel is normally found, e.g. in the cadence of an even *Śloka* pāda. As has been stated (§59), there are *Śloka* pādas in Thī which do not have the characteristic cadence ⏑ — ⏑ ⏓, and it must be concluded that Simon's assertions are not entirely without doubt.

(a) *br*: Simon maintained that *br* made position in *brahā*, *brahmā*, *bravīti* and *brūheti*, but not in *anubrūh-* and *brāhmaṇa*. The position in Thī is as follows, assuming as Simon did that the metre is regular in each case:

brāhmaṇa does not make position in 64d 290b 313b 314d 323b 324b 326b 336b, and probably does not in 251b

abravi does in 404c

brahma- does not in 459c 463c, and probably does not in 244c

anubrūh- does not in 163c 206d

(b) *tv*: *tvaṃ* does not make position in 230d if we follow the reading of S I 131, and probably does not in 237a 24a 462d (but perhaps we should read *taṃ*)

(c) *dv*: *dvāra* does not make position in 73c

(d) *by/vy*: *vyāpāda* probably does not make position in 165a

vyasana does not in 217d

vyākari does not in 517d

parivyatta does in 415b

-vyādhi does in 511c

We may conclude that in initial position *by-/vy-* does not make position (= *v-*), but intervocalically it does (= *-bb-*)

(e) *nh*: *nhātaka* does not make position in 251d 290d

nhāru does not in 470b

(f) *kl*: *-klesa* probably does in 191c 345a

Alsdorf suggests (App. II, p. 246) that *klissamānassa* (which he wishes to read for *kiliss-*) does not make position in 476b. It is more likely that we should read *kili*[*s*]*s-*.

The other occurrences of conjunct consonants are in positions where the metre is not fixed.

§75. *Svarabhakti* vowels. In many words a vowel which can be shown on historic grounds to be epenthetic, evolved to resolve a consonant group, must be disregarded for the purposes of scansion. In most cases this probably results from the fact that the epenthetic vowel had not yet developed at the time the verse was composed. In other examples the phenomenon is probably that of the resolution of a long syllable rather than the disregard of a *svarabhakti* vowel. For the purposes of the following list all such ambiguous occurrences have been listed here, and not in the lists of resolved syllables (§ 60).

aṭṭhamiyā 44e
arahat 318a
ariya 171a 186(c) 193(c) 245b 310(c) 321(c) (but not 279b 280b 342d 261(b)
kayirā 61a
turiya 139c
pariy- 78a 354c
bhariyā 225(d)
viriya 161a
sattamiyā 174c
sirīmat 229d
supina 490c
sūriya 87a

In general all other words are scanned as they are spelt, except that in *d⟨u⟩ve* (456b) a *svarabhakti* vowel must be supplied for scansion purposes.

Therīgāthā

Single Verses

A certain unknown bhikkhunī

1. Sleep happily, little therī, clad in the garment which you have made; for your desire is stilled, like dried-up vegetables in a pot.

Muttā

2. Muttā, be freed from ties, as the moon is freed from the demon ("seizer") Rāhu; with mind completely freed, without debt, enjoy your alms-food.

Puṇṇā

3. Puṇṇā, be filled with good mental states, as full as the moon on the fifteenth day; with fulfilled wisdom tear asunder the mass of darkness [of ignorance].

Tissā

4. Tissā, be trained in the training; may the opportune occasions not pass you by. Unfettered from all ties, live in the world without āsavas.

Another Tissā

5. Tissā, apply yourself to good mental states; do not let the opportune moment pass you by. For those who have missed the opportune moment grieve when consigned to hell.

Dhīrā

6. Dhīrā, attain cessation, the stilling of evil notions, happiness; gain quenching, unsurpassed rest-from-exertion.

Another Dhīrā

7. You are Dhīrā because of your firm (*dhīra*) mental states; you are a bhikkhunī with developed faculties. Bear your last body, having conquered Māra and his mount.

Mittā

8. Mittā, having gone forth in faith, be one who delights in friends (*mitta*); develop good mental states for the attainment of rest-from-exertion.

Bhadrā

9. Bhadrā, having gone forth in faith, be one who delights in auspicious things (*bhadra*); develop good mental states [and] unsurpassed rest-from-exertion.

Upasamā

10. Upasamā, you should cross the flood, the realm of death which is very hard to cross. Bear your last body, having conquered Māra and his mount.

[Another] Muttā

11. I am well-released, properly released by my release from the three crooked things, from the mortar, the pestle, and my crooked husband. I am released from birth and death; everything which leads to renewed existence has been rooted out.

Dhammadinnā

12. One should be eager, determinate, and suffused with mind; one whose thought is not attached to sensual pleasures is called an "upstreamer".

Visākhā

13. Do the Buddha's teaching; having done it one does not repent; wash your feet quickly and sit down on one side.

Sumanā

14. Seeing the elements as pain, do not come to birth again; discarding desire for existence, you will wander, stilled.

Uttarā

15. I was restrained in body, speech, and mind. I have plucked out craving root and all and have become cool, quenched.

Sumanā, who went forth when old

16. Lie down happily, old lady, clad in the garment which you have made; for your desire is stilled; you have become cool, quenched.

Dhammā

17. I wandered for alms, leaning on a stick, weak; with trembling limbs I fell to the ground in that very spot. Seeing peril in the body, then my mind was completely released.

Saṅghā

18. Giving up my house, gone forth, giving up son, cattle, and whatever was dear to me, giving up desire and hatred, and discarding ignorance, plucking out craving root and all, I have become stilled, quenched.

Nandā

19. Nandā, see the body, diseased, impure, rotten; develop the mind, intent and well-concentrated, for contemplation of the unpleasant.

20. And develop the signless, cast out the latent tendency to conceit. Then by the full understanding of conceit, you will wander, stilled.

Jentī

21. I have developed all these seven constituents of awakening, the ways for the attainment of quenching, as taught by the Buddha.

22. I have indeed seen that blessed one; this is the last body; journeying-on from rebirth to rebirth has been completely annihilated; there is now no renewed existence.

A certain unknown bhikkhunī

23. I am well-released, well-released, properly released from the pestle. It [the pestle] is noxious for me like a fungus; the mortar [is noxious] for me like snakes.

24. I destroy desire and hatred with a sizzling sound. Going up to the foot of a tree, [thinking] "O the happiness", I meditate upon it as happiness.

Aḍḍhakāsī

25. My wages of prostitution were as large as the revenue of the country of Kāsi; the townspeople fixed that price and made me priceless in price.

26. Then I became disgusted with my beauty, and being disgusted I was disinterested in it. May I not run again through the journeying-on from rebirth to rebirth again and again. I have realized the three knowledges. I have done the Buddha's teaching.

Cittā

27. Although I am thin, sick, and very weak, I go along leaning on a stick, having climbed the mountain.

28. I threw down my outer robe and turned my bowl upside down; I propped myself against a rock, tearing asunder the mass of darkness [of ignorance].

Mettikā

29. Although I am pained, weak, with my youth gone, I go along leaning on a stick, having climbed the mountain.

30. I threw down my outer robe and turned my bowl upside down. I sat down on a rock. Then my mind was completely released. I have obtained the three knowledges. I have done the Buddha's teaching.

Mittā

31. The fourteenth, the fifteenth, and the eighth day of the fortnight, and a special day of the fortnight, I kept as a fast-day, which is well-connected with the eightfold precepts. I longed for rebirth in the world of deities.

32. Today with a single meal each day, with shaven head, clad in the outer robe, I do not wish for rebirth in the world of deities. I have removed the fear in my heart.

Abhayamātā

33. Mother, from the soles of the feet upwards, from the head and hair downwards, consider this impure, evil-smelling body.

34. As I dwell in this way all my desire has been rooted out; the burning fever has been cut out; I have become cool, quenched.

Abhayattherī

35. Abhayā, fragile is the body, to which ordinary individuals are attached. Attentive and possessed of mindfulness, I shall discard this body.

36. Delighting in vigilance because of many painful objects, I have obtained the annihilation of craving. I have done the Buddha's teaching.

Sāmā

37. Four or five times I went out from my cell, not having obtained peace of mind, my mind being unsubmissive.

38. This is the eighth night since my craving was completely rooted out. Delighting in vigilance because of many painful objects, I have obtained the annihilation of craving. I have done the Buddha's teaching.

Another Sāmā

39. Twenty-five years have passed since I went forth. I am not aware of having obtained peace of mind at any time.

40. Without peace of mind, my mind being unsubmissive, then I reached a state of religious excitement, remembering the teaching of the conqueror.

41. Delighting in vigilance because of many painful objects, I have obtained the annihilation of craving. I have done the Buddha's teaching. Today is the seventh day since my craving was dried up.

Uttamā

42. Four or five times I went out from my cell, not having obtained peace of mind, my mind being unsubmissive.

43. I went up to a bhikkhunī who was fit to be trusted by me. She taught me the doctrine, the elements of existence, the sense-bases, and the elements.

44. I heard the doctrine from her as she instructed me; for seven days I sat in one and the same cross-legged position, consigned to joy and happiness. On the eighth day I stretched forth my feet, having torn asunder the mass of darkness [of ignorance].

Another Uttamā

45. I have developed all these seven constituents of awakening, the ways for the obtaining of quenching, as taught by the Buddha.

46. I am an attainer of the empty, or the signless aspects of nibbāna, whichever is wanted. I am the true daughter of the Buddha, always delighting in quenching.

47. All sensual pleasures, those which are divine and those which are human, have been completely cut out. Journeying-on from rebirth to rebirth has been completely annihilated; there is now no renewed existence.

Dantikā

48. Going out from my daytime-resting-place on Mt. Gijjhakūṭa, I saw an elephant on the bank of the river, having come up after plunging in.

49. A man, taking a hook, requested the elephant, "Give me your foot." The elephant stretched forth its foot; the man mounted the elephant.

50. Seeing the untamed tamed, gone under human control, I then concentrated my mind, gone to the forest for that purpose indeed.

Ubbirī

51. Mother, you cry out "O Jīvā" in the wood; understand yourself, Ubbirī. Eighty-four thousand daughters, all with the name Jīvā, have been burned in this funeral fire. Which of these do you grieve for?

52. Truly he has plucked out my dart, hard to see, nestling in my heart, which grief for my daughter he has thrust away for me, overcome by grief.

53. Today I have my dart plucked out; I am without hunger, quenched. I go to the Buddha-sage, the doctrine, and the Order as a refuge.

Sukkā

54. What has happened to these men in Rājagaha? They remain as though they have drunk wine. They do not attend upon Sukkā when she is preaching the Buddha's teaching.

55. But the wise drink the teaching, I think, which is not repellent, never causing surfeit, of sweet flavour, as travellers drink a rain-cloud.

56. You are Sukkā because of your bright (*sukka*) mental states, being rid of desire, concentrated. Bear your last body, having conquered Māra and his mount.

Selā

57. There is no escape in the world; what will you do with seclusion? Enjoy the delights of sensual pleasures; do not repent afterwards.

58. Sensual pleasures are like swords and stakes; the elements of existence are a chopping block for them; the delight in sensual pleasures of which you speak is now no delight for me.

59. Everywhere enjoyment of pleasure is defeated; the mass of darkness [of ignorance] is torn asunder; in this way know, evil one, you are defeated, death.

Somā

60. That place, hard to gain, which is to be attained by the seers, cannot be attained by a woman with two-finger-intelligence (= very little intelligence).

61. What harm could the woman's state do to us, when the mind is well concentrated, when knowledge exists for someone rightly having insight into the doctrine?

62. Everywhere enjoyment of pleasure is defeated; the mass of darkness [of ignorance] is torn asunder; in this way know, evil one, you are defeated, death.

The Group of Four Verses

Bhaddā Kāpilānī

63. Kassapa, the son, the heir of the Buddha, well concentrated, who knows his former habitation and sees heaven and hell,

64. and has attained the destruction of rebirths, is a sage perfected in supernormal knowledge. Because of these three knowledges he is a brahman with triple knowledge.

65. In just the same way Bhaddā Kāpilānī, with triple knowledge, having left death behind, bears her last body, having conquered Māra and his mount.

66. Having seen the peril in the world, we both went forth; with āsavas annihilated, tamed, we have become cool, quenched.

Groups of Five Verses

A certain unknown bhikkhunī

67. It is twenty-five years since I went forth. Not even for the duration of a snap of the fingers have I obtained stilling of the mind.

68. Not obtaining peace of mind, drenched with desire for sensual pleasures, holding out my arms, crying out, I entered the vihāra.

69. I went up to a bhikkhunī who was fit to be trusted by me. She taught me the doctrine, the elements of existence, the sense-bases and the elements.

70. I heard the doctrine from her and sat down on one side. I know my former habitation; I have purified the divine eye;

71. and there is knowledge of the state of mind of others; I have purified the ear-element; I have realized supernormal power too; I have attained the annihilation of the āsavas; I have realized these six supernormal knowledges; I have done the Buddha's teaching.

Vimalā, the former courtesan

72. Intoxicated by my good complexion, my figure, beauty, and fame, haughty because of my youth, I despised other women.

73. Having decorated this body, very variegated, deceiving fools, I stood at the brothel door, like a hunter having spread out a snare,

74. showing my ornamentation. Many a secret place was revealed. I did various sorts of conjuring, mocking many people.

75. Today I have wandered for alms with shaven head, clad in the outer robe, and am seated at the foot of a tree; I have obtained the stage of non-reasoning.

76. I have cut out all ties, those which are divine and those which are human. I have annihilated all the āsavas; I have become cool, quenched.

Sīhā

77. Afflicted by desire for sensual pleasures, because of unreasoned thinking, previously I was conceited, my mind being unsubmissive.

78. Obsessed by the defilements, giving way to the notion of happiness, I did not obtain peace of mind, being under the influence of thoughts of passion.

79. Thin, pale, and wan, I wandered for seven years; being very pained, I did not find happiness by day or night.

80. Then taking a rope, I went into a wood, thinking, "It is better to hang myself than to lead a low life again."

81. I made a strong noose and tied it to the branch of a tree. I cast the noose around my neck. Then my mind was completely released.

Nandā

82. "See the body, Nandā, diseased, impure, rotten. Devote the mind, intent and well concentrated, to contemplation of the unpleasant.

83. "As this is, so is that; as that is, so is this. It gives out a rotten evil smell, it is what fools delight in."

84. Looking at it in this way, not relaxing day or night, then analysing it by my own wisdom, I saw.

85. Vigilant, reflecting in a reasoned manner, I saw this body as it really was, inside and out.

86. Then I became disgusted with the body, and I was disinterested internally. Vigilant, unfettered, I have become stilled, quenched.

Nanduttarā

87. I used to worship fire and the moon and the sun and divinities. I went to river-fording places and used to go down into the water.

88. Undertaking many vows, I shaved half my head; I made my bed on the ground; I did not eat night-food.

89. Delighting in ornament and decoration, by means of bathing and anointing indeed, I ministered to this body, afflicted by desire for sensual pleasure.

90. Then obtaining faith I went forth into the houseless state, seeing the body as it really was. I have rooted out desire for sensual pleasures.

91. I have cut out all existences, and wishes and longings too. Unfettered from all ties, I have attained peace of mind.

Mittakālī

92. I went forth in faith from the house to the houseless state and wandered here and there, greedy for gain and honour.

93. I missed the highest goal and pursued the lowest goal. Gone under the mastery of the defilements, I did not know the goal of the ascetic's state.

94. I experienced religious excitement, as I sat in my little cell; thinking "I have entered upon the wrong road: I have come under the mastery of craving.

95. "My life is short. Old age and sickness are destroying it. There is no time for me to be careless before this body is broken."

96. Looking at the arising and passing away of the elements of existence as they really are, I stood up with my mind completely released. I have done the Buddha's teaching.

Sakulā

97. Living in a house, I heard the doctrine from a bhikkhu and saw the stainless doctrine, quenching, the unshaken state.

98. I abandoned son and daughter and money and grain; I had my hair cut off and went forth into the houseless state.

99. Undergoing training, developing the straight way, I eliminated desire and hatred and the āsavas which are combined with these.

100. I was ordained as a bhikkhunī and recollected that I had been born before. The divine eye has been purified; it is spotless, well-developed.

101. Seeing the constituent elements as other, arisen causally, liable to dissolution, I eliminated all āsavas; I have become cool, quenched.

Soṇā

102. I bore ten sons in this material body, and then being weak and aged I approached a bhikkhunī.

103. She taught me the doctrine, the elements of existence, the sense-bases, and the elements. When I heard the doctrine from her, I cut off my hair and went forth.

104. As I underwent training the divine eye was purified. I know my former habitation, where I lived before.

105. And, intent and well concentrated, I develop the signless. I have had immediate complete release; I have become quenched without clinging.

106. When they are known, the five elements of existence stand with root cut off. Born from an enduring foundation, I am immovable. There is now no renewed existence.

Bhaddā, the former Jain

107. With hair cut off, wearing dust, formerly I wandered, having only one robe, thinking there was a fault where there was no fault, and seeing no fault where there was a fault.

108. Going out from my daytime resting-place on Mt. Gijjhakūṭa, I saw the stainless Buddha, attended by the Order of bhikkhus.

109. Having bent the knee, having paid homage to him, I stood with cupped hands face to face with him. "Come, Bhaddā," he said to me; that was my ordination.

110. I have wandered over Aṅga, and Magadha, Vajjī, Kāsi, and Kosala. For fifty years without debt I have enjoyed the alms of the kingdoms.

111. Truly he produced much merit; truly wise was that lay-follower who gave a robe to Bhaddā who is now freed from all bonds.

Paṭācārā

112. Ploughing the field with ploughs, sowing seeds in the ground, nourishing wives and children, young men find wealth.

113. Why do I, possessed of virtuous conduct, complying with the teaching of the teacher, not obtain quenching? I am not slack, nor puffed-up.

114. I washed my feet and paid attention to the waters; and seeing the foot-water come flowing downhill from the high land to the low land, then I collected my mind, as [one collects] a noble thoroughbred horse.

115. Then I took a lamp, and I entered my cell. I inspected the bed and sat on the couch.

116. Then I took a needle and drew out the wick. The complete release of my mind was like the quenching of the lamp.

Thirty bhikkhunīs

117. "Having taken pestles, young men grind corn; nourishing wives and children, young men find wealth.

118. "Do the Buddha's teaching; having done it one does not repent. Wash your feet quickly and sit down on one side. Intent on peace of mind, do the Buddha's teaching."

119. They heard her utterance, Paṭācārā's teaching; they washed their feet and sat down on one side. Intent on peace of mind, they did the Buddha's teaching.

120. In the first watch of the night they recollected that they had been born before; in the middle watch of the night they purified the divine eye; in the last watch of the night they tore asunder the mass of darkness [of ignorance].

121. Standing up they paid homage to her feet. "We have taken your advice; we shall dwell honouring you like the thirty deities honouring Inda, who is unconquered in battle. We have the triple knowledge; we are without āsavas."

Candā

122. Formerly I fared ill, a widow, without children. Without friends and relations I did not obtain food or clothing.

123. Taking a bowl and stick, begging from family to family, and being burned by cold and heat, I wandered for seven years.

124. But then I saw a bhikkhunī who had obtained food and drink, and approaching her I said, "Send me forth into the houseless state."

125. And Paṭācārā, in pity, sent me forth; then she exhorted me and urged me towards the highest goal.

126. I heard her utterance and took her advice. The noble lady's exhortation was not in vain; I have the triple knowledge; I am without āsavas.

Groups of Six Verses

Pañcasatā Paṭācārā

127. "Whose way you do not know, either coming or going, why do you lament that being [who has] come, crying 'My son'?

128. "But you do not grieve for him whose way you do know, either coming or going; for such is the nature of living creatures.

129. "Unasked he came from there, unpermitted he went from here, surely having come from somewhere or other, having lived a few days.

130. "He went from here by one road, he will go from there by another. Passed away with the form of a man he will go journeying on. As he came, so he went. What lamentation is there in that?"

131. Truly she has plucked out my dart, hard to see, nestling in my heart, who [has] dispelled my grief for my son, when I was overcome by grief.

132. Today I have my dart plucked out; I am without hunger, quenched. I go to the Buddha-sage, the doctrine, and the Order, as a refuge.

Vāsiṭṭhī

133. Afflicted by grief for my son, with mind deranged, out of my senses, naked, and with dishevelled hair, I wandered here and there.

134. I dwelt on rubbish heaps in the streets, in a cemetery, and on highways; I wandered for three years, consigned to hunger and thirst.

135. Then I saw the well-farer who had gone to the city of Mithilā, the tamer of the untamed, the awakened one, who has no fear from any quarter.

136. Regaining my mind, I paid homage to him and sat down. In pity Gotama taught me the doctrine.

137. I heard the doctrine from him and went forth into the houseless state. Applying myself to the teacher's utterance, I realized the blissful state.

138. All griefs have been cut out, eliminated, ending in this way; for I have comprehended the grounds from which is the origin of griefs.

Khemā

139. "You are young and beautiful; I also am young and in my prime. Come, Khemā, let us delight ourselves with the fivefold music."

140. I am afflicted by and ashamed of this foul body, diseased, perishable. Craving for sensual pleasures has been rooted out.

141. Sensual pleasures are like swords and stakes; the elements of existence are a chopping block for them; what you call delight in sensual pleasures is now no delight for me.

142. Everywhere love of pleasure is defeated; the mass of darkness [of ignorance] is torn asunder; in this way know, evil one, you are defeated, death.

143. Revering the lunar mansions, tending the fire in the wood, not knowing it as it really is, fools, you thought it was purity.

144. But revering the awakened one, best of men, I am indeed completely released from all pains, doing the teacher's teaching.

Sujātā

145. Ornamented, well-dressed, wearing a garland, smeared with sandalwood-paste, covered with all my ornaments, attended by a crowd of slave-women,

146. taking food and drink, food hard and soft, in no small quantity, going out from the house I betook myself to the pleasure garden.

147. Having delighted there, having played, coming back to my own house, I saw a vihāra. I entered the Añjana wood at Sāketa.

148. I saw the light of the world. I paid homage to him and sat down. In pity the one with vision taught me the doctrine.

149. And hearing the great seer, I completely pierced the truth. In that very place I attained the stainless doctrine, the state of the death-free.

150. Then knowing the true doctrine, I went forth into the houseless state. I have obtained the three knowledges; the Buddha's teaching was not in vain.

Anopamā

151. I was born in an exalted family, which had much property and much wealth. I possessed a good complexion and figure, being Majjha's own daughter.

152. I was sought after by kings' sons, longed for by merchants' sons; one sent my father a messenger, saying, "Give me Anopamā.

153. "However much that daughter of yours Anopamā weighs, I will give you eight times that amount of gold and jewels."

154. I saw the awakened one, who was supreme in the world, unsurpassed. I paid homage to his feet and sat down on one side.

155. In pity Gotama taught me the doctrine. Seated on that seat I attained the third fruit.

156. Then I cut off my hair and went forth into the houseless state. Today is the seventh night since my craving was dried up.

Mahāpajāpatī Gotamī

157. Buddha, hero, homage to you, best of all creatures, who released me and many other people from pain.

158. All pain is known; craving as the cause is dried up; the noble eightfold way has been developed; I have attained cessation.

159. Formerly I was mother, son, father, brother, and grandmother; not having proper knowledge, I journeyed-on without respite.

160. I have indeed seen that blessed one; this is the last body; journeying on from rebirth to rebirth has been completely eliminated; there is now no renewed existence.

161. I see the disciples all together, putting forth energy, resolute, always with strong effort; this is homage to the Buddhas.

162. Truly Māyā bore Gotama for the sake of many. He has thrust away the mass of pain of those struck by sickness and death.

Guttā

163. Guttā, giving up your son and the wealth [which are] dear [to you], devote yourself to that very thing for the sake of which you went forth. Do not go under the influence of mind.

164. Creatures, deceived by mind, delighting in Māra's realm, run through the journeying on of numerous rebirths, ignorant.

165. Desire for sensual pleasures, and malevolence, and the false view of individuality, misapprehension about rules of virtuous conduct and vows, and uncertainty fifth —

166. bhikkhunī, abandoning these fetters, which lead to the lower-world, you will not come to this again.

167. Avoiding desire, pride, and ignorance, and conceit, cutting the fetters, you will put an end to pain.

168. Annihilating journeying on from rebirth to rebirth, comprehending and giving up renewed existence, you will wander in the world of phenomena, without hunger, stilled.

Vijayā

169. Four or five times I went forth from my cell, not having obtained peace of mind, my mind being unsubmissive.

170. I approached a bhikkhunī, honoured her, and questioned [her]. She taught me the doctrine, and the elements, and sense-bases,

171. the four noble truths, the faculties, and the powers, the constituents of awakening, and the eightfold way for the attainment of the supreme goal.

172. I heard her utterance, took her advice, and in the first watch of the night I recollected that I had been born before.

173. In the middle watch of the night I purified the divine eye. In the last watch of the night I tore asunder the mass of darkness [of ignorance].

174. And I then dwelt suffusing the body with joy and happiness. On the seventh day I stretched forth my feet, having torn asunder the mass of darkness [of ignorance].

Uttarā

175. "Young men take pestles and grind corn; nourishing wives and children, young men find wealth.

176. "Strive after the Buddha's teaching; having done it one does not repent. Wash your feet quickly and sit down on one side.

177. "Summoning up the mind, intent and well-concentrated, consider the constituent elements as other, and not as self."

178. Having heard her utterance, the advice of Paṭācārā, having washed my feet, I sat down on one side.

179. In the first watch of the night I recollected that I had been born before; in the middle watch of the night I purified the divine eye;

180. in the last watch of the night I tore asunder the mass of darkness [of ignorance]. Then I stood up with the triple knowledge. Your advice has been taken.

181. I shall dwell honouring you like the thirty deities honouring Inda, who is unconquered in battle. I have the triple knowledge; I am without āsavas.

Cālā

182. Summoning up mindfulness, a bhikkhunī with developed faculties, I pierced the peaceful state, the stilling of the constituent elements, happiness.

183. "Following whose teaching have you shaved your head? You seem like an ascetic, but you do not approve of sectarians. Why do you practise this, being foolish?"

184. Sectarians outside this Order rely upon false views. They do not know the doctrine; they are not proficient in the doctrine.

185. The Buddha, the unrivalled one, was born in the Sakya clan. He taught me the doctrine, the complete overcoming of false views:

186. pain, the uprising of pain, and the overcoming of pain, and the noble eightfold way leading to the stilling of pain.

187. I heard his utterance and dwelt delighting in his teaching. I have obtained the three knowledges. I have done the Buddha's teaching.

188. Everywhere the enjoyment of pleasure is defeated; the mass of darkness [of ignorance] is torn asunder; in this way know, evil one, you are defeated, death.

Upacālā

189. Possessed of mindfulness, possessed of vision, a bhikkhunī with developed faculties, I pierced the peaceful state, which is not cultivated by evil men.

190. "Why do you not approve of birth? Anyone who is born enjoys sensual pleasures. Enjoy the delights of sensual pleasures; do not repent afterwards."

191. For anyone who is born there is death, the cutting-off of hands and feet, slaughter, bonds, and calamity. Anyone who is born goes to pain.

192. The unconquered awakened one was born in the Sakya clan. He taught me the doctrine, the complete overcoming of birth:

193. pain, the uprising of pain, and the overcoming of pain, and the noble eightfold way leading to the stilling of pain.

194. I heard his utterance, and I dwelt delighting in his teaching. I have obtained the three knowledges. I have done the Buddha's teaching.

195. Everywhere the enjoyment of pleasure is defeated; the mass of darkness [of ignorance] is torn asunder; in this way know, evil one, you are defeated, death.

Sīsûpacālā

196. A bhikkhunī, possessed of virtue, well-controlled in her faculties, should obtain the peaceful state, never causing surfeit, of sweet flavour.

197. "The Tāvatiṃsa and Yāma and Tusita divinities, the Nimmānarati deities, and the Vasavatti deities; apply your mind there, where you lived before."

198. The Tāvatiṃsa and Yāma and Tusita divinities, the Nimmānarati deities, and the Vasavatti deities,

199. again and again, from existence to existence, are exposed to individuality, not passing beyond individuality, going to birth and death.

200. The whole world is ablaze, the whole world has flared up, the whole world is blazing, the whole world is shaken.

201. The Buddha taught me the doctrine, unshakable, incomparable, not cultivated by ordinary people. My mind was deeply attached to it.

202. I heard his utterance, and I dwelt delighting in his teaching. I have obtained the three knowledges. I have done the Buddha's teaching.

203. Everywhere the enjoyment of pleasure is defeated; the mass of darkness [of ignorance] is torn asunder; in this way know, evil one, you are defeated, death.

The Group of Nine Verses

Vaḍḍha's mother

204. "May you not have, Vaḍḍha, craving for the world at any time. Child, do not share in pain again and again.

205. "The sages dwell happily indeed, Vaḍḍha, free from lust, with doubts cut off, become cool, having attained self-taming, being without āsavas.

206. "Vaḍḍha, devote yourself to the way practised by those seers for the attainment of insight, for the putting of an end to pain."

207. "Confident indeed you speak this matter to me, mother. Now indeed, I think, craving is not found in you, mother."

208. "Whatever constituent elements, Vaḍḍha, are low, high, or middle, no craving, even minute, even of minute size, for them is found in me."

209. "All my āsavas have been annihilated as I meditate, vigilant. I have obtained the three knowledges. I have done the Buddha's teaching.

210. "Truly my mother, because she was sympathetic, applied an excellent goad to me, namely verses connected with the highest goal.

211. "I heard her utterance, my mother's instruction, and I reached a state of religious excitement in the doctrine, for the attainment of rest-from-exertion.

212. "Being resolute for exertion, not relaxing day or night, urged on by my mother, I attained supreme peace."

The Group of Eleven Verses

Kisāgotamī

213. The state of having noble friends has been praised by the sage with reference to the world; if he resorted to noble friends, even a fool would be wise.

214. Good men are to be resorted to; in this way the wisdom of those who resort to them increases. Resorting to good men one would be released from all pains.

215. One should know pain, and the uprising of pain, and its cessation, and the eightfold way, even the four noble truths.

216. The state of women has been said to be painful by the charioteer of men who are to be tamed; even the state of being a co-wife is painful; some, having given birth once,

217. even cut their throats; [some] tender ones take poisons; [some] having entered the belly are murderers; both suffer misfortunes.

218. Going along, about to bring forth, I saw my husband dead; having given birth on the path, I had not yet arrived at my own house.

219. Two sons dead and a husband dead upon the path for miserable me; mother and father and brother were burning upon one pyre.

220. Miserable woman, with family annihilated, you have suffered immeasurable pain; and you have shed tears for many thousands of births.

221. I dwelt in the middle of the cemetery; then the flesh of my sons was caused to be eaten; with my family destroyed, despised by all, with [my] husband dead, I attained the death-free.

222. I have developed the noble eightfold way leading to the death-free; I have realized quenching; I have looked at the doctrine as a mirror.

223. I have my dart cut out, my burden laid down; I have done that which was to be done. The therī Kisāgotamī, with mind completely released, has said this.

THE GROUP OF TWELVE VERSES

Uppalavaṇṇā

224. The two of us, mother and daughter, were co-wives; I experienced religious excitement, amazing, hair-raising.

225. Woe upon sensual pleasures, impure, evil-smelling, with many troubles, wherein we, mother and daughter, were co-wives.

226. I saw the peril in sensual pleasures, and I saw renunciation of the world as firm security; I went forth at Rājagaha from the house to the houseless state.

227. I know my former habitation; I have purified the divine eye; and there is knowledge of the state of mind of others; I have purified the ear-element;

228. I have realized supernormal power too; I have attained the annihilation of the āsavas: I have realized these six supernormal knowledges; I have done the Buddha's teaching.

229. I fashioned a four-horsed chariot by supernormal power, paid homage to the Buddha's feet, the glorious protector of the world, and I stood on one side.

230. "Going up to a tree with well-flowered top, you stand there alone at the foot of the tree; you do not even have a companion; child, are you not afraid of rogues?"

231. Even if a hundred thousand rogues like you were to come together, I should not move a hair's breadth, I should not even shake. What will you alone do to me, Māra?

232. I shall disappear, or I shall enter into your belly; I shall stand between your eyebrows; you will not see me standing there.

233. I have mastery over my mind; I have developed the bases of supernormal power well; I have realized the six supernormal knowledges. I have done the Buddha's teaching.

234. Sensual pleasures are like swords and stakes; the elements of existence are a chopping block for them; what you call "delight in sensual pleasures" is now "non-delight" for me.

235. Everywhere enjoyment of pleasure is defeated; the mass of darkness [of ignorance] is torn asunder; in this way know, evil one, you are defeated, death.

Puṇṇikā

236. "I am a water-carrier; even in the cold weather I have always gone down to the water, terrified by fear of punishment from noble ladies, harrassed by fear of [verbal] abuse and displeasure.

237. "What are you afraid of, brahman, when you constantly go down to the water? With trembling limbs you experience very great cold."

238. "But you already know the answer, lady Puṇṇikā; you ask one who is doing good action and thereby blocking off evil action.

239. "Whoever, whether young or old, does an evil action, even he is released from his evil action by ablution in water."

240. "Who indeed told you this, ignorant to the ignorant: 'Truly he is released from his evil action by ablution in water'?

241. "Now if this is true all frogs and turtles will go to heaven, and alligators and crocodiles, and the other water-dwellers.

242. "Sheep-butchers, pork-butchers, fishermen, animal-trappers, thieves and executioners, and other evil-doers, even they will be released from their evil action by ablution in water.

243. "If these streams carried away the evil you had previously done, they would carry away your merit too; thereby you would be devoid of both.

244. "Do not do the very thing, brahman, for fear of which you have always gone down to the water, brahman; may the cold water not strike your skin."

245. "Noble lady, you have brought me, entered upon the wrong way, back into the noble way. I give you this water-ablution robe."

246. "Keep the robe for yourself; I do not want the robe; if you are afraid of pain, if pain is unpleasant for you,

247. "do not do an evil action either openly or in secret. But if you do or will do an evil action,

248. "there is no release from pain for you, even if you fly up and run away. If you are afraid of pain, if pain is unpleasant for you,

249. "go to the venerable Buddha as a refuge, to the doctrine, and to the Order; undertake the rules of virtuous conduct; that will be to your advantage."

250. "I go to the venerable Buddha as a refuge, to the doctrine, and to the Order; I undertake the rules of virtuous conduct; that will be to my advantage.

251. "Formerly I was a kinsman of Brahmā; today I am truly a brahman. I possess the triple knowledge, I am endowed with knowledge, and I am versed in sacred lore; and I am washed clean."

Ambapālī

252. My hair was black, like the colour of bees, with curly ends; because of old age it is like bark fibres of hemp; not false is the utterance of the speaker of truth.

253. Covered with flowers my head was fragrant like a perfumed box; now because of old age it smells like dog's fur; not false is the utterance of the speaker of truth.

254. Thick as a well-planted grove, made beautiful, having the ends parted by comb and pin; because of old age it is thin here and there; not false is the utterance of the speaker of truth.

255. Possessing fine pins, decorated with gold, adorned with plaits, it looked beautiful; because of old age that head has been made bald; not false is the utterance of the speaker of truth.

256. Formerly my eyebrows looked beautiful, like crescents well painted by artists; because of old age they droop down with wrinkles; not false is the utterance of the speaker of truth.

257. My eyes were shining, very brilliant like jewels, very black and long; overwhelmed by old age they do not look beautiful; not false is the utterance of the speaker of truth.

258. In the bloom of my youth my nose looked beautiful like a delicate peak; because of old age it is like a flower-spike of long pepper; not false is the utterance of the speaker of truth.

259. My ear-lobes looked beautiful, like well-fashioned and well-finished bracelets; because of old age they droop down with wrinkles; not false is the utterance of the speaker of truth.

260. Formerly my teeth looked beautiful, like the colour of the bud of the plaintain; because of old age they are broken indeed and yellow; not false is the utterance of the speaker of truth.

261. Sweet was my warbling, like a cuckoo wandering in the grove in a jungle-thicket; because of old age it has faltered here and there; not false is the utterance of the speaker of truth.

262. Formerly my neck looked beautiful like a well-rubbed delicate conch-shell; because of old age it is broken and bowed-down; not false is the utterance of the speaker of truth.

263. Formerly both my arms looked beautiful, like round crossbars; because of old age they are weak as the Pāṭalī tree; not false is the utterance of the speaker of truth.

264. Formerly my hands looked beautiful, with delicate signet rings, decorated with gold; because of old age they are like onions and radishes; not false is the utterance of the speaker of truth.

265. Formerly both my breasts looked beautiful, swelling, round, close together, lofty; now they hang down like empty water-bags; not false is the utterance of the speaker of truth.

266. Formerly my body looked beautiful, like a well-polished sheet of gold; now it is covered with very fine wrinkles; not false is the utterance of the speaker of truth.

267. Formerly both my thighs looked beautiful like an elephant's trunk; because of old age they are like stalks of bamboo; not false is the utterance of the speaker of truth.

268. Formerly my calves looked beautiful, possessing delicate anklets, decorated with gold; because of old age they are like sticks of sesame; not false is the utterance of the speaker of truth.

269. Formerly both my feet looked beautiful, like shoes full of cotton wool; because of old age they are cracked and wrinkled; not false is the utterance of the speaker of truth.

270. Such was this body; now it is decrepit, the abode of many pains; an old house, with its plaster fallen off; not false is the utterance of the speaker of truth.

Rohiṇī

271. "Lady, you fell asleep saying 'Ascetics'; you wake up saying 'Ascetics'; you praise only ascetics; assuredly you will be an ascetic.

272. "You bestow much food and drink upon ascetics; Rohiṇī, now I ask you: Why are ascetics dear to you?

273. "Not dutiful, lazy, living on what is given by others; full of expectation, desirous of sweet things, why are ascetics dear to you?"

274. "Truly for a long time you have been questioning me about ascetics, father; I shall praise to you their wisdom, virtuous conduct, and effort.

275. "They are dutiful, not lazy, doers of the best of actions; they abandon desire and hatred; therefore ascetics are dear to me.

276. "They shake off the three roots of evil, doing pure actions; all their evil is eliminated; therefore ascetics are dear to me.

277. "Their body-activity is pure; and their speech-activity is likewise; their mind-activity is pure; therefore ascetics are dear to me.

278. "They are spotless like mother-of-pearl, purified inside and out; full of good mental states; therefore ascetics are dear to me.

279. "Having great learning, expert in the doctrine, noble, living in accordance with the doctrine; they teach the goal and the doctrine; therefore ascetics are dear to me.

280. "Having great learning, expert in the doctrine, noble, living in accordance with the doctrine, with intent minds, they are possessed of mindfulness; therefore ascetics are dear to me.

281. "Travelling far, possessed of mindfulness, speaking in moderation, not conceited, they comprehend the end of pain; therefore ascetics are dear to me.

282. "If they go from any village, they do not look back longingly at anything; they go without longing indeed; therefore ascetics are dear to me.

283. "They do not deposit their property in a storeroom, nor in a pot, nor in a basket, rather seeking that which is cooked; therefore ascetics are dear to me.

284. "They do not take gold, coined or uncoined, or silver; they live by means of whatever turns up; therefore ascetics are dear to me.

285. "Those who have gone forth are of various families and from various countries; nevertheless they are friendly to one another; therefore ascetics are dear to me."

286. "Truly for our sake, lady, you were born in our family, Rohiṇī; you have faith in the Buddha and the doctrine, and keen reverence for the Order.

287. "You indeed comprehend this unsurpassed field of merit; these ascetics will receive our gift too. For among them an extensive sacrifice will be set up for us."

288. "If you are afraid of pain, if pain is unpleasant for you, go to the venerable Buddha as a refuge, to the doctrine, and to the Order; undertake the rules of virtuous conduct; that will be to your advantage."

289. "I go to the venerable Buddha as a refuge, to the doctrine, and to the Order; I undertake the rules of virtuous conduct; that will be to my advantage.

290. "Formerly I was a kinsman of Brahmā, now I am truly a brahman. I possess the triple knowledge, and am versed in sacred lore, and have complete mastery of knowledge, and I am washed clean."

Cāpā

291. "Formerly I carried an ascetic's staff; now I am a deer-hunter; because of craving I have not been able to go from the terrible mire to that far shore.

292. "Thinking me very enamoured of her, Cāpā has kept our son happy; having cut Cāpā's bond I shall go forth again."

293. "Do not be angry with me, great hero; do not be angry with me, great sage; for there is no purity for one overcome by anger, how much less is there austerity."

294. "I shall indeed go out from Nālā; who will live here at Nālā? At Nālā women bind ascetics who live in accordance with the doctrine, by means of their figure[s]."

295. "Come, Kāḷa, turn back, enjoy sensual pleasures as before; I shall be under your control, and also whatever relatives I have."

296. "If indeed a quarter of this were as you say, Cāpā, truly that would be excellent for a man in love with you."

297. "Kāḷa, like a sprouting Takkārī tree in flower on the crest of a mountain, like a flowering Dālikā creeper, like a Pāṭalī tree in the middle of an island,

298. "with my body smeared with yellow sandalwood paste, wearing my best muslin garments, being beautiful, why do you go away abandoning me?"

299. "Just as a fowler wishes to snare a bird, so do you by means of your charming figure; but you will not fasten me."

300. "But this child-fruit of mine, Kāḷa, begotten by you, why do you go away abandoning me with this child?"

301. "Wise men leave their sons and their relatives and their wealth; great heroes go forth, like an elephant which has broken its fastening."

302. "Now I shall knock down to the ground on the spot this son of yours, with stick or knife; because of grief for your son you will not go."

303. "If you give our son to the jackals and dogs, you will not turn me back again for the child's sake, you wretched one."

304. "Then fare you well now. Where will you go, Kāḷa? To what village, town, city, royal capital?"

305. "Formerly we were leaders of groups, not ascetics although thinking ourselves ascetics; we wandered from village to village, to cities and royal capitals.

306. "But it will be different now, for the blessed one, the Buddha, alongside the River Nerañjarā, has taught the doctrine to living creatures for the abandonment of all pain. I shall go to his presence; he will be my teacher."

307. "You should utter my greeting now to the unsurpassed protector of the world, and having circumambulated him you should dedicate my gift."

308. "This is indeed proper for us, as you say, Cāpā; now I should utter your greeting to the unsurpassed protector of the world, and having circumambulated him I shall dedicate your gift."

309. And then Kāḷa went out alongside the River Nerañjarā; he saw the awakened one teaching the state of the death-free:

310. pain, the uprising of pain, and the overcoming of pain, and the noble eightfold way leading to the stilling of pain.

311. He saluted his feet, circumambulated him, dedicated the gift for Cāpā, and went forth into the houseless state. He has obtained the three knowledges. He has done the Buddha's teaching.

Sundarī

312. "Lady, formerly [when] causing to be eaten your sons who had passed away, you mourned excessively day and night.

313. "Today, when you have caused to be eaten seven children in all, brahman-lady Vāseṭṭhī, why do you not mourn greatly?"

314. "Many hundreds of sons, and hundreds of groups of relatives of mine and yours have been [caused to be] eaten in the past, brahman.

315. "Knowing the escape from birth and death, I do not grieve or lament; nor do I mourn."

316. "You speak such a truly amazing utterance, Vāseṭṭhī; whose doctrine do you know when you say such a thing?"

317. "That awakened one, brahman, near the city of Mithilā, has taught the doctrine to living creatures for the abandonment of all pain.

318. "I have heard that arahat's doctrine [which is] without basis for rebirth, brahman, and knowing the true doctrine there, I have thrust away grief for my son[s]."

319. "I too shall go near the city of Mithilā; perhaps that blessed one may release me from all pain."

320. The brahman saw the Buddha, completely released, without basis for rebirth. The sage who has reached the far shore of pain taught him the doctrine:

321. pain, the uprising of pain, and the overcoming of pain, and the noble eightfold way leading to the stilling of pain.

322. Knowing the true doctrine there, he found pleasure in going forth; after three nights Sujāta attained the three knowledges.

323. "Come, charioteer, go, take back this chariot; bid the brahman-lady good health and say, 'The brahman has now gone forth. After three nights Sujāta has attained the three knowledges.' "

324. And then taking the chariot and a thousand pieces too the charioteer bade the brahman-lady good health and said, "The brahman has now gone forth. After three nights Sujāta has attained the three knowledges."

325. "Hearing that the brahman has the triple knowledge, I give you this horse and chariot and a thousand pieces too, a full bowl as a present for bringing good news."

326. "Keep the horse and chariot, and the thousand pieces too, brahman-lady; I too will go forth in the presence of the one who has excellent wisdom."

327. "Abandoning elephants, cows and horses, jewels and rings, and this rich domestic wealth, your father has gone forth. Enjoy enjoyments, Sundarī; you are the heir in the family."

328. "Abandoning elephants, cows and horses, jewels and rings, and this delightful domestic wealth, my father has gone forth, afflicted by grief for his son. I too shall go forth, afflicted by grief for my brother."

329. "May the intention, which you seek, prosper, Sundarī. [There are] leftover scraps and gleanings as food, and a rag from a dust-heap as a robe. Making do with these you will be free from āsavas in the next world."

330. "Noble lady, the divine eye is purified as I undergo training; I know my former habitation, where I lived before.

331. "Relying on you, lovely one, who makes beautiful the Order of therīs, I have obtained the three knowledges. I have done the Buddha's teaching.

332. "Permit me, noble lady; I wish to go to Sāvatthi; I shall roar a lion's roar in the presence of the excellent Buddha."

333. "Sundarī, see the teacher, golden-coloured, with golden skin, the tamer of the untamed, the awakened one, who has no fear from any quarter."

334. "See Sundarī coming, completely released, without basis for rebirth, rid of desire, unfettered, her task done, without āsavas."

335. "Gone out from Bārāṇasī, and come into your presence, your disciple Sundarī pays homage to your feet, great hero.

336. "You are the Buddha, you are the teacher, I am your daughter, brahman, your true child, born from your mouth, my task done, without āsavas."

337. "Then welcome to you, good lady; you are not unwelcome. For in this way the tamed come, paying homage to the master's feet, rid of desire, unfettered, their task done, without āsavas."

Subhā, the smith's daughter

338. "I was young, with clean clothes, when previously I heard the doctrine. Being vigilant, I obtained comprehension of the four truths.

339. "Then I attained great non-delight in all sensual pleasures; seeing fear in individuality, I longed only for renunciation of the world.

340. "I left the group of my relatives, the slaves, and servants, the rich fields and villages, and delightful and pleasant possessions, and I went forth, abandoning no small wealth.

341. "Since I renounced the world in faith in this way, and the true doctrine has been well preached, it would not be fitting for me, once I had laid aside gold and silver, to take them back again, for I desire the state of having nothing.

342. "Silver or gold are not conducive to awakening or peace. This is not proper for ascetics; this is not the wealth of the noble ones.

343. "This is being greedy, and intoxication, stupefaction, increase of defilement, full of suspicions and with many troubles; there is here no permanent stability.

344. "Many men who are infatuated with this and careless, with defiled minds, being obstructed one by another, make a quarrel.

345. "Slaughter, bonds, calamity, loss, grief, and lamentation; much misfortune is seen for those who have fallen into sensual pleasures.

346. "Why do you, my relatives, like enemies, urge me on towards sensual pleasures? You know that I have gone forth, seeing fear in sensual pleasures.

347. "The āsavas do not diminish because of gold, coined or uncoined; sensual pleasures are enemies, murderers, hostile, binding with ropes.

348. "Why do you, my relatives, like enemies, urge me on towards sensual pleasures? You know that I have gone forth, with shaven head, clad in the outer robe.

349. "Leftover scraps and gleanings as food, and a rag from a dust-heap as a robe; this indeed is proper for me, the basic essentials for a houseless one.

350. "The great seers have rejected sensual pleasures, those which are divine and those which are human. Those seers are completely released in the place of security; they have arrived at unshakable happiness.

351. "May I not meet again with sensual pleasures, in which no refuge is found; sensual pleasures are enemies, murderers, like a mass of fire, painful.

352. "Greed is an obstacle, full of fear, full of annoyance, full of thorns, and it is very disagreeable; it is a great cause of stupefaction.

353. "Sensual pleasures are like a frightful attack, like a snake's head, which fools delight in, blind ordinary individuals.

354. "For people are attached to the mud of sensual pleasures; many in the world are ignorant; they do not know the end of birth and death.

355. "Because of sensual pleasures men enter very much upon the way which goes to a bad transition, bringing disease to themselves.

356. "In this way sensual pleasures are enemy-producing, burning, defiling, the lures of the world, constraining, the bonds of death.

357. "Sensual pleasures are maddening, deceiving, agitating the mind; a net spread out by Māra for the defilement of creatures.

358. "Sensual pleasures have endless perils, they have much pain, they are great poisons, they give little enjoyment, they cause conflict, drying up the virtuous party.

359. "Since I have caused such misfortune because of sensual pleasures, I shall not return to them again; I shall always delight in quenching.

360. "Having been in conflict with sensual pleasures, being desirous of the cool state, I shall dwell vigilant, in the annihilation of their fetters.

361. "I shall follow that griefless, stainless, secure, noble, eightfold, straight way, by which the great seers have crossed."

362. See this Subhā, the smith's daughter, standing firm in the doctrine. Having entered the immovable state she meditates at the foot of a tree.

363. Today is the eighth day. She went forth full of faith, beautiful by reason of the true doctrine, instructed by Uppalavaṇṇā, with triple knowledge, leaving death behind.

364. This one is a freed slave, without debt, a bhikkhunī with developed faculties, unfettered from all ties, her task done, without āsavas.

365. Sakka, the lord of beings, approaching by supernormal powers with a group of deities, reveres that Subhā, the smith's daughter.

The Group of Thirty Verses

Subhā Jīvakambavanikā

366. A rogue stopped the bhikkhunī Subhā as she was going to the delightful Jīvakamba wood; Subhā said this to him:

367. "What wrong have I done you, that you should stand obstructing me? For it is not fitting, sir, that a man should touch a woman who has gone forth.

368. "This training was taught by the well-farer, in my teacher's severe teaching. Why do you stand obstructing me? I possess the purified state, without blemish.

369. "Why do you, with disturbed mind and with passion, stand obstructing me? I am undisturbed, with passion departed, without blemish, with mind completely released in every respect."

370. "You are young and not ugly; what will going-forth do for you? Throw away your yellow robe. Come, let us delight in the flowery wood.

371. "The towering trees send forth a sweet smell in all directions with the pollen of flowers; the beginning of spring is a happy season; come, let us delight in the flowery wood.

372. "At the same time the trees with blossoming crests cry out, as it were, when shaken by the wind. What delight will there be for you if you plunge alone into the wood?

373. "You wish to go without companion to the lonely, frightening, great wood, frequented by herds of beasts of prey, disturbed by cow-elephants, who are excited by bull-elephants.

374. "You will go about like a doll made of gold, like an accharā in Cittaratha. O incomparable one, you will shine with beautiful garments of fine muslin, with excellent clothes.

375. "I should be at your beck and call if we were to dwell in the grove; for there is no creature dearer to me than you, O nymph with pleasant eyes.

376. "If you will do my bidding, being made happy, come, live in a house; you will dwell in the calm of a palace; let women do attendance upon you.

377. "Wear garments of fine muslin, put on garlands and unguents; I shall make much varied adornment for you, of gold, jewels, and pearls.

378. "Climb onto a bed with a coverlet well washed of dirt, beautiful, spread with a woollen quilt, new, very costly, decorated with sandalwood, having an excellent smell.

379. "Just as a blue lotus with beautiful blossoms rising up from the water is touched by non-human water-spirits, so you, liver of the holy life, will go to old age with your limbs untouched by any man."

380. "What is it that you approve of as essential here in the body, which is full of corpses, filling the cemetery, destined to break up? What is it that you have seen when you look at me, being out of your mind?"

381. "Your eyes are indeed like those of Turī, like those of a nymph inside a mountain; seeing your eyes my delight in sensual pleasures increases all the more.

382. "Seeing your eyes in your face, to be compared with the bud of a blue lotus, spotless, like gold, my sensual pleasure increases all the more.

383. "Even though you have gone far away, I shall remember you; you with the long eyelashes, you with the pure gaze; for no eyes are dearer to me than you, you nymph with pleasant eyes."

384. "You wish to go by the wrong path; you seek the moon as a plaything; you wish to jump over Mt. Meru, you who have designs upon a child of the Buddha.

385. "For I do not now have any object of desire anywhere in the world, including the deities; whatever sort it might be, it has been smitten root and all by the eightfold way.

386. "It has been scattered like sparks from a pit of burning coals; it is as valueless as a bowl of poison. Whatever sort it might be, it has been smitten root and all by the eightfold way.

387. "Try to seduce someone who has not observed this, or has not served the teacher; but if you seduce this one who knows, you will suffer distress.

388. "For my mindfulness is established in the midst of both reviling and praise, happiness and pain; knowing that conditioned things are disgusting, my mind does not cling to anything at all.

389. "I am a disciple of the well-farer, travelling in the eightfold vehicle which is the way. With my dart drawn out, without āsavas, gone to a place of solitude, I rejoice.

390. "For I have seen well-painted puppets, or dolls, fastened by strings and sticks, made to dance in various ways.

391. "If these strings and sticks are removed, thrown away, mutilated, scattered, not to be found, broken into pieces, on what there would one fix the mind?

392. "This little body, being of such a kind, does not exist without these phenomena; as it does not exist without phenomena, on what there would one fix the mind?

393. "Just as you have seen a picture painted on a wall, smeared with yellow orpiment; on that your gaze has been confused; so the perception of men is useless.

394. "You blind one, you run after an empty thing, like an illusion placed in front of you, like a golden tree at the end of a dream, like a puppet-show in the midst of the people.

395. "An eye is like a little ball set in a hollow, having a bubble in the middle, with tears; there is eye secretion here too; various sorts of eyes are rolled into balls."

396. Removing her eye, the good-looking lady, with an unattached mind, was not attached to it. She said, "Come, take this eye for yourself." Straightway she gave it to this man.

397. And straightway his passion ceased there, and he begged her pardon. "Become whole again, liver of the good life. Such a thing will not happen again.

398. "In smiting such a person, in embracing a blazing fire, as it were, in seizing a poisonous snake, as it were, could there be any safety? Forgive me."

399. And then that bhikkhunī, released, went to the presence of the excellent Buddha. When she saw the one with the marks of excellent merit, her eye was restored to its former condition.

The Group of Forty Verses

Isidāsī

400. In the city named after a flower, Pāṭaliputta, in the best part of the earth, there were two bhikkhunīs, members of the Sakya clan, possessed of good qualities.

401. One of them was called Isidāsī; the second was called Bodhī. Both possessed virtue, delighted in meditation and study, and had great learning. They had shaken off defilements.

402. When they had wandered for alms, made their meal, and washed their bowls, seated happily in a lonely place, they uttered these words:

403. "You are lovely, noble Isidāsī, your youth has not yet faded. What fault have you seen in household life that you are then intent on renunciation of the world?"

404. Asked in this way in the lonely place, Isidāsī, proficient in the teaching of the doctrine, said: "Hear, Bodhī, how I went forth.

405. "In Ujjenī, best of cities, my father was a merchant, restrained by virtuous conduct. I was his only daughter, dear, and charming, and beloved.

406. "Then from Sāketa came men, belonging to a most noble family, to woo me; a merchant with many jewels sent them. To him my father gave me as a daughter-in-law.

407. "Approaching morning and evening I did obeisance with my head to my father-in-law and mother-in-law; I paid homage to their feet, as I had been instructed.

408. "Seeing my husband's sisters, or his brothers, or his retinue, even my one and only beloved, I trembled and gave them a seat.

409. "I gratified them with food and drink and hard food and whatever was stored there; I brought it forth and gave what was fitting to each.

410. "Arising in good time I approached my lord's house; having washed my hands and feet, upon the threshold I approached my husband, with cupped hands.

411. "Taking a comb, decorations, collyrium, and a mirror, I myself adorned my lord, like a servant-girl.

412. "I myself prepared the rice-gruel; I myself washed the bowl; I looked after my husband as a mother her only son.

413. "My husband offended against me, who in this way had shown him devotion, an affectionate servant, with humbled pride, an early riser, not lazy, virtuous.

414. "He said to his mother and father, 'I will take leave and go; I will not be able to live together with Isidāsī in one house.'

415. " 'Do not speak in this way, son; Isidāsī is learned, clever, an early riser, not lazy. Why does she not please you, son?'

416. " 'She does me no harm, but I will not live with Isidāsī; to me she is just odious; I have had enough; having taken leave I will go.'

417. "Hearing his utterance my father-in-law and mother-in-law asked me, 'What offence have you committed? Tell us confidently how it really was.'

418. " 'I have not offended at all; I have not harmed him; I have not said any evil utterance; what can be done when my husband hates me?' I said.

419. "Downcast, overcome by pain, they led me back to my father's house, saying, 'While keeping our son safe, we have lost the goddess of beauty incarnate.'

420. "Then my father gave me to the kinsmen of a second [= another] rich man, belonging to a noble family, for half the bride-price for which the merchant had taken me.

421. "In his house too I lived a month, then he too rejected me, although I served him like a slave-girl, not harming him, possessed of virtue.

422. "And my father spoke to one who was wandering for alms, a tamer of others and self-tamed, 'Be my son-in-law; throw away your cloth and pot.'

423. "He too, having lived with me for a fortnight, then said to my father, 'Give me my cloth and pot and cup; I will beg for alms again.'

424. "Then my father, mother, and all the group of my relatives said to him, 'What has not been done for you here? Say quickly, what may be done for you.'

425. "Spoken to in this way, he said, 'Even if I myself were honoured, I have had enough; I will not be able to live together with Isidāsī in one house.'

426. "Allowed to go, he departed. I for my part, all alone, thought, 'I shall ask leave and go to die, or I shall go forth as a wanderer.'

427. "Then the noble lady Jinadattā, expert in the discipline, with great learning, possessed of virtue, came to my father's house on her begging round.

428. "Seeing her in our house, I rose up from my seat and offered it to her; I paid homage to her feet when she had sat down, and I gave her food.

429. "I satisfied her completely with food and drink and hard food and whatever was stored there, and I said, 'Noble lady, I wish to go forth.'

430. "Then my father said to me, 'Practise the doctrine in this very place, child; satisfy ascetics and twice-born brahmans with food and drink.'

431. "Then lamenting and cupping my hands I said to my father, 'Evil indeed was the action I did; I shall destroy it.'

432. "Then my father said to me, 'Attain awakening and the foremost doctrine, and obtain quenching, which the best of men realized.'

433. "I saluted my mother and father, and all the group of my relatives, and seven days after going forth I attained the three knowledges.

434. "I know my last seven births; I shall relate to you the [action] of which this is the fruit and result; listen to it with attentive mind.

435. "In the city of Erakaccha I was a goldsmith, possessing much wealth. Intoxicated by pride in my youth, I had sexual intercourse with another's wife.

436. "I fell from there and was cooked in hell; I cooked for a long time; and rising up from there I entered the womb of a female monkey.

437. "A great monkey, leader of the herd, castrated me when I was seven days old; this was the fruit of that action for me, because of having seduced another's wife.

438. "I fell from there, and dying in the Sindhava forest, I entered the womb of a one-eyed, lame she-goat.

439. "Castrated, and carrying children around for twelve years, I was worm-eaten, tailless, unfit, because of having seduced another's wife.

440. "I fell from there and was born in a cow belonging to a cattle-dealer; a lac-red calf, castrated, for twelve months

441. "I drew a great plough, and I pulled a cart, blind, tailless, unfit, because of having seduced another's wife.

442. "I fell from there and was born of a household-slave in the street, as neither a woman nor a man, because of having seduced another's wife.

443. "In my thirtieth year I died; I was born as a little girl in a carter's family, which was poor, with little wealth, much oppressed by creditors.

444. "Then, because of the large amount of interest which had accumulated, a caravan-leader removed me from the family-hous and dragged me off wailing.

445. "Then in my sixteenth year, his son, Giridāsa by name, saw me as a maiden of marriageable age and took me as his wife.

446. "He had another wife, virtuous, possessed of good qualities, and famous, affectionate towards her husband; I stirred up enmity with her.

447. "This was the fruit of that action for me, that they went rejecting me, although I served them like a slave-girl. Even of that I have now made an end."

Sumedhā

448. In the city of Mantāvatī there was Sumedhā, a daughter of King Koñca's chief queen; she was converted by those who comply with the teaching.

449. Virtuous, a brilliant speaker, having great learning, trained in the Buddha's teaching, going up to her mother and father she said, "Listen, both of you.

450. "I delight in quenching; existence is non-eternal, even if it is as a deity; how much more non-eternal are empty sensual pleasures, giving little enjoyment and much distress.

451. "Sensual pleasures, in which fools are bemused, are bitter, like a snake's poison. Consigned to hell for a long time, those fools are beaten, pained.

452. "Because of evil action they grieve in a downward transition, being evil-minded, without faith; fools are unrestrained in body, speech, and mind.

453. "Those fools, unwise, senseless, hindered by the uprising of pain, not knowing, do not understand the noble truths, when someone is teaching them.

454. "They, the majority, not knowing the truths taught by the excellent Buddha, rejoice in existence [, mother]; they long for rebirth among the deities.

455. "Even rebirth among the deities is non-eternal; it is in the impermanent existence; but fools are not afraid of being reborn again and again.

456. "Four downward transitions and two upward transitions are obtained somehow or other; but for those who have gone to a downward transition there is no going-forth in the hells.

457. "Permit me, both of you, to go forth in the teaching of the ten-powered one; having little greed I shall strive for the elimination of birth and death.

458. "What have I to do with existence, with delight, with this unsubstantial worst of bodies? For the sake of the cessation of craving for existence, permit me, I shall go forth.

459. "There is arising of Buddhas; the inopportune moment has been avoided; the opportune moment has been seized. As long as life lasts I would not infringe the rules of virtuous conduct and the living of the holy life."

460. So Sumedhā speaks to her mother and father; "Meanwhile I shall not take food as a householder; if I do not go forth I shall indeed have gone into the influence of death."

461. Pained, her mother laments; and her father, smitten [by grief], strives to reconcile her, [as she lies] fallen to the ground on the roof of the palace.

462. "Stand up, child; what do you want with grieving? You are bestowed. In Vāraṇavatī is King Anīkaratta, who is handsome; you are bestowed upon him.

463. "You will be the chief queen, the wife of King Anīkaratta. The rules of virtuous conduct, the living of the holy life, going-forth, are difficult to perform, child.

464. "In kingship there are orders to give, wealth, authority, happy enjoyments; you are young; enjoy the enjoyments of sensual pleasures; let your marriage take place, child."

465. Then Sumedhā spoke to them, "May such things not be; existence is unsubstantial. Either there will be going-forth for me or death; not marriage.

466. "Should I cling, like a worm, to this foul body, impure, smelling of urine, a frightful water-bag of corpses, always flowing, full of impure things?

467. "What do I know it to be like? A body is repulsive, smeared with flesh and blood, food for worms, vultures, and other birds. Why is it given to us?

468. "The body is soon carried out to the cemetery, devoid of consciousness; it is thrown away like a log by disgusted relatives.

469. "When they have thrown it away in the cemetery as food for worms, one's own mother and father wash themselves, disgusted; how much more do common people?

470. "They are attached to the unsubstantial body, an aggregate of bones and sinews, to the foul body, full of saliva, tears, excrement, and urine.

471. "If anyone, dissecting it, were to turn it inside out, even one's own mother, being unable to bear the smell of it, would be disgusted.

472. "Reflecting in a reasoned manner that the elements of existence, the elements, the sense-bases are compounded, have rebirth as their root, and are painful, why should I wish for marriage?

473. "Let three hundred new[ly sharpened] swords fall on my body every day. Even if the striking lasted a hundred years it would be better [than not being struck], if in this way there were destruction of pain.

474. "He should submit to this striking who in this way knows the teacher's utterance, 'Journeying-on is long for you, being killed again and again.'

475. "Among deities and among men, in the realm of animals, and in the world of asuras, among ghosts and in hells, unlimited beatings are seen.

476. "There are many beatings in hells for a defiled one who has gone to a downward transition. Even among the deities there is no protection; there is no [happiness] superior to the happiness of quenching.

477. "Those who are intent upon the teaching of the ten-powered one have attained quenching; having little greed [for sensual pleasures] they strive for the elimination of birth and death.

478. "This very day, father, I shall renounce the world; what have I to do with unsubstantial enjoyments? I am disgusted with sensual pleasures; they are like vomit, made like a topless palm-tree."

479. In this way she spoke to her father, and at the same time Anīkaratta, to whom she was betrothed, surrounded by young men, came to the marriage at the appointed time.

480. Then Sumedhā cut her black, thick, soft hair with a knife, closed the palace door, and entered on the first meditation.

481. Just as she entered on it, Anīkaratta arrived at the city; in that very palace Sumedhā developed notions of impermanence.

482. Just as she was pondering, Anīkaratta went up into the palace quickly. With his body adorned with jewels and gold, with cupped hands, he begged Sumedhā,

483. "In kingship there are [giving of] orders, wealth, authority, happy enjoyments; you are young; enjoy the enjoyments of sensual pleasures; happiness from sensual pleasures is hard to obtain in the world.

484. "My kingship has been bestowed upon you; enjoy enjoyments; give gifts; do not be depressed; your mother and father are pained."

485. Then Sumedhā, unconcerned with sensual pleasures, and free from delusion, said this: "Do not rejoice in sensual pleasures; see the peril in sensual pleasures.

486. "Mandhātar, king of the four continents, the foremost of those who had enjoyment of sensual pleasures, died unsatisfied, nor were his wishes fulfilled.

487. "If the rainy one were to rain the seven jewels all around in the ten directions, there would still be no satisfaction with sensual pleasures; men die unsatisfied indeed.

488. "Sensual pleasures are like a butcher's knife and chopping block; sensual pleasures are like a snake's head; they burn like a fire-brand; they are like a bony skeleton.

489. "Sensual pleasures are impermanent, unstable; they have much pain, they are great poisons; they are like a heated ball of iron, having evil as the root, having pain as the fruit.

490. "Sensual pleasures are like the fruits of a tree, like lumps of flesh, painful; they are like dreams, delusive; sensual pleasures are like borrowed goods.

491. "Sensual pleasures are like swords and stakes, a disease, a tumour, evil destruction, like a pit of coals, having evil as the root, fear, slaughter.

492. "In this way sensual pleasures have been said to have much pain, to be hindrances. Go! I myself have no confidence in existence.

493. "What will another do for me when his own head is burning? When old age and death are following closely one must strive for their destruction."

494. Opening the door, and seeing her mother and father and Anīkaratta seated on the ground lamenting, she said this:

495. "Journeying-on is long for fools and for those who lament again and again at that of which the end is immeasurable, at the death of a father, the slaughter of a brother, and their own slaughter.

496. "Remember the tears, the milk, the blood, the journeying on as being that of which the end is immeasurable; remember the heap of bones of beings who are journeying on.

497. "Remember the four oceans compared with the tears, milk, and blood; remember the heap of bones of one man for one eon, equal in size to Mt. Vipula.

498. "Remember the earth, Jambudīpa, compared with that which is without beginning and end for one who is journeying on. Split up into little balls the size of jujube kernels the number is not equal to his mother's mothers.

499. "Remember the leaves, twigs, and grass compared with his fathers as being without beginning and end. Split up into pieces four inches long they are indeed not equal to his father's fathers.

500. "Remember the blind turtle in the eastern sea, and the hole in the yoke to the west; and remember the putting on of it [= the yoke] as a comparison with the obtaining of human birth.

501. "Remember the form of this worst of bodies, unsubstantial, like a lump of foam. See the elements of existence as impermanent; remember the hells, giving much distress.

502. "Remember those filling up the cemetery again and again in this birth and that. Remember the fears from the crocodile; remember the four truths.

503. "When the death-free exists, what do you want with drinking the five bitter things? For all the delights in sensual pleasure are more bitter than the five bitter things.

504. "When the death-free exists, what do you want with sensual pleasures which are burning fevers? For all delights in sensual pleasures are on fire, aglow, seething.

505. "When there is non-enmity, what do you want with sensual pleasures which involve much enmity? Being similar to kings, fire, thieves, water, and people [who are] unfriendly, they involve much enmity.

506. "When release exists, what do you want with sensual pleasures, in which are slaughter and bonds? For in sensual pleasures, unwilling, people suffer the pains of slaughter and bonds.

507. "A grass fire-brand, when kindled, burns the one who holds it and does not let go; sensual pleasures are truly like fire-brands; they burn those who do not let go.

508. "Do not abandon extensive happiness for the sake of a little happiness from sensual pleasures; do not suffer afterwards, like a puthuloma fish which has swallowed the hook.

509. "Rather, just control yourself among sensual pleasures. You are like a dog bound by a chain; assuredly sensual pleasures will treat you as hungry outcasts treat a dog.

510. "Intent upon sensual pleasures you will suffer both unlimited pain and very many distresses of the mind; give up unstable sensual pleasures.

511. "When [that which is] free from old age exists, what do you want with sensual pleasures, in which are old age and death? All births everywhere are bound up with death and sickness.

512. "This is free from old age, this is death-free, this is the state [which is] free fom old age and death, without grieving, without enmity, unobstructed, without stumbling, without fear, without burning.

513. "This death-free has been attained by many, and this is to be obtained even today by one who rightly applies himself; but it cannot be attained by one who does not strive."

514. So Sumedhā spoke, not obtaining delight in the constituent elements. Conciliating Anīkaratta, Sumedhā simply threw her hair on the ground.

515. Standing up, Anīkaratta with cupped hands requested her father, "Let Sumedhā go, in order to go forth; she will be one with insight into the truths of complete release."

516. Allowed to go by her mother and father, she went forth, frightened by grief and fear; she realized the six supernormal powers while still undergoing training, and also the foremost fruit.

517. Marvellous, amazing was that quenching of the king's daughter; as she explained at the last moment her activities in her former habitations.

518. "In the time of the blessed one Koṇāgamana, in the Order's pleasure park, in a new residence, we three friends, women, gave a gift of a vihāra.

519. "Ten times, one hundred times, ten hundred times, one hundred hundred times we were reborn among the deities. But what need is there to talk about rebirth among men?

520. "We had great supernormal powers among the deities. But what need is there to talk about powers among mankind? I was the queen of a seven-jewelled king; I was his wife-jewel.

521. "That was the cause, that the origin, that the root; that very delight in the teaching, that first meeting, that was quenching for one delighting in the doctrine."

522. So they say who have faith in the utterance of the one who has perfect wisdom; they are disgusted with existence; being disgusted with it they are disinterested in it.

Notes

1. The rubric to this verse states *ittham sudam aññatarā therī apaññātā bhikkhunī gātham abhāsitthā ti*. At the end of his explanation of the verse Dhammapāla explains (Thī-a 7,23–25): *aññatarā therī apaññātā nāma-gottādi-vasena apākaṭā, ekā therī-lakkhaṇa-sampannā bhikkhunī imaṃ gāthaṃ abhāsi ti adhippāyo*. In the preliminary story, however, he takes *Therikā* as a proper name, possibly extracting it from the verse, but nevertheless giving a reason for the therī being so called: *taṃ thira-santa-sarīratāya therikā ti vohariṃsu* (Thī-a 5,11). In the cty on the verse he states: *therike ti idaṃ yadi pi tassā nāma-kittanaṃ. pacurena anvattha-saññā-bhāvato pana thire sāsane thira-bhāva-ppatte thirehi sīlādi-dhammehi samannāgate ti attho* (Thī-a 6,6–8). At the end of the cty (Thī-a 272,21) Dhammapāla states *Subhūti-ādayo therā, theriyo Therikādayo*, again apparently taking *Therikā* as a proper name.

Thī-a 5,33: *sukhan ti bhāva-napuṃsaka-niddeso*. Ñāṇamoli (1994, s.v.) explains this term as meaning "neuter gender abstract noun (grammatical)", but we should probably regard *sukhaṃ* as being an accusative used adverbially. Mrs Rhys Davids misunderstood *bhāva-napuṃsakaṃ* where it occurs at Spk I 191 in the explanation of *accantaṃ* (S I 130). She translated (KS I 163, n.) "This is a sexless state".

Thī-a 5,33–35: *supāhī ti āṇatti-vacanaṃ. therike ti āmantana-vacanam. katvā coḷena pārutā ti appicchatāya niyojanaṃ.*

Thī-a 6,8–10: *katvā coḷena pārutā ti paṃsu-kūla-coḷehi cīvaraṃ katvā acchādita-sarīrā taṃ nivatthā c' eva pārutā ca. hi-saddo hetv-attho.*

For *therīke* m.c. to give the cadence ⏑ – – ⏓ (*pathyā*) see § 69 (c). B[e] and C[e] read *therike*.

All the editions except P conclude this verse, and all other verses or groups of verses, with *ti*. Similarly all verses and groups in Th conclude with *ti*. In P, however, only the groups **35–36 63–66 213–23 224–35 338–65 366–99 400–47 448–522** end in *ti*. There appears to be no reason for this.

2. The rubric to this verse states *ittham sudam Bhagavā Muttaṃ sikkhamānaṃ imāya gāthāya abhiṇhaṃ ovadati*. At the end of his explanation of the verse Dhammapāla explains: *abhiṇhaṃ ovadatī ti ariyamaggappattiyā upakkilese visodhento bahuso ovādaṃ deti*. This and **19–20** are the only verses which actually include in the rubric a statement that the verses were uttered to the therīs named rather than by them (§ 3). The introductory story relates how the verse was uttered by the Buddha, and the conclusion of the cty indirectly refers to the word *sikkhamānaṃ*: (Thī-a 9,10–12): *arahattaṃ pana patvā sā tam eva gāthaṃ udānesi. paripuṇṇa-sikkhā upasampajjitvā apara-bhāge parinibbāna-kāle pi tam eva gātham paccabhāsi.*

The rubric to this verse in Thī states: *itthaṃ sudaṃ Bhagavā Muttaṃ sikkhamānaṃ imāya gāthāya abhiṇhaṃ ovadati.* At the end of his explanation of the verse Dhammapāla explains (Thī-a 8,30–31) : *abhiṇhaṃ ovadatī ti ariya-maggappattiyā upakkilese visodhento bahuso ovādaṃ deti.*

The introductory story relates how the verse was uttered by the Buddha, and the conclusion of the cty indirectly refers to the word *sikkhamānaṃ*: (Thī-a 9,10–12): *arahattaṃ pana patvā sā tam eva gāthaṃ udānesi. paripuṇṇa-sikkhā upasampajjitvā apara-bhāge parinibbāna-kāle pi tam eva gātham paccabhāsi.*

The cty does not comment on the all the words in the rubric here or on any of the words in the rubric to **19–20**, although it does comment on the rubric to **1** (see the note on **1**). For comments related to the word *sikkhamānaṃ*, see Thī-a 11,14–16 (ad **4**) where *sikkhassu sikkhāya* is glossed: *adhisīla-sikkhādikāya tividhāya sikkhāya sikkha, magga-sampayuttā tisso sikkhāyo sampādehī ti attho.* In **99** *sikkhamānā* is not glossed, but Thī-a 97,2–3 (ad **104**) explains: *sikkhamānāyā ti tisso pi sikkhā sikkhamānā.* The three *sikkhā* are explained as *adhisīla-*, *adhicitta-*, and *adhipaññā-sikkhā* at D III 219 A I 234 foll. Nett 126. There is a pun upon the name Muttā and the unexpressed past participle *muttā* from the verb *muccassu* (§ 7(c)).

Thī-a 8,19–20: *muccassu yogehī ti magga-paṭipāṭiyā kāma-yogādīhi catūhi yogehi mucca. tehi vimutta-cittā hohi.* For the four *yogā* see EV I, p. 142 (ad Th 32). For another meaning of *yoga* see the note on **4**.

B^{e} and C^{e} read *Rāhu-ggahā* for *-ggaho*, and there is no doubt that an ablative is easier to translate here, but by the principle of lectio difficilior we should presumably follow P's reading. Thī-a 8,21–22: *cando Rāhu-ggahā ivā ti Rāhu-saṅkhātato gahato cando viya upakkilesato muccassu.* One possible way to explain P's reading would be to assume that the original reading was *Rāhu-*[g]*gah*⟨*at*⟩*o*, which scanned because of resolution of the fourth syllable. Normalisation, to produce an eight-syllable line, could have produced P's reading. Alternatively, the original version could have had a locative form *-ggahe* "in the grasp", which was misunderstood at the time of translating into Pāli as a nominative, and changed into *-ggaho* (cf. EV I, p. 236 (ad Th 546) and Lüders, 1954, §§ 20–21). We should, however, certainly expect an ablative in such a context, cf. *cando va Rāhu-gahaṇā pamuttā* Sn 465 498; *cando yathā Rāhumukhā pamutto*, Ja IV 330.

Thī-a 8,22–24: *vippamuttena cittenā ti ariya-maggena samuccheda-vimuttiyā suṭṭhu vimuttena cittena. itthaṃ-bhūta-lakkhaṇaṃ c' etaṃ karaṇa-vacanaṃ.* I find it hard to believe that the cty is suggesting that *cittena* be taken as an instrumental in the sense of the ablative, and therefore presume that the reference is to *yogehi*, i.e. "from your bonds", not "by your exertions". Dhammapāla apparently did not realise that in this context the ending *-ehi* was ablative, although he takes *khujjehi* in **11** as ablative when it is probably instrumental. For other apparent changes of case see the notes on **104 112 314**.

Thī-a 8,24–29: *anaṇā bhuñja piṇḍakan ti kilesa-iṇaṃ pahāya anaṇā hutvā raṭṭha-piṇḍaṃ bhuñjeyyāsi. yo hi kilese appahāya satthārā anuññāta-paccaye paribhuñjati so sāṇo bhuñjati nāma. yathāha āyasmā Vakkulo*: *sattāhaṃ eva kho ayaṃ āvuso sāṇo raṭṭha-piṇḍaṃ bhuñjin ti* (cf. M III 127). *tasmā sāsane pabbajitena kāma-cchandādi-iṇam pahāya anaṇena hutvā saddhā-deyyaṃ paribhuñjitabbaṃ*. The word *anaṇa* recurs in **110 364**. Freedom from monetary debt is a prerequisite for ordination, but debt is also interpreted in other senses. For the use of the word *anaṇa* in a Buddhist context see EV I, p. 271 (ad Th 789) and Norman, 2000, where I refer to Hara 1996A and 1996B.

Note the construction of *anaṇa* with *bhuñjāhi piṇḍakaṃ* and with *raṭṭhapiṇḍaṃ abhuñji* in **110**. Cf. *anaṇo bhuñjāmi bhojanaṃ*, Th 882. This may be a continuation of the idea, pointed out by Hara, that in Indian society subjects were considered to be indebted to their master-king by the fact that they were paid a salary (*bhartṛ-piṇḍa*). Royal servants became free from debt by guarding their master in critical moments. Those who had died in battle could be described as *gatāḥ svāmi-piṇḍānṛṇyam* (Vīnāvāsavadatta 2.24 prose) "They have repaid the rice-ball of their master".

In pāda d there is resolution of the first syllable (§ 60).

3. In this verse there is a pun upon the name Puṇṇā and the unexpressed past participle *puṇṇā* from the verb *pūrassu* (§ 7(c)). Although the rubric makes no reference to the fact that this verse was spoken to the therī in the first place (§ 2), the introductory story in the cty states that it was uttered by the Buddha. Thī-a 10,10,26 states: *sā taṃ gātham sutvā vipassanaṃ vaḍḍhetvā arahattaṃ pāpuṇi. … arahattaṃ pana patvā sā therī tam eva gātham udānesi*.

Thī-a 10,3–4: *cando pannarase-r-ivā ti ra-kāro pada-sandhi-karo*. For the use of sandhi *-r-* with *iva* cf. Geiger (2000, § 73.3). The combination is especially common in Thī, e.g. *saṇha-kambu-r-iva* **262**, *tila-daṇḍakā-r-iva* **268**, *turiyā-r-iva* **381**, *kinnariyā-r-iva* **381**, *visa-patto-r-iva* **386**, *jana-majjhe-r-iva* **392**, *vaṭṭani-r-iva* **395**. Cf. *dubbalo-r-iva* Th 501; *go-r-iva*, Ja V 15; *kūṭahatā-r-iva* Ja V 17; *nigaho-r-iva* Ja V 18; *vijju-r-iva*, Ja V 14; *jalanta-r-iva*, Ja V 322; *sikhi-r-iva nadi-r-iva* Ja V 445; *dharaṇī-r-iva* Ja VI 526 Ap 460 508. The usage presumably began in contexts where there was a historic reason for the presence of *-r-*, e.g. after nominatives of *-i* and *-u* stems where the original final *-s* became *-r* before a vowel, e.g. *kambur-iva*, and was extended to other nominatives, e.g. *dubbalo-r-iva*, and finally to all case forms. Similarly other usages began in contexts where there was a historic reason, e.g. *puna-r-āgami* **14**, *puna-r-ehisi* **166**, *puna-r-āgame* **341**, and then extended to other forms, e.g. *dhi-r-atthu* **225**. See also Chalmers (p. xvi, n. 2).

For the use of the sandhi consonant *-m-* in Thī see the note on **48**.

C^e reads *paṇṇaraso* in the text and lemma, but agrees with B^e in explaining: *pannarase puṇṇa-māsiyaṃ sabbāhi kalāhi paripuṇṇo cando viya* (Thī-a 10,4–5). Cf. EV I, p. 235 (ad Th 546). PTC III 115 follows C^e and amends to *-raso*.

Thī-a 10,2–3: *pūrassu dhammehī ti satta-tiṃsa-bodhi-pakkhiya-dhammehi paripuṇṇā hohi*. Thī-a 12,18–19 (ad **5**) explains: *dhammehī ti samatha-vipassanā-dhammehi ariyehi bodhi-pakkhiya-dhammehi,* and Thī-a 13,12–13 (ad **9**): *kusale, bodhi-pakkhiya-dhamme*. For the 37 *bodhi-pakkhiya-dhammā* see EV I, p. 177 (ad Th 166) and p. 285 (ad Th 900), where 165 should be 166 in the 1st ed.. For other meanings of *dhamma* see EV I, p. 130 (ad Th 2) and cf. the explanations given in Thī-a 13,1–2 (ad **7**): *tejussadehi ariya-magga-dhammehi*; Thī-a 13,7–8 (ad **8**): *dhamme ti ariya-magga-dhamme*; Thī-a 59,26 (ad **56**): *dhammehī ti lokuttara-dhammehi*; and Thī-a 207,34 foll. (ad **278**): *puṇṇā sukkāna dhammānan ti ekanta-sukkehi anavajja-dhammehi paripuṇṇā. asekkhehi sīla-kkhandādīhi samannāgatā ti attho*.

Thī-a 10,5–6: *paripuṇṇāya paññāyā ti soḷasannaṃ kiccānam pāripūriyā paripuṇṇāya arahatta-magga-paññāya*. I translate "fulfilled" to get a jingle with "filled", although this translation is not really appropriate in English. The meaning is nearer "completed".

4. Although the rubric makes no reference to the fact that this verse was spoken to the therī in the first place (§ 2), the introductory story in the cty states that it was uttered by the Buddha. Thī-a 11,23–24 concludes: *sā taṃ gāthaṃ sutvā vipassanam vaḍḍhetvā arahattaṃ pāpuṇī ti ādi-nayo heṭṭhā vutta-nayen' eva veditabbo*.

For the *sikkhā* see the note on **2**.

There is a pun upon the two meanings of *yoga* in the verse. Thī-a 11,16–19: *mā tam yogā upaccagun ti manussattaṃ indriyāvekallaṃ buddhuppādo saddhā-paṭilābho ti ime yogā samayā dullabha-kkhaṇā taṃ mā atikkamuṃ*. It is clear that *yoga* in *sabba-yoga-visaṃyuttā* must refer to *kāma-yoga*, etc. (see the note on **2**), but the cty also suggests the possibility of understanding this meaning in pāda b, and gives an alternative gloss for *upaccaguṃ*: *abhibhaveyyuṃ*. I am not persuaded by Mrs Rhys Davids' suggestion that there is a pun here upon Tissā and *tisso* "three [trainings]". There could, however, well be a reference to the astronomical conjunction between her birthday nakkhatta *Tissa* and the sun or moon.

For *khaṇa* see the note on **5**.

For *anāsava* see EV I, p. 148 (ad Th 47).

5–10. Thī-a 11,29–30 states that the introductory stories of these six therīs resemble that of Tissā, the author of **4**, except for that of the author of **7**. Despite the rubric, therefore, we may suppose that the Buddha uttered these verses in the first place (§ 2), and the therīs later repeated them.

5. Thī-a 12,18–19: *yuñjassu dhammehī ti samatha-vipassanā-dhammehi ariyehi bodhi-pakkhiya-dhammehi ca yuñja yogaṃ karohi.* For the various translations of *dhamma* see the note on **3**.

Thī-a 12,19–23: *khaṇo taṃ mā upaccagā ti yo evaṃ yoga-bhāvanaṃ na karoti taṃ puggalam paṭirūpa-dese uppatti-kkhaṇo channam āyatanānam avekalla-kkhaṇo buddh'-uppāda-kkhaṇo saddhāya paṭiladdha-kkhaṇo sabbo pi ayam khaṇo atikkamati nāma.* Cf. the note on **4**. Thī-a 88,28–29 (ad **95**) explains: *na me kālo pamajjituṃ, ayaṃ kālo aṭṭh'-akkhaṇa-vajjito, navamo khaṇo so pamajjituṃ na yutto ti.* Thī-a 258,6–7 (ad **459**) explains: *buddhānam uppādo laddho, vivajjito niray'-uppatti-ādiko aṭṭha-vidho akkhaṇo. khaṇo navamo khaṇo laddho ti yojanā.* For the use of the past participle *paṭiladdha* as an action noun "The opportunity of receiving faith", see the note on **261**.

Th-a II 92,4–5 (ad Th 231) glosses: *khaṇā ti Buddh'-uppādādayo brahma-cariya-vāsassa okāsā.* Th-a II 171,39 foll. (ad Th 403) explains in almost exactly the same terms as Thī-a 12,19–23, except that *buddhānaṃ vacanaṃ* replaces *yoga-bhāvanaṃ* and *sammā-diṭṭhiyā* replaces *saddhāya*. The *aṭṭha akkhaṇā asamayā brahma-cariya-vāsāya* are enumerated at A IV 225–27 D III 287, and the *eko khaṇo samayo ca brahma-cariya-vāsāya*, i.e. *Tathāgato loke uppanno hoti* is given at A IV 227. Nine *akkhaṇā* are enumerated at D III 263–65.

6. C^e reads *phussehi* for *phusehi* (cf. P v.l.). This reading is somewhat strange, for the ending *-ehi* implies the causative, which in the case of *phus-* should be *phass-* < Skt *sparśayati*. PED does not list *phussati* although, under the simple verb *phusati,* it quotes *aphussayi* as an aorist middle (!) at Pv 57, although E^e first edition actually reads *phussasi* (for the alternation *y/s* see the note on **84**), and it quotes the past participle of *phasseti* as *phassita* or *phus*(*s*)*ita*. It is possible that the original reading in all contexts for the causative was *phass-*, but it was inevitable that, with practically no difference in meaning between simple and causative verb (see Norman, 1962, pp. 324–26), a contamination of *phass-*

by *phus-* was bound to occur. The same confusion can be seen elsewhere in Thī. In **149** C^e reads *phussayiṃ*, and the vv.ll. in P show that there is support for a reading with *-ss-*. Thī-a 133,26 (ad **149**): *phusayin ti phusi*. Historically we might expect *phassayiṃ*.

In **155** C^e reads *phusayiṃ*, but the vv.ll. in P support the reading *phassayiṃ*. In **212** the vv.ll. again contain *-ss-*, but here the metre supports *aphusiṃ* (glossed: *adhigacchiṃ*) as the correct reading. In **322–24** all editions read *aphassayi*. In **433** all editions read *aphassayi(ṃ)*, glossed *phus(s)i sacchākāsi*.

The cadence of pāda a is – ⏑ – ⏓, without the usual caesura after the fourth syllable (see Warder, PM §242). This perhaps supports the correction to *phu⟨s⟩sehi* (§63(b)) or *phassehi*, which would give the cadence –, – – ⏓. See also the note on **98**.

Thī-a 12,27–29: *saññā-vūpasamaṃ sukhaṃ ārādhayāhi nibbānan ti kāma-saññādīnaṃ pāpa-saññānaṃ upasama-nimittaṃ accanta-sukhaṃ nibbānaṃ ārādhehi*. Cf. *saññāya uparodhanā evaṃ dukkha-kkhayo hoti* Sn 732, glossed at Pj II 505 as: *kāma-saññādīnaṃ*. For *kāma-*, *vyāpāda-*, and *vihiṃsā-saññā* as the three *akusala-saññā* see Vbh 369 and Vbh-a 499.

For the translations "idea" and "notion" for *saññā* see Wayman (p. 152).

For the alternation *p/s* see EV I, p. 149 (ad Th 49). There are other examples of the confusion of these two letters in Thī and Thī-a, e.g. *paññā/saññā* **393**, *Pakulā/Sakulā* (author of **97–101**), *padīpito/padīsito* **200**, *paṇha-/saṇha-* **255**, *pati/sati* **258**, *pattali-/sattali-* **260**, *-pahita-/-sahita-* **265**, *-kalāpito/-kalisiyo* **265**, *-upamā/-samā* **351**, *api/asi* **383**, *anupāsito/anusāsito* **387**, *pajjittha/sajjittha* **396**, *pakkh-/sakkh-* **414** **425**, *hohi pi/so hi si* **422**, *vināpessāmi/vināsessāmi* **431**, *paññāpetuṃ/saññāpetuṃ* **461**, *pi/si* **468** **483**, *paññāpentī/ saññāpentī* **514**. Cf. *kheḷāpaka/ kheḷāsaka*, Vin II 188/Sp 1275.

For *yoga-kkhema* see EV I, p. 142 (ad Th 32). The word recurs in **8**, where Thī-a 13,8–9 explains: *yoga-kkhemassa arahattassa nibbānassa ca*; in **9** where Thī-a 13,11–12 glosses: *catūhi yogehi khemam anuppadavaṃ*; and in **211** where the cty makes no comment.

7. There is some doubt about the name of the author of this verse. Although the rubric in P states the author was *aññatarā Dhīrā*, in B^e and C^e she is called *Vīrā*. For the alternation *v/dh* see Chopra (p. 96, n. 25) and cf. *avibhūta/ adhibhūta* **419**, *vāreyya/dhāreyya* (see the note on **464**), *vīra/dhīra* EV I, p. 309 (ad Th 1083), *vamma/dhamma* (see PTC II 420, s.v. *dhamma*[4]), *van-/dhan-* (see PED, s.v. *dhanāyati*), *Yuvañjaya/Yudhañjaya*, Ja IV 119–123 (cf. Skt *Yudhājit*, *Yaudhājaya*).

The alternation *c/v* (see the note on **12**) has also led to an alternation *c/dh*, e.g. *ca/dha* (see EV I, p. 191 (ad Th 237)), *camma/dhamma* S V 6.

The cty states that the introductory story to this verse differs from the others in the group **5–10** in that the Buddha did not utter an *obhāsa-gāthā* to the therī. This statement is presumably connected in some way with the fact that there is no vocative in this verse, although it is impossible to tell whether the cty deduced the story from the lack of a vocative, or an original vocative has been changed because of the cty's story. For a comparable verse without a vocative cf. **56**. Thī-a 13,4–5 explains the imperative in pāda c by saying that the therī was addressing herself: *therī aññaṃ viya katvā attānam dasseti*.

There is a pun upon Dhīrā and *dhīrehi* (or *Vīrā* and *vīrehi*) (§ 7(c)).

Thī-a 13,1–2: *vīrehi dhammehī ti viriya-ppadhānatāya vīrehi tejussadehi ariya-magga-dhammehi*. The fact that the gloss includes *viriya-* tends to favour the reading *vīra-*. For *tejussada* see PED, s.v. *ussada*.

Thī-a 13,3: *sa-vāhanaṃ kilesa-māraṃ jinitvā*. See EV I, p. 180 (ad Th 177).

For *dhamma* see the note on **3**.

8. There is a pun upon the name Mittā and *mitta-* (§ 7(c)).

For *yoga-kkhema* see the note on **6**.

For *dhamma* see the note on **3**.

9. There is a pun upon the name Bhadrā and *bhadra-* (§ 7(c)).

For *yoga-kkhema* see the note on **6**.

For *dhamma* see the note on **3**.

10. By classical standards the opening ⏓ ⏑ ⏑ – should be avoided (cf. EV I, p. 152 (ad Th 61)). There are, however, several pādas in Thī where it is tolerated, although frequently the metre could be corrected without difficulty, e.g. *mā puna jāti-* **26** (? read *punā* or *puno*), *arati dāni* **58 141 234** (? read *aratī*), *iddhi pi me* **71 228** (? read *iddhī*), *vicari 'haṃ* **92** (? read *vicāri* or *vicarī*), *tattha ramitvā* **147** (? read *rāmitvā*), *saṃsari 'haṃ* **159** (? read *saṃsarī*), *pītisukhena* **174** (? read *pītī-* or *-su⟨k⟩khena*), *ghaṭatha buddha-* **176** (? read *ghaṭātha*), *upavijaññā* **218** (? read *-vi⟨j⟩jaññā*), *sabhariyā* **225** (? read *sabhāriya*), *Rohiṇi dāni* **272** (? read *Rohiṇīdāni*, i.e. < *idāni*), *āharimena* **299** (? read *āhārimena*), *addasa brāhmaṇo* **320** (? read *addasā*). There are, however, pādas where this opening is avoided, e.g. *satīmatī* **189**, *rukkhapphalūpamā* **490**. It is probable that the authors of Thī had different ideas about this, and we should accordingly be very cautious about correcting on metrical grounds alone (§ 62). See also the notes on **44** and **74**.

Thī-a 13,15: *maccu ettha dhīyati ti maccu-dheyyaṃ*. Cf. EV I, p. 342 (ad Th 1278).

Thī-a 13,16–17: *saṃsāra-mahoghaṃ tare ariya-magga-nāvāya tareyyāsi*, i.e. *tare* is a second person singular optative.

11. Thī-a 15,3–7 makes it clear that the three *khujja* things are *udukkhala*, *musala*, and *pati*: *iti tāni sa-rūpato dassentī udukkhalena musalena patinā khujjakena cā ti āha. udukkhale hi dhaññaṃ pakkhipantiyā parivattentiyā musalena koṭṭentiyā piṭṭhi onāmetabbā hotī ti. khujja-kāraṇa-hetutāya tad ubhayaṃ khujjan ti vuttaṃ. sāmiko pan' assā khujjo eva.*

In Skt the root *muc-* is constructed with the ablative or the instrumental, rarely with the genitive (see MW, s.v. *muc*). It is possible, therefore, that *tīhi* and *khujjehi* may be either ablative forms or instrumentals. For the construction of *muc-* with the genitive see the note on **23**.

Thī-a 15,11 explains *bhava-netti* as *bhavassa netti nādikā taṇhā*. See EV I, p. 170 (ad Th 135).

In pāda c there is resolution of the sixth syllable (§ 60)

12. The Buddha ranked Dhammadinnā as foremost among the preachers of the doctrine: *etad aggaṃ dhamma-kathikānaṃ, yad idaṃ Dhammadinnā* (A I 25).

All oriental editions and mss read *avasāyī*, but P reads *avasāye*, on the assumption (p. 176) that *avasāyī* was corrupt. The verse recurs with masculine forms at Dhp 218, where, however, *anakkhāte* replaces *avasāyī*. Thī-a 19,6–9: *avasāyī ti avasāyo vuccati avasānaṃ niṭṭhānaṃ, tam pi kāmesu appaṭibaddha-cittatāya uddhaṃsotā ti vakkhamānatta samaṇa-kiccassa niṭṭhānaṃ veditabbaṃ* (B[e] inserts *na*) *yassa kassaci*. It is clear, therefore, that *avasāyī* is masculine, and we can see its equivalent in BHS at Udāna-v 2.9, which like Dhp has all words in the masculine, reading *avasrāyī* for *avasāyī*. We can, therefore, deduce that the author of **12** transposed her verse from one which already existed, referring to a man. She was able to change all nominatives in *-o* to *-ā* without damaging the metre in any way, but found it impossible to write the correct form *avasāyinī* and retain the metre unharmed. She therefore kept the masculine form, no doubt hoping that the ending *-ī* might be mistaken for a feminine. CPD (s.v. *avasāyin*) says that this is a feminine, which cannot be correct. Cf. the note on *nibbindaṃ* in **26**.

Thī-a 19,6: *tattha chanda-jātā ti agga-pphal'-atthaṃ jāta-cchandā*. Cf. EV I, p. 302 (ad Th 1029) where *chanda-jāto* is quoted as a gloss on *chandikato*, and Pj II 513 (ad Sn 767) where *chanda-jātassa* is glossed: *jāta-taṇhassa*. For *phala* cf. *rukkha-pphalūpama* **490**, and *sukha-pphalāni* D III 178.

Instead of *phuṭā* C^e reads *phuṭhā* and K^e S^e *phuṭṭhā*. Thī-a 19,11–12: *phuṭā* (C^e *phuṭhā*) *phusitā bhaveyya*. This gloss would seem to suggest that the cty was explaining a text with the reading *phuṭṭhā* (or *phuṭhā* m.c.) with which *phusitā*, as the alternative form of the past participle of *phusati,* would be entirely synonymous. For *phu*[*ṭ*]*ṭhā* m.c. see § 65(b).

In his first edition of Dhp (p. 39) Fausbøll read *kāme ca appaṭibaddha-citto*; in his second edition (p. 50) he read *kāmesu ca* (v.l. *va*), with a footnote "are we to read *kāmappaṭi-*?" He presumably thought the pāda was a śloka, and was trying to produce eight syllables. If, however, we read *cā* (or *vā*) in Dhp 218 we have a perfectly regular triṣṭubh pāda. I should therefore suggest following Dhp here and reading *kāmesu* ⟨*cā*⟩ or ⟨*vā*⟩ (§ 66(a)).

For the alternation *c*/*v* see EV I, pp. 136 foll. (ad Th 15), and cf. *cāpi*/*vā* pi **23**, *ca*/*va* in **31 89 260 294 353 372 379 395 439 481 514**, *ce*/*ve* in **33**, *ca*/*vata* in **111 238**, and *yācat' assā*/*yāva tassā* in **515**. The confusion between the syllables for *c* and *v* dates from the time of the Aśokan inscriptions.

Thī-a 19,13–16: *uddhaṃsotā ti uddham eva magga-soto saṃsāra-soto ca etissā ti uddhaṃsotā. anāgāmino hi yathā agga-maggo uppajjati, na añño. evaṃ Avihādīsu uppannassa yāva Akaniṭṭhā uddham eva uppatti hotī ti.*

13. The cty makes no reference to the fact that *pāda* is usually masculine in Pāli, but includes *pāde* in the explanation here and on **118**. No explanation is given for **154 176 311 337** (but see the note on the last). The usual form *pāde* occurs in **44 174 178 335**. Other masculine plural forms in *-āni* are found in Thī, e.g. *kesāni* **156** (although *kese* occurs in **40**), *petāni* **312**, *puttāni* **312–13**, *dāsa-kamma-karāni* **340**. The cty ad **156** makes no reference to *kesāni*, but Thī-a 219,15–16 (ad **312**) states: *puttānī ti liṅga-vipallāsena vuttaṃ. pete putte ti attho.* Similarly Thī-a 224,31–32 (ad **340**) states: *dāsa-kamma-karāni cā ti dāse ca kamma-kare ca. liṅga-vipallāsena h' etaṃ vuttaṃ*. For such forms in *-āni* see Geiger (2000, § 76). There is, of course, no need to follow the cty in believing that these are actual examples of a change of gender. It is much more likely that we are dealing with Eastern masculine plural endings in *-āni* which predate the translation of the Buddhist canon into Pāli (§ 27). Such endings are found in the Aśokan inscriptions (see Hultzsch, pp. lxii and lxxvi) and in BHS (see BHSG, § 8.98). Cf. also *dumāni* in Th 528 (see EV I, p. 232 (ad Th 528)). For feminine plurals in *-ni* see the note on **518**. For other apparent changes of gender see the note on **209**.

14. Thī-a 20,12–14: *dhātuyo dukkhato disvā ti santatiṃ patiyāpannā dukkhādi-dhātuyo itarā pi ca udaya-bbayassa paṭipīḷanādinā dukkhā ti ñāṇa-cakkhunā disvā*. For *dhātuyo* as an accusative plural see Geiger (2000, § 76).

Bᵉ and Cᵉ read *jāti⟨ṃ⟩*, and the correctness of this reading is shown by Thī-a 20,14–15: *puna jātiṃ āyatiṃ punabbhavaṃ mā upagacchi*, and by such contexts as *na punar jāti-jarām upeṣyasi* Udāna-v 29.57. The same verse at Dhp-a III 117 has *lokaṃ* for *jāti⟨ṃ⟩*.

Thī-a 20,15–16: *bhave chandaṃ virājetvā ti kāma-bhavādike sabbasmiṃ bhave taṇhā-chandaṃ virāga-saṅkhātena maggeṇa pajahitvā*. For *virāga* see EV I, p. 252 (ad Th 673). For *chanda* see the note on **12**.

For sandhi *-r-* see the note on **3**.

15. Thī-a 21,3: *udā ti atha*. PED states (s.v.) that *uda* is a disjunctive particle, but in Skt it is both disjunctive and conjunctive: "and, also, even, or " (MW). It is clearly conjunctive here.

Thī-a 21,15–16: *sīti-bhūt' amhi nibbutā ti sabbaso kilesa-pariḷāhābhāvena sīti-bhāva-ppattā anupādi-sesa-nibbāna-dhātuyā nibbutā amhi*. Thī-a 74,16–17 (ad **66**) explains: *tato eva kilesa-pariḷāhābhāvato sīti-bhūtā sa-upādi-sesāya nibbāna-dhātuyā nibbutā ca amha bhavāma*. For *anupādi-sesa* and *sa-upādi-sesa* see EV I, p. 132 (ad Th 5).

16. Thī-a 22,3–4: *gāthāya pana vuḍḍhike ti vuḍḍhe; vayo-vuḍḍhe ti attho. ayaṃ pana sīlādi-guṇehi pi vuḍḍhā*. In Skt *vṛddha* is found in the sense of "religious mendicant" (MW, s.v.), and the same is probably true of *vuḍha* in the Aśokan inscriptions (see Norman, 1967, p. 168). It is possible that the same is true here, in which case *vuḍḍhike* would mean exactly the same as *therike* in **1**, i.e. "little therī". It may be, therefore, that the statement *vuḍḍha-pabbajitā* in the rubric is based upon a misunderstanding of the word.

17. Thī-a 22,22 explains *daṇḍaṃ olubbha* as *yaṭṭhi-upatthambhena*. Thī-a 32,27 (ad **27**) explains: *kattara-yaṭṭhiṃ ālambitvā*. The cty ad **29** is silent. Burrow (1956, p. 195) explains *olubbha* as being from *lubh-* "to disturb" + *ava-* "to collapse down on".

Thī-a 22,23–24: *chamā ti chamāyam bhūmiyaṃ*. From the instrumental *chamā* < Skt *kṣamā* a new nominative *chamā* was formed, from which in due course a new locative *chamāyaṃ* was made. Thī-a 86,28–29 (ad **88**) explains *chamāya* (= locative) as *bhūmiyā*. Thī-a 113,21–22 (ad **112**) explains: *chamā ti chamāyaṃ. bhummatthe hi idam paccatta-vacanam*. For such apparent changes of case see the note on **2**. PED (s.v. *paccatta*) says that *paccatta-vacana* is the accusative case. This is clearly not so here. See also Ñāṇamoli (1960, p. 317).

The cty ad **461** makes no reference to *chamā*; Thī-a 262,22 (ad **494**) explains: *chaman ti chamāyam*. Alsdorf, however, suggests reading *chamā* (with P v.l.). See the note on **494**.

18. Pādas abcd occur again at S I 15 with some slight differences. There *agāraṃ* is read instead of *ghare*, but the latter was certainly in Dhammapāla's text since he explains (Thī-a 23,8–10): *ghare ti gehaṃ. ghara-saddo hi ekasmim pi abhidheyye kadāci bahūsu bījaṃ viya rūḷhī-vasena voharīyati*. The word is therefore either neuter singular or masculine plural, just like Skt *gṛha* (see MW, s.v.).

Thī-a 23,10–11: *hitvā puttaṃ pasuṃ piyan ti piyāyitabbe putte c' eva go-mahiṃsādike pasū ca tap-paṭibandha-chanda-rāga-ppahānena pahāya*. The glossing of *puttaṃ* by a plural is strange. Thī-a 154,31 (ad **163**) glosses it as a singular (see the note on **163**).

Thī-a 23,13–15: *avijjañ ca virājiyā ti sabbākusalesu pubbaṅgamaṃ mohaṃ ca virājetvā, maggena samugghāṭetvā icc eva attho*. Cf. the explanation of *virājetvā* in the note on **14**.

19–20. The rubric states that these verses were uttered to Nandā (§ 2) by the Buddha while she was undergoing training (for *sikkhamānā* see the note on **2**). Although the rubric calls her Nandā, the cty calls her Abhirūpa-nandā, and explains (Thī-a 24,10–11) that she was so called because of her great beauty: *sā atta-bhāvassa ativiya rūpa-sobhagga-ppattiyā abhirūpā dassanīyā pāsādikā*.

19. There is resolution of the first syllable in pāda c (§ 60). Cf. **82** and Th 1225.

20. With pāda a cf. **46**a and **105**a and S I 188. Spk I 272 explains: *animittañ ca bhāvehī ti niccādīnaṃ nimittānaṃ ugghatitattā cupassanā animittā nāma. taṃ bhāvehī ti vadati*. See also EV I, p. 333 (ad Th 1226).

21. Thī-a 26,28 foll.: *ye ime satta bojjhaṅgā ti ye ime satti-dhamma-vicaya-viriya-pīti-passaddhi-samādhi-upekkhā-saṃkhātā bodhiyā yathā-vuttāya dhamma-sāmaggiyā bodhissa vā bojjhaṅgassa samaṅgino puggalassa aṅga-bhūtattā bojjhaṅgā ti laddha-nāmā satta dhammā*. Cf. **45** and see EV I, p. 175 (ad Th 161).

Thī-a 27,3–6: *bhāvita te mayā sabbe yathā buddhena desitā ti te satta-tiṃsa bodhi-pakkhiya-dhammā sabbe pi* (B^e and C^e *sabbehi*) *mayā yathā buddhena bhagavatā desitā tathā mayā uppāditā vaḍḍhitā ca*. For the 37 *bodhi-pakkhiya-dhammā* see the note on **3**.

23–24. The rubric in P states that these verses are by *aññatarā therī-bhikkhunī apaññātā*, but the cty begins (Thī-a 27,16) and ends with the statement: *Sumaṅgala-mātāya theriyā gāthā*. Possibly because of this the rubric in Bᵉ calls the author of the verses *Sumaṅgala-mātā therī*. We must assume that the cty is following a different tradition from that of the rubric-writers in this (§31), since there is nothing in the verses to connect the author with Sumaṅgala, except that the verses resemble somewhat those attributed to Sumaṅgala (Th 43 — actually two verses, but not recognised as such by the *saṅgītikārā* (see EV I, p. 147 (ad Th 43)). The fact that the rubric was known to Dhammapāla in the form in which it appears in P is proved by the fact that he states (Thī-a 27,21–22): *yasmā pan' assā nāmaṃ gottaṃ na pākaṭaṃ, tasmā aññatarā bhikkhunī apaññātā ti pāḷiyaṃ vuttā*.

The metre of these verses is probably old āryā. Warder (PM §47) calls it gīti, presumably meaning old gīti, since it differs from the later gīti in the position of the caesura. The metre, is however, very corrupt (see Alsdorf, App. II, p. 234, n. 2). It would be kinder to ignore Mrs Rhys Davids' remark (Sist., p. 25, n. 2) that **24** is in śloka metre, with *sukhato* "an obvious gloss". For the scansion of old āryā verses in AMg see Alsdorf (1958, pp. 252–53).

23. There is some doubt about the reading of the first two words. P reads the first word as a vocative and the second as a nominative; Cᵉ reads them both as vocatives; Bᵉ reads them both as nominatives. It is probable that Bᵉ is correct, for Thī-a 28,2–3 agrees with Bᵉ in the gloss: *sumuttikā ti sumuttā. ka-kāro pada-pūraṇa-mattaṃ*. Moreover, had the verse included a vocative form, the cty would almost certainly have taken it as a personal name. I follow Bᵉ in the translation.

Thī-a 28,7: *musalassā ti musalato*. In the first edition I suggested that we were dealing here not with a genitive, but with an ablative, i.e. *-assa* < *-assā* < Skt *-asmāt*. Cf. the comparable *kula-gharassa* in **444**, which Thī-a 249,2–3 glosses: *jāta-kula-gehato*. The ending *-asa* < *-asmāt* occurs in GDhp (Brough, p. 187) and could have occurred in Thī as the result of borrowing from a dialect where *-sm-* > *-ss-*. For this development and the weakening of the final vowel see EV I, p. 191 (ad Th 239), and p. 247 (ad Th 640), where it is suggested that *-assa* could be derived <*-asmin*.

Nevertheless, although it is possible that *-assa* is an ablative form, there is no need to assume this change in this verse, since the Skt verb *muc-* is sometimes constructed with the genitive (see the note on **11**).

Thī-a 28,9–16: *ahiriko me ti mama sāmiko ahiriko nillajjo. so mama na ruccatī ti vacana-seso. pakatiyā va kāmesu viratta-cittatāya kāmādhimuttānaṃ pavattiṃ jigucchantī vadati. chattakaṃ vā pī ti jīvita-hetukena karīyamānaṃ chattakam pi me na ruccatī ti attho. vā-saddo avutta-samuccayattho. tena peḷā-caṅgoṭakādiṃ saṅgaṇhāti. veḷu-daṇḍādīni gahetvā divase divase chattādīnaṃ karaṇa-vasena dukkha-jīvitaṃ jigucchantī vadati. ahitako me vāto vātī ti keci vatvā ahitako jarā-vaho gihi-kāle mama sarīre vāto vāyatī ti atthaṃ vadanti. apare pana ahitako paresam duggandha-taro ca mama sarīrato vāto vāyati ti atthaṃ vadanti.*

The v.l. in pāda c gives the possibility of several different translations:

(i) (adopting the lexicographical use of *vā* followed by the cty) "my shameless [man], even his sunshade, etc. (= *vā*) [disgust me]".

(ii) (assuming that *vā pi* is an early variant of *cāpi* (for the alternation *c/v* see the note on **12**)) "my shameless (man) and his sunshade too (disgust me)".

(iii) "an unpleasant wind blows for me".

(iv) "my unpleasant wind blows, i.e. an unpleasant wind blows from me".

PED (s.v. *chattaka*) states "nickname of sunshade-makers", but Thī-a 29,11–12 does not seem to provide any authority for this statement.

In pāda d B^{e} and C^{e} read *deḍḍubhaṃ vāti* for *daḷidda-bhāvā ti*, and the explanation at Thī-a 28,17–19 confirms that Dhammapāla had this reading: *ukkhalikā me deḍḍubhaṃ vātī ti me mama bhata-pacana-bhājanaṃ cira-pārivāsika-bhāvena aparisuddhatāya, udaka-sappa- gandhaṃ vāyati.* Cf. *deḍḍubhassā ti udaka-sappassa* Ja VI 194.

Although the Pāli dictionaries give the meaning "pot" for *ukkhalikā*, it seems possible that there is a connection with Pkt *ukkhala* "mortar" (= Skt *udūkhala*), i.e. it is a variant of *udukkhala* in **11**). This would make a good pair with *musala* "pestle", as in **11**.

In the first edition I followed Thī-a closely in my translation, but Wright (1999) has pointed out that *vāti* could be < *vā ti* (= *va* + *ti*), which would balance *vāpi* (= *va api*), although the cty clearly takes *vāti* as a verb. If we follow Wright, then pādas cd are two comparisons. There are, however, problems in both. In pāda c there is the problem of not knowing what *ahiriko* refers to. Thī-a takes it as referring to the husband, but I think it more likely that it refers to *musala*. Against this is the problem that *ahiriko* is not a very obvious epithet to apply to a pestle. Wright postulates the *-aṃ* ending, and translates "pertaining to a snake", i.e. as a development of *ahi*, thus providing a word for "snake" in both pādas. I am reluctant to follow Wright, and I should rather see a slightly different meaning for *ahirika* — "disgusting" or "shameful". The v.l. *ahitako* which the cty mentions might be the reading to adopt. MW gives "noxious, hostile" for *ahita*. I take *chattaka* in the meaning "mushroom" (cf. Skt *chattraka*). Both *duṇḍubha* and *dundubha* in Skt are masculine, so I assume that *deṇḍubhaṃ* is a mistake for *-ā*. The reading *daḷidda-bhāvā ti* gives some evidence for reading *-bhā vā ti* in this verse.

The metre of this verse seems to be old āryā. Pāda a can be corrected by reading *sûmuttike sumuttîkā*; pāda b is correct if we read *sādhû* (§70(d)); because of the v.l. in pāda c it is difficult to correct. If we follow P's reading we must scan *ahitikŏ me vāto vāti*. In pāda d the reading of B^e and C^e is metrical if we scan *mĕ* (§72(d)).

24. B^e and C^e read *cicciṭi cicciṭī ti vihanāmi* in pāda b, and the fact that the first part of this reading, at least, was read by Dhammapāla is shown by his explanation (Thī-a 28,22–23): *iminā saddena saddhiṃ vihanāmi vināsemi vijahāmi*. I am not, however, convinced that *vihanāmi* is a better reading than *viharāmi*. Although PED does not list it in this sense, *viharati* does occur in Pāli with the meaning "remove, get rid of" (see EV I, p. 133 (ad Th 10)). If this word were taken in its usual sense of "dwell, remain", then P's reading could easily have evolved because a present participle seemed necessary: "I remain cutting" (see Geiger, 2000, §174). Scribes unacquainted with the meaning "to destroy" for *viharati* could easily have replaced it by the very similar *vihanati*. The original author probably meant nothing more than "I destroy *rāga* and *dosa* with a sizzling sound". The cty, however, sees a connection between this sound and the sound made by her husband while weaving baskets (Thī-a 28,23–26): *sā kira attano sāmikaṃ jigucchantī tena divase divase phāliyamānānaṃ sukkhānaṃ veḷu-daṇḍādīnaṃ saddaṃ garahantī tassa pahānaṃ rāga-dosa-pahānena samam katvā avoca*.

The third person pronoun *sā* with a first person verb or with *ahaṃ* is very common in Thī. The combination also occurs in **32 43 53 75 98 132 154 226 232** (*esā*) **315 359 389**. It would be possible to translate "[that same] I" if it were thought necessary to indicate the presence of the third person pronoun. The combination of *so* with *ahaṃ* or a first person verb also occurs in **212 290 319 435 436 438 440 442**. A first person plural verb occurs with *te* in **66**. A second person verb occurs with *sā* in **313** and with *so* in **387**. We find *taṃ maṃ* in **298 444**; *tassā me* in **38 85 94 104 224**; and *tassā te* in **337**. Cf. *taṃ maṃ* Sn 425 (see Pj II 386: *dvīhi pi vacanehi attānam eva niddisati*). See also GD, p. 173 (ad Sn p. 15,23).

The metre of this verse seems to be old āryā. Pāda a in P is metrical as it stands; pāda b is unmetrical in P, but if we read *vicchindantī* the sixth gaṇa would be ⏑, i.e. we should have an udgīti stanza. The reading of B^e and C^e quoted above is, however, metrical. Pāda c is metrical; in pāda d we must scan *ahŏ su⟨k⟩khan* and *sukhatŏ* m.c. (§§64(b), 72(d)). Alsdorf (1958, p. 252 note 6) does not quote ⏓, ⏑ – for the fourth gaṇa in AMg, but Warder (PM § 221) seems to allow it for Pāli, in which case we could scan *aho* without change.

25–26. Were it not for the cty and the canonical references to Aḍḍhakāsī, it would not be unreasonable to take the name as meaning "rich Kāsī" or "rich inhabitant of Kāsī", deriving *aḍḍha* < *āḍhya* as Neumann did (p. 277, n. 3). The introductory story in the cty tells how she was born in Kāsī in a wealthy family (*Kāsi-raṭṭhe uḷāra-vibhave seṭṭhi-kule nibbattitvā* (Thī-a 29,7–8)), and we could take *negamo* in **25** (so read with Bᵉ and Cᵉ) to be her father or guardian ("the mayor"). *Suṇka* would be her bride-price, cf. *upaḍḍha-suṅkena* **420**. For high bride-prices, cf. the reference to eight times the daughter's weight in **153**. For this particular price ("the size of Kāsī", or "the revenue of Kāsī" as the cty states), cf. the Jain references *jai vi ya ṇaṃ sā sayaṃ rajja-sukkhā*, Nāya-dhammakahāo § 75 (Sutt. p. 1022) Vivāga-sutta § 176 (Sutt. p. 1278): "even if she requires a dowry of my whole kingdom".

The cty, however, tells how Aḍḍhakāsī became a *gaṇikā* in consequence of having reviled a therī in a previous existence by calling her a *gaṇikā*. For the explanation of her name see the note on **25**. There are references to the *gaṇikā* Aḍḍhakāsī in the canon (Vin II 277), where she is said to have been ordained by special messenger, and her fame is shown by the reference to her at Ja V 447: *na bahūna(ṃ) kantā ti Aḍḍhakāsī-gaṇikā viya na bahunnaṃ piyā manāpā*. Thī-a 31,18 explains *negamo*: *nigama-vāsī jano*, cf. Sp 1114 *negamo ti kuṭumbika-gaṇo*, and in the explanation on the same page: *nāgarā*. We are reminded by the phrase *negamo ṭhapesi maṃ* (**25**) of the reference to Sālavatī: *Rākagahako negamo Sālavatiṃ kumāriṃ gaṇikaṃ vuṭṭhāpesi* (Vin I 268–2), where Miss Horner translates *negama* "urban council" (BD IV 379–80).

25. Thī-a 31,7–20: *yāva Kāsi-janapado suṅko me tattako ahū ti Kāsīsu janapadesu bhavo suṅko Kāsi-janapado. so yāva yattako, tattako mayhaṃ suṅko ahu ahosi. kittako pana so ti? sahassa-matto. Kāsī-raṭṭhe kira tadā suṅka-vasena eka-divasaṃ rañño uppajjanaka-āyo ahosi sahassa-matto. imāya pi purisānaṃ hatthato eka-divasaṃ laddha-dhanaṃ tattakaṃ. tena vuttaṃ yāva Kāsi-janapado suṅko me tattako ahū ti. sā pana Kāsi-suṅka-parimāṇatāya Kāsī ti samaññaṃ labhi. tattha yebhuyyena manussā sahassaṃ dātuṃ asakkontā tato upaḍḍhaṃ datvā divasa-bhāgam eva ramitvā gacchanti. tesaṃ vasenāyaṃ Aḍḍhakāsī ti paññāyittha. tena vuttaṃ taṃ katvā negamo agghaṃ aḍḍhen'* (Ce *agghen'*) *agghaṃ ṭhapesi man ti. tam pañca-sata-mattaṃ dhanaṃ agghaṃ katvā negamo nigama-vāsī jano itthi-ratana-bhāvena anagghaṃ pi samānaṃ aḍḍhena* (Ce *agghena*) *agghaṃ nimittaṃ Aḍḍhakāsī ti samaññā-vasena maṃ* *ṭhapesi, tathā maṃ voharī ti attho*. The variation between B^{e} and C^{e} *bhavo* and the v.l. *gato* in B^{e} is probably due in part, at least, to the alternation *g*/*bh*. For other examples of this in Thī, cf. *gaṇḍa*/*bhaṇḍa* **54**, *gaṇanti*/*bhaṇanti* **217**, *ukkāgāriṃ*/*ukkābhāriṃ* **297**, *vigata*/*vibhava* **327–28**, *uggata*/*ubbhata* **379**, *gaṇāmi*/*bhaṇāmi* **418**, *gatta*/*bhasta* **466**. See also EV I, p. 176 (ad Th 164).

It is noteworthy that the cty does not state that *Kāsi-janapada* means 1000, but only that the revenue of Kāsī amounted to 1000. The cty seems to be taking *Kāsi-janapado* as an adjective, but I think we should rather see a split compound *Kāsi-janapado suṅko* = *Kāsi-janapada-suṅko* (see the note on **147**), with *suṅka* to be taken in two senses: "my wages from prostitution were as large as the revenues of the country of Kāsī." PED does not list these two meanings for *suṅka*, but see MW, s.v. *śulka*. If her fees were equal to the rest of the revenue, then she was in fact the equivalent of half of Kāsī. There is, however, elsewhere in Pāli a belief that *kāsika* means 1000, cf. *aḍḍha-kāsikaṃ kambalaṃ pāhesi uppaḍha-kāsīnaṃ khamamānaṃ* (Vin I 281). Sp 1119 explains: *aḍḍha-kāsiyan ti ettha kāsī ti sahassaṃ vuccati, taṃ agghanako kāsiyo, ayam pana pañca-satāni agghato, tasmā aḍḍha-kāsiyo ti vutto. ten' āha upaḍḍha-kāsīnaṃ khamamānam*. See Miss Horner's note (BD IV p. 398, n. 1). CPD, however, states (s.v. *aḍḍha-kāsika*) "it seems originally to mean a sort of 'half-muslin', but here it is taken in the sense of 'a piece of stuff sufficient for half the people of Kāsī' ". Rhys Davids and Oldenberg translated "a woollen garment made half of Benares cloth" (VT II 195).

It is hard to accept the cty's explanation of pāda d, since it contains both *aḍḍhena* and *anagghaṃ*, although the syllable *na* can only belong to one word in the text. CPD (s.v. [1]*aggha*) recognised this, and proposed to read *aḍḍhe*[*na*] in the cty, but nevertheless wanted to read *aḍḍhaṃ agghen' agghaṃ* in the text. See also CPD s.v. [1]*aḍḍha*. I personally prefer to read as P, and would assume that the reading *aḍḍhena* came into existence because of the name Aḍḍhakāsī.

The cty's explanation of her name is interesting, despite these difficulties, because there is a variant of this story in Mvu III 375–76, where we read of a *gaṇika* named Kāśikā, so called not because she lived in Kāśī but because "she was worth [as a fee] the whole sum of 1000" (to follow Edgerton's translation of *sarvāṃ kāśi-bhūmiṃ kṣamati*). Her sister was named Uparddha-kāśikā, because "she was worth half of 1000" (*uparddha-*(mss for *upārdha-*)*kāśiṃ kṣamati*). It is debatable whether the Skt version has made two women from one. I am, however, not at all certain that I can accept Edgeton's translations of *bhūmi* and *kṣaṃ-*. As mentioned above, CPD prefers "is sufficient" for *kham-*, although PED agrees with Edgerton in translating "worth". For further discussion of the name Aḍḍhakāsi see Bollée, 1970, pp. 110–11.

26. Thī-a 31,21–23: *atha nibbind' aham rūpe ti evaṃ rūpūpajīvinī hutvā ṭhitā atha pacchā sāsanaṃ nissāya rūpe ahaṃ nibbindiṃ "iti pi rūpaṃ aniccaṃ, iti p' idaṃ rūpaṃ dukkhaṃ asubhan" ti passantī tattha ukkaṇṭhiṃ*). PED does not list the aorist form *nibbindiṃ*. I take *rūpa* in the sense of "beauty, [woman's] figure".

Thī-a 31,24–25: *nibbindañ ca virajj' ahan ti nibbindantī cāhaṃ tato paraṃ virāgaṃ āpajjiṃ*. Presumably *virajj'* stands for *virajjiṃ*, also aorist, although once again PED does not list this form, although it occurs at Thī-a 85,23 (ad **86**). It is clear that *nibbindaṃ* cannot stand for *nibbindantī*, as the cty claims. There are two possible explanations for *nibbindaṃ*; firstly the pāda may have been taken over from a context where it was appropriate, i.e. with a masculine subject, cf. *nibbindaṃ virajjati* S II 125, and see the note on **12**.

Alternatively we could see here a *ṇamul*-type absolutive. In this connection it should be noted that the comparable sentiment in **522** is expressed with an absolutive *nibbinditvā*, although a present participle would have been equally metrical. Other possible examples of *ṇamul* forms in Thī are: *ogāhaṃ* **48**, *ubbandhaṃ* **80**, *kasaṃ* < **kāsaṃ* and *pavapaṃ* < **pavāpam* **112**, *paricaraṃ* < **paricāraṃ* **143**, *anibbisaṃ* < **anibbesam* **159**. For other examples of *ṇamul* absolutives see EV I, p. 139 (ad Th 22). In his review of EV I de Jong (1972) has added *ālumpa-kāraṃ* Dhp-a II 55 and *sannidhi-kāraṃ* D I 6. *Jayaṃ* < **jāyaṃ* in Th 70 (= Dhp 201 etc.) could also be taken as a *ṇamul*, as could *saraṃ* < **sāraṃ* S I 140 and *jānaṃ passaṃ* A I 149. Cf. *sampassaṃ* at Ja IV 134 (glossed *sampassantā*). Other possible *ṇamul* absolutives in Th are: *samācāraṃ* 727 (no need to emend to *samācaraṃ*), *avadehakaṃ* in *udarāvadehakaṃ* 935 (cf. D III 238 M I 102–3 A III 222 249 Vbh 378) which is explained by another *ṇamul udara-pūraṃ* at Th-a III 78,26 and Mp III 325, and by an absolutive *avadihitvā* at Mp III 307. Cf. *kucchi-pūraṃ* Ja III 268. For another *ṇamul* from the root *dih-* (*diha upacaye* Dhātupāṭha 336 Dhātumañjarī 500, cf. Skt (lex.) "to increase, accumulate" (MW, s.v.)), cf. *pheṇ'-uddehakaṃ* A I 141 IV 134, Vism 56, glossed (Mp IV 65): *uddihitvā*. For *ṇamul* absolutives in *-aka* see BHSG § 35.5, and cf. *sannidhi-kārakaṃ* Vin I 209 IV 87 D III 235 M I 523 A III 109 IV 370, *ālumpa-kārakaṃ* D III 85 Vism 417, and the group of eleven at Vin II 214 IV 195–98: *piṇḍukkhepakaṃ*, *kabaḷāvacchedakaṃ*, *avagaṇḍa-kārakaṃ*, *hattha-biddhūnakaṃ*, *sitthāva-kārakaṃ*, *jivhā-nicchārakaṃ*, *capu-capu-kārakaṃ*, *suru-suru-kārakaṃ*, *hattha-nillehakaṃ*, *patta-nillehakaṃ*, *oṭṭha-nillehakaṃ*, all of which are explained at Sp 893–94 by reiterated absolutives: *ukkhipitvā ukkhipitvā*, *avacchinditvā avacchinditvā*, etc. Cf. *dant'-ullehakaṃ* M III 167.

For *punâ* (or *puno*) m.c. in pāda c to avoid the opening ⏓ ⏑ ⏑ – see § 70(a) and the note on **10**. Although PED (s.v. *puna*) states that *puno* is a Sanskritisation, found only at Thī-a 70,14* 71,2*, it does in fact occur at **292 397**. See also EV I, p. 151 (ad Th 57), and the note on **423**.

27. For *kiñcāpi* in the sense of "although" see PED (s.v. *kiṃ*), and Geiger (2000, § 111, n.). the same meaning is found in Th 947 Sn 230 232 D I 237. See also **29**.

For *olubbha* see the note on **17**.

28. Thī-a 33,4–6 explains *tamo-kkhandha* by *moha-kkhanda*, and the same explanation is given at Thī-a 157,31 (ad **174**). The splitting is done *dīghena addhunā* here, but *agga-magga-ñāṇāsinā* in **174**. Thī-a 47,19–20 (ad **44**) explains: *anavasesa-moha-kkhandhaṃ agga-maggena padāletvā*. There is no comment on *tamo-kkhanda* in **59** (= Sn I 130). Spk I 191 explains: *tamo-kkhando ti avijjā-kkhando. padālito ti ñāṇena bhinno*. There is no comment on *tamo-kkhando* in **142**. See also EV I, p. 169 (ad Th 128).

Thī-a 33,4–7: *khambesi attānaṃ, attānaṃ atta-bhavaṃ khambhesi mama sattānaṃ āyatiṃ anuppatti-dhamma-tāpa-dānena vikkhambhesī ti attho*. For *atta-bhāva* see the note on **270**.

The cadence –, – – ⏓ usually has the opening ⏓ – ⏑ – (or ⏓ ⏑ – –), so we should probably read *khambhesim* (§ 68(b)(iii)) and obtain the cadence ⏑ – – ⏓ (*pathyā*). The same cadence is found elsewhere in Thī, e.g. *saṃvegaṃ āpādiṃ* **40** (? read *saṃvegam*), *Sundariṃ āyantiṃ* **334** (? read *Sundarim*), *bālānaṃ saṃsāro* **495** (? read *bālāna*[*ṃ*], cf. *sukkāna dhammānam* in **278**). Conversely we should probably read *sa*[*ṃ*] in **283** to give the opening ⏓ – ⏑ – with the cadence – , – – ⏓ .

29. For *kiñcāpi* see the note on **27**.

For *olubbha* see the note on **17**.

31–32. I translate *deva* as "deity" (cf. **121 181 475–76**) and *devatā* as "divinity" (see **87**). I translate *deva-kāya* as "world of deities". Cf. *asurakāya* **475**.

31. This verse recurs at S I 208 A I 144–45 VV 12 17 19 20 26 35 51 Ja IV 320 VI 118 DhA IV 21. A similar verse, but in jagatī metre, occurs at Sn 402.

B^{e} and C^{e} read *cātuddasiṃ pañcadasiṃ* for *cātuddasī pañcadasī*, and this reading is also found at S I 208 Vv 12 17 26 35 51 Dhp-a IV 21. A I 144–45 reads as P. Vv 19 20 Ja IV 320 VI 118 read as B^{e} and C^{e} in pāda a but read *aṭṭhamiṃ* for *aṭṭhamī* in pāda b. This corruption must be old, since it is found in the BHS version at Mvu III 1. It is clear that we must read accusatives in pāda a since the cty states: *cātuddasiṃ pañcadasin ti catuddasannaṃ pūraṇī cātuddası, pañcadasannaṃ pūraṇī pañcadasī, taṃ cātuddasiṃ pañcadasiṃ ca. pakkhassā ti sambandho. accanta-saṃoye c' etaṃ upayoga-vacanaṃ*, i.e. this is the accusative case in the sense of continuous period of time. The same comment is made at Vv-a 72.

In pāda b several versions read *va* for *ca* (for the alternation *c*/*v* see the note on **12**), and some editors print *yāva*, e.g. at S I 208 A I 144–45 Vv 19 26 Ja IV 320 VI 118. This interpretation must be old since *yāvat* occurs at Mvu III 1, and *yāva* at Mvu III 2. It is clear from Ce that Dhammapāla read *yā* as a relative pronoun: *yā ca pakkhassa aṭṭhamī, taṃ cā ti yojanā*. Vv-a 72 also has ⟨*taṃ*⟩ as a v.l.

In pāda c B^e and C^e S I 208 A I 144–45 Sn 402 Ja IV 320 VI 118 read *-hāriya-* for *-hārika-*. For the alternation *k*/*y* see the note on **43**. All versions except P read *pāṭi-* for *pāri-*. For the alternation *pāri-*/*pāṭi-* see Emeneau (pp. 33–39).

Edgerton (BHSD, s.v. *prātihāraka-pakṣa*) wrote of "wholly discordant glosses in the (Pāli) cties: at least one of them is a baseless guess". He pointed out that in BHS *pakṣa* always refers to half a month. Spk I 307 gives two explanations: *pāṭihāriya-pakkhañ cā ti manussā aṭṭhamī-uposathassa paccuggamanañ ca anuggamanañ ca karissāmī ti sattamiyā pi navamiyā pi uposath'-aṅgāni samādiyanti. cātuddasī-paṇṇarasīnaṃ paccuggaman'-anugamanaṃ karontā terasiyā pi pāṭipade pi samādiyanti. vassa-vāsassa anuggamanaṃ karissāmī ti dvinnaṃ pavāraṇānaṃ antare aḍḍha-māsaṃ nibaddh'-uposathikā bhavanti. idaṃ sandhāya vuttaṃ pāṭhāriya-pakkhañ cā ti.* Mp II 234 gives only the first of these explanations; Thī-a 36,10–13 Vv-a 71 Ja IV 321 VI 118 give only the second; Pj II 378 gives the second and adds: *ettha pana vassūpanāyikāya purima-bhāge Āsāḷha-māso, anto-vasse tayo māsā, Kattika-māso ti ime pañca māsā pāṭihāriya-pakkho ti vuccanti*; *Āsāḷha-Kattika-Phagguṇa-māsā tayo evā ti apare*. It concludes: *yaṃ ruccati, taṃ gahetabbaṃ, na puññena bhāsitabbaṃ*. PED does not list *anu(g)gamana* or *paccuggamana* in the meanings "day following" or "day preceding" respectively.

PED quotes *pakkha* (s.v.), with reference to time, only in the meaning "fortnight", and the fact that some of the cties include an explanation depending upon another meaning is probably in its favour. In the context it seems clear that the reference must be to individual days of the fortnight. Cf. Vv-a 109: *bhariyā pun' assa aṭṭhamiṃ catuddasiṃ pannarasiṃ pāṭihārika-pakkhesu* (v.l. *-pakkhaññu*) *uposathaṃ upavasi, visesato sīlācāra-sampannā ahosi,* where again the context makes the meaning "days" more likely. In Pkt, however, *pakkha* is used in a comparable way, whether by change of meaning to *tithi*, as Jacobi (Kalp,

Index, p. 152, s.v. *pakkha*) implied, or because of the reversal of the members of a compound, as Hultzsch thought (p. 128, n. 5), e.g. Kalp, § 2 (p. 1) *chaṭṭhī-pakkheṇaṃ*, § 30 (p. 41) *terasī-pakkheṇaṃ*, § 120 (p. 63) *dasamī-pakkheṇaṃ*, § 124 (p. 64) *pannarasī-pakkheṇaṃ*, Aśoka's Pillar Edict V *aṭhamī-pakhāye*, all to be translated "on the ...th day of the fortnight".

I assume that *pāṭihāriya* is connected with *pāṭihīra* "wonder, marvel", and I therefore translate "special, extra-ordinary day of the fortnight".

Thī-a 36,14–16: *aṭṭhaṅga-susamāgatan ti pāṇātipātā veramaṇī-ādīhi aṭṭhahi aṅgehi suṭṭhu samannāgataṃ uposathaṃ upāgañchin ti upagamiṃ upavasin ti attho*. The cty quotes Sn 400–401 to illustrate this. S I 208 reads *susamāhita* for *susamāgata*.

Thī-a 36,25–26: *deva-kāyābhinandinī ti tatrūpapatti-ākaṅkhā-vasena cātu-mahārājika-deva-kāyaṃ abhipatthentī uposathaṃ upāgañchin ti yojanā.*

For *-dd-* in *pañca-ddasiṃ* see § 64(a).

32. Thī-a 36,31–37,1: *vineyya hadaye daran ti citta-gataṃ kilesa-darathaṃ samuccheda-vasena vinetvā ti attho*. For *dara* and *daratha* see Brough (GDhp, pp. 185–86).

For *sā* with a first person verb see the note on **24**.

33–34. The introductory story to these verses relates how the author bore a son by king Bimbisāra of Magadha (§ 24). The son grew up to become the thera Abhaya (Th 26 98). His mother one day heard him preaching, went forth from the world, and later became an arahat. She then repeated a verse with which her son had admonished her (for her love of bodily beauty), and added her own verse to it (Thī-a 38,12–14): *arahattaṃ pana patvā attano puttena Abhaya-therena dhammaṃ kathentena ovāda-vasena yā gāthā bhāsitā udāna-vasena sayam pi tā eva paccudāharantī āha* (§ 4).

33. B^e and C^e read *ve* for *ce* in pāda b. For the alternation *c/v* see the note on **12**.

34. Thī-a 39,6: *pariḷāho, kilesa-pariḷāho.*

35–36. These verses presumably follow **33–34** because of the apparent connection between Abhayamātā and Abhayā (§ 13(b)). This is the first group of verse in P to be followed by *ti* (see the note on **1**).

35. Thī-a 41,19–22: *bhiduro ti bhijjana-sabhāvo anicco ti attho. yattha sattā puthujjanā ti yasmiṃ khaṇe bhijjana-sīle asuci-duggandha-jigucchā-paṭikūla-*

sabhāve kāye ime andha-puthujjanā sattā laggā laggitā. The cty seems to be taking *yattha* in the sense of "when". See the note on **225**.

For *satīmatī* m.c. see § 69(c).

36. Thī-a 41,25–26: *bahūhi dukkha-dhammehi jāti-jarādīhi anekehi dukkha-dhammehi phuṭṭhāya ti adhippāyo*.

37–38. This group presumably follows **35–36** because both groups have a verse in common (§ 13(a)).

37. The cadence – – – ⏓ without a caesura after the fifth syllable is quite irregular by classical standards. It can be avoided here, in **42**, and in **169**, by reading *pañca[k]khattuṃ* (§ 65(b)). See also the note on **519** where the metre (āryā) shows that we must read -*[k]khattuṃ* four times in that verse. The cadence – – – ⏓ is found elsewhere in Thī, e.g. *vasī-hūtāhaṃ* **233** (? read *vasī-*), *bahu-dukkhā kāmā* **492** (? read -*du[k]khā*).

P reads -*vattini* here and in **40 42 77 169**. This form would be the loc. sing. neuter, in agreement with *citte*; see CPD, s.v. [2]*a-vasa-vatti(n)*. C^{e} and S^{e} agree with P in all verses. K^{e} reads -*ī* in **77** and **169** only; B^{e} reads -*ī* in all verses. This form would be the nom. sing. fem.; see CPD, s.v. [1]*a-vasa-vatti(n)*.

Thī-a 42,28–29: *citte avasavattinī ti vīriyasamatāya abhāvena mama bhāvanācitte na vasavattinī. sā kira ativiya paggahitavīriyā ahosi*. Cf. Thī-a 78,12–13 (ad **77**): *citte avasavattinī ti pubbe mama citte mayhaṃ vase avattamāne*. Cf. **40 42 77 169**.

38. For *tassā me* see the note on **24**.

39–41. This group of verses is presumably first in the *tika-nipāta* because of the apparent resemblances with **37–38**. The groups have more than a verse in common (§ 13(a)), and are both by therīs called Sāmā (§ 13(b)).

39. The syntax of pāda b is rather strange, but the cty makes no reference to it.

40. For *saṃvegam* m.c. (with C^{e}) to give the cadence ⏑ – – ⏓ (*pathyā*) see § 68(b) (iii) and the note on **28**.

For *avasavattini* see the note on **37**.

42–44. This group probably follows **39–41** because the two groups have two pādas (**40**ab and **42**cd) in common (§ 13(a)).

The introductory story in the cty tells how Uttamā went forth from the world in the presence of Paṭācārā (**112–16**), but required admonition from her before she could obtain arahatship. The bhikkhunī mentioned in **43** is identified as Paṭācārā by the cty.

42. For *avasavattini* see the note on **37**.

43. Ce reads *ahū* for *ahu*. Historically *ahū* is to be expected, but there is no obvious reason for shortening > *ahu* here, nor in **57**d **190**d **204**d **338**d. The shortening may, however, be m.c. in **94**a to avoid the cadence – , – – ⏓ with the opening ⏓ – – ⏑ ; in **116**d to give the cadence ⏑ – ⏑ ⏓ ; in **204**b to avoid the opening ⏓ – ⏑ – ; in **224**c to avoid the cadence – , – – ⏓ with the opening ⏓ – – ⏑ ; in **270**a where a short syllable is required in a rathoddhatā pāda.

I leave *bhikkhunī* untranslated for the same reasons which persuaded me not to translate *bhikkhu* in Th (see EV I, p. 132 (ad Th 6)).

Thī-a 47,5–6: *yā me saddhāyikā ahū ti yā mayā saddhātabbā saddheyya-vacanā*. Sv III 809 (ad D II 320) explains: *saddhāyikā ti aham tumhe saddahāmi, tumhe mayhaṃ saddhāyikā, saddhāyitabba-vacanā ti attho*. Mp V 58 (ad A V 170) explains: *saddhāyiko ti saddhāya āgama-karo pasādāvaho,* saddhātabba-vacano vā. Thī-a 47,8 gives a v.l.: *yā me sādhāyikā ti pi pāṭho* (§ **35**).... *yā mayhaṃ padatthassa sādhikā ti attho*.

The word occurs in the form *saddhāyita* at Pv 22, and Pv-a 109 glosses: *saddhāyitabbaṃ*. That this reading is not merely a scribal error is shown by the existence of BHS *śraddhayita* (see BHSD, s.v.). This alternation of -*k*- and -*t*- and elsewhere of -*k*- and -y-, and -*t*- and -*y*-, presumably arose from a dialect where -*k*- and -*t*- coincided with -*y*- (see Bollée, 1969), and it may therefore possibly pre-date the translation of the Buddhist canon into Pāli (§ 27), although the simple scribal confusion of *k* and *t* cannot be ignored. Other possible examples of these alternations may be seen in Thī, e.g. *pārihārika-/pārihāriya-* **31**, *icchakaṃ/icchitaṃ* **46**, *pakāsikaṃ/pakāsitaṃ* **74**, *akampitaṃ/akampiyaṃ* **201**, *ajānako/ajānato* **240**, *lekhikā/lekhitā* **256**, **upakuliyā/*upakulitā* **258**, *khaṇḍitā/khaṇḍiyā* **260**, *dubbalikā/-bbalitā* **263**, *phuṭikā/phuṭitā* **269**, *upamānite/upamāniye* **382**, *panaccakā/panaccitā* **390**, *pasādikā/pasāditā* **448**. See EV I, p. 151 (ad Th 57) and Lüders (1954, §§ 133–38).

For *khandāyatana-dhātuyo* see EV I, p. 338 (ad Th 1255) and the note on **472**.

44. Thī-a 47,19–21: *pāde pasāresiṃ ... pallaṅkaṃ bhindantī* (§ **35**) *pāde pasāresiṃ*. No explanation is given of *pallaṅka*. Elsewhere two different comments are made: Sp 953 (ad Vin I 1) explains: *eka-pallaṅkenā ti sakim pi* *anuṭṭhahitvā yathā ābhujitena eken' eva pallaṅkena* (i.e. a particular posture). In some contexts, however, *pallaṅka* is used in the sense of "seat". Bv-a 99 (ad Bv 10) explains: *pallaṅkaṃ ābhujitvā ti kata-pallaṅko hutvā puppha-rāsimhi nisīdin ti attho*. Cf. Sp 66: *atha nāgarājā attano ratanamayaṃ pallaṅkaṃ āharāpetvā therassa paññāpesi. nisīdi thero pallaṅke*. In so far as it seems possible to distinguish between these two usages in Pāli it seems probable that the original usage was to use the locative case in the meaning "seat", and the instrumental in the meaning "posture". If this was still so at the time of the composition of this verse, then the instrumental would be more correct, and it is interesting to note that there is a v.l. (P n.) *-pallaṅkena*. To read this and at the same time to preserve the metre we should need to read [*ni-*]*sīdi*. For the alternation *-na*/*ni-* cf. EV I, p. 238 (ad Th 568).

Ce omits *pīti-* in pāda d, which leaves pādas cd as śloka, with resolution of the fourth syllable in pāda d (§ 60). If, however, we read *sattāham* (§ 68(b)(iii)) and *eka-pa*[*l*]*laṅke* (§ 65(b)(ii)) in pāda c, then we have a triṣṭubh pāda in a śloka verse, and pāda d is quite regular. Pāda e has nine syllables (§ 61) even when we scan *aṭṭham*^{i}*yā* (§ 75). Cf. **174**c.

The opening ⏓ ⏑ ⏑ ⏑ in pāda d is irregular by classical standards (cf. EV I, p. 199 (ad Th 286)), and it is avoided in **88**, where the cty notes that *bahū-vata-samādānā* is m.c. (see the note on **88**). The opening is, however, tolerated in several other pādas in Thī, although the metre could frequently be corrected without difficulty, e.g. *abbuhi vata* **52** **131** (? read *abbuhī*), *vyādhi-maraṇa-* **162** (? read *vyādhī-*), *jāti-maraṇa-* **199** (? read *jātī-*), *aṇu pi aṇu-matto* **208** (? read *aṇū*), *pabbaji anagāriyaṃ* **311** (? read *pabbajī*), *duggati-gamanaṃ* **355** (? read *duggatī-*), *gacchatha na* **492** (? read *gacchātha*). We could correct the metre here by reading either *pītî-* (§ 70(e)) or *-su*⟨*k*⟩*kha-* (§ 64(b)). See also the notes on **10** and **74**.

45–47. This group of verses presumably follows **42–44** because both authors have the name Uttamā (§ 13(b)).

45. For the seven *bojjhaṅgas* see the note on **21**.

46. Be and Ce read *icchakaṃ* for *icchitaṃ* (for the alternation *k*/*t* see the note on **43**). Thī-a 48,18–21: *suññatassānimittassa lābhinī 'haṃ yad icchakan ti suññata-samāpattiyā animitta-samāpattiyā ca ahaṃ yad icchakaṃ lābhinī. tattha yaṃ yaṃ samāpajjituṃ icchāmi yattha yattha yadā yadā taṃ taṃ tattha tattha samāpajjitvā viharāmī ti attho. yadi pi hi suññatāppaṇihitādi-nāmakassa yassa kassaci pi maggassa suññatādi-bhedaṃ tividham pi phalaṃ sambhavati. ayaṃ pana therī suññatānimitta-samāpattiyo va samāpajjati*. For *suññata* as an adjective see BHSD, s.v. *śūnyatā*, and cf. Vin III 92: *vimokkho ti, suññato vimokkho animitto vimokkho appaṇihito vimokkho.* For *animitta* see the note on **20**.

For *dhītā* applied to a follower of the Buddha cf. **336**. In **384** Subhā Jīvambavanikā describes herself as *Buddha-sutaṃ*, glossed (Thī-a 238,8): *buddhassa bhagavato orasaṃ dhītaraṃ.* In **63** Kassapa is described as *putto buddhassa*, glossed; *buddhānubuddha-bhāvato sammā-sambuddhassa anujāta-bhūto.* For this use of *putta* see EV I, p. 145 (ad Th 41). In Thī-a 272,18–19 Dhammapāla describes all the theras and therīs as *dhamma-rājassa satthuno orasā mukha-jā puttā.* The cty ad **46** does not gloss *orasā*, but Thī-a 221,31 (ad **336**) states: *tuyhaṃ urasā manasā janitābhijātitāya orasā.*

48. Thī-a 50,19–21: *nāgaṃ ogāha-m-uttiṇṇan ti hatthi-nāgaṃ nadiyaṃ ogāhaṃ katvā ogayha tato uttiṇṇaṃ. ogayha-m-uttiṇṇan ti vā pāṭho. ma-kāro pada-sandhi-karo.* For other examples of sandhi *-m-* see *vana-m-antaraṃ* **80**, *orambhāga-m-anīyāni* **166** (Thī-a 156,11: *ma-kāro pada-sandhi-karo*), *abhinīla-m-āyata* **257**, *puno-m-ahaṃ* **292**, *roga-m-āvahaṃ* **355**.

It is, however, not at all certain that in this verse *-m-* is a sandhi consonant. If the cty is correct, we have here a tatpuruṣa compound "risen up from a plunge". The v.l. *ogayha* mentioned by the cty can, however, be paralleled by *nāgānaṃ ogayha uttarantānaṃ* at Vin III 109 on which Sp 513 comments: *nāgānaṃ ogāhaṃ uttarantānan ti ogayha ogāhitvā puna uttarantānaṃ.* This suggests the possibility that *ogāhaṃ* (> *ogāham* before a vowel) is a *ṇamul* absolutive "risen up having plunged". For other possible examples of *ṇamul* absolutives see the note on **26**. Against this is the fact that Mp IV 203 (ad A IV 435) takes *ogāha* as a noun: [*nāgassa*] *ogāham otiṇṇassā ti ogāhitabbattā ogāhan ti laddha-nāmaṃ udaka-titthaṃ.* It is also a noun in the phrase *ogāhā uttiṇṇassa* at Ud 41–42, with the v.l. *ogāhañ* (before *ca*). Ud-a 250 shows knowledge of both endings: *ogāhā ti titthato*; *ogāhan ti pi pāḷi.* It would seem likely that the accusative *ogāhaṃ* should occur with *otiṇṇa*, and the ablative *ogāhā*, or the absolutive *ogayha*, should occur with *uttiṇṇa*, but scribal confusion led to errors.

PED (s.v. *ogāha*) states that *ogāha* is found only in the form *pariyogāha*.

For the use of *-r-* as a sandhi consonant see the note on **3**.

49. There is resolution of the first syllable in pāda a (§ 60).

For *āruhi* m.c. to give the cadence ⏑ — ⏑ ⏓ see § 71.

50. Thī-a 51,1–2: *khalū ti avadhāraṇatthe nipāto. tato hatthidassanato pacchā. tāya hatthino kiriyāya hetu-bhūtāya vanaṃ araññaṃ gatā.* As P (p. 180) stated, this makes it quite clear that Dhammapāla read *khalu tāya* as two words. P nevertheless wished to read *khalutāya*, and to take it as the instrumental of a noun **khalutā* "certainty, surety". MW quotes *khalutas* "certainly", so perhaps *khalutāya* as a noun is not impossible "in certainty". Neumann (p. 284 note 5) suggested reading *tayā vasaṃgatā*. The cty suggests that *tāya* is instrumental "because of that (action)". I would suggest, however, that if the reading *tāya* is correct, it can only be a dative of purpose: "(gone to the wood) for that purpose".

Although *khalu* as first word of a pāda is unusual, MW states that "[*khalu*] is only exceptionally found at the beginning of a phrase".

51–53. The introductory story in the cty (Thī-a 51,25 foll.) tells how Ubbirī had a daughter called Jīvantī (Mrs Rhys Davids calls her Jīvā (Sist., p. 39)), who died. The Buddha heard Ubbirī lamenting her daughter's death, and consoled her by uttering **51** (§ 2). There are difficulties in the story, since *Jīvā ti* can stand only for *Jīva* + *ti* or *Jīvā* + *ti* and neither *Jīva* nor *Jīvā* can be the vocative of *Jīvā* or *Jīvantī*, although the reading *Jīvatī ti* in C[e] looks like an attempt to correct this discrepancy. This reading is, however, unmetrical. For the suggestion that Dhammapāla has misunderstood the meaning of *jīvā ti* and made up a story to fit his interpretation, see the note on **51**.

51. Pādas ab are vaitālīya; pādas cdef are śloka. For [*amma*] m.c. see § 67(a) and cf. **454**a. The corruption must be old, since Thī-a 52,5–6 explains: *amma Jīvā* (C[e] *Jīvatī*) *ti māt'-upacāra-nāmena dhītuyā ālapanaṃ. idaṃ c' assā vippalapanākāra-dassanaṃ.* Since *amma* is hypermetric, and probably unoriginal, it is perhaps superfluous to consider how it should be translated. The cty's suggestion that it is a mark of Ubbiri's confusion is not very likely, although Mrs Rhys Davids accepts it and translates accordingly. I think that it is more likely to have been uttered to Ubbirī by the author of **51**, either the Buddha, using the word as an expression of politeness, or perhaps more likely by a child of Ubbirī.

Jīva can only be the imperative from *jīv-* "live", or the vocative of *jīva*. The latter would make no sense as a daughter's name, but could mean "o living creature". I would suggest that there is a play upon the two meanings of the word here. Ubbirī had said to her dead daughter, "Live"; the other speaker says, "You have had 84,000 daughters (in previous existences) all having the name 'living creature'". Dhammapāla misunderstands this, and explains (Thī-a 52,9): *sabbā Jīva-sanāmikā ti tā sabbā pi jīvantiyā samāna-nāmikā*, assuming that *jīva-* was actually the child's name.

Thī-a 52,7–8: *attānam adhigaccha Ubbirī ti Ubbiri tava attānam eva tāva bujjhassu yathāvato jānāhi.*

B^e reads *cullāsīti-* for *cūḷāsīti-*. Both readings seem to be Eastern forms with *-l-* for *-r-* (cf. Pkt *culāsīi* (Pischel, 1900, §446)). *Catul-* has developed > *caul-* > *col-* > *cūl-*, and B^e shows the secondary change > *cull-*. There seems to be no historic reason for retroflex *-ḷ-*.

52. Thī-a 54,21 foll.: *yaṃ me sokaparetāyā ti yasmā sokena abhibhūtāya mayhaṃ dhītusokaṃ byapānudi anavasesato nīhari.*

See also **131**, where *yā* replaces *yaṃ* in pāda c.

For *abbuhî* m.c. to avoid the opening ⏓ ⏑ ⏑ ⏑ see §70(e) and the note on **44**. B^e and C^e read *abbahī.*

There is resolution of the fourth syllable in pāda b (§60). B^e reads -[*ni-*]*ssitaṃ*, but this is probably later normalisation.

53. For *sā ahaṃ* see the note on **24**. See also **132**.

The cty makes no mention of *nicchātā* here or in the comment ad **132**, but Thī-a 156,23 (ad **168**) glosses: *nicchātā, nittaṇhā.*

For *parinibbuta* see EV I, p. 132 (ad Th 5) and p. 332 (ad Th 1218).

Thī-a 55,3: *munin ti sabba-ññu-buddhaṃ*. For *muni* see EV I, p. 154 (ad Th 68) and the note on **205**. In this context *muniṃ* is presumably an adjective qualifying *buddhaṃ*, although rather removed from it. For *buddha-muni* see the note on **231**. See also the note on *buddhaṃ tādisaṃ* in **249–50**.

54. In this verse pāda a is triṣṭubh; pādas bcd are śloka. It recurs at S I 212, although pādas cd differ slightly there.

Thī-a 59,1–2: *kiṃ 'me katā Rājagahe manussā ti ime Rājagaha-manussā kiṃ katā, kismiṃ nāma kicce vyāvatā*. Spk I 315 explains: *kim me katā ti kiṃ ime katā? kiṃ karontī ti attho*. We should probably read *k' ime* (with C^e) for *kiṃ ime*. Possibly the original version had a split compound *kim ime katā* (for *kiṃkatā ime*) with resolution of the first syllable of the pāda, and then by metrical haplology (see CPD p. 548, s.v. *accupati*, and cf. the note on **166**) one *-im-* was omitted and the resulting *kime* changed to *kiṃ me*. I assume that the meaning is "Made into what?", i.e. "What has happpened to?" For split compounds see the note on **147**.

Thī-a 59,2–6: *madhuṃ* (Ce *madhu*) *pītā va acchare ti yathā bhaṇḍa-madhuṃ* (Ce *gaṇḍa-madhuṃ* (for the alternation *g*/*bh* see the note on **25**)) *gahetvā madhuṃ pītavanto visaññino hutvā sīsaṃ ukkhipituṃ na sakkonti, evaṃ ime pi dhamma-saññāya visaññino hutvā maññe sīsaṃ ukkhipituṃ na sakkonti, kevalaṃ acchanti yevā ti attho*. S I 212 reads *madhu-pītā va seyyare*, and Spk I

316 explains: *gaṇḍa-madhu-pānaṃ pītā viya sayanti. gaṇḍa-madhu-pānaṃ pīto kira sīsaṃ ukkhipituṃ na sakkoti, asaññī hutvā sayate va.* PED does not list *gaṇḍa* in the sense of "honeycomb" s.v. *gaṇḍa*, but see s.v. *madhu-gaṇḍa*.

55. Thī-a 59,10–14: *taṃ ca appaṭivāniyan ti tañ ca pana dhammaṃ ani-vattanīya-bhāvāvahaṃ niyyānikaṃ abhikkantatāya vā yathā-sotu-jana-savaṇa-manohara-bhāvena anapanīyaṃ asecanakaṃ anāsittakaṃ pakatiyā va mahā-rasaṃ tato c' eva ojavantaṃ. osadhan ti pi pāṭho. vaṭṭa-dukkha-vyādhi-ti-kkicchāya osadha-bhūtaṃ.* Thī-a 164,7–9 (ad **196**) explains: *asecanakam ojavan ti kenaci anāsittakaṃ ojavantaṃ sabhāva-madhuraṃ sabbassa pi kilesa-rogassa vūpasamato osadha-bhūtaṃ ariya-maggaṃ nibbānam eva.* The reading *thāsotu-* in M can be seen to be merely an error (§ 35), and Morris's attempt to explain this (1884, p. 82) can be disregarded.

Thī-a 59,14–17: *pivanti maññe sappaññā, valāhakam iv' addhagū ti valāhakantarato nikkhantaṃ udakaṃ nirudakakantāre pathagā viya taṃ dhammaṃ sappaññā paṇḍitapurisā pivanti maññe pivantā viya suṇanti.*

For *asecanaka* and *ojavant* see Brough (GDhp, p. 193).

The cty's explanation of *ca* by *pana* makes it clear that we are to take it in the disjunctive sense "but" here. See EV I, p. 145 (ad Th 41), and cf. **128 144 183 416 455–56 487 513** (where Thī-a 167,2 includes *pana* in the explanation).

56. For the form of pāda a cf. **7**.

For *Māraṃ savāhanam* see the note on **7**.

For *dhamma* see the note on **3**.

57–59. Verse **57** was uttered by Māra; **58–59** by the therī (§ 2). A similar set of verses in S I 128 is ascribed to Āḷavikā. The introductory story in the cty states that Selā was born in Āḷavī as the king's daughter, and adds (Thī-a 60,13–14): *Āḷavikassa pana rañño dhītā ti katvā, Āḷavikā ti pi naṃ voharanti.* It would seem then that Selā and Āḷavikā are two names of the same therī, but in S I 134 a different set of verses is ascribed to Selā (§ 20). For different definitions of Āḷavika see CPD, s.vv. *Āḷavika, Āḷavikā*.

57. For *ahu* see the note on **43**.

Thī-a 63,4–8: *tass' attho: imasmiṃ loke sabba-samayesu pi upa-rikkhiyamānaṃ nissaraṇa-nibbānaṃ kiṃ vivekaṃ nāma n' atthi. tesaṃ tesaṃ samaṇa-brāhmaṇānaṃ chandaso paṭiññāyamānaṃ vā cha-vatthuṃ ev' etaṃ, tasmā kiṃ vivekena kāhasi eva-rūpe sampanna-paṭhama-vaye ṭhitā iminā kāya-vivekena kiṃ karissasi?*

Thī-a 63,8–9: *bhuñjāhi kāma-ratiyo, vatthu-kāma-kilesa-kāma-sannissitā khiḍḍā-ratiyo paccanubhohi.*

58. B^e and C^e read *khandhāsaṃ* for *khandhānaṃ*. So do S I 128 and Spk I 189, although Spk-pṭ I (B^e) 223 reads as P [LSC]. P does not record *khandhāsaṃ* as a v.l. here, but he does for **141** and **234** where the verse recurs. Thī-a 63,23: *khandhā ti upādānakkhandhā. āsan ti tesaṃ.* Cf. *sabb' āsaṃ sokā nassanti*, Ja VI 522, explained as *sabbe etesaṃ sokā*. It seems probable, therefore, that we should read *khandhāsaṃ*, and explain it as *khandhā āsaṃ*. For *āsaṃ* (= the masculine genitive plural of the demonstrative pronoun *ayaṃ*) see CPD (s.v. *ayaṃ*) and NPED (s.v. *idaṃ*), and cf. Geiger (2000, § 108), where only the feminine usage is listed.

Thī-a 63,23–25: *adhikuṭṭanā ti chindanādhiṭṭhānā accādhāna-ṭṭhānan ti attho. yato khandhe accādhāya sattā kāmehi chejja-bhejjaṃ pāpuṇanti.* See CPD (p. 548) s.v. *accādhāna*. Spk I 189 glosses: *adhikuṭṭanā, adhikuṭṭana-gaṇḍhikā.*

For *aratî* m.c. (with C^e) to avoid the opening ⏓ ⏑ ⏑ – see § 70(e) and the note on **10**. C^e also reads *aratī* in **234**, but *arati* in **141**.

59. The cty does not comment on *nandi*, but Spk I 191 (ad S I 130) explains: *sabbattha vihatā nandī ti sabbesu khandhāyatana-dhātu-bhava-yoni-gati-ṭhiti-nivāsesu mama taṇhā-nandī vihatā.*

For *tamo-kkhandha* and *padālita* see the note on **28**.

In pāda d there is resolution of the first syllable (§ 60).

60–62. Thī-a 64,25 foll. explains that **60** was uttered by Māra (§ 2) and **61–62** by the therī (Thī-a 65,10 foll.). The verses ascribed to Somā in the Bhikkhunī-saṃyutta (S I 129) include two which are almost identical with **60–61**.

60. The cty does not mention *ṭhāna*, but Spk I 189 (ad S I 129) glosses: *ṭhānan ti arahattaṃ.*

Thī-a 65,1–2: *sīla-kkhandhādīnam esan'-aṭṭhena isīhi laddha-nāmehi buddhādīhi mahā-paññehi pattabbaṃ.* The attempt to derive *isi* < *is-* "to seek" is interesting. It does not seem to be repeated elsewhere in Thī-a, for there is no comment on *mahesissa* in **149**, the gloss on *isīhi* in **206** is *khīṇāsavehi* (Thī-a 167,2), that on *mahesīhi* in **350** is *buddhādīhi* (Thī-a 226,28), and that on *mahesayo* in **361** is *buddhādayo* (Thī-a 228,20). Dhammapāla, however, repeats it in other cties, e.g. Pv-a 98 (ad Pv 19): *yama-niyamādīnaṃ esan'-atthena isayo*; Pv-a 163 (ad Pv 32): *jhānādīnaṃ guṇānaṃ esan'-atthena isi*; Pv-a 265 (ad Pv 64): *asekkhānaṃ sīla-kkhandhādīnaṃ esan'-atthena isiṃ*; Th-a III 18,1 (ad Th 724): *adhisīla-sikkhādīnaṃ esan'-aṭṭhena isino*; Th-a III 195,5–6 (ad Th 1234): *asekkhānaṃ sīla-kkhandādīnaṃ esita-bhāvena isi*. The suggested etymology was also known to the authors of other cties, e.g. Bv-a 51 (ad Bv 5): *esati gavesati kusale dhamme ti isi* [IBH]; Bv-a 98 (ad Bv 10): *mahante sīla-samādhi-paññā-khandhe esi gavesī ti mahesi*; Dhp-a IV 232 (ad Dhp 422): *mahantānaṃ sīla-kkhandhādīnaṃ esitattā mahesiṃ*; Nidd II 224 *mahantaṃ sīla-kkhandhaṃ ... esi gavesi pariyesī ti mahesi*. An alternative explanation, also based on the supposed connection with *is-* "to seek", is given at Nidd II 224: *mahesakkhehi vā sattehi esito ti mahesi*. Cf. *kahaṃ Buddho, kahaṃ Bhagavā, kahaṃ narāsabho ti mahesi*, Nidd I 343 (= Nidd II 225).

It is, however, very doubtful whether the commentators really thought that *isi* meant "seeker" rather than "seer", and even more doubtful whether the original authors of the verses used the word with this meaning. To anyone speaking or writing a MIA dialect in which Skt *ṛ* had disappeared, the apparent connection with the root *is-* was the only help towards providing an etymology for *isi*. It is, however, noteworthy that *mahesi* is a MIA innovation < *mahā* + *isi*. The expected historic development *mahā* + *ṛṣi* > *maharṣi* > MIA *mahassi* does not seem to have occurred, although *rayerṣayu* occurs in GDhp 196 as the development of *rājarṣayo*. Even so, the equivalent of *ṛṣi* in GDhp (236) is *iṣi*.

Thī-a 65,2–3: *durabhisambhavaṃ dunnipphādanīyaṃ*. This latter word does not occur in PED. Spk I 189 (ad Spk I 129) glosses: *durabhisambhavan ti duppasaham*.

Thī-a 65,4–9: *na taṃ dvaṅguli-paññāya itthiyā pāpuṇitum sakkā. itthiyo hi satt'-aṭṭha-vassa-kālato paṭṭhāya sabba-kālaṃ odanaṃ pacantiyo pakkuthite udake taṇḍule pakkhipitvā ettāvatā odanam pakkan ti na jānanti. pakkuthiyamāne pana taṇḍule dabbiyā uddharitvā dvīhi aṅgulīhi pīḷitvā jānanti, tasmā dvaṅguli-paññāyā ti vuttā*. Spk I 189 (ad S I 129) explains: *dvaṅgula-paññāyā ti paritta-paññāya*; *yasmā vā dvīhi aṅgulehi kappāsa-vaṭṭim gahetvā suttaṃ kantanti. tasmā itthī dvaṅgula-paññā ti vuccati*. Of these three suggestions, that referring to the size of a woman's sense seems to me to be the most likely. Cf. also *itthikā, dvaṅgula-buddhikā* Vv-a 96, and *dvyaṅgula-prajñāye strī-mātrāye* Mvu III 391, translated by Jones (III 391) as "two-inch wit".

61. For the scansion of *kay*^{i}*rā* (by metathesis from **karyā*) see §75. S I 129 normalises the pāda by omitting *no*. Dhammapāla, however, certainly read *no* since he includes *amhākaṃ* in his explanation (Thī-a 65,16).

62. See the note on **59**.

63–66. Mrs Rhy Davids points out (Sist., p. 47, n. 1) that we should rather read *Kāpilānī* (cf. Vin IV 227 290 292) in the rubric to these verses, and assume that it is a matronymic from *Kapilā*. *Kāpilānī* is in fact read by B[e] C[e] K[e] and S[e]. P's reading doubtless arose because in **65** we have to read *kapilānī* m.c. (see the note on **65**). The Buddha ranked Bhaddā as foremost among those who remembered that they had been born before: *etad aggaṃ pubbe-nivāsaṃ anussarantīnaṃ*, *yad idaṃ Bhaddā Kapilānī* (A I 25 (E[e] so, v.l. *Kāpilānī*)).

This group of verses ends in *ti* in P (see the note on **1**).

63. For *putta* see the note on **46**.

Thī-a 73,30–33: *pubbe-nivāsam yo vedi ti yo Mahā-kassapa-thero pubbe-nivāsam attano paresañ ca nivuttha-kkhandha-santānaṃ pubbe-nivāsānussati-ñāṇena pākaṭaṃ katvā avedi aññāsi paṭivijjhi*. Spk I 231 (ad S I 167) explains: *vedī ti pubbe-nivāsa-ñāṇena jātiṃ paṭivijjhi*. It is of interest that, as far as I am aware, wherever the phrase occurs (cf. **70 104 227 330 517** Th 332 379 516 562) including BHS (e.g. Udāna-v 33.47) *-nivāsaṃ* is always in the singular. The same applies to *pubba-jāti* (see the note on **100**. Occasionally reference is made to a particular number of existences being remembered, e.g. *jānāmi attano satta jātiyo* **434**. Cf. M I 278 *so aneka-vihitaṃ pubbe-nivāsaṃ anussarati, seyyathīdaṃ*: *ekam pi jātiṃ*, *dve pi jātiyo*, *tisso pi jātiyo* ... *jāti-sata-sahassam pi*.

64. For *br-* not making position in *brāhmaṇo* see § 74(a). For *tevijja* see the note on **251**.

65. There is resolution of the sixth syllable in pāda a (§ 60). For *Kapilānī* m.c. to give two short syllables, so that such resolution may take place, see § 71 and the note on **63–66**.

The cty does not explain *maccu-hāyinī* here or in **363**. For this see EV I, p. 169 (ad Th 129). For *tevijja* see the note on **251**.

66. Thī-a 74,13–15: *ty amhā*, *te mayaṃ amha*. For *te mayaṃ* see the note on **24**.

Geiger notes (2000, § 71.1(c)) that in external sandhi monosyllabic words such as *te*, *me*, *so*, *yo*, and *kho*, *-e* and *-o* become *-y* and *-v*; a following open syllable is always lengthened, and a closed one optionally. It is clear that from the historical point of view *-e* and *-o* should not become *-y* and *-v*, nor is there any reason for the lengthening of a short vowel after them.

This development, however, becomes regular if we assume that for some reason *-e* and *-o* were treated in sandhi positions, not as developments < *-ay* and *-av*, but as though they were *-ya* and *-va*. This could have occurred on the analogy of the guṇa grades of *-i-* and *-u-*, which occur in the forms *-ya-* and *-va-* as well as *-e-* < *-ay-* and *-o-* < *-av-* respectively (see Norman, 1958A, p. 47, n. 8). This view of the development would explain the lengthening of the following vowel. We should note that in this type of sandhi a following short vowel is lengthened even if it is followed by a double consonant, and hence by the "Law of two morae" should not be lengthened. See Norman, 1988 and 1993.

This type of sandhi is more widespread than might be realised from reference to the grammars and dictionaries. I have noted the following examples: *ke*: *kyāhaṃ* Cp 87, *kyāssa* Sn 961; *ko*: *kvattho* (? read *kvāttho*) Vv 46 (E^e *kīvattho*), *kvajja* Ja IV 446; *kho*: *khvāssa* M I 68 A IV 169, *khvāyaṃ* M I 97 S I 11 II 17 III 134 A III 306 404–5 408, *khvāhaṃ* D II 52 S I 2 133 214 III 155 239 Sn p. 32, *khvesa* A IV 174; *te*: *tyāmhā* Ja V 352, *tyāhaṃ* M I 13, *tyāyaṃ* S I 144, *tyāssa* M III 25 A I 154 IV 363 Dhp-a I 116, *tyāssu* D II 287 A III 44 239, *tyāhutiṃ* S I 141, *tyāpare* A III 346; *me*: *myāyaṃ* S I 136 221–22 III 108 V 353–54; *yo*: *yvāssa* M I 137, *yvāyaṃ* M I 296 S I 139 204; *so*: *svājja* Sn 998 Ja VI 500, *svāhaṃ* S II 167 Ja I 167, *svāyaṃ* Vin I 29 Ja V 232 340 (see also EV I, p. 133 (ad Th 9) and p. 277 (ad Th 837)). See also PTC, s.vv. ty^{2} and ty^{3}.

The development is not restricted to monosyllabic words, e.g. *ito*: *itveva* Th 869; *kāmesu ahaṃ* > *kāmesvāhaṃ* Ja III 242 (unmetrical); *nanu ayaṃ* > *nanvāyaṃ* A V 207; *pabbate ahaṃ* > *pabbatyāhaṃ*, Ja VI 92; *yato*: *yatvādhikaraṇaṃ* D I 70 M I 180 269. We should, then, probably read *tyāmhā* here and *tyātthu* in **157**.

For *āsava* see the note on **4**.

For *sīti-bhūtā* and *nibbutā* see the note on **15**.

67–71. The rubric to these verses states *aññatarā bhikkhunī apaññātā*, and the cty begins and ends *aññatarāya theriyā gāthā*. The introductory story relates how the therī was Mahāpajāpatī's nurse, and adds: *Vaḍḍhesī nāma, gottato pana apaññātā ahosi*, clearly trying to explain why the rubric called her *apaññātā*. It would seem that here Dhammapala had access to traditional material which was unknown to the rubric-writers (§ 31). The story tells how she was converted by Dhammadinnā, and the bhikkhunī mentioned in verse **69** is identified accordingly.

67. B^e and C^e read ⟨*n'*⟩ *accharā-saṃghāta-mattaṃ*, and although it is possible to make sense of the pada without reading ⟨*n'*⟩, as in A I 10–11 34–35 etc. [IBH], Thī-a 75,15–16 explains: *na ajjhagaman ti yojanā. na paṭilabhī ti attho*. The following verse too makes it clear that no peace of mind was obtained: *aladdhā cetaso santiṃ* **68**. For ⟨*n'*⟩ see § 66(d).

P's reading *citassa* must be a mistake for *cittassa* which the other editions read (§63(c)).

There are nine syllables in pāda c (§61), although no normalised version of the pāda seems to have arisen as in the case of Th 405 (see EV I, p. 215 (ad Th 405)).

68. Thī-a 75,17–18: *kāma-rāgen' avassutā ti kāma-guṇa-sabkhātesu vatthu-kāmesu daḷhatarābhinivesitāya bahulena chanda-rāgena tinta-cittā.* See CPD, s.v. *avassuta.*

69. For *saddhāyikā* see the note on **43**. The bhikkhunī is said to be Dhamma-dinnā (see the note on **67–71**).

70. For *pubbe-nivāsaṃ* see the note on **63**.

71. Thī-a 75,20: *ceto-paricca-ñāṇañ cā ti ceto-pariyaya-ñāṇaṃ.* Thī-a 190,11–12 (ad **227**) gives the same explanation. For *ceto-paricca* cf. *para-sattānam para-puggalānam cetasā ceto paricca pajānāti* M II 19,15–16, translated "he comprehends with the mind the mind of other beings" (MLS II 219). For *ceto-pariyaya-ñāṇa* see EV I, p. 299 (ad Th 997). For *sota-dhātu* see D I 79 (= M II 19), which is explained at Vism 407.

For *iddhî* m.c. to avoid the opening ⏓ ⏑ ⏑ — see §70(e) and the note on **10**.

72. Thī-a 76,18–20: *yobbanena c' upatthaddhā ti yobbana-madena uparūpari thaddhā* (Ce *-tthaddhā*); *yobbana-nimittena ahaṃ-kārena upatthaddha-cittā anupasanta-mānasā.*

Thī-a 76,20–23: *aññā samatimaññi 'han ti aññā itthiyo attano vaṇṇādi-guṇehi sabbathā pi atikkamitvā maññiṃ ahaṃ. aññāsam vā itthīnam vaṇṇādi-guṇe atimaññiṃ, atikkamitvā amaññiṃ avamānaṃ akāsiṃ.* Since the cty thus explains both *aññā samatimaññi* and *aññāsam atimaññi*, Mrs Rhys Davids' comments and corrections (pp. xli note 1 and 192) are not quite to the point.

73. For the cadence — ⏑ ⏑ ⏓ in pāda b see §59(d). Be Ce Ke and Se read bālă-lâpanaṃ (§§70(e) and 72(e)) which gives the usual śloka cadence. Thī-a 76,24–26: *bāla-lāpanan ti ... mamā ti bālānaṃ lāpanato vācanato bāla-lāpanaṃ.* It is, however, possible that the reading *bāla-lāpanaṃ* is merely a normalised reading, since there exists in BHS the word *ullāpana* "deceitful, deceptive" (cf. *ullapana* **357**), and the compounds *bāla-ullāpana* and *bālollāpana* are found as epithets of lusts, worldly life, especially royal pleasures, "deceiving tools" (see BHSD, s.v.). It would seem, therefore, to be a very appropriate description of a woman's body. The comparison with BHS is particularly interesting because *ullāpana* is found in BHS compounded with *uccagghana*, cf. *ujjhagghantī* **74**.

Since the cadence – – – ⏑̄ without a caesura after the fifth syllable would be irregular, we can be certain that *dv* does not make position in *-dvāramhi* (§ 74(c)).

74. Thī-a 76,32–77,1: *pilandhanam vidaṃsentī guyhaṃ pakāsikaṃ bahun ti ūru-jaghana-thana-dassanādikaṃ guyhañ c' eva pāda-jānu-sirādikam pakāsañ cā ti guyhaṃ pakāsikañ ca bahuṃ nāna-ppakāram piḷandhanaṃ ābharaṇaṃ dassentī*. PED does not list *pakāsa* nor *pakāsikā* (nor *pakāsaka* of which the latter is presumably the feminine (see PTC III 1)). Nor is it clear what *pakāsikā* would mean in the context, nor how a feminine is to be fitted into the syntax. These difficulties disappear if we assume that pāda b is quite separate from pāda a, and we take *pakāsikaṃ* as *pakāsitaṃ* "revealed". For the alternation *k/t* see the note on **43**.

Thī-a 77,1–5: *akāsiṃ vividhaṃ māyaṃ ujjhagghantī bahuṃ janan ti yobbana-mada-mattaṃ bahuṃ bāla-janaṃ vippalambhetuṃ hasantī gandha-mālā-vatthābharaṇādīhi sarīra-sabhāva-paṭicchādanena hasa-vilāsa-bhāvādīhi tehi ca vividhaṃ nāna-ppakāraṃ vañcanaṃ akāsiṃ*. Aspirated *-jjh-* cannot be correct historically, and we should probably read *-jj-*. For the use of the word in close connection with *ullāpana* see BHSD, s.v. *uccagghati* "laugh at, mock, sneer, deride".

By classical standards the opening ⏑̄ – ⏑ – should be avoided in the posterior pādas of a śloka verse (cf. EV I, p. 160 (ad Th 90)), but this opening is found elsewhere in Thī, although it is sometimes possible to correct the metre, e.g. *icchā ca patthanā* **91** (? read *cā*), *tiṭṭhanti chinna-* **106** (? read *tiṭṭhantī*), *karotha buddha-* **118** (? read *karothā*), *akaṃsu buddha-* **119** (? read *akaṃsū* or *akaṃsu⟨ṃ⟩*), *sakkāya-diṭṭhiṃ* **165** (? read *-⟨d⟩diṭṭhiṃ*), *ajj' amhi saccaṃ* **251** (? read *amhī*), *saṅghe ca tibba-* **286** (? read *cā*), *katvāna naṃ* **311** (? read *katvāna⟨ṃ⟩* or *karitvā*), *punappunaṃ* **495** (? read *punappuna*[*ṃ*]). See also the notes on **10** and **44**. We could correct the metre here by reading *pâkāsikaṃ* (§ 70(e)).

75. Thī-a 77,10–11: *dutiya-jjhāna-pādakassa agga-phalassa adhigamena avitakkassa lābhinī*. See EV I, p. 248 (ad Th 650).

76. For *yogā* see the note on **2**.

The cty does not comment on *khepetvā* here, but Thī-a 156,22–23 (ad **168**) explains: *pariyosāpetvā*. See EV I, pp. 209 foll. (ad Th 364). The definitions given by PED for *pariyosāpeti* (s.v.) do not seem entirely satisfactory. The meaning "to make fulfil" is given for Vin III 155 225 229 where the phrase *attanā/parehi vippakataṃ parehi/attanā pariyosāpeti* occurs. Miss Horner translates "finishes" (BD I 264). "Bring to an end, finish" is quoted by PED for Vism 244: *maggo dvīha-tīhena pariyosāpetabbo hoti*. Ñāṇamoli translates "finish" (1956, p. 264), and the same translation suits Sv I 241: *navahi māsehi cārikaṃ pariyosāpeti*.

77. B[e] and C[e] read *aṭṭitā* for *additā*. K[e] and S[e] read *addhitā*. See also the notes on **89 328**. PED (s.v. *addhita*) states that this reading at Pv 18 is to be corrected to *aṭṭita* (with Pv-a 94 v.l.). Thī-a 78,11–12: *kāma-rāgena aṭṭitā ti kāma-guṇesu chanda-rāgena pīḷitā*.

In pāda a there is resolution of the sixth syllable (§ 60), giving the cadence ⏑ — — ⏓ (*pathyā*).

For *avasa-vattini* see the note on **37**.

78. B[e] and C[e] read *subha-*. Thī-a 78,15–17: *subha-saññānuvattinī ti rūpādisu subhan ti pavattāya kāma-saññāya anuvattana-sīlā*.

Thī-a 78,17–19: *cittassa samaṃ, ceto-samatha-citt'-ekaggataṃ na alabhiṃ*.

For the scansion of *pariyantaṃ* see § 75.

79. Thī-a 78,20–22: *kisā paṇḍu vivaṇṇā ca evaṃ ukkaṇṭhita-bhāvena kisā dhamaṇi-santhata-gattā uppaṇḍuppaṇḍuka-jātā tato eva vivaṇṇā vigatachavi-vaṇṇā ca hutvā*. See BHSD, s.v. *utpāṇḍūtpāṇḍu(ka)*.

For *cāri* m.c. to give the cadence ⏑ — ⏑ ⏓ see § 69(c).

80. For the sandhi *-m-* in *vana-m-antaram* see the note on **48**.

PED gives this reference s.v. *ubbandhati*, implying that it is the nom. sing. masc. of the present participle, which makes no sense in the context. Thī-a 78,31–32: *imasmiṃ vanantare ubbandhaṃ bandhitvā maraṇaṃ me varaṃ seṭṭhan ti attho*. CPD suggests reading *ubbaddhaṃ* which would be a past participle used as an action noun (see the note on **261**), or taking it a a *ṇamul* absolutive (see the note on **26**). It is perhaps better to believe that we are dealing with the equivalent of Skt *udbandha* (m.) "hanging, hanging one's self" (see MW, s.v.) with a change of gender perhaps occasioned by the idea that it should agree with *varaṃ*.

81. Ce reads *daḷhaṃ pāsaṃ* for *daḷha-pāsaṃ*.

82–86. The introductory story (Thī-a 79,2 foll.) tells how Nandā was the Buddha's (half-)sister, and was called Sundarī because of her beauty. The name Sundarī-Nandā-therī is given at both Thī-a 79,1 and 85,26. The Buddha assigned to her the foremost place among those who meditate: *etad aggam jhāyīnaṃ, yad idaṃ Nandā* (A I 25). As in the case of the other Nandā (**19–20**), also renowned for her beauty, the Buddha showed her a body gradually ageing.

82–84. The cty states that these three verses were uttered by the Buddha (§ 2).

82. Cf. **19**. There is resolution of the first syllable in pāda c (§ 60).

83. For pāda d see EV I, p. 212 (ad Th 394).

84. If the cty is correct in assigning this verse to the Buddha (see the note on **82–84**), then *dakkhisaṃ* cannot be correct since a second person singular verb would be required. C[e] reads *dakkhisi* in the text, and P has *rakkhasi* (clearly a mistake for *dakkhasi*) as a v.l. Thī-a 85,15, however, has *dakkhisaṃ* in the lemma, explained as *passissaṃ*, in all editions. If this is correct, *dakkhisaṃ* must be a future with *-s-* for *-ss-* m.c. (see § 65(a) and EV I, p. 157 (ad Th 78)), and this verse must be attributed to Nandā. I am not convinced that a future makes very good sense if the verse was uttered by Nandā, and I should rather assume that *dakkhisaṃ* is an aorist, and either the cty is wrong in glossing *passissaṃ*, or this is a scribal error for *passisaṃ*. See Mrs Rhys Davids' note (Sist., p. 56, n. 2).

P also quotes a v.l. *dakkhiyaṃ*. For the alternation *y/s(s)* cf. *aphussayi/phussasi* in the note on **6**, *vihariyāma/viharissāma* **121**, *keḷāpayi/keḷāyasi* **292**, *-yo ānehi/sobhaṇehi* **331**, *-koṭṭhāsaya-/-koṭṭhāsassa* **358**, *palobhaya/palobhassa* **387**, *gaṇhiya/gaṇhissaṃ* **398**, *pakkhiyaṃ/pakkhissaṃ* **414**, *āhariya/āharissaṃ* **460**.

Here P reads *avekkhantī*, but in **96** *apekkhantī* and **222** *apekkhi*, although the other editions read *avekkh-* in all contexts, except C[e] at **222**, which has *apekkh-*. For the alternation *p/v* cf. *kapana-paññāta/parama-avaññāta* **220**, *passi taṃ/vasitā* **221**, *apalepa/avalepa* **270**, *pi cittena/vicitena* **271**, *apāpuritvā/avāpuritvā* **494**.

Thī-a 85,13–14: *sakāya bhāvanāmayāya paññāya yāthāvato ghana-vinibbhoga-karaṇena abhinibbijja* (C[e] so, B[e] *-nibbijjha*). See CPD, s.v. *abhinibbijja*.

85. For the cadence in pāda b see § 59(a). We can correct the metre by reading *vicinantiyă* (§ 72(e)).

86. C^e reads *nibbindi 'haṃ* for *nibbind' ahaṃ*. Thī-a 85,21–23: *nibbind' ahaṃ kāye vipassanā-sahitāya magga-paññāya atta-bhāve nibbindiṃ, visesato va ajjhatta-santāne virajji virāgaṃ āpajjiṃ*. For *nibbind-* followed by *virajj-* see the note on **26**.

For *atta-bhāva* see the note on **270**.

87–91. As Mrs Rhys Davids pointed out (Sist., p. 57, n. 3) the introductory story in the cty says nothing which would explain the practices outlined in **89** (§29), although it says that Nanduttarā was born in a brahman family (cf. the brahmanical rites mentioned in **87**), and then became a Jain (cf. the rites mentioned in **88**). For other references to Jains being converted to Buddhism see the notes on **107–11 236–51 400–47** and EV I, p. 158 (ad Th 81). For the rejection of brahmanical rites see the notes on **112–16 143 236–51** and **283**.

87. PED does not list *oruhati*, nor *ruhati*. Presumably this is m.c. (§71) for *orūhati = orohati*. Cf. *āruhi* in **49**d **482**b.

For *devatā* "divinity" see the note on **31–32**.

For the scansion of *sūr^iyañ* see §75.

88. Thī-a 86,24–25: *bahū-vata-samādānā ti pañca-tāpa-tappanādi-bahuvidha-vata-samādānā*. The compound can be taken as an ablative "because of the undertaking of ...", or as a nominative singular feminine. I follow the second alternative.

For *bahū-* m.c. to avoid the opening ⏓ ⏑ ⏑ ⏑ see §69(c) and the note on **44**. Thī-a 86,25: *gāthā-sukhatthaṃ bahū ti dīgha-karaṇaṃ*.

Thī-a 86,29–30: *rattiṃ bhattaṃ na bhunji 'han* (C^e so; B^e *bhuñj' ahan*) *ti rattūparatā hutvā rattiyam bhojanaṃ na bhuñjiṃ*. Perhaps we should read *ratti⟨ṃ⟩* (with Be) and translate "I did not eat food at night". For this Jain prohibition see the note on **87–91**.

89. Since there is no obvious reason for reading *vibhūsa-* we should probably read *vibhūsā-* with B^e and C^e. Thī-a 87,1: *vibhūsāyam maṇḍane ca ratā*.

Although no edition reads *va* in pāda b we should probably read this instead of *ca*. For the alternation *c/v* see the note on **12**.

B^e and C^e read *aṭṭitā* for *additā*; K^e and S^e read *addhitā*. See the note on **77**.

90. In pāda c I read *yathābhūtaṃ*, in place of *tathābhūtaṃ*, with B^e C^e Thī-a.

91. For *câ* m.c. to avoid the opening ⏓ – ⏑ – in pāda b see §79(e) and the note on **74**.

For *pāpuṇi*[*ṃ*] (with B^e and C^e) to give the cadence ⏑ – ⏑ ⏓ see §§ 59(a), 68(b) (ii).

92. Pāda b has nine syllables (§ 61). We could correct the metre by reading *agārasmānagāriyaṃ* with B^e and C^e. See EV I, p. 147 (ad Th 46) and cf. **226**d.

For *vicarî* m.c. in pāda c (with C^e) to avoid the opening ⏓ ⏑ ⏑ – see § 70(e) and the note on **10**. We could also read *vicâri*.

Thī-a 88,$_{9–10}$: *tena tena bāhusacca-dhamma-kathādinā lābhuppāda-hetunā*. The cty is presumably taking *tena tena* in the sense of "on account of this and on account of that" = "for this reason and that". Thī-a 122,$_{7–8}$ (ad **133**), however, explains: *tena tenā ti gāmena gāmam nagarena nagaraṃ vīthiyā vīthiṃ vicariṃ ahaṃ* (? = "here and there"). For such reduplicated adverbial phrases see Sen (§ 31), and cf. *kulā kulaṃ* **123**, *bhavā bhavaṃ* **199**, *kālam kālaṃ* **199**, *gāmena gāmaṃ* **305**.

93. B^e reads *na bujjhi 'haṃ* and C^e reads *na bujjh' ahaṃ* for *nirajji 'haṃ*. Thī-a 88,$_{15–16}$: *sāmaññatthaṃ samaṇa-kiccaṃ na bujjhiṃ na jāniṃ ahaṃ*. The gloss shows clearly that Dhammapāla was reading *na bujjh-*, not *nirajj-*, and we should probably accept this reading, although P's reading is acceptable if we assume that *-atthaṃ* is an ablative in *-aṃ* (see EV I, p. 271 (ad Th 788) and Brough (GDhp, p. 274)), since *nirajjati* seems to occur only with the ablative (PED s.v.). Alternatively we could read *nirajjhi*, since *niradh-* occurs rarely in Skt (MW s.v.) in the sense of "deliver up, surrender". PED (s.v. *nirajjati*) rejects Kern's suggestion (1916B, p. 176) *virajjhi*, but this seems to me to be quite possible.

S^e quotes a v.l. *asevitaṃ* for *asevi 'haṃ*. Clearly Dhammapāla read *asevi*, since Thī-a 88,$_{14}$ explains: *pariseviṃ ahaṃ*, but for the variation *'haṃ*/*-taṃ* see the note on **261**.

94. For *ahu*, possibly to avoid the cadence –, – – ⏓ with the opening ⏓ – – ⏑, see § 71, and the note on **43**.

Thī-a 88,$_{17}$: *vihārake ti vasanaka-ovarake* (see also the note on **115**). PED states that the etymology of *ovaraka* is uncertain, but on this see Bailey (1954, p. 28).

95. C^e reads *jarāya* for *purāyaṃ* in text and lemma, and explains: *ayaṃ kāyo bhijjati jarāya*. The presence of *ayaṃ* in the explanation suggests that *purāyaṃ* stands for *purā ayaṃ*, and Thī-a 88,$_{27}$ (B^e) explains: *ayaṃ kāyo bhijjati purā*. In Skt *purā* is found with the present, in the sense of the future (see MW s.v., quoting Pāṇini III.3.4).

Thī-a 88,26 quotes *maddare* as a v.l. for *maddati*, which is explained as *nimmathati*

Thī-a 88,28–29: *na me kālo pamajjituṃ, ayaṃ kālo aṭṭha-kkhaṇa-vajjito, navamo khaṇo so pamajjituṃ na yutto ti*. For *khaṇa* see the note on **5**.

96. B^e^ C^e^ K^e^ and S^e^ all read *avekkhantī* for *apekkhantī*, and we should adopt this reading. For the alternation *p*/*v* see the note on **84**.

97–101. The author's name is given as *Sakulā*, although P records *Pakulā* as a v.l The name is *Sakulā* at A I 25 where the therī is placed foremost among those who possess the deva-eye: *tad aggaṃ dibba-cakkhukānaṃ, yad idaṃ Sakulā*. For the alternation *p*/*s* see the note on **6**.

97. Thī-a 92,25: *vānato nikkhantattā nibbānaṃ*. For this etymology of *nibbāna* see EV I, p. 254 (ad Th 691).

98. There is no caesura after the fourth syllable of pāda a (see also the note on **6**), which would support the reading *putta⟨ṃ⟩ dhītarañ ca* (§ 70(e)) with B^e^ K^e^ and S^e^. C^e^ reads *puttañ ca dhītañ ca* (cf. P v.l.).

For *sāhaṃ* = *sā* + *ahaṃ* see the note on **24**.

99. B^e^ and C^e^ read *santī* for *santiṃ*. It is clear that Dhammapāla had this reading since Thī-a 92,30 glosses: *sikkhamānā va samānā*. For *sikkhamānā* see the note on **2**.

Thī-a 92,31–32: *bhāventī maggam añjasan ti majjhima-paṭipatti-bhāvato añjasaṃ upari-maggaṃ uppādentī*. For *añjasa* see EV I, p. 143 (ad Th 35).

Thī-a 92,32–93,2: *tad-ekaṭṭhe ca āsave ti rāga-dosehi sahajekaṭṭhe pahānekaṭṭhe ca tatiya-magga-majjhe āsave pahāsi samucchindi*. Cf. *tad-ekaṭṭhatāya sabbesaṃ kilesa-dhammānaṃ vūpasama-siddhito tathā hi vuccati*

> "*uddhacca-vicikicchāhi yo moho sahajo mato*
> *pahān'-ekaṭṭha-bhāvena rāgena saraṇo hi so*" *ti* (Thī-a 7,7–11)

I do not know whether *tad-ekaṭṭha* is to be derived < *tad-ekārtha* "having the same goal, meaning" or < *tad-eka-stha* "standing together with, combined with that". Ultimately there is probably very little difference in meaning between the two.

100. Edgerton noted that in BHS *pūrve-jāti* is substantially equal to *pūrve-nivāsa* (BHSD s.v. *pūrve-jāti*), and the same is probably true of Pāli (see the note on **63**). The word recurs in **120 172 179**.

101. Thī-a 93,8: *parato ti anattato*. Cf. *parato, no ca attato* **177**. Spk I 271 (ad S I 188) explains: *parato passā ti aniccato passa*.

Thī-a 93,8–9: *hetu-jāte ti paccuppanne*.

Thī-a 93,9: *palokine ti palujjana-sabhāve*. For the alternation *paloka*/*paloga* see Lüders (1954, § 131). The fact that Dhammapāla could correctly derive the word from the root *luj-* would seem to indicate that he had access to a commentarial tradition which ante-dated the translation of the canon into Pāli (§ 27) and knew of a Pkt where the devoicing of intervocalic consonants took place. For comparable examples of devoicing in Pāli see CPD (s.v. *aciravatī*) and see the note on *kata*/*gata* in **219**.

For the ending *-ine* see Geiger (2000, § 95.2). It can be regarded as the accusative plural of a new formation with the suffix *-ina*, as Geiger says, or as a Māgadhism for *-ino*. Cf. *pāṇine* Sn 220, *tādine* (= locative singular of **tādina* < *tādin*) Th 1173, and *māla-dhārine* Ja VI 543.

102–6. The Buddha placed Soṇā as foremost for capacity of effort: ... *etad aggaṃ āraddhaviriyānaṃ, yad idaṃ Soṇā* (A I 25).

102. Thī-a 96,12: *rūpa-samussaye ti rūpa-saṅkhāte samussaye sarīre ti attho*. I take the word to mean much the same as *rūpa-kāya*, i.e. "form-body, material body", as opposed to *dhamma-kāya*.

104. Thī-a 97,1–2: *tassā ti vā, tassā santike. puna vā tassā ti karaṇe sāmivacanaṃ. tāyā ti attho*. For such apparent changes of case see the note on **2**. I see no reason for assuming anything other than an ordinary possessive genitive or genitive absolute here.

For *sikkhamānāya* see the note on **2**.

For *pubbe-nivāsaṃ* see the note on **63**.

For *tassā me* see the note on **24**.

105. For *animitta* see the note on **20**.

Thī-a 97,4–9: *anantarā-vimokkhāsin ti anantarā uppanna-vimokkhā āsiṃ. rūpī rūpāni passatī ti ādayo hi aṭṭha pi vimokkhā anantarā-vimokkhā nāma na honti. magganantaraṃ anuppattā ti phala-vimokkhā pana samāpatti-kāle pavattamānā pi paṭhama-magganantaram eva samuppattito taṃ upādāya anantara-vimokkho nāma. yathā magga-samādhi anantarika-samādhī ti vuccati*. For the eight *vimokkhas* see PED (s.v. *vimokkha*).

Thī-a 97,9–10: *anupādāya nibbutā ti rūpādīsu kiñci agahetvā kilesa-parinibbānena nibbutā āsiṃ*. See also EV I, p. 341 (ad Th 1274).

106. For *tiṭṭhantî* m.c. in pāda b to avoid the opening ⏓ – ⏑ – see § 70(e) and the note on **74**. For *-kkh-* see § 63(a).

B^e^ and C^e^ read *dhi tav' atthu jare jamme* (better *jammi*) in pāda c, and it is clear that Dhammapāla had this reading too since Thī-a 97,15–16 explains: *aṅgānaṃ sithila-bhāva-karaṇādinā jare jamme lāmake hīne tava tuyhaṃ dhi atthu dhi-kāro hotu.* As P states (p. 184), this pāda seems quite out of place here.

107–11. The rubric states that Bhaddā was formerly a Jain, and the cty recognises that the practices mentioned in **107** are appropriate to that sect (see the note on **107**). The introductory story in the cty (Thī-a 99,17 foll.) tells how the events leading up to Bhaddā's conversion to Buddhism took place in Sāvatthi, which, as Mrs Rhys Davids says (Sist., pp. xviii and 67 note 3) does not agree with the reference to Gijjhakūṭa in **108** (§ 37). The Buddha ranked Bhaddā foremost of those whose intuition was swift: *etad aggaṃ khippābhiññānaṃ, yad idaṃ Bhaddā Kuṇḍala-kesā* (A I 25). As Mrs Rhys Davids says (Sist., p. 67 note 4), Dhammapāla stresses (Thī-a 297,4 foll.) Bhaddā's importance as having been ordained by the *ehi-bhikkhuni* formula.

For other references to Jains being converted to Buddhism see the note on **87–91**.

107. Thī-a 105,8–12: *lūna-kesī ti lūnā luñcitā kesā mayhan ti lūna-kesī. nigaṇṭhesu pabbajitā laṭṭhinā luñcita-kesā, taṃ sandhāya vadati. paṅka-dharī ti danta-kaṭṭhassa akhādanena dantesu mala-paṅka-dhāraṇato paṅka-dharī. eka-saṭī ti nigaṇṭha-cāritta-vasena eka-sāṭikā. pure carin ti pubbe nigaṇṭhī hutvā evaṃ vicariṃ.* See the note on **107–11**.

Thī-a 105,12–14: *avajje vajja-matinī ti nhān'-ucchādana-danta-kaṭṭha-khādanādika anavajje sāvajja-saññā. vajje cāvajja-dassinī ti māna-makkha-palāsa-vipallāsādike sāvajje anavajja-diṭṭhī.* For the construction cf. *asāre sāra-matino, sāre cāsāra-dassino* Dhp 11, and see the note on *-mānin* in **305**.

108. For the inconsistency between the mention of Sāvatthi in the introductory story in the cty and the reference to Gijjhakūṭa here see the note on **107–11**.

For *purakkhata* see the note on **199**.

109. B^e^ and C^e^ read ⟨*maṃ*⟩ *avaca*. The same reading is found at Thī-a 269,27, and since it is slightly preferable metrically it should be adopted (§ 66(d)). We then have resolution of the seventh syllable (§ 60).

For the cadence ⏑ ⏑ ⏑ ⏓ in pāda b see § 59(b). We can correct the metre by reading *pañjalî* (§ 70(e)).

C^{e} reads *jāṇuṃ* for *jānuṃ*. For the retroflex -*ṇ*- cf. *jaṇṇu*(*ka*) (PED, s.v.). For the alternation *jāṇu*/*jaṇṇu* see Turner (1970, p. 172).

110. There is resolution of the first syllable in pāda c (§ 60).

For *anaṇā … raṭṭhapiṇḍaṃ abhuñj' ahaṃ* see the note on **2**.

111. This verse closely resembles S I 213, which however reads *vata* for *ca* in pāda a. This reading is also found in B^{e}, and is guaranteed by the metre (vaitālīya). For the alternation *c*/*v* see the note on **12**. For *va*⟨*ta*⟩ m.c. see § 66(b). The reading is also found in the lemma of Thī-a (C^{e}), the text and lemma of Thī-a (B^{e}), and as a v.l. in P.

It is clear from the context that the *upāsaka* produced the merit, so a first person verb is out of place. B^{e} K^{e} and S^{e} read *pasavi*[*ṃ*], but the metre requires *pa*⟨*s*⟩*savî* (§§ 65(b), 70(c)), which occurs as a v.l. in P. P also lists *pasavī* as a v.l.

In pāda b we must read *vat' ăyaṃ* (§§ 60(c), 72(c)) m.c.

In S I 213 the verse continues as vaitālīya, although pāda c is a posterior pāda, not a prior. There I would suggest that pādas c and d be reversed, and that we read *sabba-gantha-vippamuttiyā* in the new pāda c, giving the syncopated opening – ⏑ – ⏑ (for – – ⏑ ⏑). This would presumably be a dative of purpose "he heaped up merit for the release from … ". Here, however, it does not seem possible to scan the rest of the verse as vaitālīya, although pāda c would (as in S I 213) become a posterior vaitālīya pāda if we reversed the order of *cīvaram adāsi*. B^{e} and C^{e} read *vippamuttāya* for *muttāya*, possible because of S I 213, but this does not seem to help the metre. If we read *Bhaddāyâ* m.c. (§ 70(d)), then we get, possibly by accident, the prior *pādayuga* of an āryā verse, in the posterior position, as in the gīti.

For -*ganthehi* for -*gandhehi* (with B^{e} C^{e} and K^{e}) see EV I, p. 267 (ad Th 768).

112–16. These verses do not tell us sufficient about Paṭācārā to be able to judge whether the introductory story told by Dhammapāla is appropriate or not, but since the first part of that story agrees closely with Kisā-gotamī's verses (**213–23**) it would seem likely that the story has somehow in the tradition become attached to the wrong therī. Possibly Paṭācārā was a member of the Gotama gotra, which could have led to a confusion between her clan name Gotamī and Kisā-gotamī's name.

The Buddha ranked Paṭācārā foremost of those who were versed in the rules of the Order: *etad aggaṃ vinaya-dharānaṃ, yad idaṃ Paṭācārā* (A I 25). Several therīs relate how Paṭācārā's teaching converted them to Buddhism, e.g.

the group of 30 therīs (**117–21**), Candā (**122–26**), Uttarā (**175–81**). The cty tells how others were so converted, e.g. Uttamā (**42–44**), the group of 500 (**127–32**, but see the note on these verses). The group of 30 and Uttarā actually quote Paṭācārā's teaching almost verbatim (**117 175**). As I understand it, her teaching was an attack upon the brahmanical teaching, in particular the householder stage of a brahman's life, which meant that a man who stayed at home and carried out all the usual duties of a householder was nevertheless coming nearer to his goal in life, i.e. *dhanaṃ vindati*. For comparable attacks upon various aspects of the brahmanical religion see the note on **87–91**.

112. Thī-a 113,20–21: *kasan ti kasi-kammaṃ karontā. puthutthe hi idaṃ eka-vacanaṃ. pavapan ti bījāni vapantā.* It is probable that we have here a patch-work verse, made up from floating pādas by an author with no eye for consistency, but it is possible that *kasaṃ* and *pavapaṃ* are derived from **kāsaṃ* and **pavāpaṃ*, i.e. *ṇamul* type absolutives, with *-ā-* shortened > *-a-* m.c. See the note on **26**.

For *chamā* see the note on **17**.

Thī-a 113,23–27: *ime māṇavā sattā naṅgalehi phālehi khettaṃ kasantā yathādhippāyaṃ khetta-bhūmiyaṃ pubbaṇṇāparaṇṇa-bhedāni bījāni vapantā taṃhetu taṃnimittaṃ attānaṃ putta-dārādīni posentā hutvā dhanaṃ paṭilabhanti. evaṃ imasmiṃ loke yoniso payutto paccatta-purisa-kāro nāma saphalo sa-udayo.*

B^e^ K^e^ and S^e^ read *māṇavā*. In the first edition I took *māṇavā* here and in **117** (= **175**) to refer in this context specifically to young brahmans. It is clear, however, that the cty takes the word as referring to young men in general since it states that those doing these jobs which are described as inferior work (see the note on **117**), nevertheless gain wealth, while Paṭācārā, although virtuous, does not attain nibbāna (**113**).

114. Thī-a 114,2 includes *āsittesu udakesu* in the explanation, which seems to indicate that we should read *udakesu* as one word (with B^e^ C^e^ and K^e^). S^e^ reads *sukarom'* as one word, but I do not know what this would mean.

K^e^ and S^e^ read *asso bhadro va jāniyo* in pāda f, and P mentions this as a v.l. Thī-a 114,6–9, however, explains: *tato cittaṃ samādhesiṃ, yathā assaṃ bhadraṃ ājāniyaṃ kusalo sārathi sukhena sāreti, evaṃ mayhaṃ cittaṃ sukhena eva samādhesiṃ vipassanā-samādhinā samāhitaṃ akāsiṃ.* Cf. *bhadrāśvam iva sārathiḥ*, Udāna-v 19.13–14. B^e^ and C^e^ punctuate *v' ajāniyaṃ*, and we should accept this punctuation. For *ajāniyaṃ* in place of *ājāniyaṃ* m.c. see § 71.

115. Thī-a 114,10 explains *vihāraṃ* by *ovarakam*. See the note on **94**.

116. For *padīpasseva*, showing the contraction of *-a* + *iva* > *-eva*, see EV I, p. 166 (ad Th 118), and cf. *kaṭṭhakasseva* Dhp 164; *amitteneva* Dhp 207 S I 57; *jambonadasseva* Dhp 230; *nigrodhasseva* S I 207.

For the simile of the lamp cf. D II 157 S I 159 Th 906 A I 236 IV 3. A similar idea is found in Sn 235.

For *ahu* see § 71 and the note on **43**.

117–21. There is no reason to doubt the story in the cty (Thī-a 114,$_{31}$ foll.) that these therīs were converted after hearing Paṭācārā preach. Verse **117** closely resembles Paṭācārā's own verse **112**, and the therī's name is actually mentioned in **119**.

117. Thī-a 115,$_{7–11}$: *ime sattā jīvitahetu musalāni gahetvā paresaṃ dhaññaṃ koṭṭenti, udukkhala-kammaṃ karonti. aññam pi edisaṃ nihīna-kammaṃ katvā putta-dāraṃ posentā yathārahaṃ dhanam pi saṃharanti. taṃ pana nesaṃ kammaṃ nihīnaṃ gammaṃ pothujjanikaṃ dukkhaṃ anattha-sañhitañ ca.*

B^{e} K^{e} and S^{e} read *māṇavā*. See the note on **112**.

Cf. **175**.

118. There is resolution of the sixth syllable in pāda e (§ 60).

For *karothâ* in pāda f to avoid the opening ⏓ – ⏑ – see § 70(e) and the note on **74**.

119. There is resolution of the sixth syllable in pāda 3 (§ 60).

For *akaṃsû* or *akamsu⟨ṃ⟩* in pāda f to avoid the opening ⏓ – ⏑ – see § 70(e) and the note on **74**.

120. For *pubba-jāti* see the note on **100**.

121. In pāda e B^{e} reads *vihassāma*, C^{e} *vihariyāma*, and K^{e} and S^{e} *viharissāma*. The last reading must be a gloss which has come into the text, since it is unmetrical, showing resolution of the fifth syllable in the cadence – – – ⏓, without a caesura after the fifth syllable. The reading of C^{e} must be a mistake for the same reading; for the alternation *y*/*s*(*s*) see the note on **84**. The pāda recurs in **181**, where P reads *vihissāmi*, but B^{e} and C^{e} read *vihassāmi*. The same is true of **360**, where K^{e} and S^{e} read *viharissāmi*. Geiger (2000, § 153.1) derives *vihassāmi* < **viharṣyāmi*. The forms with *-hiss-* (if genuine; there also occurs *vihessati* Th 257 *āhissaṃ* Ja VI 523) could be derived < **vihṛṣyāmi*.

Thī-a 116,14–17: *indaṃ va devā tidasā saṅgāme aparājitan ti devāsura-saṅgāme aparājitaṃ vijitāviṃ indaṃ tāvatiṃsā devā viya mahātheri, mayaṃ taṃ purakkhatvā viharissāma aññassa kattabbassa abhāvato.*

"Thirty" is therefore, as commonly, the equivalent of "thirty-three".

For *deva* "deity" see the note on **31–32**.

122–26. The introductory story in the cty (Thī-a 117,2 foll.) relates that Candā was converted after hearing Paṭacārā preach (see the note on **112–16**), and the therī's name is actually mentioned in **125**.

122. Thī-a 117,19: *duggatā ti daliddā.* Cf. Vv-a 101 (ad Vv 17): *daliddā ti duggatā.*

Thī-a 117,22–23: *vidhavā ti dhavo vuccati sāmiko, tad-abhāvā vidhavā mata-patikā ti attho.*

Thī-a 117,24–27: *bhatta-coḷassa nādhigan ti bhattassa coḷassa ca pāripūriṃ nādhigacchi, kevalaṃ pana bhikkhā-piṇḍassa pilotikā-khaṇḍassa ca vasena ghāsa-cchādana-mattam eva alatthan ti adhippāyo.* This explanation makes it clear that Dhammapāla was reading the genitive *-coḷassa*, which he tried to explain by understanding *pāripūriṃ*. It seems most unlikely that *adhigacchati* would be constructed with a genitive, and I would suggest that *-coḷassa* is to be derived < *-coḷaṃ sa*, where *sa* is the particle < Skt *sma* (see EV I, p. 189 (ad Th 225)). For *-ṃs-* > *-ss-* cf. *kissa* < *kiṃ sa* in **417** and Chopra's suggestion (p. 40, n. 2) of reading *cittaṃ sya* for *cittasya* at Mvu III 1. See also EV I, p. 156 (ad Th 77). Possibly the same explanation can be given for *kissa* = "why" (see the note on **467**), although the wide extent of use of the derivatives of *kissa* in the various Pkts is perhaps against this.

123. Thī-a 117,30: *kulā kulan ti kulato kulaṃ.* See the note on **92** and Sen (§ 54).

For *cāri* in pāda d m.c. see § 69(c).

124. Be and Ce agree with P in reading *puna*. Thī-a 117,32–33: *punā ti pacchā satta-saṃvaccharato apara-bhāge.* Nevertheless, it is possible that *puna* should be taken here in the sense of "but", as rarely in Pāli (see PED s.v. and Brough (GDhp, pp. 109–10)), and I translate accordingly.

In pāda d *pabbajiṃ* must be wrong, and probably arises from contexts such as **137**b. Be and Ce read *pabbajjaṃ*. Gombrich (1974) suggests reading *ayāciṃ* for *avocaṃ*. This is an attractive suggestion, since *yāc-* is found elsewhere with *pabbajjaṃ*, e.g. Th 624 829. It is not, however, clear why a verb commonly found with *pabbajjaṃ* should be changed to *avocaṃ*, which makes no sense in the context. The most common phrase is *anagāriyaṃ* with the verb *pabbajati.*

The vv.ll. *pabbajiṃ* and *pabbaja* suggest that there should be a form from *pabbajati* here, and it seems clear from the occurrence of *pabbājesi* in **125**b that what Candā said was "Cause me to go forth", i.e. the imperative of the causative of *pabbajati*. Cf. *pabbājehi* Th 476. We should therefore probably read *pabbājeh'* here.

There is no *ti* to mark the end of Candā's words, but this is frequently omitted in Thī, e.g. **460**.

125. For the cadence of pāda b see § 59(c). Cᵉ reads *Paṭācārā*.

126. There are nine syllables in pāda c (§ 61). Bᵉ reads *ayyāy'* and Cᵉ *'yyāya* to correct the metre.

127–32. The rubric in P reads *pañca-satā Paṭācārā*, and the cty on these verses concludes (Thī-a 120,3–6): *pañca-satā Paṭācārā ti Paṭācārāya theriyā santike laddha-ovādatāya paṭācārāya vuttaṃ avedisun ti katvā Paṭācārā ti laddha-nāmā pañca-satā bhikkhuniyo. pañca-sata-mattānaṃ therīnam gāthā-vaṇṇanā samattā.* The introductory story gives a very brief account of how the therīs each lost a child, went to Paṭācārā, and were comforted by her.

Mrs Rhy Davids (Sist., p. 77, n. 1) rejected Neumann's attempt (p. 302, n. 1) to see in *pañca-satā*, not a numeral, but an adjective "die fünfmal Feine", and yet I believe that Neumann was more likely to be correct than Mrs Rhys Davids allowed. In the first place P had already pointed out (p. 121) that although the 30 therīs who were followers of Paṭācārā (**117–21**) are included in the total number of therīs in the *uddāna* verse, the 500 are not. Secondly, since the verses uttered by Paṭācārā to the 30 have plural verbs, plural verbs would be expected in these verses uttered to the 500, but they are all singular. Thirdly, we should not have expected *Paṭācārā* to mean "follower of Paṭācārā", or alternatively, if it did mean this we should have expected it to be applied to the 30 also. I have, therefore, no hesitation in assuming that these verses were uttered by one therī only, whose name was Paṭācārā, to whom the epithet *pañca-satā* (whatever its meaning) was given to distinguish her from the other Paṭācārā (**112–16**). The lack of detail in Dhammapāla's introductory story seems to me to indicate that it has no real value, but was made up to suit the (supposed) 500 authors. I would suggest that the real story is that given for Kisā-gotamī (**213**–23), while the latter's story has been incorrectly attached to the other Paṭācāra (**112–16**). See the note on **213–23**.

As for the epithet *pañca-satā*, I would suggest that this means "mindful about the five", and would assume the "five" refers either to the five *khandhas* or the five *nīvaraṇas* (cf. D II 300–2).

127–30. Thī-a 118,14 states that these four verses were uttered by the therī to whom the 500 went.

127. B^e, C^e and Thī-a (text) have *sattaṃ* for *puttaṃ* in pāda c, and since Thī-a 119,7–9 includes *sattaṃ* in the rubric and the explanation we can assume that Dhammapāla had this reading.

Thī-a 119,7–10: *taṃ kuto c' āgataṃ sattan ti taṃ evaṃ aviññātāgata-gata-maggaṃ kuto ci gatito āgata-maggaṃ āgacchantena antarāmagge sabbena sabbaṃ akata-paricaya-samāgata-purisa-sadisaṃ sattaṃ kevalaṃ mamattaṃ uppādetvā mama putto ti kuto kena kāraṇena rodasi.*

B^e and Thī-a (in the text and lemma) read *kuto c'* making *kuto* indefinite: "come from somewhere or other". Cf. *kuto ci/pi* in **129**. Thī-a (B^e and S^e, but not C^e and M) includes the word *kuto* twice in the explanation: *kuto ci* is glossed *kuto ci gatito*, and *kuto* is glossed *kuto kena kāraṇena*. I assume that the reading of Thī-a (text) and C^e in **127** is correct, and the gloss indicates that *kuto* means "why?" and the verse is therefore a question "why do you mourn?", although it is not clear why *kuto* should be the second word in the pāda. The gloss *kuto kena kāraṇena* is the original text, and *c'* in WP and B^e and the gloss *kuto ci gatito* in the cty are later insertions, influenced by **129**.

128. Thī-a 119,12–14: *maggañ ca kho 'ssa jānāsī ti assa tava puttābhimatassa sattassa āgata-maggaṃ ca gatassa gata-maggaṃ ca atha jāneyyāsi. na naṃ samanusocesī ti evam pi naṃ na samanusoceyyāsi.* The cty seems therefore to be taking the verse as implying a condition "if you knew, you would not grieve". I do not think that it is necessary to do this. If we follow the cty and take *assa* as the third person pronoun (Geiger, 2000, § 108.1) we can translate "you know this one's way; you do not grieve".

Alternatively, the parallelism between **127** and **128** is so close that we would expect *assa* to = *yassa* and *naṃ* to = *taṃ*. If we assume that *assa* is an Eastern form for *yassa*, then we can translate "you do not grieve for him whose way you know". For *assa* = *yassa* see WD, p. 115 (ad Dhp 179), and Norman, 1994B, pp. 215–16. For relative pronouns without *y-* in the Aśokan inscriptions see Norman, 1967, pp. 165–67. The correlative to *ya* is usually *ta*, but *na* is occasionally found. Cf. *yassa ... naṃ* M 134; *naṃ ... yāyaṃ* [= *yā ayaṃ*] Th 124. Note E^e and C^e at A III 346: *yaṃ manussā namassanti sabbadhammāna pāraguṃ, devā pi taṃ* (C^e E^e *naṃ*) *namassanti.*

A third possibility is to assume that *ssa* is < Skt *sma*. For the use of this particle after *kho*, cf. *sa kho so bhikkhave kumāro* at M I 266. For the developments of *sma* in Pāli see EV I p. 189 (ad Th 225).

For *ca* = *tu* in pāda a see the note on **55**.

129–30. B^e and C^e allot the first line of P's **130** to **129**.

129. B^e C^e and Thī-a (text) read *kuto ci*; S^e agrees with P in reading *kuto pi*. Thī-a 119,20–21: *kuto cī ti nirayādito yato kuto ci gatito*.

Thī-a 119,21: *nūnā ti parisaṅkāyaṃ*.

B^e and C^e read *tat' āgacchi* for *tato 'gacchi*, and I follow this reading. Thī-a 119,19 includes *āgacchi* in the explanation, and quotes *āgato* as a v.l.

In pāda b there is resolution of the first syllable (§60) in *ananuññāto* which is read by P C^e and S^e. B^e reads *nānuññāto*.

130. B^e and C^e read *aññena gato* which makes better sense than P's reading; "he went from here by another [road]". In pāda b Thī-a 119,23–25 takes *gacchati* as a future: *tato aññena gacchatī ti tato pi bhavato aññena gamissati aññam eva upagamissati*, "he will go from his next existence by another [road]". For *gacchati* as a future see EV I, p. 136 (ad Th 14), and cf. **306 426**.

131–32. The cty explains that these verses were uttered by the 500 therīs.

131. This differs from **52** in having *yā* instead of *yaṃ* in pāda c.

132. See the note on **53**.

133. For the phrase *tena tena* see the note on **92**.

Thī-a 121,6: *vidhūta-kesatāya pakiṇṇa-kesī*. PED lists only *pakiṇṇaka*, but cf. Skt *prakīrṇa-keśa* (MW, s.v.).

Thī-a 121,4: *aṭṭā ti aṭṭitā. ayam eva vā pāṭho. aṭṭitā ti pīḷitā*. The alternative reading would seem to be unmetrical.

134. C^e reads *vasiṃ* for *vīthi-* in pāda a, cf. vv.ll. *vasi-* and *vasī-* in P (n.). We should probably adopt this reading.

135. Thī-a 121,9: *athā ti pacchā*. Thī-a 200,23 (ad **253**) and Thī-a 244,28 (ad **406**) give the same gloss. Thī-a 238,19 (ad **385**) glosses: *athā ti nipāta-mattaṃ*, as does Thī-a 245,20–21 (ad **403**).

Thī-a 121,10–11: *sugatan ti sobhaṇa-gamanattā sundaraṃ ṭhānaṃ gatattā sammā gatattā sugataṃ bhagavantaṃ*. Thī-a 234,32 (ad **368**) explains: *sugatena sammā-sambuddhena*. See also EV I, p. 181 (ad Th 185).

Thī-a 121,11–12: *Mithilaṃ gatan ti Mithilābhimukhaṃ, Mithilā-nagarābhimukhaṃ gacchantan* (M *gacchitan* (§35)) *ti attho*. B^e and C^e read *pati* for *gataṃ*, and it is possible that this is the correct reading (cf. **317 319**) and *gataṃ* has come into the text because of *gacchantaṃ* in the cty. The vv.ll. *gati* and *pathi* in P (n.) probably arise from a reading *pati*.

For *akutobhaya* cf. **333** and see EV I, p. 200 (ad Th 289).

136. Thī-a 121,13–14: *saṃ* (Bᵉ Cᵉ and Kᵉ read *sa-*) *cittaṃ paṭiladdhānā ti buddhānubhāvena ummādaṃ pahāya attano pakati-cittaṃ paṭilabhitvā*. Bᵉ and Cᵉ presumably doubt the existence of *sa-* as an adjective "one's own", but see EV I, p. 249 (ad Th 659).

138. Thī-a 121,19–21: *etadantikā ti etaṃ idāni mayā adhigataṃ arahattaṃ anto pariyosānaṃ etesan ti etadantikā sokā. na dāni tesaṃ sambhavo atthī ti attho.* Spk I 191 (ad S I 130) explains: *purisā etadantikā ti purisā pi me etadantikā va. yo me putta-maraṇassa anto, purisānam pi es' ev' anto. abhabbā aham idāni purisaṃ gavesitun ti.* The word must therefore mean "having this as an end, ending in this, ending thus".

For *sokāna* m.c. in pāda d see § 68(b)(i).

139–33. Khemā was ranked by the Buddha as foremost of those who possessed great knowledge: *etad aggaṃ mahā-paññānaṃ, yad idaṃ Khemā* (A I 25). The introductory story to Vijayā's verses (**169–74**) relates how Khemā's preaching converted her to Buddhism (§ 22). Dhammapāla discloses (Thī-a 128,6–9) that there was a difference in the tradition about Khemā as related in the aṭṭhakathā and in the Apadāna: *sā gāthā-pariyosāne saha paṭisambhidāhi arahattaṃ pāpuṇī ti aṭṭha-kathāsu āgataṃ. Apadāne pana imaṃ gāthaṃ sutvā sotāpatti-phale patiṭṭhitā rājānaṃ anujānāpetvā pabbajitvā arahattaṃ pāpuṇī ti āgataṃ* (§ 30).

139. Thī-a 131,21 foll. explains that this verse was uttered by Māra, in the form of a young man (§ 2).

There is resolution of the first syllable in pāda a (§ 60).

For the scansion of *tur^{i}yena* see § 75.

140. Bᵉ and Cᵉ read *aṭṭiyāmi* for *addiyāmi*, and PED (s.v. *aṭṭiyati*) seems to prefer this spelling. For the alternation *add-/aṭṭ-* see the note on **77**. The cty does not comment on the word, but Spk I 191 (ad S I 131) glosses: *aṭṭiyāmī ti aṭṭā pīḷitā homi. harāyāmī ti lajjāmi.* PED (s.v. *harāyati*) would seem to be wrong in giving the meaning "don't worry" to *mā hari* at Th 1173 and listing it under *harāyati*. *Mā hari* should be read as *māhari* and is for *mā āhari* "do not offend" (see PED s.v. *āharati*, where the context is also listed).

141. See the note on **58**. C[e] reads *arati* here.

142. See the note on **59**.

143. Thī-a 132,15–16 glosses *paricaraṃ* as *paricaranto* and does not explain the occurrence of a singular particple between the two plural forms *namassantā* and *ajānantā*. We are probably dealing with a patchwork verse, made up from floating pādas by an author with no eye for consistency, but it is possible that *paricaraṃ* is derived from **paricāraṃ*, i.e. a *ṇamul* type absolutive, with *-ā-* shortened > *-a-* m.c. (see the note on **26**).

For the rejection of brahmanical rites see the note on **87–91**.

Thī-a 132,11–12: *yathā-bhuccaṃ ajānantā ti pavattiyo yathā-bhūtaṃ aparijānantā*. Thī-a 137,12–13 (ad **159**) explains: *yathā-bhuccaṃ ajānantī ti pavatti-hetu-ādi yathā-bhūtaṃ anavabojhantī*.

144. For *ca* = *tu* see the note on **55**.

There is resolution of the first syllable in pāda c (§60).

145. Thī-a 133,17: *candanokkhitā ti candanānulittā*. Although PED lists this reference under *okkhita*, I am not persuaded that there is necessarily any real difference between *ukkhita* and *okkhita*. For the alternation *u*/*o* before a double consonant cf. *aggi-hutta* (Th 341) and see EV I, p. 207 (ad Th 341).

For *purakkhata* see the note on **199**.

146. Thī-a 133,21–22: *abhihārayin ti upanesi*. CPD accepts this, but in the context it is more likely that we should see here the meaning "betake oneself" (with PED s.v.), cf. Sn 414 (Pj II 383 glosses: *āruhi*), 708 (Pj II 495: *gaccheyya*).

147. For *râmitvā* m.c. to avoid the opening ⏓ ⏑ ⏑ – see § 70(e) and the note on **10**.

B[e] and C[e] read *daṭṭhuṃ* for *dakkhiṃ* in pāda c.

Thī-a 133,23–24: *Sākete Añjanaṃ vanan ti Sāketa-samīpe Añjana-vane vihāraṃ pāvisi*. It seems, therefore, that we are to take *Añjaraṃ vanaṃ* as a split compound, or as an example of the lengthening of a syllable by nasalisation m.c. to give the cadence ⏑ – ⏑ ⏓. See EV I, p. 146 (ad Th 42) and the notes on *Kāsi-janapado suṅko* **25**, *kim 'me katā* **147**, *amataṃ padaṃ* **149 309**, *udakābhisecanam sāṭaṃ* **245**, *dhuvaṃ ṭhiti* **343**, *kuṇapaṃ bhastaṃ* **466**.

149. For *mahesissa* see the note on *isi* in **60**.

Thī-a 133,26: *phu(s)sayin ti phusi*. C^e reads *phussayiṃ*, and the vv.ll. in P (n.) show that there is support for a reading with *-ss-*. See the note on **6**.

The cty makes no comment on *amataṃ padaṃ* here or in **309**. Elsewhere, however, *amata* is a synonym for *nibbāna* (see PED and CPD s.v.), and I assume that it is a noun here, rather than an adjective. We have, then, a tatpuruṣa compound "state of the death-free" which has been split m.c. For such split compounds see the note on **147**. As CPD notes, *amataṃ padaṃ* at Th 1110 is not m.c.

For *amata* "death-free" see Norman, 1994A, p. 219. Cf. **221 222 309 503 504 513**. Cf. *amara* **512** and *amaraṇa* **512**. Cf. *ajara* "free from old age" **511–12**, and see Norman, 1994A, p. 220.

C^e reads *appaṭivijjh'*. See also P v.l. For the meaning of *paṭivijjhati* see the note on **182**.

151–56. This group of verses is included in MIAR (pp. 27, 151–52).

151. For *mahaddhane* m.c. in pāda b to give the cadence ⏑ – ⏑ ⏓ see § 64. Thī-a 134,22–24: *mahaddhane ti nidhāna-gatass' eva. cattārīsa-koṭi-parimāṇassa mahato dhanassa atthi-bhāvena mahaddhane ahaṃ jātā ti yojanā.*

Thī-a 134,24–25: *vaṇṇa-rūpena sampannā ti vaṇṇa-sampannā c' eva rūpa-sampannā ca*, i.e. *vaṇṇa-rūpa* is a *dvandva* compound.

Thī-a 134,26–27: *atrajā ti orasā*. PED (s.v.) states "this form occurs only in Jātaka and similar sources, i.e. popular lore".

152. For *Anopamā* = *Anūpamā* with *o/ū* m.c. (as MIAR (p. 151) points out) to give the cadence ⏑ – ⏑ ⏓ both here and in **153** see § 69(c), and cf. the note on **374**.

B^e and C^e read *pesayī* for *pesayi*, giving the cadence ⏑ – – ⏓ (*pathyā*).

153. For *Anopamā* m.c. see § 69(c) and the note on **152**.

154. For *sāham* = *sā aham* see the note on **24**.

155. C^e reads *phusayiṃ* here despite reading *phussayiṃ* in **149**. The vv.ll. in P, however, support the reading *phassayiṃ*. See the note on **6**.

The "third fruit" is *anāgāmi-phala*. See PED (s.v. *phala*).

156. C^e reads *ajja* for *sājja* in pāda c.

For *kesāni* = *kese* see the note on **13**.

157–62. Mahāpajāpatī Gotamī was sister of, and co-wife with, Māyā, the Buddha's mother. She was ranked by the Buddha as foremost of those who were of long standing: *etad aggaṃ ratta-ññūnaṃ, yad idaṃ Mahāpajāpatī Gotamī* (A I 25). For the meaning of *ratta-ññu* see Norman, 1987, pp. 165–67.

157. For the development *te atthu* > *tyātthu* see the note on **66**.

158. I take *hetu-taṇhā* to mean "craving as the cause", although the equivalent occurs in Skt (MW, s.v. *tṛṣṇā*) with the meaning "external world of the senses", i.e. that which has craving as the cause.

B^e reads *bhāvito* for *ariy'*-, and K^e and S^e read *bhāvit'*-, which P quotes as a v.l. This can be translated "the eightfold way has been developed", which seems preferable to following P's text, and taking *maggo* and *nirodho* in apposition.

159. For *saṃsarî* m.c. (with C^e) to avoid the opening ⏒ ⏑ ⏑ – see § 70(e) and the note on **10**. B^e reads *saṃsariṃ 'haṃ*, which gives the same scansion, but the prodelision of *ahaṃ* > *'haṃ* after an anusvāra seems doubtful.

Thī-a 137,24–25: *anibbisan ti saṃsārasamudde patiṭṭhaṃ avindantī alabhantī.* No explanation is given for the apparent change of gender. Since a form in *-aṃ* cannot be a feminine participle, it is probable that it was taken over without change by a tradition which did not fully understand the form. For such a taking over, see the note on **26** (ad *nibbindaṃ*).

Pāda b has a partial parallel in *sandhāvissaṃ anibbisaṃ* Th 78. Th-a I 182,19 explains: *anibbisan ti, tassa nivattaka-ñāṇaṃ avindanto, alabhanto.* Dhp-a III 128 (ad Dhp 153) gives a similar explanation. See WD, p. 100 (ad Dhp 153).

The BHS equivalent of Th 78 (Udāna-v 31.6) has *saṃdhāvitvā punaḥ punaḥ*. If *punaḥ punaḥ* is a genuine equivalent to *anibbisaṃ*, it implies a meaning such as "not ceasing, not putting an end to". I would suggest that *-bb-* is m.c. (for the unhistoric doubling of consonants m.c. see § 64(a)) and *anibbisaṃ* stands for *a-nivisaṃ* < *niviś-*, in which case we might compare Skt *aniviśamāna* "not retiring to rest, restless" (see MW, s.v.). We could therefore translate "not resting, without respite". Thomas translates "unceasingly", taking the word as an adverb (1949, p. 75.1), possibly because of the Udāna-v reading.

It is possible that, since *nibbisa* occurs in Pāli in the sense of *nirveśa*, *anibbisaṃ* could be the equivalent of *anirveśam*, i.e. an adverbial accusative or possibly a *ṇamul* absolutive (with *-besaṃ* > *-bisaṃ* m.c.), with the meaning "not having expiated [my] sins". For this suggestion see EV I, p. 244 (ad Th 606). For *ṇamul* absolutives see the note on **26**.

In my translation I follow the interpretation "without respite", but it is possible that more than one meaning is intended. For such puns see the note on **5**.

161. For the scansion of *-vir^{i}ye* see § 75. In pāda a there is resolution of the sixth syllable (§ 60). For *buddhāna* m.c. in pāda d see § 68(b)(i).

Thī-a 137,24–25: *pahitatte ti nibbānaṃ pesita-citte*. Dhammapāla seems here to be influenced by Buddhaghosa's confusion between *pahita* < *padahati* and *pahita* < *pahiṇati* (see PED, s.v. *pahita*^{I}). The same confusion is shown in the explanation of *padhāna-pahitatto* at Thī-a 168,26–27 (ad **212**): *catubbudha-samma-ppadhāna-yogena nibbānaṃ pati pesitatto*. For a comparable confusion on the part of the cty, cf. the suggestion that *isi* is to be derived from the root *is-* "to seek" in the note on **60**.

B^{e} and C^{e} reads *passe* for *passa*. This is presumably the first person middle "I see", and the reading *passe* possibly developed because of the difficulty of fitting *passāmi* into the metre. The cty in fact seems to be reading an indicative rather than an imperative: *sāvake ti ime maggaṭṭhā ime phalaṭṭhā ti yāthāvato passati*.

Thī-a 137,28–32: *esā buddhāna vandanā ti sā satthu dhamma-sarīra-bhūtassa ariya-sāvakānaṃ ariya-bhāva-bhūtassa ca lokuttara-dhammassa attha-paccakkha-kiriyā esā sammā-sambuddhānaṃ sāvaka-buddhānaṃ ca vandanā yathāva-toraṇa-ninnatā*. We find Skt and Pkt *toraṇa* in the sense of "festoon", and we may well have the same sense here.

162. For *vyādhî-* m.c. to avoid the opening ⏓ ⏑ ⏑ ⏑ see § 70(e) and the note on **44**.

PED derives *tunna* < *tud-* (s.v. *tunna*^{I}, where this reference is given wrongly). It derives *abhitunna*, however, < *abhi-tūrv-*, following Kern (1916A, p. 4). For this latter suggestion see BHSD (s.vv. *abhitunna* and *abhitūrṇa*), where it is pointed out that in Skt neither *tud-* nor *turv-* is found compounded with *abhi-*. In Pāli *abhituṇṇa* is found as well as *abhitunna*, and the correctness of the form with retroflex *-ṇṇ-* seems to be guaranteed by Pkt *abhiduṇa* in GDhp 261, since the Gāndhārī dialect normally writes *-n-* for *-nn-* (Brough, GDhp § 45). The Pāli equivalent of GDhp 261 (Dhp 288) has *abhibhūta*, which is a sufficiently close synonym of *abhitunna* to make it certain that *abhiduṇa* is the equivalent of *abhitunna*.

I would suggest that Pāli *abhituṇṇa* and BHS *abhitūrṇa* are to be derived < *abhi-tṛ-* "to come near, to overtake", with the past participle **-tūrṇa* instead of *-tīrṇa*. For this alternation cf. Skt *jīrṇa* and *jūrṇa* < *jṛ-*, and Pkt *tūha* < **tūrtha* (see Burrow, 1955, p. 45), and Pkt *aṇṇa-utthiya* < **anya-tūrthika*. The meaning is "overtaken" = "overcome", and there is no connection between Pāli *tunna* and *abhitunna*, except that the change *abhituṇṇa* > *-tunna* is probably due to an imagined connection between the two.

163–68. The introductory story in the cty relates how these verses were first uttered by the Buddha (§ 2), and then repeated by the therī, whereupon they became her verses (Thī-a 156,25–27): *evaṃ satthārā imāsu gāthāsu bhāsitāsu gāthā-pariyosāne therī saha paṭisambhidāhi arahattaṃ patvā udāna-vasena bhagavatā bhāsita-niyāmen' eva imā gāthā abhāsi. ten' etā theriyā gāthā nāma jātā* (§ 4).

163. Thī-a 155,29–30: *yad-atthaṃ, yassa kilesa-parinibbānassa khandha-parinibbān-assa ca atthāya.* Cf. *yad-attho* Th 60, *yad-atthiya* Th 1274.

Thī-a 155,29–156,1: *tam eva anubrūhehī ti mama sāsane pabbajjā brahma-cariya-vāso icchito tam eva vaḍḍheyyāsi sampādeyyāsi.* We must presumably understand a genitive or dative of the second person pronoun, "there was ordination [for you] having left ... ". For *br-* not making position in *anubrūh-* see § 74(a) and EV I, p. 139 (ad Th 23), and cf. **206**.

Bᵉ and Cᵉ read *vasuṃ piyaṃ* for *samussayaṃ*, and P lists *samuppiyaṃ*, *samusiyaṃ*, and *samappiyaṃ* as vv.ll. Thī-a 155,30–31: *hitvā puttaṃ vasuṃ piyan ti piyāyitabbaṃ ñāti-parivaṭṭaṃ bhoga-kkhandhañ ca hitvā.* In the first edition I adopted the reading *samappiyaṃ* and translated it as "those who are equally dear". In view of the cty's gloss *bhoga-kkhandhañ* I now follow WP in reading *puttaṃ vasuṃ piyaṃ*, in the belief that if the reading had been *pasuṃ* (perhaps taken over from **18**) we might have expected to see a gloss on *pasuṃ* in the cty. Cf. *putte c' eva go-mahiṃsādike pasū ca* in the note on **18**.

165. These are the five *oraṃbhāgiya saṃyojanas* (see the note on **166**). The BHS equivalent is *avara-bhāgīya* (see BHSD, s.v.). For the absense of *-ṃ-* cf. BHS *ūrdhva-bhāgīya* (see the note on **167**).

The cty makes no mention of *sakkāya* here, but Thī-a 165,13 (ad **199**) explains: *sakkāyasmin ti khandha-pañcake*, and Thī-a 224,28 (ad **339**) explains *upādāna-kkhanda-pañcake.* Cf. M I 299–300. See also BHSD, s.v. *satkāya*. For *parāmāsa* see EV I, p. 207 (ad Th 342), PED (s.v. *sīla*), and BHSD (s.v. *śīla-vrata-parāmāsa*).

Since the cadence –,– – ⏓ does not usually have the opening ⏓ – – – (PM § 242), we can assume that *by-* does not make position in *byāpāda* (§ 74(d)). We thus have the cadence ⏑ – – ⏓ (*pathyā*).

For *ku-⟨d⟩diṭṭhiṃ* m.c. in pāda b to avoid the opening ⏓ – ⏑ – see § 64(b) and the note on **74**.

166. Thī-a 156,8–11: *orambhāgamanīyānī ti rūpārūpa-dhātuto heṭṭhā-bhāge kāma-dhātuyaṃ manussa-jīvassa hitāni upakārāni, tattha paṭisandhiyā paccaya-bhāvato. ma-kāro pada-sandhi-karo.* This suggests that we are to take the word as *orambhāga-m-anīyāni*, but I am unable to suggest what *anīyāni* might be. The cty quotes the v.l. (not gloss, as PED states) *oramāgamanīyāni*, with the same meaning, and it is possible that the cty's statement refers to this form, i.e. *ora-m-āgamanīyāni*.

For sandhi *-m-* see the note on **48**.

CPD (Vol. I, p. 548, s.v. *accupati*) suggests that the original reading was *orambhāga-gamanīyāni*, from which *-ga-* was omitted by (metrical) haplography (see the note on **54**). If this is correct, then there would have been resolution of the fourth syllable.

Thī-a 156,11–14: *na-y-idam puna-r-ehisī ti orambhāgiyānaṃ samyojanānaṃ pahānena idaṃ kāma-ṭṭhānaṃ kāma-bhavaṃ paṭisandhi-vase na puna-r-āgamissasi. ra-kāro pada-sandhi-karo.*

For the sandhi consonant *-y-* before *i-* in *na-y-idaṃ* cf. *na-y-ito* Th 359, and see Geiger, 2000, § 72.2.

For sandhi *-r-* see the note on **3**. For *kāma-bhava* "state of desire" see BHSD, s.v. *avara-bhāgīya*.

167. Thī-a 156,16–20: *rāgan ti rūpa-rāgañ ca arūpa-rāgañ ca. saṃyojanāni chetvānā ti etāni rūpa-rāgādīni pañc'-uddhambhāgiyāni saṃyojanāni arahatta-magena samucchinditvā.* By thus understanding *rāga* as *rūpa-* and *arūpa-rāga* the cty is able to see all five *uddhambhāgiya saṃyojanas* here (see PED, s.v. *saṃyojana*).

The BHS equivalent of *uddhambhāgiya* is *ūrdhva-bhāgīya* (see BHSD, s.v.). For the absence of *-m-* cf. BHS *avara-bhāgīya* (see the note on **165**).

168. The cty makes no comment on *pariññāya*, but cf. AMg *pariṇṇāya* "abandoning after careful consideration", e.g.

aimāṇaṃ ca māyaṃ ca taṃ pariṇṇāya paṃḍie
gāravāṇi ya savvāṇi nivvāṇaṃ saṃdhae muṇi (Sūyag, I.9.36).

The cty on Sūyag explains: *parijñāya, pratyākhyāna-parijñayā pariharet.* Cf. Jacobi's observation (SBE XXII, p. 1, n. 2) "knowledge (*parijñā*) is twofold: comprehension and renunciation".

For *nicchāta* see the note on **53**. For *khepetvā* see the note on **76**.

169. For *avasavattini* see the note on **37**.

170. The bhikkhunī is said to be Khemā (**139–44**).

The cty makes no comment on *sakkaccaṃ*. For absolutives in *-ṃ* see Norman (1958B, p. 313), EV I, p. 336 (ad Th 1242), and cf. *peccaṃ* (PED, s.v. *pecca*) and *upapajjaṃ* (NPED, s.v. *upapajjati*).

171. Thī-a 157,24–25: *bojjhaṅg'-aṭṭhaṅgikaṃ maggan ti satta-bojjhaṅgañ ca aṭṭhaṅgikañ ca ariya-maggaṃ*. The cty seems to be taking *bojjhaṅg'-aṭṭhaṅgikaṃ* as a *dvandra* adjective "possessing the [seven] *bojjhaṅgas* and being eightfold". I should rather assume that *bojjhaṅg'* is for *bojjhaṅgā*, i.e. accusative plural neuter. For the gender of *bojjhaṅga* see BHSD, s.v. *bodhyaṅga*. In **21** *bojjhaṅga* is masculine. If this suggestion is correct we should rather punctuate *bojjhaṅg' aṭṭhaṅgikaṃ*.

For the scansion of *ariya* see § 75.

172. For *pubba-jāti* see the note on **100**.

174. For *pītī-* or *-su⟨k⟩khena* to avoid the opening ⏓ ⏑ ⏑ – see §§ 64(b), 70(e) and the note on **10**.

In pāda c there are nine syllables (§ 61) even when we scan *sattamiyā* (§ 75). Cf. **44**e.

For *pāde pasāremi* see the note on **44**. For *tamo-kkhandha* see the note on **28**.

175. See the notes on **112** and **117**.

176. For *ghaṭetha* (read by Bᵉ Cᵉ Kᵉ and Sᵉ) to avoid the opening ⏓ ⏑ ⏑ – see the note on **10**. It would perhaps be better to read *ghaṭâtha* (see § 70(e) and the note on **461**).

177. For the phrase *parato no ca attato* see the note on **101**.

Thī-a 158,31–32: *cittaṃ upaṭṭhapetvānā ti bhāvanā-cittaṃ kamma-ṭṭhāne upaṭṭhapetvā*. Thī-a 160,29–30 (ad **182**) explains: *satiṃ upaṭṭhapetvānā ti sati-paṭṭhānaṃ bhāvanā-vasena kāyādīsu asubha-dukkhāniccānanta-vasena satiṃ suṭṭhu upaṭṭhitaṃ katvā*. See BHSD, s.v. *upasthāpayati*.

178. For the reference to Paṭācārā see the note on **112–16**.

179. For *pubba-jāti* see the note on **100**.

181. Bᵉ and Cᵉ read *vihassāmi* for *vihissāmi* (see the note on **121**). Kᵉ and Sᵉ read *viharāmi*.

For *deva* "deity" see the note on **31–32**. For *tidasā* see the note on **121**.

182–203. The cty makes no reference to the fact that the verses by Cālā, Upacālā, and Sīsūpacālā are assigned to different authors in the Bhikkhunī-saṃyutta (= S I 132–34) (§ 19).

182. Thī-a 160,32–33: *padaṃ santan ti santaṃ padaṃ nibbānaṃ sacchi-kiriyāya paṭivedhena paṭivijjhi sacchākāsi.*

For *satiṃ upaṭṭhapetvāna* see the note on **177**.

183. Thī-a 161,4–5: *imasmiṃ loke bahū samayā tesañ ca desetāro bahū eva titthakarā, tesu kaṃ nu kho tvaṃ uddissa muṇḍā si muṇḍita-kesā asi.* In pāda a Bᵉ and Thī-a (text) read *kaṃ* and Cᵉ reads *kan* for *kin*. I follow the reading *kaṃ*. For *uddissa* "pointing, looking to [as a teacher]", see NPED s.v. *uddisati.*

Thī-a 161,6–8: *na ca rocesi pāsaṇḍe ti tāpasa-paribbājakādīnaṃ ādāya-bhūte pāsaṇḍe te te samayantare n' eva rocesi.* Thī-a 161,13–14 (ad **184**) explains: *te hi sattānaṃ taṇhāpāyaṃ diṭṭhi-pāsann ca ḍenti oḍḍentī ti pāsaṇḍā ti vuccanti.* Spk I 193 (ad S I 133) gives a similar explanation: *pāsaṃ oḍḍentī ti pāsaṇḍā. sattānaṃ cittesu diṭṭhi-pāsaṃ khipantī ti attho. sāsanaṃ pana mocesi, tasmā pāsaṇḍo ti na vuccati. ito bahiddhā yeva pāsaṇḍā honti.* For an etymology of *pāsaṇḍa* see Bailey (1952, pp. 427–28).

The comparable verse at S I 133 has *pāsaṇḍaṃ* for *pāsaṇḍe*. Since *pāsaṇḍā* occurs in the following verse, it is very likely that this is an example of *-aṃ* as an accusative plural (see EV I, p. 159 (ad Th 83)). Another example of this ending, with *-a* for *-aṃ* m.c., can be seen in *sabba-saṃyoga* (Eᵉ *-saṃyoge*) *visajja* Sn 522 = Spk I 77, on which Spk-pṭ (Bᵉ) I 113 comments: *sabba-saṃyogā ti vibhatti-lopena niddeso*; *sabba-saṃyoge ti attho* [LSC].

For *ca* = *tu* see the note on **55**.

Thī-a 161,8–10: *kim idaṃ carasi momuhā ti kiṃ nām' idaṃ, yaṃ pāsaṇḍa-vihitaṃ ujuṃ nibbāna-maggaṃ pahāya ajja kālikaṃ kumaggaṃ paṭipajjantī ativiya mūḷhā carasi paribbhamasī ti.* The cty is interpreting *kiṃ idaṃ* as "why is this, that (*yaṃ*) … ". It would be possible to see here the adverbial use of *idaṃ*. For this see NPED s.v. *idaṃ* 4, and MW s.v. ²*idam*. I prefer to take *idaṃ* as the object of *carasi*: "why do you practice this?"

For *momuhā* m.c to give the cadence ⏑ – ⏑ ⏓ see § 71.

There is resolution of the first syllable in pāda d (§ 60).

186. Bᵉ, Cᵉ and Thī-a read *ariyaṃ c' aṭṭhaṅgikaṃ* in pāda c here and in **193 310 321**. Since this reading produces an apparently nine-syllable line, it is more likely to be original than the normalised eight-syllable pāda in P. Udāna-v 27.34 reads *āryam cāṣṭāṅgikaṃ*.

For the scansion of *ariyaṃ* see **6 75**.

188. See the note on **59**.

189–95. These verses probably follow **182–88** because Upacālā was Cālā's sister (§ 13(b)). For the different attribution of these verses in the Bhikkhunī-saṃyutta (= S I 132–34) see the note on **182–203**.

189. For *satīmatī* m.c. to avoid the opening ⏓ ⏑ ⏑ – see § 69(c) and the note on **10**. For *paṭivijjhiṃ* see the note on **182**.

Thī-a 162,7–8: *akāpurisa-sevitan ti alāmaka-purisehi uttama-purisehi ariyehi buddhādīhi sevitaṃ.*

Thī-a 162,4–5: *cakkhumatī ti paññā-cakkhunā samannāgatā.* Cf. Bv-a 33: *ñāṇa-cakkhu pañca-vidhaṃ, buddha-, dhamma-, samanta-, dibba-, paññā-cakkhu* [IBH].

190. The cty states that this verse was uttered by Māra (§ 2).

For *ahu* see the note on **43**.

191. For *-pādāna* m.c. to give the cadence ⏑ – ⏑ ⏓ see § 68(b)(i).

For *-kl-* making position in *pariklesa* to give the cadence ⏑ – – ⏓ (*pathyā*) see § 74(f). Cf. **345**.

193. See the note on **186**.

195. See the note on **59**.

196–203. For the different attribution of these verses in the Bhikkhunī-saṃyutta (= S I 132–34) see the note on **182–203**.

196. For *asecanaka* and *ojava* see the note on **55**.

197. Thī-a 164,15–16 states that this verse was uttered by Māra (§ 2).

Thī-a 164,17–24: *tattha saha-puñña-kārino tettiṃsa janā yattha uppannā taṃ ṭhānaṃ Tāvatiṃsan ti. tattha nibbattā sabbe pi deva-puttā Tāvatiṃsā. keci pana Tāvatiṃsā ti tesaṃ devānam nāmam evā ti vadanti. dvīhi devalokehi visiṭṭhaṃ dibbaṃ sukhaṃ yātā upayātā sampannā ti Yāmā, dibbāya sampattiyā tuṭṭhā pahaṭṭhā ti Tusitā. pakati-paṭiyattārammaṇato atirekena nimmita-kāmatā-kāle yathā-rucite bhoge nimminitvā ramantī ti vattantī ti Vasavattino*. It seems clear that the cty is taking *Vasavattino* as the equivalent of *Para-nimmita-vasavattino*, although DPPN does not list *Vasavattino* in this sense. Edgerton (BHSD, s.v. *Vaśavartin*) states that there is "a deceptive appearance of the use of this as a name for the whole class of *paranirmitavaśavartin* gods, see s.v. *Suyāma*".

There seems, however, no doubt from this occurrence, which recurs in S I 133, that *Vasavattin* is so used in Pāli.

199. Thī-a 165,12–13: *kālaṃ kālan ti taṃ taṃ kālaṃ. bhavā bhavan ti bhavato bhavaṃ*. For such reduplicated adverbial phrases see the note on **92**, and Sen (§ 11).

For *sakkāya* see the note on **165**.

Thī-a 165,13–14: *purakkhatā ti purakkhāra-kārino*. P is wrong (p. 194) in rejecting this reading simply because the cty misunderstands it (§ 37). For *purakkhata* see EV I, p. 144 (ad Th 37). It occurs in the normal sense of "honoured, attended" in **108 145**.

Thī-a 165,19: *avītivattā sakkāyaṃ nissaraṇābhimukhā ahutvā sakkāya-tīram eva anuparidhāvantā*.

Thī-a 165,19–20: *jāti-maraṇa-sārino, rāgādīhi anugatattā punappunaṃ jāti-maraṇam eva anusaranti*.

For *jātî-* m.c. to avoid the opening ⏓ ⏑ ⏑ ⏑ see § 70(e) and the note on **44**.

200. Pāda b has nine syllables (§ 61). B^e^ and C^e^ read *pa[ri]dīpito* (§ 67(d)). P has *padisito* and *padīsito* as vv.ll., which support the same reading (for the alternation *p/s* see the note on **6**). The verse recurs at S I 133 with the reading *padhūpito*. Spk I 193 glosses: *padhūpito ti santāpito*. This gloss confirms that Buddhaghosa was reading *dhūp-*, or *dhūm-* (see EV I, p. 222 (ad Th 448)), but Dhammapāla's gloss (Thī-a 165,23) *tehi yeva punappunaṃ ādīpatāya paridīpito* seems to imply that he was reading a form with *dīp-*.

201. B^e^ reads *akampiyaṃ* for *akampitaṃ*, and P states (p. 195) that this reading is perhaps preferable to that given in his text. It is supported by the explanation at Thī-a 165,26–28: *kenaci pi kampetuṃ cāletuṃ asakkuṇeyyatāya akampiyaṃ. guṇato ettako ti tuletuṃ asakkuṇeyyatāya attanā sadisassa abhāvato ca atuliyaṃ*. S I 133 reads *akampitaṃ acalitaṃ*, but Spk does not comment. For the alternation *t/y* see the note on **43**.

203. See the note on **59**.

204–12. These verses are ascribed to Vaḍḍha's mother, although it is clear, and the cty recognises, that some of the verses (**207 210–12**) are by Vaḍḍha himself. This raises the question why these verses are not included among Vaḍḍha's verses (Th 335–39). For Winternitz's suggestion that originally **204–12** and Th 335–39 were a whole which has been arbitrarily divided, see § 16 and EV I,

p. 206 (ad Th 335–39). Although the cty does not say so, it is probable that **209** is by Vaḍḍha too (see the note on **209**).

204. Thī-a 166,22–23: *sū ti nipāta-mattaṃ*. In view of this statement we are probably correct in seeing *su* in the sense of Skt *sma* here, cf. Brough (GDh, p. 264) and EV I, p. 189 (ad Th 225). See also the notes on **255 481**.

For *ahu* in pāda b, where it is third person, and in pāda c, where it is in second person, see § 71 and the note on **43**.

Thī-a 166,22–24: *vanatho*, *kilesa-vanatho*. See EV I, p. 207 (ad Th 338).

In pāda b there is resolution of the first syllable (§ 60).

205. Thī-a 166,30–31: *moneyya-dhamma-pasannāgamena munayo*. For *muni* see the note on **53** and EV I, p. 154 (ad Th 68).

Thī-a 166,31: *ejā-saṅkhātāya taṇhāya abhāvena anejā*. The same explanation is given by Spk I 224 (ad S I 159). Cf. Ps III 440: *anejo nittaṇho*, whereas Mp III 19 glosses: *anejā niccalā nāma* [IBH]. For *aneja* as a noun see the note on **362**.

206. For *isi* see the note on **60**.

For *-br-* not making position in *anubrūhaya* see § 74(a) and the note on **163**.

207. The cty states that this verse was uttered by Vaḍḍha (§ 16).

Thī-a 167,13–15: *maññāmi nūna māmike vanatho te na vihatī ti nūna māmike mayhaṃ amma geha-sita-pema-matto pi vanatho tuyhaṃ mayi na vijatī ti maññāmi. na māmikā ti attho*.

208. For *aṇû* m.c. (with Bᵉ and Cᵉ) to avoid the opening ⏓ ⏑ ⏑ ⏑ see § 70(e) and the note on **44**.

209. Thī-a 167,32–33: *appamattassa jhāyato ti appamattāya jhāyantiyā. liṅga-vipallāsena h' etaṃ vuttaṃ*. For other explanations by the supposition of a change of gender see the note on **13**. The need for such a change here can be avoided by recognising that the verse was uttered by Vaḍḍha, not his mother (§ 2).

210–12. The cty recognises that these verses were uttered by Vaḍḍha (§ 16).

210. Thī-a 168,17–18: *patodan ti ovāda-patodaṃ. samavassarī ti sampavattesi. vatā ti yojanā*. For *-ss-* in *samavassari* m.c. see § 64(a). Cf. *avaṃsari*, Sn 685.

Cᵉ reads -*saṃhitā*; Bᵉ Kᵉ and Sᵉ read -*sañhitā*, cf. *upasañhita* in Th 968. The western convention is to spell the past participle passive of *saṃdhā-* as *saṃhita*, and we should adopt this spelling here. Cf. Dhp 101.

There is resolution of the first syllable in pāda c (§ 60).

For *yathāpi* see the note on **437**.

211. For *yoga-kkhema* see the note on **6**. PED does not list *anusiṭṭhi*.

212. Thī-a 168,26–27: *padhāna-pahitatto ti catubbidha-samma-ppadhāna-yogena nibbānaṃ pati pesita-citto*. For *pati* see the note on **258**. For *pahitatto* see the note on **161**.

The cty does not comment on *santo* here. It could be either the present particple of the verb "to be", taken with *codito* "being urged", or the past participle of *sam-* < Skt *śānta* "calmed". See also EV I, p. 183 (ad Th 198). The jingle between *santa* and *santi* might well be intended.

Thī-a 168,28: *aphusiṃ*, *adhigacchiṃ*. See the note on **6**.

There is resolution of the sixth syllable in pāda a (§ 60).

213–23. Mrs Rhys Davids notes (Sist., p. 110, n. 1) that the metre of these verses is not the śloka, and is too irregular to be easily classifiable. The metre is in fact gaṇacchandas (see Alsdorf, App. II, p. 233, and Warder, § 1). All the verses are āryā except **213**abc and **218**ab which are śloka, and **216** which is gīti. Leumann seems to have been the first to notice that the āryā metre occurs in Thī, and even he seems not to have identified the metre of these particular verses, since Hardy (p. xxiii, note 4) states that the āryā portion of Thī is **400** to the end, excluding **488–92**.

For *ti* at the end of the group see the note on **1**.

The Buddha ranked Kisā-gotamī as foremost among those who wore rough garments: *etad aggaṃ lūkhacīvara-dharānaṃ, yad idaṃ Kisā-gotamī* (A I 25). The cty refers to this in the introductory story, but the remainder of the story hardly accords with what we can deduce from the verses (**29**). There is in particular a discrepancy between the story of her one dead child and the two which she herself mentions in verse **219**. The story which may be deduced from her verses so closely resembles that told for Paṭācārā (**112–16**) that it seems most likely that a mistake has been made. Dhammapāla recognises the resemblance and states (Thī-a 172,25–26): *upavijaññā gacchantī tiādikā dve gāthā Paṭācārāya theriyā pavattiṃ ārabbha bhāsitā*. The story which is told here for Kisā-gotamī would seem to be more appropriate for Paṭācārā pañcasatā (**127–32**); the first part of Paṭācārā's story should belong here; and only the latter part of her story, dealing with the trickling water, originally belonged to that therī. It should be noted that the confusion is as old as Ap, where the story which is told agrees with Dhammapāla's.

213. Pādas abc are śloka; pāda d is āryā. There is resolution of the seventh syllable in pāda a, and of the sixth syllable in pāda c (§ 60).

Thī-a 171,15–16: *kalyāṇa-mittatā ti kalyāṇo bhaddo sundaro mitto etassā ti kalyāṇa-mitto*, i.e. taking it as a bahuvrīhi compound. The cty continues: *yo yassa sīlādi-guṇa-samādapena aghassa ghātāhitassa vidhātā evaṃ sabbā-kārena upakāro mitto hoti* (i.e. taking it as a tatpuruṣa compound), *so puggalo kalyāṇa-mitto. tassa bhāvo kalyāṇa-mittatā, kalyāṇa-mitta-vantatā* (i.e. taking it as both types).

For the sentiment of the verse cf. Th 75c.

214. For *tathă* m.c. see § 72(d). For [*pa-*]*vaḍḍhatî* m.c. see § 67(c) and § 70(d). For [*pi*] m.c. see § 67(c). For *du*[*k*]*khehi* m.c. see § 65(b).

B[e] and C[e] read [*pa-*]*vaḍḍhati* and ⟨*pa-*⟩*mucceya*. For the reading of S[e] (followed by K[e]) see Alsdorf (App. II, p. 238, n.).

Thī-a 171,30–31: *tathā paññā vaḍḍhati brūhati pāripūriṃ gacchati.*

215. B[e] and C[e] read *nirodhaṃ* at the end of pāda b, correctly (§ 57(c)), but exclude *ca*, incorrectly. For ⟨*ca*⟩ in pāda c and ⟨*pi*⟩ in pāda d m.c. (with B[e] and C[e]) see § 66(c). For *vijāneyyâ* m.c. see § 70(d).

216. This verse is gīti. For *itthî-* m.c. (with C[e]) and for *sâpattikaṃ* m.c. (with Kern (1916B, p. 73)) see § 70(d).

Thī-a 172,11–12: *app ekaccā sakiṃ vijātāyo ti ekaccā itthiyo eka-vāram eva vijātā paṭhama-gabbhe vijāyana-dukkhaṃ asahantiyo. galake api kantantī ti attano gīvam pi chindanti.* The presence of *pi* in the explanation supports the reading *api* instead of *apa-*.

217. Thī-a 172,15–19: *jana-māraka-majjha-gatā ti jana-mārako vuccati mūḷha-gabbo mātu-gāma-janassa mārako, majjha-gatā jana-mārakā kucchi-gata-mūḷha-gabbhā ti attho. ubho pi vyasanāni anubhontī ti gabbho gabbhinī cā ti dve pi janā maraṇa-māraṇantika-vyasanāni pāpuṇanti. apare pana bhaṇanti* (M *apadassa na gaṇantī ti* (for the alternation *g*/*bh* see the note on **25**)) *jana-mārakā nāma kilesā.* The inclusion of *gabbho gabbhinī ca* makes it clear that the cty believes that pāda c refers to the embryo, and *ubho* refers to the mother and her unborn child.

For *gal⟨ak⟩e* m.c (with B^e^ C^e^ K^e^ and S^e^) see § 66(c). Kern (1916A, p. 84) suggested *kalale* (cf. M, p. 176 n.), but see CPD, s.v. *apakantati*. For *apakantantî* m.c. see § 70(d).

In pāda b *sukhumāliniyo* is strange with the *-inī* ending, but cf. *-iniyo* at Mil 68. K^e^ and S^e^ read *sukhumāliyo*. Perhaps we should read *sukhumālīyo* m.c.

In pāda d *vy-* counts as a single consonant in *vyasanāni* m.c. (see § 74(d) and Alsdorf, App. II p. 238).

218. Pādas ab are śloka; pādas cd are āryā. B^e^ and C^e^ read *panthamhi* at the beginning of pāda c, correctly (§ 57(c)). K^e^ and S^e^ read *panthe* in the same position. For *panthamhi* instead of *panthe* m.c. see § 66(c).

Thī-a 172,26–27: *upavijaññā gacchantī ti upagata-vijāyana-kāle maggaṃ gacchantī appattā sakaṃ gehaṃ panthe vijāyitvā*. This explanation shows that the cty knew the correct line division.

For *upavi⟨j⟩jaññā* m.c. to avoid the opening ⏓ ⏑ ⏑ – in pāda a see § 64(b) and the note on **10**. For *vijāyitvā[na]* m.c. see § 67(c).

219. For *kāla[ṅ]katā* m.c. (with B^e^ C^e^ K^e^ and S^e^) see § 68(a)(ii). For [*ca*] m.c. see § 67(c). For *patî* (with B^e^ and C^e^) and *ḍayhantî* m.c. see § 70(d).

The very similar verse at Thī-a 108,4–5 (= Ap 559) is in śloka metre.

For the possible confusion between *-k-* and *-g-* in *kāla-kata* cf. *priyaṃ mṛtaṃ kāla-gataṃ* Udāna-v 5.7 and see the notes on **101** and **413**. See also PED (s.v. *gata*), BHSD (s.v. *-kṛta*), and CPD (s.v. *anabhāva*). For *gata* see the note on **450**.

220. Thī-a 172,33–35: *khīṇa-kulīne ti bhogādīhi pārijuñña-ppatta-kule. kapaṇe ti parama-avaññātaṃ* (M *kapana-paññātaṃ* (for the alternation *p/v* see the note on **84**) *patte*; *ubhayaṃ c' etaṃ attano eva āmantana-vacanaṃ*. K^e^ and S^e^ read *-kulamhi* for *-kuline*, presumably understanding *kapaṇe* as a locative too.

For the idea of tears being shed for thousands of births see **495–97**, and cf. Anamatagga-saṃyutta (S II 178 foll.) [IBH].

For *assû* (with B^e^) and *jātî-* m.c. see § 70(d). For *du[k]khaṃ* m.c. (with B^e^) see § 65(b).

221. Pāda a does not scan in P, and Alsdorf suggests (App. II p. 239) reading [*taṃ*] (§ 67(c)). He points out that *vasitā* (found in B^e^ and C^e^) scans equally well, "I dwelt", and I follow this reading. Thī-a 173,6–7: *vasitā susāna-majjhe ti manussa-maṃsa-khādikā sunakhī si(ṅ)gālī ca hutvā susāna-majjhe vusitā. Vasitaṃ me* is used passively in Th 602. For the alternation *p/v* in *passitaṃ/vasitaṃ* see the note on **84**.

Thī-a 173,7–8: *khāditāni putta-maṃsānī ti vyaggha-dīpi-biḷārādi-kāle putta-maṃsāni khāditāni*. The cty clearly understands that she herself ate her children, but I take *khāditāni* to be the past participle of the causative *khādayati*, i.e. "caused to be eaten" = "exposed [for animals to eat]". Cf. the notes on **312** and **314**.

Pāda b is unmetrical and Alsdorf suggests reading *khā[di]tāni* (§ 67(c)), cf. Pkt *khāya* < Skt *khādita*. It is equally possible to read *khăditāni* (§ 72(d)), cf. Pkt *khaiya* (Erz, p. 49 line 32), and Skt *khad-* = *khād-* (Dhātupāṭha).

Pāda c is unmetrical and Alsdorf suggests reading *su-* for *sabba-garahitā*. All the editions, however, read *sabba-*, and its antiquity is guaranteed by the fact that the cty explains: *sabbehi pi garahitā garaha-ppattā*. We could perhaps still retain *sabba-* and yet correct the metre by reading *hata-kul[ik]ă* (see §§ 67(c), 72(d)). The sense of *garahita* here is possibly "despised, condemned" (see MW, s.v. *garhita*).

For *amata* see the note on **149**.

222. Thī-a 173,14–15: *bhāvito ti vibhāvito uppādito vaḍḍhito bhāvanābhi-samaya-vasena paṭiladdho*.

For ⟨*saṃ-*⟩*bhāvito* m.c. see Alsdorf (App. II p. 239, n.) and § 66(c). For *apekkhî* m.c. see § 70(d). For the alternation *p/v* (read by B^e K^e and S^e) see the note on **84**. M (text) reads *avekkhitaṃ* for *avekkhi 'haṃ*. For the alternation *-itaṃ/-i 'haṃ* see the note on **261**. For *mĕ* m.c. see § 72(d). I presume that Alsdorf's reading *amaya-* for *amata-* is merely a misprint.

For *amata* see the note on **149**.

223. Thī-a 173,17: *kanta-sallā ti samucchinna-rāgādi-sallā*. For *kanta* see PED s.v.

For *aham* (with C^e) m.c. see § 68(b)(iii). For *mĕ* m.c. see § 72(d). C^e reads *hi*, which is also metrical. For *Kîsā-* (with S^e and N^e v.l.) see § 70(d). For *-gotamĭ* m.c. see § 72(d). For [*su-*]*vimutta-* (with B^e and C^e) m.c. see § 67(c). For ⟨*a*⟩*bhaṇī* (with C^e) m.c. see § 66(c).

224–35. The Buddha ranked Uppalavaṇṇā as foremost among those who had supernormal powers: *etad aggaṃ iddhi-matīnaṃ, yad idaṃ Uppalavaṇṇā* (A I 25). See also Lévi's note on Utpalavarṇā (p. 159, n. 5).

For *ti* at the end of the group see the note on **1**.

As Mrs Rhys Davids points out (Sist., p. 115, n.), the cty divides these verses up into four episodes: **224–26**, **227–28**, **229**, **230–35**. As in the case of Ānanda and some other theras (see EV I, § 10), verses uttered at different times have been collected together with no attempt made to produce an organic whole.

224. For co-wives see VI, s.v. *sapatnī*.

For *tassā me* see the note on **24**.

For *ahu* see § 71 and the note on **43**.

For *abbhuta* see the note on **316**. The cty does not comment on the word here.

225. PED (s.v. *dhi*[1]) states that *dhi* is constructed with either the accusative or the genitive case. It is not at all clear that we have the accusative here. Although PED (s.v. *kāma*) states that *kāma* can be masculine or neuter, *asucī* can hardly be neuter. The cty is clearly taking *kāmā* as masculine and nominative, since *te kāmā* is included in the explanation. It is probable then that we should have a mark of punctuation after *dhi-r-atthu*, and translate "woe upon it; sensual pleasures are ... ". See MW (s.v. *dhik*). For sandhi *-r-* see the note on **3**.

Thī-a 190,4: *yatthā ti yesu kāmesu paribhuñjitabbesu*. See also the note on **35**.

For *sabhâriyā* m.c. to avoid the opening ⏓ ⏑ ⏑ – see § 70(e) and the note on **10**. This, however, then gives the opening ⏓ – ⏑ –, which is also irregular by classical standards (see the notes on **74** and **299**). We could obtain a regular opening by reading *sabharīyā*, but the lengthening of a svarabhakti vowel is unparalleled elsewhere in Thī or Th (see EV I, p. 261 (ad Th 739)). K^{e} and S^{e}, however, read *saha-bhariyā* for *sa-bhariyā*, and if we scan *-bhariyā* (§ 75) we have the opening ⏓ ⏑ – –. The reading with *sa-* doubtless arose to avoid the apparently nine-syllable pāda.

Thī-a 190,4–5: *sa-bhariyā ti samāna-bhariyā sa-pattiyo ti attho*.

226. For *-u* > *-v* in *kāmesv* see § 73(a), and cf. *hotv* **326**, *kāmesv* **485**, *-pitusv* **499**. For *-i* > *-y* see the note on **248**.

For pāda d see the note on **92**.

B^{e} C^{e} K^{e} and S^{e} read *daṭṭhu* for *daḷha-*. This is the reading of Th 458. The cty is silent.

C^{e} reads *pabbaji* for *pabbajiṃ*. The cty is silent. See Mrs Rhys Davids' note (Sist., p. 113, n. 1). For *sā* and a first person verb see the note on **24**.

The cty makes no comment on *nekkhamma* here, but Thī-a 224,29–30 (ad **339**) glosses: *pabbajjā-nibbāna* and Thī-a 245,21 (ad **403**): *pabbajjaṃ*.

227–28. Thī-a 190,10–11: *pubbe-nivāsan ti ādikā dve gāthā attano adhigata-visesaṃ paccavekkhitvā pīti-somanassa-jātāya theriyā vuttā*.

227. For *pubbe-nivāsa* see the note on **63**.

For *ceto-paricca-ñāṇa* and *sota-dhātu* see the note on **71**.

228. For *iddhī* m.c. to avoid the opening ⏓ ⏑ ⏑ – see § 70(e) and the note on **10**. In pāda c there is resolution of the seventh syllable (§ 60).

229. For Uppalavaṇṇā's pre-eminence in *iddhi* see the note on **224–35**. The cty relates that she worked this miracle before the Buddha, with his permission.

This verse contains no finite verb. Thī-a 190,22 understands *ekamantaṃ aṭṭhāsiṃ*.

For the scansion of *sirīmato* see § 75.

230–35. Thī-a 191,1 foll. states that **230** was uttered by Māra (§ 2), and **231–35** by the therī. The same episode is included in the Bhikkhunī-saṃyutta (S I 131–32), although there are differences of reading.

230–31. These two verses are not in śloka metre. The first is in mixed triṣṭubh/jagatī metre, and the second in triṣṭubh. The comparable verses at S I 131–32 differ slightly.

230. Pāda a is jagatī; pādas bcd are triṣṭubh. The comparable verse at S I 131 has five pādas, all triṣṭubh.

Thī-a 190,28–30: *na cāpi te dutiyo atthi kocī ti tava sahāya-bhūto ārakkhako koci pi n' atthi. rūpa-sampattiyā vā tuyhaṃ dutiyo koci n' atthi.* S I 131 reads *na c' atthi te dutiyā vaṇṇa-dhātu*, and the cty's alternative explanation seems to be referring to a reading which resembles this. See also BHSD, s.v. *varṇa-dhātu*.

Pāda d has the opening ⏓ – – – which Warder (PM, § 278) calls "very rare". S I 131 reads *bāle na tvaṃ*, instead of *na tvaṃ bāle*, which gives the common opening ⏓ – ⏑ – if we either assume that *tv-* does not make position in *tvaṃ* or read *t*[*v*]*aṃ* (§ 74(b)). The opening ⏓ – – – is perhaps not as rare as Warder states. It occurs in S (to consider one text only) I 19 22 (twice) 42 (twice) 46 52 92 (twice) 126 137 141 (three times) 168 (twice) 181 214 (twice, although some of these openings could be "corrected" to ⏓ – ⏑ – without difficulty. B^{e} reads as S I 131.

231. The metre is triṣṭubh. B^{e} C^{e} and S I 132 read *sahassāni* which is preferable syntactically, and better metrically. For *sahassāna*(*ṃ*) m.c. see § 68(b)(ii).

Thī-a 191,19: *yādisako tvaṃ edisakā evarūpā*, which seems to be a gloss upon *tādisika* rather than *edisaka*. S I 132 reads *tādisikā* for *edisakā*. Spk I 192 explains: *idhāgatā tādisikā bhaveyyun ti yathā tvaṃ idh' āgatā kiñci santhavaṃ vā sinehaṃ va na labhasi, evam evaṃ te pi tayā va sadisā bhaveyyuṃ.*

Thī-a 191,20–21: *lomaṃ na iñje na pi sampavedhe ti loma-mattam pi na iñjeyya na sampavedheyya*, taking *iñje* as an optative. The fact that *iñje* is the first person singular middle indicative is confirmed by the reading *iñjāmi* at S I 132. Cf. *lomam pi na tattha iñjaye* S I 107, which Spk I 173–74 explains: *tatthā ti tesu bheravesu suññāgāra-gato buddha-muni loma-calana-mattakam pi na karoti*. See also BHSD (s.v. *iñjate*).

232. For *esā* with a first person verb see the note on **24**.

Thī-a 191,24–27: *tass' attho: Māra, esāhaṃ tava purato ṭhitā va antara-dhāyāmi adassanaṃ gacchāmi, ajānantass' eva te kucchiṃ vā pavisāmi, bhamukantare vā tiṭṭhāmi, evaṃ tiṭṭhantiṃ ca maṃ tvaṃ na passasi*. S I 132 reads: *pakhumantarikāyam pi* for *bhamukantare tiṭṭhāmi*. Spk I 192 explains: *pakhumantarikāyan ti dvinnaṃ akkhīnaṃ majjhe nāsa-vaṃse pi tiṭṭhantiṃ mam na passasi*.

B^{e} C^{e} and S I 132 read *dakkhasi* for *dakkhisi*.

233. Thī-a 191,28–29 explains *vasī-bhūtāhaṃ* as: *mayhaṃ cittaṃ vasī-bhāva-ppattaṃ*. One would expect *vasī-bhūta* to have the opposite meaning to *vasī-kar-*, and Edgerton (BHSD, s.v. *vaśī-bhūta*) points out that the Buddhist meaning is the opposite of the usual Skt one "subjected, subdued". The Buddhist meaning probably arose because the compound was taken as two separate words *vasī bhū-* "to be possessing power, powerful". See BHSD, s.v. *vaśin*.

For *vasĭ-* m.c. to give the cadence ⏑ – – ⏓ (*pathyā*) see § 72(e) and the note on **37**.

In pāda c there is resolution of the seventh syllable (§ 60. B^{e} normalises by reading *chaḷ-abhiññā*, and K^{e} and S^{e} by reading *cha me 'bhiññā*.

234. See the note on **58**.

235. See the note on **59**.

236–51. The rubric calls the author of these verses Puṇṇikā, and this name actually occurs in **238**. In the introductory story in the cty, however, she is called Puṇṇā. The rubric in Ap calls her Puṇṇikā, but the name Puṇṇā occurs in Ap 612.

Verses **236–37 240–44 246–49** are by Puṇṇikā; **238–39 245 250–51** are by the brahman (§ 2). Thī-a 198,4–5 explains how the verses subsequently became hers: *ettha ca brāhmaṇena vutta-gātha pi attanā vutta-gāthā pi pacchā theriyā pacceka-bhāsitā ti sabbā theriyā gāthā eva jātā* (§ 4).

The verses constitute an attack upon brahmanical ritual, particularly the ritual washing away of sins. For comparable attacks upon brahmanism see the note on **87–91**. For a Jain attack upon ritual bathing see the note on **241–43**.

Thī-a 195,14 foll. relates how Puṇṇikā, going down to the river for water in very cold weather, saw a brahman engaged in ritual bathing, his teeth chattering (*danta-vīṇaṃ vādayamānaṃ*, cf. MW, s.v. *danta-vīṇā*). She explains (**236**) that she goes down to the river for fear of punishment; she asks (**237**) what he fears that makes him go down to the river.

236. There is resolution of the first syllable of pāda a, and of the sixth syllable in pāda c (§ 60). The same resolution of the first two syllables of *udaka-* occurs in **239–40 242 245**. Bᵉ reads *uda*[*ka*]- on each occasion, but this is probably mere normalisation. Although Warder (PM, § 47) and PED (s.v. *oka*) both draw attention to Geiger's suggestion (2000, § 20) that *oka* exists as a contraction of *udaka*, and Warder suggests that it could be read in these contexts m.c., the phenomenon of resolution is so common that there is no need to doubt the reading *udaka-* here. There is moreover every reason to doubt the existence of *oka* in the sense "water". PED points out that *oka* at Vin I 253 is probably corrupt since there is a v.l. *ogha*. The same is probably true of Dhp 34, for the BHS version at Udāna-v 31.2 has *okād oghāt* in place of *oka-m-okata*. We may therefore assume either that the Pāli version is corrupt, or more likely that it reflects a borrowing from a dialect which, like Gāndhārī, blurred the distinction between aspirated and unaspirated consonants and also, on occasion, replaced *-g-* by unhistoric *-k-*.

237. Thī-a 195,23–24: *sītaṃ vedayase bhusaṃ, sītaṃ dukkhaṃ ativiya dukkhaṃ paṭiveddayasi paccanubhavasi*. PED lists two meanings for *vedeti*: "to know" and "to experience", but only one, "to make known, to declare, to anounce" for *paṭivedeti*. It is clear from this gloss that *paṭivedeti* can also have the meaning of *paccanubhavati*, " to experience".

There is nothing to tells us whether *br-* makes position in *brāhmaṇa* or not (§ 74). Since the opening ⏓ – – ⏑ is not usual with the cadence – , – – ⏓ it seems likely that *tv-* does not make position in *tvaṃ* (§ 74(b)). We therefore have the cadence ⏑ – – ⏓ (*pathyā*).

238. Bᵉ and Cᵉ read *vata maṃ* for *ca tuvaṃ* in pāda a, and the verse is easier to translate with *maṃ* in agreement with *karontaṃ* and *rudhantaṃ*. The cty's explanation includes both *tvaṃ* and *maṃ*. For the alternation *s*/*v* see the note on **12**.

For *kamma* m.c. see § 68(b)(i). It is, of course, historically correct.

239. B[e] C[e] K[e] and S[e] omit the first *vā* in pāda a, and in view of the authority for this reading it should probably be adopted. On the other hand it is not impossible that *vā* was excluded to give an eight-syllable pāda. This can be achieved by assuming resolution of the sixth syllable (§ 60).

There is resolution of the first syllable in pāda c (§ 60). See also the note on **236**. C[e] (lemma) reads *dakābhisecanā*.

240. There are nine syllables in pāda b (§ 61). The pāda can be normalised by reading *ajānantass'* with K[e] (§ 67(d)). C[e] and S[e] read ajānako for ajānato. For the alternation *k*/*t* see the note on **43**. For *ajānato* m.c. see § 68(a)(i).

There is resolution of the first syllable in pāda c (§ 60). See also the note on **236**. C[e] reads *dakābhisecanā*.

241–43. The Jains have a comparable view of the uselessness of ritual bathing, and a passage in Sūyag closely resembles these verses:

udageṇa je siddhim udāharaṃti, sāyaṃ ca pāyaṃ udagaṃ phusaṃtā,
udagassa phāseṇa siyā ya siddhī, sijjhiṃsu pāṇā bahave 'dagaṃsi:
macchā ya kummā ya sirīsivā ya maggū ya uṭṭā 'daga-rakkhasā ya.
aṭṭhānam eyaṃ kusalā vayaṃti, udageṇa je siddhim udāharaṃti.
udayaṃ jai kamma-malaṃ harejjā, evaṃ suhaṃ. icchā-mittam eva.
aṃdhaṃ va ṇeyāram aṇusarittā, pāṇāṇi c' evaṃ viṇihaṃti maṃdā.
pāvāiṃ kammāiṃ pakuvvato hi sīodagaṃ tu jai taṃ karijjā,
sijjhiṃsu ege 'daga-satta-ghātī; musaṃ vayaṃte jala-siddhim āhu.

I, 7, 14–17

For other Jain references see the note on **87–91**.

241. Thī-a 196,10–11: *te pi saggaṃ nūna gamissanti, deva-lokaṃ upapajjissanti maññe*. The juxtaposition of *sagga* and *deva* lends weight to the view that the reference in Aśoka's Minor Rock Edict to *adeva-misa* men becoming *deva-misa* is merely an alternative way of expressing what elsewhere appears in the form *sagaṃ ārādhetave* (see Filliozat (p. 225) and Meile (p. 193)). Brough has already pointed out that GDhp 344 makes it clear that *svarga* was an acceptable second-best to *nirvāṇa* for Buddhists (GDhp, p. 282). The point is made even more clearly by the Buddha himself at M I 142: *ye te bhikkhū dhammānusārino saddhānusārino, sabbe te sambodhi-parāyanā. yesaṃ mayi saddhā-mattaṃ pema-mattaṃ, sabbe te sagga-parāyanā*. Cf. *saggaṃ sugatino yanti parinibbanti anāsavā* Dhp 126, quoted by Hultzsch, p. liv.

Thī-a 196,9–10: *ye c' aññe udake-carā ti ye c' aññe pi vāri-gocarā maccha-makara-nandi-y-āvattādayo ca*. PED does not list any appropriate meaning for *nandi-y-āvatta*, although MW quotes the meaning "a species of large fish" from the lexica for *nandy-āvarta*.

Thī-a 196,8: *nāgā ti vajjhasā*. The latter word is not in PED, nor is *vijjhasā* which is the gloss in Be. Ce reads: *nakkā ti jhasā*. *Nakka* is not quoted in PED, but it is quoted for Pāli by CDIAL (7038), probably from Childers, where it is quoted from Abh 674. *Nākra* exists in Skt with the sense "crocodile" (MW, s.vv.), and *ṇakka* is quoted for Pkt in PSM (s.v.). PED does not quote *jhasa* except in the meaning "window", but it is quoted by Childers from Abh 671 in the sense "fish". *Jhaṣa* exists in Skt with this meaning (MW, s.v.), as does *jhasa* in Pkt (PSM, s.v.). *Jhaṣa* is found in Hindī with the meaning "alligator". Since I know of no evidence to support the view that *nāga* exists in the sense "water-snake", which would be essential here, I would suggest that we follow the reading of Ce here, for both text and gloss.

242. Thī-a 196,13–15: *orabhikā ti urabbha-ghātakā. sūkarikā ti sūkara-ghātakā. macchikā ti kevaṭṭā. miga-vadhikā ti māgavikā. vajjha-ghātā* (Ce *-ghātakā*) *ti vajjha-ghāta-kamme niyuttā*. PED (s.v. *orabbhika*) points out that Skt *aurabhrika* is later and differs in meaning; the Pāli meaning, however, is found in BHS (BHSD, s.v. *aurabhrika*). The same is true of *sūkarika* (see BHSD, s.v. *saukarika*).

There is resolution of the first syllable in pāda e (§ 60). See also the note on **236**. Ce reads *dakābhisecanā*.

243. The metre of this verse is āryā (see Alsdorf, App. II, p. 239). For *nadîyo* and *tenâ* m.c. see § 70(d). For [*tvaṃ*] m.c. see § 67(c). We should also read *te* at the end of pāda b instead of in pāda a.

I do not think that we need to read *hañce* with Alsdorf for *sace*. In EV I, p. 212 (ad Th 386) I stated that the first gaṇa of an āryā pādayuga is occasionally one mora short (cf. PM §§ 206, n. 1, 214, 226). I now think that I was wrong in the case of Th 386, and we should perhaps in all cases emend the first gaṇa from ⏑ – to – –. In this case we could correct the metre equally well by reading *sa⟨c⟩ce* (see § 64(b)). Comparable non-historic doublings can be postulated for **420**c **436**c (*ta⟨t⟩to*, cf. Pkt *tatto*); **428**c (*ni⟨s⟩sinnāya*; **486**c (*a⟨t⟩titto*; **510**a (*a⟨p⟩pari-*).

Thī-a 196,19–25: *tena tvaṃ paribāhiro assa, tathā sati, tena puñña-kammena tvaṃ paribāhiro virahito va bhaveyyā ti. na c' etaṃ yuttan ti adhippāyo. yathā vā udakena udakorohakassa puñña-pavāhanaṃ na hoti, evaṃ pāpa-pavāhanam pi na hoti eva. kasmā? nhānassa pāpa-hetūnaṃ appaṭipakka-bhāvato. yo yaṃ vināseti, so tassa paṭipakkho. yathā āloko andha-kārassa, vijjā ca avijjāya, na evaṃ nhānaṃ pāpassa. tasmā niṭṭhaṃ ettha gantabbaṃ "na udakābhisecanā pāpato parimuttī" ti.* For the phrase *niṭṭhaṃ gantabbaṃ* "we must come to the conclusion that ... " in the cty's explanation, see MW (s.v. *niṣṭhā*). PED does not list this meaning.

The text is therefore saying that if water washed away sin, it would also wash away merit, and a man would lose that too (= *paribāhira* "be outside it, be excluded from it"). The cty explains this, and gives a further reason for saying that the idea is absurd: it is only things which are mutually opposed which can destroy one another, e.g. light and dark. Water and sin are not so opposed, therefore water cannot destroy sin. For the comparable Jain idea of water washing away both bad and good, see the note on **241–43**.

244. Thī-a 196,31–32: *brahme, brāhmaṇa.* Since the opening ⏓ – – – is not usual with the cadence –, – – ⏓, we can deduce that *br-* does not make position in *brahme* here (§74(a)). Similarly, since the opening ⏓ ⏑ – ⏑ is not common with the cadence –, – – ⏓, we can deduce that *tv-* does not make position in *tvaṃ* here (§74(b)). We should probably read *t*[*v*]*aṃ* (see EV I, §50(b)).

Thī-a 196,30–32: *tam eva brahme mā kāsī ti yato pāpato tvaṃ bhīto tam eva pāpam brahme brāhmana tvaṃ mā kāsi.* I presume that this verse follows on from **243**: you bathe from fear of not gaining merit, but if bathing washes away merit together with de-merit you are doing the very thing, i.e. not gaining merit, for fear of which you bathe.

Thī-a 196,32–197,2: *udakorohanaṃ pana īdise sīta-kāle kevalaṃ sarīram eva bādhati. ten' āha; mā te sītaṃ chaviṃ hane ti īdise sīta-kāle udakābhisecanena jāta-sītaṃ tava sarīra-cchaviṃ mā haneyya mā bādhesī ti attho.* I take *sītaṃ* as the subject of *hane*, although the meanings "cold, coldness, cold water" are only only quoted from the lexica for Skt *śīta* (see MW, s.v.)

245–49. The verse divisions in this section of the group are not entirely satisfactory. Verse **247**ab makes better sense if taken with **246**cd; **248**ab should go with **247**cd (cf. Udāna-v 9.3–4); **248**cd should go with **249**; **246**ab should presumably go with **245**. C^e does not number the verses, but divides the poem up into pairs of pāda-yugas, except that **248**cd and **249** are printed as one six-pāda verse. This arrangement, however, means that **243** is split between two different verses, although its metre (āryā) guarantees that it is an organic whole. B^e follows the same verse divisions as P, where only **242** has six pādas.

245. The cty unfortunately makes no reference to *udakābhisecanaṃ* in pāda c, and there is consequently some doubt about how it should be taken. It could be in apposition to *kumaggaṃ* in pāda a, but the distance between the two words and the fact that *ariya-maggaṃ* comes between them is against this suggestion. Alternatively we could assume that the ending *-aṃ* is for the ablative (see EV I, p. 271 (ad Th 788)): "you have led me back to the path from ... ". Alternatively we could regard *udakābhisecanaṃ sāṭaṃ* as a split compound (see the note on **147**): "my robe for bathing". In favour of the second explanation is the fact that C^e^ reads *udakābhisecanā*, which, whether a genuine reading or not, seems to indicate that somewhere in the tradition the word was interpreted as an ablative. In favour of the last suggestion is the fact that it would be natural for the brahman to give away the particular robe for which he would have no further need, i.e. his bathing-robe.

There is resolution of the first syllable of pāda c (§60). See also the note on **236**. Here C^e^ reads *udakā-*.

For the scansion of *ariya-* see §75.

248. Thī-a 197,20–22: *upecca sañcicca. palāyato pi te tato pāpato mutti mokkho n' atthi. gati-kālādi-paccayantara-samavāye sati vipaccate evā ti attho. uppaccā ti vā pāṭho. uppatitvā ti attho.* Spk I 307 (ad S I 209) explains: *uppaccā pī ti uppatitvā pi. "sace sakuṇo viya uppatitvā palāyasi, tathā pi te mokkho n' atthī" ti vadati.* Spk-pṭ (B^e^) I 313 confirms this: *uppatitvā ti ākāse uppatitvā* [LSC]. We find *uppaccā* at Dhp-a IV 21 and Pv 21 (B^e^ so, E^e^ *upaccha* with v.l. *upacca*). Pv-a 103 explains: *upaccha uppatitvā. upeccā ti pi pāḷi, sañcicca.* The BHS version (Udāna-v 9.4) has *utplutyāpi*, and the idea of springing up is so appropriate in the context that we might well feel that *uppacca* is the superior reading. We find, however, only *upecca* at Nett 131 and Ud 51, and Ud-a 295 explains: *upecca, sañcicca.*

For *-i* > *-y* in *pamuty* see §73(a) and cf. *anunenty* in **514**. For *-u* > *-v* see the note on **226**.

249–50. Thī-a 197,25–27: *tādinan ti diṭṭhādi-sutādi-bhāva-ppattaṃ yathā vā puri-makā sammā-sambuddhā passitabbā, tathā passitabbato tādisaṃ buddhaṃ saraṇaṃ upehī ti yojanā. dhamma-saṃghesu pi es' eva nayo. tādinaṃ vara-buddhādīnaṃ dhammaṃ aṭṭhannaṃ ariya-puggalānam saṃgha-samūhan ti yojanā.* If we take *tādinaṃ* as an accusative singular, the phrase is exactly parallel to *buddhaṃ dhammañ ca saṅghañ ca upemi saraṇam muniṃ* **53 132**. If we take it as a genitive plural we can translate "the order of the venerable ones" (see EV I, p. 145 (ad Th 41)).

251. Thī-a 198,1–4: *idāni sabbaso bāhita-pāpatāya brāhmaṇo paramattha-brāhmaṇo, vijja-ttayādhigamena tevijjo, magga-ñāṇa-saṃkhātena vedena samannāgatattā veda-sampanno, niratta-sabba-pāpatāya bhātako ca amhī ti.*

For comparable Buddhist interpretations of brahmanical terms including *sotthiya*, which the cty does not explain here or on **290**, see EV I, p. 140 (ad Th 24). For the attempt at an etymology for the word *brāhmaṇa* see EV I, p. 188 (ad Th 221). For the Buddhist use of *nhātaka* cf. *ninhāya sabba-pāpakāni ... tam āhu nhātako ti* Sn 521 and *visnāpiya sarva-pāpakāni ... punar āhu snātako ti* Mvu III 397 (see Jones, III 396, n. 6).

That the Buddhists knew the correct brahmanical use of these words is shown by the comment in Thī-a 197,35–36: *tathā iru-bbedādīnaṃ ajjhenādi-mattena tevijjo*.

For the cadence of pāda b see § 59(a). We can normalise by reading *sacca[ṃ]* m.c. (with B^{e} and C^{e}) (§ 68(b)(ii) and assuming that *br-* does not make position in *brāhmaṇo* (§ 74(a)). For *amhî* m.c. to avoid the opening ⏓ — ⏑ — see § 70(e) and the note on **74**.

For *nh-* not making position in *nhātako* see § 74(e) and Warder (PM, § 50). It would not seem possible to read *nahātako* here, nor can I see that such a reading would be metrical at Sn 518 521. I would suggest that the irregular cadence reflects the fact that the pāda was originally composed in a dialect which converted initial *sn-* > *n-*, cf. Skt *nāpita* < **snāpita*, Pkt *ninneha* < *niḥsneha* (Erz, p. 52, line 15; Utt 14.49) and *niddha* < *snigdha* (Pischel, 1900 § 313). Cf. *nusā* Ja VI 584 586 Sadd 198 (B^{e} reads *suṇhā*). and the vv.ll. *nināya* and *nātako* at Sn 521.

252–70. Although the rubric does not call Ambapālī a *purāṇa-gaṇikā* (cf. the note on **25–26**), the introductory story tells how, as the result of calling a therī a *gaṇikā* in a previous birth, in her final birth (*carimatta-bhāve*) she was appointed as a courtesan (*gaṇikā-ṭhāne ṭhapesuṃ*). We read in Vin I 268 that she charged fifty pieces a night for her services (*paññāsāya ca rattiṃ gacchati*) and as a result the city of Vesālī became very prosperous. She bore a son by King Bimbisāra who became the thera Vimala-kondañña (author of Th 64). For the thera's punning reference to his parentage see EV I, p. 153 (ad Th 64). Having heard her son preach the doctrine, she strove for insight, using her own ageing body as a symbol of impermanence.

This poem is in rathoddhatā metre (see PM § 166, note 1), and since the structure of this metre is fixed within very narrow limits it is possible to identify unmetrical pādas without difficulty, and also to propose emendations which stand a good chance of being correct. These verses were examined by Kern, who proposed many corrections (VG, XV, 163–69), and more recently by Bollée (1969, pp. 148–49).

Although Macdonell (1927, p. 234) shows the rathoddhatā cadence as being – ⏑ – ⏑ – –, Warder (PM, § 287) shows the final syllable as anceps, as one would expect. Only in one pāda (**257**a) does any edition show a long vowel (in *maṇī*) where P reads a short vowel. It would, however, be a simple matter to read *mamā* or *mama⟨ṃ⟩* in **256**b **260**b **262**b **263**b **264**b **265**b **266**b **267**b **268**b **269**b, *-bhū* in **253**b, *patī* in **258**b, *viyā* in **258**c, and *ivā* in **268**c if it were thought necessary.

252. Thī-a 200,11–15: *vellit'-aggā ti kuñcit'-aggā. mūlato paṭṭhāya yāva aggā kuñcitā vellitā ti attho. muddha-jā ti kesā. jarāyā ti jarā-hetu jarāya upahata-sobhā. sāṇa-vāka-sadisā ti sāṇa-sadisā vāka-sadisā ca sāṇa-vāka-sadisā c' eva makaci vāka-sadisā cā ti pi attho.* The cty is clearly taking *sāṇa-vāka* as a dvandva compound, but in Skt *śaṇa-valka* means "bark of hemp", and presumably **śāṇa-valka* would mean the same, i.e. her hair looked like the bark-fibres of the hemp-plant.

Thī-a 200,15–18: *sacca-vādi-vacanaṃ anaññathā ti sacca-vādino avitatha-vādino sammā-sambuddhassa "sabbaṃ rūpaṃ aniccaṃ jarābhibhūtan" ti ādi vacanam anaññathā yathā-bhūtam eva. na tattha vitathaṃ atthī ti.*

For *-sâdisā* m.c. in pāda a (with Bᵉ and Cᵉ) and in pāda c (with Bᵉ) see § 70(a). For *vellit'-aggă* and *săṇa-* m.c. (with Kern) see § 72(b).

253. Thī-a 200,19–20: *vāsito va surabhī karaṇḍako ti puppha-gandha-vāsa-cuṇṇādīhi vāsito vāsaṃ gahāpito pasādhana-samuggo viya sugandhi.* It is clear that Bᵉ and Cᵉ are correct in separating *surabhi* (*surabhī* m.c., see below) from *karaṇḍako*. *Surabhi* is neuter, agreeing with *uttam'-aṅgaṃ*.

Thī-a 200,20–22: *puppha-pūraṃ mama uttam'-aṅga-jo ti campaka-sumana-mallikādīhi pupphehi pūrito pubbe mama kesa-kalāpo* (PED quotes this compound in the plural only). *nimmalo ti attho.* It seems clear that neither *uttam'-aṅga-jo*, nor *-bhūto* (which is also read by Kᵉ and Sᵉ), nor Bollée's suggestion *-jā* can be correct, since *-pūtaṃ* and *taṃ* (in pāda c) require a neuter to agree with. The reading *-bhūto* is, moreover, unmetrical. Kern follows P's reading, but *-bhu* is difficult to translate since *taṃ* in pāda c must refer to it, and yet *taṃ* is glossed: *tan ti uttam'-aṅgaṃ.* I would suggest that we punctuate *uttam'-aṅg' abhu*, and assume either that *abhu* is a mistake for *ahu*, since *h* and *bh* can be confused in Sinhalese script according to Alsdorf (see CPD s.v. *uttamaṅga*), or possibly a genuine historical development < Skt *abhūt*, unattested elsewhere in Pāli. This would give a neuter singular subject *uttamaṅgaṃ* for *-pūraṃ* to agree with, and would seem to be supported by the gloss.

For *pūra* in the sense of "filled (here = covered?)" see PED and BHSD (s.v.). The same meaning is given for *pūra* by Th-a II 117,12 (ad Th 279) (see EV I, p. 1797(ad Th 279)). Cf. **380**.

In pāda c B[e] and P (v.l.) read *jarāy' atha sa-loma-gandhikaṃ*. This reading is supported by Thī-a 200,23–25: *atha pacchā etarahi sa-*(C[e] *sasa-*)*loma-gandhikaṃ pākatika-loma-gandham eva jātaṃ. atha vā sa-*(C[e] *sasa-*)*loma-gandhikan ti meṇḍaka-*(C[e] *matthaka-*)*lomehi samāna-gandhaṃ. eḷaka-loma-gandhan ti pi vadanti.* I do not know of *sa-* in the sense of *meṇḍaka* or *eḷaka*, but *sa* < *Skt śvan-* (cf. *sa-pāka*) would make good sense here.

For *surabhî* m.c. (with B[e] and C[e]) see § 70(a). For *-pūra*[*ṃ*] m.c. (with B[e] and C[e]) see § 68(b)(ii). According to Alsdorf (CPD s.v. *uttamaṅga*) *pūra* is m.c. for *pūro* (agreeing with *karaṇḍako*).

254. Thī-a 200,26–28: *kānaṃ va sahitaṃ suropitan ti suṭṭhu ropitaṃ sahitam ghana-sannivesaṃ uddham eva uṭṭhitaṃ ujuka-dīgha-sākhaṃ upavanaṃ viya.* Kern suggested reading *surohitaṃ* for *suropitaṃ*, but I see no need for this. For *sahita* see BHSD (s.v.), Kern (VG II, p. 247), and cf. **265**.

Thī-a 200,28–29: *koccha-sūci-vicitagga-sobhitan ti pubbe kocchena suvaṇṇa-sūciyā ca kesa-jaṭā-vijaṭanena vicitaggaṃ hutvā sobbhitaṃ.* For *koccha* see the note on **411**. PED gives no etymology for *koccha*[2]. It is probably connected with Skt *kūrca* and Pkt *kucca*, both of which, however, mean "brush", although the difference between that and "comb" is probably not great. See CDIAL 3408 (s.v. *kūrca*), where Pāli *koccha* is not listed. The cty gives an alternative explanation, which seems to be based upon the meaning of *koccha*[1], "thicket": *ghana-bhāvena koccha-sadīsaṃ kutvā phala-*(B[e] *paṇa-* (see PED, s.v. *paṇaka* = *phaṇaka*))*danta-sūcīhi vicit'-aggatāya sobhitaṃ.* This explanation seems to depend upon the separation of *koccha* from the remainder of the compound, and upon the assumption that it stands for *kocchaṃ* m.c., whereas I should prefer to follow the cty's first explanation but separate *sobhitaṃ* from the first part of the compound and assume that *-vicit-agga* is m.c. for *-vicit'-aggaṃ*.

Thī-a 200,30–31: *tan ti uttam'-aṅga-jaṃ.* I see no reason for supposing that the subject has changed since the previous verse, where it was *uttam'-aṅgaṃ*. I think this is confirmed by the gloss: *viraḷaṃ tahiṃ tahin ti tattha tattha ciraḷam vilūna-kesaṃ*, where I take *vilūna-kesaṃ* to be a bahuvrīhi compound, i.e. "[My head] possessing cut off (= fallen out) hair". Cf. the note on **255**.

255. B[e] and C[e] read *kaṇha-khandhaka-* for *saṇha-gandhaka-*. Thī-a 200,33–35: *kaṇha-kandhaka-suvaṇṇa-maṇḍitan ti suvaṇṇa-vajirādīhi vibhū-sitaṃ kaṇha-kesa-puñjakaṃ ye pana saṇha-*(M *paṇha-* (for the alternation *p*/*s* see the note on

6))*kaṇḍaka-suvaṇṇa-maṇḍitan ti paṭhanti, tesaṃ saṇhāhi suvaṇṇa-sūcīhi jaṭā-vijaṭanena maṇḍitan ti attho*. Neither of these explanations mentions the word *gandhaka*, which must therefore be a mistake in P. It seems clear that if we follow the first of these readings and explanations, we should separate *kaṇha-khandhaka* from the remainder of the compound and assume that it is m.c. for *-khandhakaṃ*. If we follow the second reading, the separation of the compound is not essential but it leads to an easier translation, i.e. *saṇha-kaṇḍaka* is taken as a bahuvrīhi agreeing with *siraṃ*. Compounds beginning with *saṇha-* and ending with *-suvaṇṇa-maṇḍitā* occur in **264 268**. In both cases the sentence makes good sense if the compounds are divided up (see the notes on **264 268**).

PED does not list *khandhaka* in the sense of "small pile", nor is the meaning "pin" given specifically for *kaṇḍaka*, although it is said to be the equivalent of *kaṇṭaka* for which "instrument with a sharp point" is given.

Thī-a 200,36–37: *sobhate su veṇīhi 'laṅkatan ti sundarehi rāja-rukkha-phala-sadisehi kesa-veṇīhi alaṅkataṃ hutvā pubbe virājate*. The cty seems to be taking *su* as being compounded with the following noun here and in **256 258**. In **259**, however, *mama* follows *su*, and the cty glosses: *su iti nipāta-mattaṃ*, and the explanation *su* = *sundara* does not occur again. At Thī-a 202,7 (ad **265**) *sobhate* is explained: *atītatthe vattamāna-vacanaṃ*. There can be no doubt that Kern was correct (VG, Vol. XV, p. 169 note) in assuming that *su* was the equivalent of Skt *sma*, and that it could be used, as *sma* in Skt, to turn a present tense verb into a past tense. Cf. **256 258–60 262–69**. See also the notes on **204** and **481**.

Kern suggested reading *khalatī* m.c., but B^e C^e K^e and S^e all read *khalitaṃ* (§70(a)), and there is no doubt that this is the correct reading. Thī-a 200,37–39: *taṃ jarāya khalitaṃ siraṃ katan ti taṃ tathā sobhitaṃ siraṃ idāni jarāya khalitaṃ khaṇḍitākhaṇḍitaṃ vilūna-kesaṃ kataṃ*.

For the – / ⏑ ⏑ equivalence in *veṇihi* see §52(c)(iii). For *veṇîhi* m.c. (with B^e K^e and S^e) see §70(a). For [*a*]*laṅkataṃ* m.c. (with B^e and C^e) see §67(b).

For *sobhate*, glossed *virājate*, in the sense of "looks well on" see BHSD, s.v. *śobhate*.

256. Thī-a 201,1–2: *citta-kāra-sukatā va lekhikā ti citta-kārena sippinā nīlāya vaṇṇa-dhātuyā suṭṭhu katā lekhā viya sobhate*. The confusion *k/t* probably goes back to a version in a dialect which reduced both *-k-* and *-t-* > *-y-*. See the note on **43**. Although the meaning "drawn" makes sense in the context, a better sense is obtained by assuming that *lekhiya* < *lekhya* can have the same meaning as Skt *lekhā*, i.e. "crescent of the moon" (MW, s.v.). This would make an excellent simile for eyebrows.

Thī-a 201,2–3: *su-bhamukā pure mamā ti sundarā bhamukā pubbe mama sobhanaṃ gatā*. For the cty's interpretation of the particle *su* as being compounded with the following noun see the note on **255**.

Although *bhamukā* is plural, the cty makes no reference to *sobhate* being singular. See the note on **259**. Bᵉ reads *sobhare*, i.e. plural.

For *sobhate* m.c. see § 68(a)(i). For ⟨*p*⟩*palambitā* m.c. (with Bᵉ) see § 63(b). Alternatively we could read *valihî* (§ 70(a)). Cᵉ Kᵉ and Sᵉ read *valīhi*, but this is not metrical. Cf. **259**.

257. Thī-a 201,5–7: *bhassarā ti pabhassarā. abhinīla-m-āyatā ti abhinīlā hutvā āyatā ca*. For sandhi *-m-* see the note on **48**.

Bᵉ and Cᵉ read *maṇī*. See the note on **252–70**.

Bᵉ reads *nett' ăhesum*, and we should read this m.c. (§§ 68(b)(iii), 72(b)). For *sobhate* m.c. see § 68(a)(i).

258. Thī-a 201,9–10: *saṇha-tuṅga-sadisī cā ti saṇhā tuṅgā sesa-mukhāvayavānaṃ anurūpā ca*. The cty is, therefore, taking the compound as a dvandva, i.e. "delicate, high, and in keeping with the rest". Theoretically this is quite possible, but since in every other occurrence of *sadisa-* in this poem a comparison is made, I think that on the grounds of style we must assume that a simile is intended here, i.e. "like a *saṇha-tuṅga* (= delicate hill?)". Thī-a 201,10–11: *sobhate ti vaṭṭetvā* (Cᵉ *vaḍḍhetvā*) *ṭhapita-haritāla-vaṭṭi viya mama nāsikā sobhate*. The word is obviously connected with *tuṅga-nāsikā* found in Skt and at S II 284, meaning "with a long or prominent nose". Spk II 120 explains: *tuṅga-nāsā ti laddha-vohāram ghānaṃ vaṭṭetvā ṭhapita-haritāla-vaṭṭi viya maññanti*. Cf. *garul'-āyaya-ujju-tuṅga-nāsa*, Ova 16. I think *tuṅga-nāsa* must mean "[having] a nose which is a *tuṅga*", i.e. long and thin and pointed like a stick of yellow orpiment. The translation given for *tuṅga-nāsa* at PTC II 244 seems to be the result of a confusion with *tuṇḍa-nāsa*. PED does not list *tuṅga* as a noun, but it is found in Skt with the meaning "hill" (MW).

Thī-a 201,11: *su-abhiyobbanaṃ patī ti sundare abhinava-yobbana-kāle*. All the editions except P read *pati* for *paṭi*, and this seems to be the correct spelling for the word when it is used as a postposition (see PTC III 117). It is spelt *pati* in **306 309 317 319**. The phrase *nibbānaṃ pati* occurs in Cᵉ at Thī-a 168,26–27 (ad **212**). See also EV I, p. 229 (ad Th 517). M (v.l.) reads *sati* for *pati*. For the alternation *p*/*s* see the note on **6**.

For *su* see the note on **255**.

Thī-a 201,11–12: *sā nāsikā idāni jarāya nivārita-sobhatāya pariseditā viya varattā viya ca jātā*. The cty therefore understands the verse to mean: her nose, which was long and pointed, has now become like a moistened leather strap, i.e. drooping. PED does not quote this meaning for *parisedita*, but see PED s.v. *sedita*. It is not, however, at all clear how *upakūlita* could get this meaning. We might suppose that *upakūlita* is connected with *upakūla* [IBH], and could perhaps mean "sloping down", just as *ukkūla* means "sloping up, steep, high", i.e. nearly synonymous with *tuṅga*. Nevertheless, as a matter of style we should note that in other pādas c in this poem *-sadisa*, *yathā*, *iva*, and *va* are used only with nouns, not past participles. The likelihood therefore is that *upakūlita* is not a past participle. I venture to suggest, with no great conviction that I am correct, that it is to be derived < Skt *upakulyā* "piper longum". This could develop > **upakuliyā*, and then > **upakulitā* (for the alternation *y/t* see the note on **43**). The change *-u-* > *-ū-* would then be m.c. The meaning would be that her nose looks like the fruit spike of a long pepper. This is described by Bentley and Trimen (p. 244) as follows: "Fruit … fused together into a solid, cylindrical, slightly tapering, reddish-brown, spike-like cone about 1½″ long and ¼″ thick." This is not too much of a contrast with a stick of yellow orpiment as the description of a nose, and yet clearly would indicate a deterioration.

259. Thī-a 201,13–14: *kaṅkaṇam va sukataṃ suniṭṭhitan ti suparikamma-kataṃ suvaṇṇa-kaṅkaṇaṃ viya. vaṭṭula-bhāvaṃ sandhāya vadati*. The reference is, then, to the roundness of her earlobes.

In pāda b B^e reads *sobhare*. Thī-a 201,14–15: *sobhate* (B^e *sobhare*) *ti sobhante. sobhante ti vā pāṭho*. It is strange that the cty did not make a similar gloss on **256**. See the notes on **256** and **265**.

It was clearly impossible for the cty to take *su mama* as a compound, which explains the gloss: *su iti, nipāta-mattaṃ* (see the note on **255**). It may be that the cty did not realise until this verse that *su* could not be part of a compound. Although *su* recurs in all the remaining verses of this poem except **261** and **270**, the cty does not again explain *su* as *sundara*.

Thī-a 201,15–16: *kaṇṇa-pāliyo* (B^e *-pāḷiyo*) *ti kaṇṇa-pattā* (B^e *-gaṅghā*). PED does not list *pāli* (cf. Skt *pāli* "ear-lobe" (MW)) s.v. *pāli*, but it does occur s.v. *kaṇṇa*. I do not understand the gloss in B^e.

Thī-a 201,16–17: *valihi palambitā ti tahiṃ tahiṃ uppanna-valihi valitā hutvā vaḍḍhaniyā paṇāmita-cattha-khandhā viya bhassantā* (C^e *āsannā*) *olambanti*.

For *sobhate* m.c. see § 68(a)(i). For [*pure*] m.c. (with B^e and C^e) see § 67(b). For ⟨*p*⟩*palambita* m.c. (with B^e) see § 63(b). Alternatively we could read *valihî* (§ 70(a)). C^e (lemma) K^e and S^e read *valīhi*, but this is not metrical. Cf. **256**.

260. Thī-a 201,18–19: *pattali-makula-vaṇṇa-sadisā ti kadali-*(C^e^ *kandali-*) *makula-sadisā vaṇṇā*. Kern (1916B, p. 35) suggested reading *sattali-* for *pattali-* (for the alternation *p/s* see the note on **6**), doubtless because *sattali* at Ja IV 440 is explained: *kandala-puppha* (Ja IV 442). In a description of teeth a reference to the *kandala* would be very appropriate as having white flowers (see MW, s.v.), and the word is so employed in Jain literature, e.g. *kaṃdala-siliṃdha-dantā* "having white tusks" as an epithet of elephants (Nāyā-dhamma-kahāo 9.87 = Sutt. I, p. 1039). At Vism 253 *te sabbe pi kandala-makula-saṇṭhānā* is used of shape rather than colour. Ñāṇamoli translates (1956, p. 272): "[sinews] all the shape of yam shoots". See also the note on **263**. For *sattali* see PED (s.v.).

The cty makes no comment upon *sobhate* or *su*. B^e^ reads *sobhare*. For *su* see the note on **255**.

B^e^ and C^e^ read *khaṇḍitā* for *khaṇḍā*. Thī-a 201,19: *khaṇḍitā ti bhedana-patanehi khaṇḍitā khaṇḍa-bhāvaṃ gatā*.

B^e^ reads *cāsitā* for *yava-pītakā*, and C^e^ reads *ca pītakā*. The reading of B^e^ does not seem to be metrical. Thī-a 201,19–20: *pītakā* (B^e^ *asitā*) *ti vaṇṇa-bhedena pīta-*(B^e^ *asita-*)*bhāvaṃ gatā*. If either B^e^ or C^e^ is correct, it is not easy to see how P's reading came about. I would suggest that we read *khaṇḍiyā va pītakā*, where *khaṇḍiyā* is a past participle taken from a dialect where *-t-* > *-y-*. For the alternation *t/y* see the note on **43**. I take *va* to equal *eva*, although *ca* (with C^e^) would be possible. For the alternation *c/v* see the note on **12**. We must read *kha[ṇ]ḍiyā* m.c. (§ 68(a)(ii)). Alternatively we could read *khaṇḍā va pītakā*, but this would not explain the presence of the syllable *ya* in P.

For the alternation ⏑̄/⏑ ⏑ in *dantā* (and in *khaṇḍā* if the last suggestion is followed) see § 52(c)(iii).

For *pattalî-* and *-sâdisā* m.c. (with B^e^ and C^e^) see § 70(a).

Kern suggested reading *khaṇḍā vipītakā*, and for *vipītakā* compared Skt *vipaṇḍu*, *vibaṇḍura*, *vipāṭala*, and *vilohita*. Bollée suggests *khaṇḍă ca pītakā*, but the metre of this does not seem to be entirely satisfactory.

For *sobhate* m.c. see § 68(a)(i).

261. Thī-a 201,21–23: *kānanamhi vana-saṇḍa-cārinī kokilā va madhuraṃ nikūji 'han ti vana-saṇḍe gocara-caraṇena* (C^e^ *gocaraṃ caratī ti*) *vana-saṇḍa-cārinī kānane anusaṅgīta-nivāsinī kokilā viya madhurālāpaṃ nikūji 'haṃ kathesiṃ ahaṃ* (B^e^ omits). It seems clear that Dhammapāla was interpreting whatever reading he had as a first person singular aorist, and yet on grounds of style I would reject the reading *nikūji 'haṃ* (or Bollée's suggestion *nikūjisaṃ*). Pāda c begins with *taṃ* (glossed: *tan ti taṃ nikūjitaṃ ālāpaṃ*), and since in every other verse the pronoun at the beginning of pāda c refers back to the noun in pādas ab, I think that we must read a neuter noun in pāda b of this verse, and assume that *nikūji 'haṃ* has crept into the verse from the gloss. I concede that this then strains the sense somewhat, since we must translate "sweet was my warbling, like a kokila", whereas we should expect "sweet was my warbling, like a kokila's". I do not, however, think that this presents any great difficulty. The replacement of *nikūjitaṃ* by *nikūji 'haṃ* was probably helped by the fact that there are other examples in Thī of a confusion between the suffix *-itaṃ* and the aorist ending *-i 'haṃ*, e.g. P's v.l. *āsevitaṃ* for *āsevi 'haṃ* **93**, M (text) *avekkhitaṃ* and P's v.l. *taṃ* for *'haṃ* after *apekkhi* **222**, P's v.l. *taṃ* for *'haṃ* after *āsevi* **435**.

For the use of the past participle as an action noun see EV I, p. 143 (ad Th 36). For other examples in Thī cf. *paṭiladdha* at Thī-a 12,22 (ad **5**), *jāta* at Thī-a 213,18 (ad **294**), *pabbajita* **363**, *apaccavekkhita* **387**, *akkuṭṭha-vandita* **388**, *bhatti-kata* **413**, *abhinandita* **458**, *socita* **462**, *āgata-bhāva* at Thī-a 260,26 (ad **480**), *saṃsarita* **496**, *paṭimukka* **500**. See also the note on **80**. Cf. *uppanna-kālato* Ja II 415. For *nikūjita* cf. Mvu III 438 and Jones' note (III 440, n. 7).

PED does not list *anusaṅgita*, which occurs in the cty's explanation, and the meaning given in CPD (s.v.) does not suit here.

Thī-a 201,24–25: *khalitaṃ tahiṃ tahin ti khaṇḍa-dantādi-bhāvena tattha tattha pakkhalitaṃ jātaṃ*. PED does not list *pakkhalita*.

For *kānanasmi[ṃ]* m.c or *kānanamhi* (with Bᵉ and Cᵉ) see § 68(b)(ii).

262. Bᵉ and Cᵉ read *-kambu-r-iva* for *-kampurī va*, and in view of the existence of the compound *kambu-gīva* (see PED, s.v. *kambu*) this reading must be correct. Kᵉ and Sᵉ, however, read *saṇṭhakaṃmudī va*. Thī-a 201,26–27: *suṭṭhu pamajjitā saṇhā suvaṇṇa-saṅkhā viya*. For sandhi *-r-* see the note on **3**.

All editions except P read *vināmitā* for *vināsitā*. Thī-a 201,27–28: *bhaggā vināmitā ti maṃsa-parikkhayena vibhūta-sirā-jālatāya bhaggā hutvā vinatā*. For the alternation *m/s*, cf. *viharessasi* / *viharemasi* **375**.

For the alternation –/⏑ ⏑ in *gīvā* and *bhaggā* see § 52(c)(iii).

For *-kambu-r-ĭva* m.c. see § 72(b).

For *su* see the note on **255**.

263. Thī-a 201,29–30: *vaṭṭa-paligha-sadisopamā ti vaṭṭena parigha-daṇḍena sama-samā. tā ti tā ubho pi bāhāyo*. The cty makes no reference to the singular verb *sobhate* with a plural subject. Bᵉ reads *sobhare*.

Bᵉ reads *pāṭali-bbalitā* and Cᵉ Kᵉ and Sᵉ read *pāṭali-ppalitā* for *pāṭalī dubbalikā*. All three readings are unmetrical. Thī-a 201,30–31: *jajjara-bhāvena palita-pāṭalī-sākhā-sadisā*. I am not certain what the cty is trying to explain, but on the assumption that a contrast is intended between the former state of her arms ("as strong as door-bars") and their present weak state, I should like to read *abalikā*, on which P's *dubbalikā* could be a gloss. I conjecture that the pāda could have been *tā jarāy' abalikā va pāṭalī*. I do not know why the *pāṭalī* should be chosen as a symbol of weakness. The *kadalī* would be more appropriate, and it could be that the original had *pattalī* (for *sattāli* (see the note on **260**)). The cty would then be explaining that her arms were weak and shrivelled like the plantain after it had fruited (following M's reading *phalitā*). A pun could be intended with the alternative meaning of *phalita* "broken" [IBH].

For the alternation *k/t* see the note on **43**.

Kern suggested reading *yathă pāṭalī-viṭā*, comparing Skt *viṭa* in *viṭapa*. For *yathă* m.c. (with Bᵉ) see § 72(b). For *sobhate* m.c. see § 68(a)(i).

For the alternation –/⏑ ⏑ in *bāhā* see § 52(c)(iii). For the alternation ⏑ ⏑/– in *-paligha-* see § 52(c)(i).

For *su* see the note on **255**.

264. Thī-a 202,1–2: *saṇha-muddikā-suvaṇṇa-maṇḍitā ti suvaṇṇa-mayāhi maṭṭha-bhāsurāhi muddikāhi vibhūsitā*. As in the case of **255** it would be possible to separate *saṇha-muddikā* from the remainder of the compound (with Kᵉ and Sᵉ) and take it as a bahuvrīhi compound agreeing with *hatthā*.

Thī-a 202,2–3: *yathā mūla-mūlikā ti mūlaka-kanda-sadisā*. Bᵉ reads *-kaṇḍa-* and Cᵉ reads *-khanda-*, but in view of *mūlaka-kanda* at Ja IV 88 491 Dhp-a IV 78 *-kanda-* must be the correct reading.

The cty does not comment on *sobhate*. Bᵉ reads *sobhare*.

For the alternation –/⏑ ⏑ in *hatthā* see § 52(c)(iii).

For *-muddikă-* m.c. (with Bᵉ and Cᵉ) and *yathă* m.c. (with Kern) see § 72(b). For *sobhate* m.c. see § 68(a)(i).

For *su* see the note on **255**.

265. Bᵉ and Cᵉ read *-sahit'-* for *-pahit'-*. For the alternation *p/s* see the note on **6**. Thī-a 202,4–5: *pīna-vaṭṭa-sahit'-uggatā ti pīnā vaṭṭā aññamaññaṃ sahitā va hutvā uggatā uddha-mukhā*. For *sahita* cf. **254**.

Thī-a 202,5–6: *sobhate su thanakā pure maman ti mama ubho pi thanā yathā-vutta-rūpā hutvā suvaṇṇa-kalasiyo* (M *-kalāpiyo*) *viya sobhiṃsu*. PED does not list the feminine form *kalasī*. For the alternation *p/s* see the note on **6**.

Bᵉ reads *sobhare* in the text, but *sobhate* in the lemma. The latter reading is essential because the cty explains: *puthutte hi idaṃ eka-vacanaṃ, atītatthe ca vattamāna-vacanaṃ*. It is clear from this that we should read *sobhate* in each verse, with both singular and plural subjects, and B^e is consequently wrong to read *sobhare*. The editors who introduced that reading did not realise that *sobhate can* be plural as well as singular if we assume that it stands for *sobha(n)te*, with the short nasalised vowel. It is very likely that in other contexts where editors have introduced the third plural middle ending *-are* m.c. it would be more correct to retain *-ante* (> *-ate* m.c.), e.g. *nhāyare* **469** *dissare* **475**.

B^e and C^e read *thevikī*, and K^e and S^e read *therī ti* for *te rindī*, but, as Bollée says, on stylistic grounds we should expect a demonstrative pronoun in pāda c. The cty explains: *te ubho pi me thanā anudakā gaḷita-jalā veṇu-daṇḍake ṭhapita-udaka-bhastā viya lambanti*. Morris (1884, p. 94) suggested *rindī was a* mistake for *rittī (va)* = *rittā iva*. Kern (VG, II, pp. 247–48) thought *rindī* was the correct reading, and he derived the word < *dr̥ti*. Bollée suggests reading **ditī* < *dr̥ti*. Th-a III 159,19 (ad Th 1134) glosses: *bhastan ti ruttiṃ*. This seems to me to indicate that there was a word in Pāli which began with *r-* and contained a doubled or nasalised dental group, and meant "water-bag". I can suggest no etymology for this *rindī*/*rutti* word, and the variations in spelling may well indicate that it is not of Indo-Aryan origin.

For *sobhate* m.c. see § 68(a)(i). For *ri[n]dī* m.c. (with Kern) see § 68(a)(ii). For *lambanti* m.c. (with B^e) or *lambantĕ* (with Bollée) see § 72(b).

For *su* see the note on **255**.

For the alternation –/⏑ ⏑ in *lambante* see § 52(c)(iii).

266. Thī-a 202,10–11: *kañcanassa phalakaṃ va sammaṭṭhan* (C^e *sumaṭṭan*) *ti jāti-hiṅgulakena makkhitvā cira-parimajjita-sovaṇṇa-phalakaṃ viya sobhate*.

Thī-a 202,11–13: *so valīhi sukhumāhi otato ti so mama kāyo idāni sukhumāhi valīhi tahiṃ tahiṃ vitato vali-ttacataṃ āpanno*.

For the alternation –/⏑ ⏑ in *kāyo* see § 52(c)(iii).

For *saṃ-* m.c. (with B^e) or *sû-* m.c. see § 70(a). For *-ma[ṭ]ṭhaṃ* m.c. see § 65(b). Bollée reads *-măṭṭhaṃ*, which is merely a different way of indicating the same phenomenon, i.e. the reading of a short vowel before a doubled consonant. For *valîhi* m.c. (with B^e C^e K^e and S^e) see § 70(a).

For *su* see the note on **255**.

267. Thī-a 202,14–15: *nāga-bhoga-sadisopamā ti hatthi-nāgassa hatthena sama-samā. hattho hi idha bhuñjati etenā ti bhogo ti vutto*. Neither MW nor PED lists *bhoga* in the sense of "elephant's trunk", although MW quotes *bhuja* in the senses of "trunk of an elephant" and "coil [of a serpent]". That "elephant's trunk" is the correct interpretation here, rather than "snake's coil", cf. *nāga-nāsa-samūpamā ūrū*, Ja V 155, and such adjectives as Pāli *karabhoru* "[a woman] with beautiful thighs" (see PED, s.v. *karabha*), and BHS *gaja-bhuja-saṃnibha-ūruṇikā* "having thighs like an elephant's trunk" (see BHSD, s.v. *-ūruṇikā*).

For *sobhate* m.c. see § 68(a)(i). For *yathă* m.c. (with Kern) see § 72(b).

For *su* see the note on **255**.

For the alternation –/⌣ ⌣ in *ūrū* see § 52(c)(iii).

268. Thī-a 202,17–18: *saṇha-nūpura-suvaṇṇa-maṇḍitā ti siniddha-maṭṭhehi* (Cᵉ *-maṭṭehi*) *suvaṇṇa-nūpurehi vibhūsitā*. As in **255** and **264** we could separate *saṇha-nūpura* from the rest of the compound, assume that *-nūpura* is m.c. for *-nūpurā*, and translate it as a bahuvrīhi compound.

Thī-a 202,18–20: *tila-daṇḍakā-r-ivā ti appa-maṃsa-lohitattā kisa-bhāvena lūnā-vasiṭṭha-visukkha-tila-daṇḍakā viya ahesuṃ. ra-kāro pada-sandhi-karo.* For sandhi *-r-* see the note on **3**.

For *sobhate* m.c. see § 68(a)(i). Bᵉ reads *sobhare*.

For *su* see the note on **255**.

For the alternation –/⌣ ⌣ in jaṅgahā see § 52(c)(iii).

269. Thī-a 202,21–22: *tūla-puṇṇa-sadisopamā ti mudu-siniddha-bhāvena simbali-tūla-puṇṇa-paliguṇṭhita-upāhaṇa-sadisā*. For shoes stuffed with cotton wool cf. *tūla-puṇṇikā* and *pāliguṇṭhima* at Vin I 186.

Bᵉ and Cᵉ read *phuṭitā* for *phuṭikā*. For the alternation *k*/*t* see the note on **43**. Thī-a 202,22–23: *te mama pādā idāni phuṭitā phalitā*. PED states (s.v. *phalita*²) that *phalita* is found only in the phrase *hadayaṃ phalitaṃ*. Cf. BHS *sphuṭita-pāṇi-pādāni* (BHSD, s.v. *utpāṇḍūtpāṇḍu*(*ka*)).

Thī-a 202,23: *valīmatā valimanto jātā*. For *valī-* m.c. see § 69(a). For *-matā* and *sobhate* m.c. see § 68(a)(i). Bᵉ reads *sobhare*.

For *su* see the note on **255**.

For the alternation –/⌣ ⌣ in *pādā* see § 52(c)(iii).

270. Thī-a 202,25: *jajjaro ti sithilābhandho*.

Thī-a 202,26–28: *so 'palepa-patito ti so ayaṃ samussayo apalepa-patito. abhisaṅkhārālepa-parikkhayena patito pātābhimukho ti attho. so pi alepa-patito ti vā pada-vibhāgo so ev' attho*. PED (s.v. *apalepa*) says that we should read *palepa-*, not *'palepa-*, here, but the cty seems to show that this view is incorrect. Morris (1886, p. 126) suggested reading *avalepa*. CPD quotes neither *apalepa* nor *avalepa*, but does list *avalepana* "daubing, plastering" and *avalitta* "be-daubed". For the alternation *p*/*v* see the note on **84**.

Thī-a 202,29–30: *jarā-gharo ti jiṇṇa-ghara-sadiso. jarāya vā ghara-bhūto ahosi*. For the comparison between the body and a house cf. Th 183–84.

Thī-a 202,33–36: *evaṃ ayaṃ therī attano atta-bhāve aniccatāya salla-kkhaṇa-mukhena sabbesu pi te-bhūmaka-dhammesu aniccataṃ upadhāretvā tad-anusārena tattha dukkha-lakkhaṇaṃ ananta-lakkhaṇaṃ ca āropetvā vipassanaṃ ussukkāpentī magga-paṭipāṭiyā arahattaṃ pāpuni.* Although quoting BHS *ātma-bhāva* in the sense "body" (see BHSD s.v.), PED does not quote any examples for Pali (s.v. *atta*). See CPD (s.v. *atta-bhāva*) and the notes on **86** and **284**.

For *ahu* see § 71 and the note on **43**. For *-du[k]khānam* m.c. (with Bᵉ) see § 65(b).

271–90. The introductory story to these verses tells how Rohiṇī was born into a brahman family, and having become a Buddhist had the discussion with her father which she later remembered in her verses. As a result of her replies her father too became a Buddhist. The cty states that the first three verses were originally uttered by her father, the next twelve by Rohiṇī, and **286–87** by her father. The cty does not comment on **288–90**, but we may deduce that Rohiṇī uttered **288**, and her father **289–90** (§ 2).

In one verse at least (**283**) Rohiṇī's reply seems to be a direct attack upon normal brahmanical customs. For such anti-brahmanical utterances see the note on **87–91**.

271. Pāda a presents difficulties. P's reading *vipassi* makes no sense, while B^e reads *supi* for *maṃ vipassi* and C^e reads *tvaṃ sayasi*. Some such reading makes good sense, i.e. "you fall asleep and you wake up saying 'ascetics'". The explanations in the various editions of Thī-a 206,22–24 are equally diverse. WP and B^e explain: *supi, supana-kāle supasi*. C^e explains: *sayasi, sayana-kāle sayasi*. Thī-a 206,33–34 (ad **272**), however, states: *sayantī pi pabujjhantī pi aññadā pi*. This would seem to support the reading *sayasi* of C^e, but it is then very difficult to explain how P's reading came into existence. In Skt there exists *vi-svap-* (MW, s.v.) with the meaning "fall asleep", from which a form **vissapati* could have evolved in Pāli. The gloss in the cty would then have been *vissapi*, *sayana-kāle supasi*, and the existing versions could all have evolved from this. B^e has generalised *sup-* in verse and cty, giving a normalised eight-syllable pāda, and producing a noun *supana* which is not listed in PED. C^e has generalised *say-* thoughout. The tradition behind P has at some stage produced *vipassi* by metathesis from *vissapi*. For such metathesis in the Aśokan inscriptions see Hultzsch (p. 38, n. 17); for examples in Pāli see Lüders (1954, § 105) and Brough (GDhp, p. 218), and cf. *yajetha* in Dhp 106 with *jayeta* in Mvu III 434. Cf. EV I, p. 205 (ad Th 316) and p. 261 (ad Th 738).

In P's text *maṃ* is hyper-metrical, and was possibly inserted to provide an object for *vipassi*. Cᵉ has inserted *tvaṃ* from the cty.

Thī-a 206,26–27: *samaṇānam eva kittesī ti sabba-kālam pi samaṇe eva samaṇānam eva vā guṇe kittesi abhitthavasi*. PED says nothing about the case used with *kitteti*, but it is found with the accusative and genitive in Skt and with the genitive at M I 146 (*kittayamāno*, middle, as rarely in Skt (see MW, s.v. *kīrt-*)).

Thī-a 206,27–30 gives two interpretations of pāda d: *samanī nūna bhavissasī ti gihī-rūpena ṭhitā pi cittena* (M *vicittena* (for the alternation *p/v* see the note on **84**)) *samaṇī eva maññe bhavissasi. atha vā samaṇī nūna bhavissasi ti idāni gihī-rūpena ṭhitā pi na ciren' eva samaṇī eva maññe bhavissasi samaṇesu eva ninna-poṇa-bhāvato.*

There is resolution of the first syllable of all four pādas (§60). Bᵉ normalises pādas abc: pāda a is mentioned above; pāda b is normalised by reading *pa[tī]bujjhasi*; pāda c is normalised by reading *samaṇān-[am] eva*. There is resolution of the seventh syllable in Cᵉ's version of pāda b. This, I must admit, is support for the belief that Cᵉ has the correct version, since a scribal emendation is not likely to have introduced a reading involving resolution.

272. Cᵉ reads *payacchasi* for *pavecchasi* (cf. P's vv.ll. *sayacchasi* (for the alternation *p/s* see the note on **6**) and *pavacchasi*). If this reading is genuine it would support Trenckner's suggestion (see PED s.v. *pavecchati*) that *pavecchati* is to be derived < *payacchati* (see also Kern, VG II pp. 258–60). None of the other suggestions given in PED is convincing. If Trenckner is correct, *pavecchati* is presumably a borrowing from another dialect, since Pali does not usually palatalise *a* > *e* after *y*, although this change is common in GDhp (see Brough, §22(a)), nor is the change *-y-* > *-v-* very common although it does occur, usually in contact with *u*, e.g. *āvudha* < *āyudha*, *āvuso* < *āyusmant-*, *pubba* < **pū-va* < *pūya*. The change *-y-* > *-v-* is, however, normal in the Eastern dialect underlying the Aśokan inscriptions (see Norman, 1970, pp. 140–41).

For *Rohiṇî* m.c. (with Bᵉ) to avoid the opening ⏓ ⏑ ⏑ – see §70(e) and the note on **10**. Since we require a vocative here we should probably read *Rohiṇīdāni*, and assume it is for *Rohiṇi* + *idāni*.

There is resolution of the first syllable in pāda a (§60).

273. Thī-a 207,2–3: *akamma-kāmā ti na kamma-kārā attano paresaṃ ca atthāva-haṃ kiñci kammaṃ na kātu-kāmā.*

Thī-a 207,4–5: *āsamsukā ti tato eva ghāsa-cchādanādīnaṃ āsiṃsanakā*. M, however, explains: *tato vuḍḍhā pajānanādinaṃ āsiṃsanakā.*

274. For *cirassaṃ* see EV I, pp. 280 foll. (ad Th 868).

Thī-a 207,12–13: *samaṇānan ti samaṇe. samaṇānaṃ vā mayhaṃ piyāyutabbaṃ* (Cᵉ *piyāyitaṃ*) *paripucchasi.* The cty seems confused by the genitive case of *samaṇānaṃ*. In Skt *paripracch-* is constructed with the accusative of the person asked, and the locative or genitive, or *prati* + the accusative, of the thing asked (MW, s.v.).

Thī-a 207,13–14: *paññā-sīla-parakkaman ti paññañ ca sīlañ ca ussāhañ ca.*

In pāda b there is resolution of the first syllable (§ 60).

275. Thī-a 207,20–22: *taṃ pana kammaṃ seṭṭhaṃ uttamaṃ nibbānāvahaṃ eva karontī ti kamma-seṭṭhassa kārakā. karontā pana taṃ paṭupattiyā avañjha-*(Bᵉ *anavajja-*)*bhāvato rāgaṃ dosaṃ pajahanti.*

276. Thī-a 207,25–26: *tīṇi pāpassa mūlānī ti lobha-dosa-moha-saṅkhātāni akusalassa tīṇi mūlāni. dhunantī ti nicchādenti* (Bᵉ and Cᵉ *nigghātenti*) *pajahantī ti attho.* PED does not list *nigghāteti*. The fact that *nicchādeti* (= *nicchodeti*) occurs in context with *nidhunāti* (see PED s.v. *nicchodeti*) possibly supports M's reading against Bᵉ and Cᵉ.

For *esaṃ* (= genitive plural of the demonstrative pronoun) see Geiger (2000, § 108 and EV I, p. 257 (ad Th 705).

278. Thī-a 207,31–32: *vimalā saṅkha-muttā vā ti sudhota-saṅkhā viya muttā viya ca vigata-malā rāgādi-mala-rahitā*, i.e. *saṅkha-muttā* is taken as a dvandva compound. PED (s.v. *saṅkha*¹) gives only the translation "mother-of-pearl", which I adopt, but in Skt *śaṅkha-muktā* has both this meaning and that of a dvandva (MW, s.v. *śaṅkha*).

Cᵉ Kᵉ and Sᵉ read *sukkehi dhammehi* for *sukkāna dhammānaṃ*, but by the principle of lectio difficilior we should retain P's reading. There is, however, no need to doubt the reading, since *pūreti* is constructed with both the genitive and the instrumental (see PED, s.v.). PED (s.v. *puṇṇa*) states that *puṇṇa* is found by itself only at D I 47 (= Sn p. 139), but cf. *pānīyena puṇṇaṃ* Pv-a 251.

For *dhamma* see the note on **3**.

For *sukkāna* m.c. to avoid the cadence – , – – ⏓ with the opening ⏓ – – – see § 68(b)(i) and the note on **28**.

279. Thī-a 208,3–5: *sutta-geyyādi bahuṃ sutaṃ etesaṃ, sutena vā* (M ca (for the alternation *c*/*v* see the note on **12**)) *uppannā ti bahussutā. pariyatti-bāhusaccena paṭivedha-bāhusaccena ca samannāgatā ti attho.*

Thī-a 208,6: *sattānaṃ ācāra-samācāra-sikkh-padena arīyantī ti ariyā.*

Thī-a 208,7–9: *attham dhammaṃ ca desentī ti bhāsitatthaṃ ca desanā-dhammaṃ ca kathenti pakāsenti. atha vā atthato anapetaṃ dhammato anapetaṃ ca desenti ācikkhanti.*

For *dhamma-ddharā* see § 64(a). All editions except P read *-dharā.*

280. For *dhamma-ddharā* see § 64(a). All editions except P read *-dharā.*

In pāda c there is resolution of the sixth syllable (§ 60).

281. Thī-a 208,11–13: *dūraṃ-gamā ti arañña-gatā; manussûpacāraṃ muñcitvā dūraṃ gacchantā. iddhānubhāvena vā yathā-rucitaṃ dūrā-ṭṭhānaṃ gacchantī ti dūraṃ-gamā.*

Thī-a 208,13: *mantā vuccati paññā. tāya bhaṇana-sīlatāya manta-bhāṇī.* For *manta-bhāṇin* and *anuddhaṭā* see EV I, p. 130 (ad Th 2).

For *satîmanto* m.c. to give the cadence ⏑ – – ⏓ (*pathyā*) see § 70(e).

282. Thī-a 208,17–18: *na vilokenti* (C[e] *nāvalokenti*) *kiñcanan ti yato gāmato pakka-manti tasmiṃ gāme kañci* (C[e] *kiñci*) *sattaṃ vā saṅkhāraṃ vā apekkhā-vasena na olokenti.* This seems to support the reading *nāvalokenti.* I take *avaloketi* here in the sense of *apaloketi.* For the confusion between *apa-* and *ava-* see CPD, s.v. *apaloketi.*

The relative pronoun would seem here to have the value of *si quis* as sometimes in Skt (see MW, s.v. *yad,* and BHSD s.v. *utpadyati*). This usage is not mentioned in PED. See also the note on **471**.

283. Thī-a 208,20–22: *na te saṃ koṭṭhe osentī ti te samaṇā saṃ attano santakaṃ sāpateyyaṃ koṭṭhe na osenti na paṭisāmetvā ṭhapenti. tādisassa parigga-hassa abhāvato.* Spk I 353 (ad S I 236) explains: *na te saṃ koṭṭhe opentī ti na te sam santakaṃ dhaññaṃ koṭṭhe pakkhipanti, na hi etesaṃ dhannñam atthi.* For *oseti* see EV I, pp. 166 foll. (ad Th 119). For the alternation *p/s* see the note on **6**.

Thī-a 208,22: *kumbhin ti kumbhiyaṃ.* S I 236 reads *kumbhā,* with vv.ll. *kumbhi* and *kumbhī.* Spk I 353 explains: *na kumbhyā ti na kumbhiyaṃ,* with vv.ll. *kkumbhī* and *kumbhe.* For the locative of *kumbhī* we should expect *kumbhiyaṃ* (see **1**). This would have become *kumbhyaṃ* here m.c., which in turn could have become *kumbhaṃ* (see Geiger (2000, § 86.2) and cf. *Naliññaṃ* Ja VI 33)). A scribe who thought that *kumbhaṃ* was a strange form to emerge from *kumbhī* could well have "corrected" to *kumbhiṃ* to maintain the vowel *-i-*. We thus have a locative form which is identical with the accusative, just as in the case of *Rohiṇiyaṃ* in Th 529 we have an accusative which looks like a locative. I misunderstood this form in EV I (1st ed.), p. 206 (see CPD, p. 549, s.v. *ajī*). Cf. *gantvāna Buddho nadiyaṃ Kakuṭṭhaṃ,* D II 135 Ud 84.

Thī-a 208,22–23: *kaḷopiyan ti pacchiyaṃ.* Spk I 353 agrees.

Thī-a 208,23–24: *pariniṭṭitam esānā ti para-kulesu paresaṃ atthāya siddham eva ghāsaṃ-pariyesantā.* Spk I 353 explains: *para-niṭṭhitam esānā ti paresaṃ niṭṭhitaṃ, para-ghare pakkaṃ bhikkhācāra-vattena esamānā, gavesamānā.* The similarity of the explanations makes it look as though Dhammapāla is reading *para-* instead of *pari-* (cf. S I 236). It is, however, likely that *pariniṭṭhitam* is the correct reading, for a very similar verse occurs in the Jain text Utt:

paresu ghāsam esejjā bhoyaṇe pariṇiṭṭhie;
laddhe piṃḍe aladdhe vā nāṇutappejja paṃḍie. (2.30)

Jacobi, presumably following the cty, translates (SBE, XLV, p. 13) "when his dinner is ready", confirming the Pāli cty's explanation *siddhaṃ*. PED is wrong in stating that *siddha* is a specific Pāli formation from *sijjati* (< *svid-*). The meaning "cooked" is merely a specialised one of *siddha* "ended, accomplished", and is found in Skt (see MW, s.v. *siddha* and BHSD, s.v. *siddhaka*).

The whole of this verse seems to be a direct denial of the first half of Manu 4.7:

kusūla-dhānyako vā syāt kumbhī-dhānyaka eva vā;
try-ahaihiko vāpi bhaved aśvastanika eva vā.

The inclusion of "granary" and "pot" (*kumbhī* in both Skt and Pāli) could be a conscious reminiscence of the instruction in Manu or some comparable brahmanical text, which would be known to the daughter of a brahman. Rohiṇī is therefore alluding directly to the fact that the Buddhists rejected the brahmanical practice. For similar attacks upon brahmanical practices see the note on **87–91**.

For bhikkhus, storing up food in this way was a *pācittiya* offence: *yo pana bhikkhu sannidhi-kārakaṃ khādaniyaṃ vā bhojaniyaṃ vā khādeyya vā bhuñjeyya vā, pacittiyan ti,* Vin IV 87 [IBH].

For *sa*[*ṃ*] m.c to give the opening ⏓ – ⏑ – with the cadence –, – – ⏓ see § 68(b)(ii) and the note on **28**.

284. Thī-a 208,25: *hiraññan ti kahāpaṇaṃ. rūpiyan ti rajataṃ.* For bhikkhus, receiving gold and silver in this way was a *nissaggiya* offence: *yo pana bhikkhu jātarūpa-rajataṃ uggaṇheyya vā uggaṇhāpeyya vā upanikkhittam vā sādiyeyya, nissaggiyaṃ pācittiyan ti,* Vin III 237 [IBH].

Thī-a 208,25–27: *paccuppannena yāpentī ti atītaṃ ananusocantā anāgataṃ ca apaccāsiṃsantā paccuppannena yāpenti attā-bhāvaṃ pavattenti.* For *atta-bhāva* see the note on **270**. The cty's explanation is a reminiscence of S I 5 (as Mrs Rhys Davids points out (Sist., p. 127, n. 2)):

atītam nānusocanti na ppajappanti 'nāgataṃ
paccuppannena yāpenti tena vaṇṇo pasīdati.

In BHS *pratyutpanna* occurs with the same meaning as *utpanna*, and I think the same meaning is to be seen here, rather than "present", i.e. "they live by [whatever] arises". Spk I 28 (ad S I 5) explains: *paccuppannenā ti yena kenaci taṃkhaṇe laddhena yāpenti.*

285. Thī-a 208,28: *aññamaññam piyāyantī ti aññamaññasmiṃ mettiṃ karonti.*

For *nānā-kula* see EV I, p. 238 (ad Th 567), and cf. *nānā-nāmā, -gottā, -jaccā,* and *-kulā* at Vin II 139.

286. Pādas cd recur at S I 34, where, however, *buddhe pasannā* replaces *saddhā buddhe ca.*

For *câ* m.c. to avoid the opening ⏓ – ⏑ – in pāda d see § 70(e) and the note on **74**.

287. Thī-a 208,32–33: *amhaṃ pī ti amhākam pi. dakkhiṇan ti deyya-dhammaṃ. etthā ti samaṇesu etesu. yañño ti dāna-dhammo. vipulo ti vipula-phalo.*

288–89. See the note on **249–50**.

290. See the note on **251**.

For *br-* not making position in *brāhmaṇo* see § 74(a). For *nh-* not making position in *nhātako* see § 74(e) and the note on **251**.

291–311. This set of verses consists of a dialogue between Cāpā and her husband, called Upaka in the introductory story, but Kāḷa in the verses. Verses **291–92 294 296 299 301 303 305–6 308** were uttered by her husband, and **293 295 297–8 300 302 304 307** by Cāpā (§ 2). Verses **309–11** round off the dialogue by relating Kāḷa's subsequent actions, and could well have been added by the *saṅgīti-kārā* (§ 5), although the cty makes no reference to this. Thī-a 211,13 accounts for the inclusion of the husband's verses with Cāpā's: *pubbe Upakena attanā ca kathita-gāthāyo udāna-vasena ekajjhaṃ katvā imā gāthā abhāsi* (§ 4).

For the geographical references in this group of verses see § 37 and Mrs Rhys Davids' note (Sist., p. 133 note 1).

291. This verse probably follows immediately after Rohiṇī's because of the jingle between **290**ab and **291**ab (§ 13(a)).

Thī-a 212,33–34: *āsāyā ti taṇhāya. āsiyā ti pi pāṭho. ajjhāsaya-hetū ti attho. palipā ti kāma-paṅkato diṭṭhi-paṅkato ca.* Th-a I 198,7–9 (ad Th 89) explains: *palipā ti gambhīra-puthulo mahā-kaddamo. asuci-bhavāpād-anena cittassa makkhanato palipo viyā ti palipo.*

Thī-a 212,35–36: *na sakkhi pāram etase ti tass' eva palipassa pāra-bhūtaṃ nibbānaṃ etuṃ gantuṃ na sakkhi na abhisambhunī ti.* B^e^ and C^e^ read *etave* for *etase*, but this is probably later normalisation.

For *so* with a first person verb see the note on **24**.

292. Thī-a 213,1–5: *sumattaṃ maṃ maññamānā ti attani suṭṭhu mattaṃ mada-ppattaṃ kāma-gedha-vasena laggaṃ pamattaṃ vā katvā maṃ sallakkhantī.* Neither PED nor MW lists *sumatta*, but *matta* occurs in Skt with the meaning "excited by sensual passion or desire" (MW, s.v.), and *sammatta* occurs with the meaning "enraptured, enamoured" (MW, s.v.). This meaning approximates closely to the cty's explanation here, and I therefore adopt it.

Thī-a 213,3–4: *Cāpā puttam atosayī ti maṃ ghaṭṭentī puttaṃ tosesi keḷāyasi* (C^e^ *keḷāpayi*). For the alternation *y*/*s*(*s*) see the note on **84**.

Thī-a 213,4–5: *supati maṃ maññamānā ti ca paṭhanti. supatī ti maṃ maññamānā ti attho.*

Thī-a 213,5–7: *Cāpāya bandhanaṃ chetvā ti Cāpāya tayi uppannam kilesa-bandhanaṃ chindetvā.*

For sandhi *-m-* see the note on **48**.

For *puno* m.c. see § 69(a). See also EV I, p. 136 (ad Th 57) and cf. **397**.

293. B^e^ and C^e^ read *kujjhi* for *kujjha* in pādas ab. Thī-a 213,10–11: *mā me kujjhī ti keli-kāraṇa-mattena mā mayhaṃ kujjhi.*

294. Although all the editions read *ca* in pāda a, Thī-a 213,17–20 explains: *ko idha Nāḷāya vasissati, Nāḷāto va ahaṃ pakkamissām' eva. so hi tassa jāta-gāmo. tato nikkhamitvā pabbaji. so ca Magadha-raṭṭhe Bodhi-maṇḍassa āsanna-padese.* We should, therefore, probably read *va* (= *eva*). For the alternation *c*/*v* see the note on **12**.

Thī-a 213,20–22: *bandhanti itthi-rūpena samaṇe dhamma-jīvino ti Cāpe tvaṃ dhammena jīvante dhammike pabbajite attano itthi-rūpena itthi-kuttākappehi bandhantī tiṭṭhasi.* Although Be reads *bandhantī*, I would suggest that Dhammapāla is wrong to take *bandhanti* as the feminine participle here. It seems better to separate *itthi* and *rūpena*, and read *itthî* (with C^e^, although there a compound is read, unmetrically since the cadence would be – – – ⏓, without a caesura after the fifth syllable) (§ 70(e)).

295. Thī-a 213,25: *kāḷa-vaṇṇatāya Kāḷa Upaka.*

Thī-a 213,27: *vasī-katā, vasa-vattino katā ti.*

296. For the cadence of pāda b see § 59(c). B^e^ and C^e^ read *tvaṃ ca me* to regularise the cadence both here and in **308**. B^e^ and C^e^ read *Cāpe* in place of *c' eva* in pāda a. It is clear that *Cāpe* occurs somewhere in the verse since Thī-a 213,28–29 includes: *Cāpe ti Cāpe.* It is also clear that *ce* must occur since Thī-a 213,21 states: *ito catubbhāgam ce piya-samudāhāraṃ kareyyāsi*, but since *ca* can = *ce* (see EV I, p. 144 (ad Th 37)) there is no way of deciding between the *ca* of *tvaṃ ca me* and the *ce* of *c' eva*. On balance I prefer the reading of B^e^ and C^e^.

297. Thī-a 214,2–10: *aṅginin ti aṅga-laṭṭhi-sampannaṃ. ivā ti* (C^e^ *iva iti*) *upamāya nipāto. takkāriṃ pupphitaṃ giri-muddhanī ti pabbata-muddhani ṭhitaṃ supupphita-dālika-laṭṭhiṃ viya. ukkāgārin ti keci paṭīhanti. aṅga-laṭṭhiṃ viyā ti attho. giri-muddhanī ti ca idaṃ kenaci anupahata-sobhatā-dassanatthaṃ vuttaṃ. keci kāliṅginin ti pāṭhaṃ vatvā tassa kumbhaṇḍa-latā-sadisan ti atthaṃ vadanti. phulladālima-laṭṭhiṃ vā ti pupphitaṃ bīja-pūra-lataṃ viya. anto-dīpe va pāṭalin ti dīpa-kabbhantare* (C^e^ *-kassanta-*) *pupphita-pāṭali-rukkhaṃ viya. dīpa-ggahaṇañ c' ettha sobhā-pāṭihāriya-dassanatthaṃ eva.* This use of *gahaṇa* in the sense of "a word mentioned or employed (e.g. *vacana-*, 'the word *vacana*')" is not listed in PED, although quoted for Skt (MW, s.v. *grahaṇa*). Cf. *ukkaṭṭha-gahaṇa*, quoted in CPD from Vjb (B^e^ 1960) 83,15.

Von Hinüber (1994, p. 142) has drawn attention to the v.l. *ukkāgāriṃ*, which would seem to be a mistake for *ukkābhāriṃ* (for the *bh*/*g* alternation see the note on **25**), "fire-bearer", perhaps a kind of tree.

These various similes are to be understood with *maṃ rūpavatiṃ* in **298**: "why do you go leaving me, as beautiful as … ".

298. Thī-a 214,12: *kāsikuttama]dhārinin ti uttama-kāsika-vattha-dharaṃ.* For *kāsika* see the note on **374**.

Thī-a 214,13–15: *kassa ohāya gacchasī ti kassa nāma sattassa kassa vā hetuno kena kāreṇena pahāya ohāya pariccajitvā gacchasi.* See also the note on *kissa* in **467**.

For *taṃ maṃ* see the note on **24**.

299. For *āharîmena* m.c. to avoid the opening ⏓ ⏑ ⏑ – see § 70(e) and the note on **10**. The reading *āhârimena* is perhaps more likely, but this would also offend against classical standards (see the notes on **74** and **225**).

300. Thī-a 214,22: *putta-phalan ti putta-saṅkhāta-phalaṃ putta-ppasavo.*

301. For the simile of the elephant breaking his bonds cf. Th 1181.

302. Thī-a 214,30–31: *bhūmiyaṃ vā nisumbheyyan ti paṭhaviyaṃ pātetvā bādhana-vijjhanādinā vibādhissāmi.* For the verb *nisumbh-* see Kern (VG II, p. 243), Geiger (2000, § 60), and CDIAL 13496. I take *va* = *eva.*

303. B^e and C^e read *putta-katte*, but this is unmetrical (for the cadence – – – ⏓ see the note on **37**). We could assume that *-kate* is m.c. for *-katte*, i.e. the vocative of *kattar-* (cf. Ja V 225 (ad *katte* at Ja V 221): *katte ti tam eva aparena nāmena ālapati*), but there is no reason for disregarding the obvious interpretation of *-kate* as being < Skt *-kṛte* (see PED, s.v. *kate*) "for the sake of". Thī-a 214,33: *putta-kate ti putta-kāraṇā.*

304. For *bhaddan te* see EV I, pp. 231 foll. (ad Th 527).

305. Thī-a 215,6–7: *asamaṇā ti na samita-pāpā. samaṇa-mānino ti samita-pāpā ti evaṃ-saññino.* For the etymology connecting *samaṇa* with the root *sam-*, cf. *samitattā hi pāpānaṃ samaṇo ti pavuccati*, Dhp 265.

For *mānin* see EV I, p. 292 (ad Th 953), where I was probably wrong about *aññāta-mānino*, and see the note on *-matin* in **107**.

In pāda b there is resolution of the first and fourth syllables, and in pāda c there is resolution of the sixth syllable (§ 60).

For *gāmena gāmaṃ* see the note on **92** and Sen (§ 36).

306. Thī-a 215,9: *Nerañjaraṃ patī ti Nerañjarāya nadiyā samīpe.* For *pati* see the note on **258**.

For *gacchaṃ* as a future see the note on **130**.

307. Thī-a 215,12–13: *vajjāsi, vadeyyāsi,* i.e. the word is an optative. See the note on **308**.

308. For the cadence of pāda b see § 59(c), and cf. the note on **296**. Although M (text) reads *taṃ ca me*, the cty includes: *tuvaṃ Cāpe ti tvaṃ Cāpe.*

Thī-a 215,20–21: *te vajjan ti tava vandanaṃ* (B^e v.l.: *tvañ ca me ti tvaṃ Cāpe*) *vajjaṃ vakkhāmi.* Despite the cty, *vajjaṃ* is in fact an optative. Cf. **307**.

309. For *pati* see the note on **258**.

For the split compound *amataṃ padaṃ* see the note on **149**.

310. See the note on **186**.

311. For *katvāna⟨ṃ⟩* or *karitvā* in place of *katvāna* in pāda b to avoid the opening ⏓ — ⏑ — see § 70(e) and the note on **74**, and cf. the note on **438**.

For *pabbajî* or *pabbâji* in pāda d to avoid the opening ⏓ ⏑ ⏑ ⏑ see § 70(e) and the note on **44**.

312–37. The interpretation of this set of verses is complicated by the cty's desire, which is followed by Mrs Rhys Davids, to see in the references to Vāseṭṭhī the same therī who was the author of **133–38**. Without any other information, however, one would normally take *brāhmaṇi* in **313** and *brāhmaṇa* in **314** to refer to husband and wife, and their close relationship is confirmed by the allusion to relatives and sons *mama tuyhañ ca* in **314**. *Vāseṭṭhī* (or *Vāsiṭṭhī*) is of course merely a *gotra* name (see Brough, 1953, p. 37), and there is nothing in common between the two Vāseṭṭhīs except their membership of the same gotra. Mrs Rhys Davids' objection (Sist., p. 136, n. 2) to Neumann's interpretation is therefore unfounded. Winternitz too (p. 108) takes the couple as husband and wife. We can therefore see that Sujāta uttered **312–13 316 319 323**; his wife uttered **314–15 317–18 325 327 329**; his charioteer uttered **326**; Sundarī uttered **328 330–36**; the Buddha uttered **337**; **320–22 324** are narrative verses.

At the end of the introductory story (Thī-a 217,20–21), the cty relates that Sundarī pronounced the verses previously uttered by her father (and presumably the others as well): *sā apara-bhāge attano paṭipattiṃ paccavekkhitvā pitarā vutta-gāthaṃ ādiṃ katvā udāna-vasena imā gāthā paccudabhāsi* (§ 4).

312. Thī-a 219,15–16: *petāni ti matāni. bhotī ti tam ālapati. puttānī ti liṅga-vipallāsena vuttaṃ. pete putte ti attho.* For *-āni* as a masculine nominative and accusative plural ending see the note on **13**.

Thī-a 219,16–18: *eko eva ca tassā putto mato. brāhmaṇo pana "cira-kālaṃ ayaṃ sokena aṭṭā hutvā vicari bahū maññe imissā puttā matā" ti evaṃ-saññī hutvā bahu-vacanen' āha.* The need to assume that the brahman was confused about the number of children who had died disappears when we ralise that there were two different Vāseṭṭhīs (see the note on **312–37**).

Thī-a 219,19–21: *puttāni khādamānā ti loka-vohāra-vasena khuṃsana-vacanaṃ etaṃ. loke hi yassā itthiyā jāta-jātā puttā maranti taṃ garahanti "putta-khādanī" ti ādi vadanti.* Dhammapāla may be correct in saying that such a woman was called *putta-khādanī*, but it is more likely that he is trying to explain an apparent reference to the mother eating her sons. See also the note on **221** where Thī-a 173,7–8 explains *khāditāni putta-maṃsāni* by saying that the childen were eaten by the mother in former existences as a wild animal. Thī-a

219,28–29 (ad **314**) gives both explanations: *khāditānī ti therī brāhmaṇena vutta-pariyāyen' eva vadati. khāditānī ti vā vyaggha-dīpi-biḷārādi-jātiyo sandhāy' evam āha*. The problem disappears when we realise that we should understand *khādamānā* to be a corruption of the causative participle *khādemānā* (from *khad-* = *khād-*?) "causing them to be eaten", i.e. exposing them in a cemetery to be eaten by wild animals, cf. *puttaṃ sigālānaṃ kukkurānaṃ padāhasi* **303**. In the same way we must read *khādetvā* in **313**, i.e. "having caused to be eaten, having exposed", and we must understand *khāditāni* in **314** as the past participle of the causative verb, "caused to be eaten, exposed".

PED does not list *khuṃsana*, but it may be connected with BHS *kuṃsana* (see BHSD, s.v.), with the alternation *k/kh* (see Geiger, 2000, § 40.1(a)). CDIAL (13661) suggests a derivation < **skōṣati* "plucks out, pokes".

313. Thī-a 219,26–27: *kena vaṇṇenā ti kena kāraṇena*. See PED (s.v. *vaṇṇa*, § 11).

B[e] and C[e] read *sata-puttāni* for *satta puttāni*, but I think that this must be incorrect. It is appropriate that in **314** the brāhmaṇī should point out that she has mourned hundreds of sons in previous existences, but here it is her husband wondering why she is not mourning her seventh child as she has mourned the others. The reading *sata-puttāni* has undoubtedly arisen because of *putta-satāni* in **314**.

For *sā* and the second person verb see the note on **24**.

For *khāditvā* as a causative (= *khādetvā*) see the note on **312**.

For the ending *-āni* = *-e* in *puttāni* see the note on **312**.

For *Vāseṭṭhī* as the name of the brahman's wife see the note on **312–37**.

For *br-* not making position in *brāhmaṇi* see § 74(a).

314. Thī-a 219,30–31: *mama tuyhaṃ cā ti mayā ca tayā ca*. The cty is presumably led into believing that *mama* and *tuyhaṃ* must be instrumentals because of the belief that *khāditāni* means "eaten [by you and me]", instead of "caused to be eaten" (see the note on **312**). I take *mama* and *tuyhaṃ* to be straight-forward possessive genitives. For such apparent changes of case see the note on **2**.

There are nine syllables in pāda a (§ 61). The metre can be corrected by reading *putta-satā*[*ni*] (§ 67(d)), although B[e] and C[e] correct by excluding [*me*].

For *br-* not making position in *brāhmaṇa* see § 74(a).

315. For *sāhaṃ* = *sā ahaṃ* see the note on **24**.

For the cadence ⏑ – – ⏓ in pāda d see § 59(c). Be and Ce read *paritappayiṃ*. Thī-a 219,33–34: *na cāpi paritappayin ti na cāpi upāyās' āsiṃ, ahaṃ upāyāsaṃ na āpajjin ti attho.*

316. Thī-a 219,35–36: *abbhutaṃ vatā ti acchariyaṃ vata. taṃ hi abbhutaṃ pubbe abhūtaṃ abhūtan ti vuccati.* There is no comment on *abbhuta* at Thī-a 189,4 foll. (ad **224**) and Thī-a 267,20 foll. (ad **517**). The belief that *abbhuta* is connected with *bhū-* doubtless explains the form *abbhūtaṃ* found in Se. See also CPD (s.v. [I]*abbhuta*). PED states (s.v. *abbhuta*) that the etymology is uncertain, but for Skt *adbhuta* see Burrow (1955, p. 108).

317. For *pati* see the note on **258**.

318. Thī-a 220,5: *nirupadhin ti niddukkhaṃ. viññāta-saddhammā ti paṭividdha-ariya-sacca-dhammā.* The more common usage of *nirupadhi* is as an epithet of persons, e.g. **320 334**, Th 516, but it is used elsewhere to describe the dhamma, e.g. Mp II 242 (ad A I 147): *ñatvā dhammaṃ nirupadhin ti sabbūpadhi-virahitaṃ nibbāna-dhammaṃ ñatvā*, and Ud-a 314 (ad Ud 59): *ñatvā dhammaṃ nirupadhin ti sabbūpadhi-paṭinissaggattā nirupadhiṃ nibbāna-dhammaṃ yathā-bhūtaṃ ñatvā nissaraṇa-vivekāsaṅkhatāmata-sabhāvato magga-ñāṇena paṭivijjhitvā.* I assume that to describe the dhamma as *nirupadhi* means that it is regarded as removing the basis for rebirth.

There are nine syllables in pāda (§ 61) even when we scan *ar^a^hato* (§ 75). The scansion can be corrected by reading *tassa* for *tassāhaṃ* (with Be and Ce) or *brahme* (with Be) or *brāhmaṇ'* (§ 67(d)). The version in Be seems to be excessively normalised, since it requires the svarabhakti vowel in *arahato* to give an eight-syllable pāda. I follow the reading *brāhmaṇ'* in the analysis (§ 58(a)(xiii)).

For *nirûpadhiṃ* (Be Ce Ke and Se) m.c. to give the cadence ⏑ – ⏑ ⏓ see §§ 59(b), 70(e).

319. For *pati* see the note on **258**.

320. For *addasâ* m.c. to avoid the opening ⏓ ⏑ ⏑ – see § 70(e) and the note on **10**. This lengthening is of course unnecessary if *br-* does make position in *brāhmaṇo* here (§ 74(a)).

For *nirupadhi* cf. **318 334**.

For *nirûpadhiṃ* (Be Ce Ke and Se) m.c. to give the cadence ⏑ – ⏑ ⏓ see §§ 59(b), 70(e).

321. See the note on **186**.

322–24. For *aphassayi* see the note on **6**.

323–24. In pāda d there is resolution of the second syllable (§ 60).
For *br-* not making position in *brāhmaṇo* see § 74(a).

324. Pāda c has nine syllables (§ 61). We could correct the metre by reading *brāhmaṇim* (§ 68(b)(iii)), and assuming resolution of the sixth syllable (§ 60).

325. Thī-a 220,14: *puṇṇa-pattan ti tuṭṭhi-dānaṃ*. See also MW (s.v. *pūrṇa-pātra*).

326. There are nine syllables in pāda a, but this problem can be overcome by assuming resolution of the seventh syllable (§ 60). B^e^ corrects the scansion by reading *hotv* for *hotu*. For the development of final *-u* > *-v* see § 73(b) and the note on **226**.
For *br-* not making position in *brāhmaṇi* see § 74(a).

327–28. These two verses consist of a mixture of śloka and triṣṭubh pādas, **327** consisting of two triṣṭubh and three śloka pādas, and **328** of two triṣṭubh and four śloka pādas. Mrs Rhys Davids described the verses as "redundant" (Sist., p. 139, n. 1), by which she possibly meant "hyper-metric". There seems to be no reason to doubt that we have here patchwork verses, made up, partly at least, from already existing pādas. There is no need to follow Mrs Rhys Davids in thinking that the "redundancy" reflects the abundance of her heritage. For a comparable hyper-metric patchwork verse, cf. **51**.

For *hatthî* (with B^e^ and C^e^) m.c. see § 70(b). Thī-a 220,20 glosses: *hatthī ti hatthino*, clearly taking the form as a nominative plural, so we should punctuate *hatthī gavassaṃ* (with B^e^ and C^e^).

Pādas b as printed in P are unmetrical, and have a redundant fourth syllable. Warder (PM, § 278) mentions only the 5 + 7 and 5 + 8 types of hyper-metric triṣṭubh and jagatī pāda, i.e. where the pāda has a caesura after the fifth syllable but then continues as though the caesura had been after the fourth, giving two fifth syllables. Where the caesura is other than after the fifth syllable, however, a redundant syllable can also arise. Although I recognised this in EV I, some of the analyses I gave in EV I §§ 26(d)(ii) and 27(d)(ii) were incorrect: Th 781c 869b 1264c can be regarded as having redundant fifth syllables; Th 1263b has redundant fifth and tenth syllables, although the second redundancy arises from a wrong reading; Th 518a 522b have redundant fourth syllables (cf. S I 25,18 *saggaṃ ca so gacchati* ... and 123,9 *anāsavo jhāyāmi* ...); Th 1270b 1274c have redundant sixth syllables (cf. S I 21,3 from bottom *bhīruṃ pasaṃsanti* ...); Th 1266a probably does not have a redundant syllable, but shows resolution of the fifth syllable.

Several apparent examples of redundant syllables can frequently be corrected by assuming shortening m.c., and then resolution: if we read *jarā̆-* m.c. in Th 518a we can then assume resolution of the fifth syllable (not fourth as stated in EV I, p. 230 (ad Th 518)); similarly there is resolution of the fifth syllable in Th 522b if we read *viha*[*ṅ*]*ga-* m.c. Here too the redundant syllable can be removed if we read *gĕha-* (§72(a)), or *gaha-* (with B[e] and C[e]), or *ghara-*. We then have resolution of the fifth syllable (§49(d)).

B[e] and C[e] read *-vibhavaṃ* for *-vigataṃ*. Thī-a 220,23: *gaha-vibhavaṃ, gehūpakaraṇaṃ*. It is very difficult to see what *vigata* could mean in this context, and although *upakaraṇa* is not a very satisfactory gloss for *vibhava*, the latter is probably the correct reading. The reading *vigata* possibly arose from a combination of two elements: the fact that *vibhava* has two meanings, i.e. "wealth" and "disappearance", with the latter of which *vigata* would be synonymous, and the alternation *g*/*bh* (see the note on **25**), which could have led to a spelling *vigava* which was then "corrected" to *vigata*.

327. I list pādas de as posterior pādas in §58(b)(xiii).

328. B[e] and C[e] read *aṭṭito* and *aṭṭitā* for *addito* and *additā*; K[e] and S[e] read *addh-*. See also the note on **77**.

329. Thī-a 220,32–221,1: *uttiṭṭha-piṇḍo ti ghare ghare patiṭṭhitvā* (C[e] *upatiṭṭhitvā*) *laddhabba-bhikkhā-piṇḍo. uñcho ti tad-atthaṃ ghara-paṭipāṭiyā āhiṇḍa-naṃ uṭṭhānañ ca, etānī ti uttiṭṭha-piṇḍādīni*. Thī-a 226,24–25 (ad **349**) explains: *uttiṭṭha-piṇḍo ti vivaṭa-dvāre ghare ghare patiṭṭhitvā labhanaka-piṇḍo. uñcho ti tad-attham uñchā-cariyā*. See also EV I, p. 174 (ad Th 155).

Thī-a 221,1–2: *abhisambhontī ti anibbiṇṇa-rūpā jaṅghā-balaṃ nissāya abhisambhavantī sādhentī ti attho*. This sense of *sādh-* is not given in PED. The cty is therefore taking *uttiṭṭha-piṇḍo*, etc., as floating nominatives: "[there are] alms, etc.; making do with these [you will be] ... ". Cf. *lūkhaṃ pi abhisambhonto* Th 351 436 (glossed: *dussaham pi paccaya-lūkhaṃ abhibhavanto adhivāsento* (Th-a II 149,5–6)). On the other hand the parallel with Th 1057 is so close that we may not be wrong in thinking that we should read *abhisambhontĭ*, take *etāni* as the subject of this, and translate "these will be sufficient" (see EV I, p. 269 ad 1057). The structural parallel with **349**c ("this is proper for me") would also support this interpratation.

330. For *sikkhamānā* see the note on **2**.

For *pubbe-nivāsa* see the note on **63**.

331. Thī-a 221,9–11: *sobhaṇe ti sobhaṇehi* (M *-yo anehi*: for the alternation *y/s* see the note on **84**) *sīlādīhi samannāgatattā sobhaṇe*. Cf. *saddhamma-sobhaṇā* in **363**, where, however, Thī-a 228,29–30 explains: *saddhammādhigamena sobhaṇā*. See MW (s.v. *śobhana*): (at the end of compounds = "beautiful by reason of"); *-ā* "a beautiful woman (often in voc.)". With the preceding genitive it could mean "o beauty (= beautiful one) of the order of therīs". It is, however, possible that *sobhaṇā* is causative in meaning "beautifier of the order of therīs, i.e. making beautiful the order". I follow the latter translation here. In **363**, however, this translation is perhaps less likely, so I follow the translation "beautiful by reason of the true doctrine" there.

332. For the cadence of pāda b see § 59(a). For *Sāvatthi*[*ṃ*] m.c. (with C[e]) see § 68(b)(ii).

The cty does not comment on *buddha-seṭṭhassa* here, but Th-a II 50,8–10 (ad Th 175) explains: *Buddhassa sambuddhassa tato eva sabbasattuttamatāya seṭṭhassa, Buddhānaṃ vā sāvaka-buddhādīnaṃ seṭṭhassa*. We may therefore translate "Buddha and best" or "best of the Buddhas, i.e. enlightened ones". In his review of EV I de Jong has given reasons for finding the first explanation more acceptable. See also the note on *vara* in **399**.

333. For *akutobhaya* see the note on **135**.

334. For *nirupadhi* cf. **318 320**.

For *Sundariṃ* (with C[e]) to give the cadence ⏑ – – ⏓ (*pathyā*) with the opening ⏓ ⏑ – ⏑ see § 68(b)(iii) and the note on **28**.

For the cadence of pāda b see § 59(b). For *nirûpadhiṃ* (B[e] C[e] K[e] and S[e]) m.c. see § 70(e).

336. For *dhītā* (*buddhassa*) see the note on **46**.

For *br-* not making position in *brāhmaṇa* see § 74(a).

337. Thī-a 222,2: *adurāgataṃ, na durāgataṃ*. The word is therefore a synonym of *svāgataṃ*. Mrs Rhys Davids presumably overlooked the cty when she translated "twas but a little way to come", since this seems to be based upon a confusion of *adurāgata* and *adūrāgata*. For the relationship between *adurāgata*, Pkt *aṇurāgaya*, and BHS *anurāgata*, and their use with *svāgata*, see Kern (1916A, p. 13) and BHSG § 4.63, and cf. Chopra (p. 46, note 13).

All editions read *satthu pādāni vandikā*. An accusative governed by *vandikā* is not impossible; B^e^ and C^e^, however, read *pādānaṃ vandikā* in the explanation, and I think we should probably read *pādāna vandikā* "praisers of the feet". For *pādāna* m.c. see § 68. For *pādāni* = *pāde* see the note on **13**.

For *tassā te* see the note on **24**.

338–65. This group of verses ends in *ti* in P (see the note on **1**).

338. Thī-a 224,21–24: *tassā me appamattāya saccābhisamayo ahū ti yasmā ca tasmā me mayhaṃ yathā-sutaṃ dhammam paccavekkhitvā appamattāya upaṭṭhita-satiyā sīlaṃ adhiṭṭhahitvā bhāvanaṃ anuyuñjantī yāva catunnaṃ ariya-saccānaṃ abhisamayo idaṃ dukkhan ti ādinā paṭivedho ahosi.*

With *suddha* cf. Skt *śuddha* "pure, white".

For *tassā me* see the note on **24**. For *ahu* see the note on **43**. For *a⟨s⟩suṇiṃ* m.c. (with B^e^ and C^e^) to give the cadence ⏑ – ⏑ ⏓ see §§ 59(b), 63(b). K^e^ and S^e^ read *āsuṇiṃ*.

In pāda a there is resolution of the first syllable (§ 60).

339. There seems to be no reason for reading *bhūsaṃ*, and we should read *bhusaṃ* with B^e^ and C^e^. Thī-a 224,27–28: *bhusaṃ ati viya aratiṃ ukkaṇṭhiṃ adhigacchi.*

For the cadence of pāda d see § 59(b). It can be normalised by reading *pîhaye* with B^e^ and C^e^ (§ 70(e)). No other edition agrees with P in reading *nekkhammaṃ yeva*. B^e^ reads *-am eva*; C^e^ reads *-añ ñeva*; K^e^ and S^e^ read *-ass' eva*. In Skt *spr̥h-* is constructed with the dative, genitive, or accusative; in Pāli *pih-* is constructed with the accusative or genitive.

For *sakkāya* see the note on **165**. For *nekkhamma* see the note on **226**.

340–41. B^e^ and C^e^ make three verses from these two.

340. Thī-a 224,31–32: *dāsa-kamma-karāni cā ti dāse ca kamma-kare ca. liṅga-vipallāsena h' etaṃ vuttaṃ*. For *-āni* = *-e* see the note on **13**.

Thī-a 224,33–35: *phītānī ti samiddhāni. ramaṇīye ti manuññe. pamodite ti pamudite. bhoga-kkhandhe hutvā ti sambandho*. PED gives only "greatly delighted, very pleased" for *pamudita* and *pamodita*.

341. Thī-a 225,10–11: *puna-r-āgame ti puna taṃ gaṇheyya*. Because of this gloss CPD (s.v. *āgame*) suggested that we should read *āgahe* (< **āgahati*). Although von Hinüber (1994, p. 36) makes a strong case for retaining *āgame*, in view of the alternative readings *āgam-* and *āvam-* at Th 1125 (see EV I, p. 317), I would suggest that we read *āvame* "take back what has been vomitted". See also the note on **359**.

B^e and C^e read *chaḍḍetvā* in the text instead of *ṭhapetvā*.Thī-a (text, rubric and gloss) reads *chaḍḍetvā*.

For sandhi *-r-* see the note on **3**.

In pāda c there is resolution of the sixth syllable (§ 60).

342. B^e C^e and Thī-a (text) read *santiyā*. P gives a v.l. *santiyā*, and it is not clear why the editor read *santaye*. I have adopted this reading.

There is resolution of the fourth syllable in pāda c (§ 60).

For the cadence of pāda d see § 59(b). It can be normalised by reading *ariya-⟨d⟩dhanaṃ* with B^e or *ariyaṃ dhanaṃ* with C^e (§§ 64(b), 70(e)).

343. Thī-a 225,24–26: *n' atthi c' ettha dhuvaṃ ṭhitī ti etasmiṃ ṭhāne dhuva-bhāvo vā ṭhiti-bhāvo vā n' atthi calācalaṃ anavatthitam evā ti attho*. Cf. EV I, p. 268 (ad Th 769). For such split compounds see the note on **147**.

344. Thī-a 225,30–32: *puthu kubbanti medhagan ti puthu sattā medhagaṃ kalahaṃ karonti*. P records *medhakaṃ* as a v.l. See EV I, p. 197 (ad Th 275). For *puthu* in the sense of "numerous, many" see PED s.v., where, however, *puthu-sattā* is said to be equal to *puthujjanā* "common people".

345. Thī-a 226,3–5: *vadho ti maraṇaṃ. bandho ti daddu-bandhanādi-bandhanaṃ. parikleso ti hattha-cchedādi-parikilesāpatti. dhanaṃ*-(B^e omits)-*jānī ti dhana-jāni c' eva parivāra-jāni ca*. Cf. **191**c.

For *-kl-* making position in *parikleso* to give the cadence ⏑ – – ⏓ (*pathyā*) see § 74(f). Cf. **191**.

346. Thī-a 226,9–10: *taṃ, maṃ, tādisaṃ maṃ*. See the note on *sā ahaṃ* in **24**.

It is not clear why *maṃ* occurs in both pādas a and b. B^e and C^e read *vo* for *maṃ* in pāda b, but this causes difficulties, since it can hardly be the enclitic form of the oblique cases of the second person pronoun. Perhaps *vo* is the alternative form of the emphatic particle *ve* (see EV I, p. 215 (ad Th 403)); the problem which arose when the particle *vo* was confused with the pronoun *vo* might well have led to the change of *vo* to *maṃ*.

Thī-a 226,9–11: *amittā va, amittā viya*.

Thī-a 226,11: *kiṃ, kena kāraṇena*.

Thī-a 226,11: *yuñjatha, niyojetha*. This sense arises easily enough from the usual sense of "join", if we translate "you are in the act of joining me to sensual pleasures, i.e. you are moving me towards, urging me towards".

347. Thī-a 226,20–21: *rāgādīnaṃ sallānaṃ bandhanato salla-bandhanā*. This explanation seems to indicate that the cty was taking the compound as a tatpuruṣa "the binding of the sallas", not as a dvandva as PED does (s.v. *salla*) "arrow and prison bond". This would seem to support Edgerton's suggestion (BHSD s.v. *śalya*) that *salla* here means "rope". We could translate "sensual pleasures which bind with ropes".

We should, however, note that *salla* is frequently found in its usual sense of "arrow, dart" in conjunction with *bandhana*, e.g. five types of *salla* and five *cetaso vinibandhā* are listed at Vbh 377 [IBH].

348. Thī-a 226,22–23: *tattha tattha nantakāni gahetvā saṃbhāṭi-cīvara-pārupanena saṃghāṭi-pārutaṃ*. PED states that the etymology of *nantaka* and *namataka* is doubtful, but *namata* "felt cloth" is probably a loan word fom Iranian. See Burrow (1937, p. 100, s.v. *namatae*), and EWA II, p. 135 and Bailey, 1979, s.v. *namata*.

349. For *uttiṭṭha-piṇḍa* and *uñcha* see the note on **329**.

Thī-a 226,25–27: *anagārūpanissayo ti anagārānaṃ pabbajitānaṃ upagantvā nissita-bbato upanissaya-bhūto jīvita-parikkhāro. taṃ hi nissāya pabba-jitā jīvanti.*

350. B^e C^e K^e and S^e read *mahesīhi* for *mahesinā*, and Thī-a 226,28 explains: *mahesīhī ti buddhādīhi mahesīhi*, which makes it clear that Dhammapāla was reading a plural form. The reading is confirmed by the plural *te* in pādas cd. For *isi* see the note on **60**.

Thī-a 226,28–29: *khema-ṭṭhāne ti kāma-yogādīhi anupaddava-ṭṭhāna-bhūte nibbāne*. Ps II 85 (ad M I 117) explains: *khemaṃ, nibbhaya-ṭṭhānaṃ*; Ps II 267 (ad M I 227) explains: *khemaṃ, arahattaṃ*. Cf. also *khemaṃ, nibbānaṃ* Nidd I 130. For *khema* as an adjective see the note on **361**.

351. C^e reads *aggi-kkhandha-samā* for *-kkhandhūpamā*, cf. P v.l. This reading presumably arose because of the misreading of *-s-* for *-p-* (see the note on **6**). Thī-a 227,2–3: *aggi-kkhandhūpamā mahābhitāpaṭṭhena. dukkhā dukkha-m-aṭṭhena.*

For *dukhā* m.c. to give the cadence ⏑ — ⏑ ⏓ see § 65(a).

352. Thī-a 227,4–5: *paripantho esa bhayo yadidaṃ kāmā nāma avidita-vipulānatthāvahattā*. M reads *paribandho* for *paripantho* in the lemma. The word also occurs in Th 1152 (see EV I, p. 323)

Thī-a 227,6–7: *gedho suvisamo c' eso ti giddhi-hetutāya gedho. suṭṭhu visamo mahā-palibodho so.* It is tempting to take *gedha* as thicket, cf. Mp II 254: *gedhan ti ghanaṃ araññaṃ saṃsatta-sākhaṃ ekābaddhaṃ mahā-vana-saṇḍaṃ* (ad A I 154), but the cty does support that suggestion.

B^e^ and C^e^ read *esa bhayo* for *eso sabhayo*. This would seem to be normalisation to avoid the nine-syllable pāda. This can be avoided by assuming resolution of the first syllable (§ 60).

353. Thī-a 227,9–10: *upasaggo bhīma-rūpo, atibhiṃsanaka-sabhāvo mahanto devatūpasaggo viya anatthakādi-*(C^e^ *appaṭikāra-*)*dukkhāvahano.* Since the explanation contains *viya*, we must assume that Dhammapāla was reading *va* not *ca*. For the alternation *v/c* see the note on **12**.

There is resolution of the first syllable in pāda a (§ 60).

354. Pāda a has nine syllables (§ 61). B^e^ and C^e^ read *kāma-paṅkena sattā hi* which gives a normal pāda. K^e^ and S^e^ read *kāma-saṃsagga-sattā*, but this cannot have been the reading which Dhammapāla had because Thī-a 227,12 explains: *kāma-saṃkhātena paṅkena sattā laggā.* For *pariyanta* cf. *pacceka-buddho bhavapariyante ṭhito*, Ja IV 340.

For the scansion of *par^i^yantam* see § 75. B^e^ normalises the apparently irregular pāda by reading *na jānanti* for *nābhijānanti*.

355. Thī-a 227,14–15: *bahun ti pāṇātipātādi-bhedana bahu-vidhaṃ.* This seems to be an attempt to take *bahuṃ* as an adjective agreeing with *maggaṃ*. It would seem preferable to take it as an adverbial accusative with the emphatic particle *ve* "very much indeed".

For *duggatî* m.c. to avoid the opening ⏓ ⏑ ⏑ ⏑ see § 70(e) and the note on **44**.

For the sandhi *-m-* in *roga-m-āvahaṃ* see the note on **48**.

356. Thī-a 227,18: *tāpanā ti santāpanakā tapanīyā ti attho.* PED does not list *tāpana.*

357. Thī-a 227,24–27: *ullapanā ti aho sukhaṃ aho sukhan ti uddhaṃ uddhaṃ lapāpanakā. ullolanā ti pi pāṭho. bhatta-piṇḍa-nimittaṃ naṅguṭṭhaṃ ullolento sunakho viya āmisa-hetu satte uparūpari lālanā, parābhavā-vaññāta-pāpanakā ti attho.* For *ullapana* see the note on **73**.

Thī-a 227,28–29: *citta-ppamāthino ti pariḷāhuppādanādinā sampati āyatiñ ca cittassa pamathana-sīlā. citta-ppamaddino ti vā pāṭho. so ev' attho. ye pana citta-ppamādino ti vadanti, tesaṃ cittassa pamādāvahā ti attho.* B^e^ reads *-ppamaddino*. PED prefers *-ppamādino*, and does not list *pamāthin.*

Cᵉ reads *khipaṃ* for *khippaṃ*. A I 33 287 has *khipaṃ* with *khippaṃ* as a v.l. S I 74 has *khippaṃ*, without v.l., but this may be m.c. to avoid the opening ⏓ – ⏑ – (see the note on **74**). Thī-a 227,31–33: *khipaṃ Mārena oḍḍitan ti kāmā nām' ete Mārena oḍḍitaṃ kuminan ti daṭṭhabbā sattānaṃ anatthāvahanato*. Spk I 140 (ad S I 74) glosses: *khipaṃ va oḍḍitan ti kuminaṃ viya oḍḍitaṃ*.

358. Thī-a 228,6–7: *raṇa-karā ti sārāgādi-saṃvaḍḍhakā*. Thī-a 228,15–16 (ad **360**), however, explains: *raṇaṃ taritvā kāmānan ti kāmānaṃ raṇaṃ taritvā tañ* (M *te*) *ca mayā kātabbaṃ ariya-magga-sampahāraṃ katvā*. As PED states (s.v. *raṇa*), the cty is giving two different meanings to *raṇa* here, i.e. "grief" and "fight". It might be thought, however, that when *raṇa* occurs twice in close proximity, each time with the root *kar-*, the same meaning is intended. Since "battle, fight, conflict" seems to be the most likely sense in **360**, I assume that a similar meaning is intended here. In BHS only the equivalence with *kleśa* seems to occur (see BHSD, s.v. *raṇa*).

Thī-a 228,5–6: *appassādā ti sattha-dhārā-gata-madhu-bindu viya paritta-ssādā*.

Thī-a 228,7: *sukka-pakkha-visosanā ti sattānaṃ anavajja-koṭṭhāsassa vināsakā* (M *-koṭṭhāsaya-vināsakā*; for the alternation *y/s(s)* see the note on **84**). For *sukka-pakkha* see BHSD (s.v. *śulka-pakṣa*).

359. For *sāhaṃ* see the note on **24**.

Thī-a 228,10: *katvā ti iti katvā yathā-vutta-kāraṇenā ti attho*. Kᵉ and Sᵉ read *hitvā* for *katvā*.

Thī-a 228,11–12: *na taṃ paccāgamissāmī ti taṃ mayā pubbe vantaṃ kāma-methunaṃ na patibhuñjissāmi*. The occurrence of *vantaṃ* in the explanation gives the possibility that we should read *paccāvam-* for *paccāgam-*, and translate "swallow back". For *vam-/paccāvam-* see EV I, p. 317 (ad Th 1125). Cf. *lokaṃ na paccāgamanti* in Ps II 167, after *vamanti*. See the note on **341**.

Despite the cty, it is not quite clear what *taṃ* refers to. In the explanation M reads *te* for *taṃ* when the pāda is quoted again. Here *te* could stand for *kāme*. Bᵉ and Cᵉ, however, retain *taṃ*.

360. Bᵉ agrees with P in reading *karitvā*. Cᵉ reads *taritvā* "having crossed over the conflict". In view of *raṇakarā* in **358**, I prefer to retain *karitvā* here. See the note on **358**. Thī-a 228,15–19, however, reads *taritvā*: *raṇaṃ taritvā kāmānan ti kāmānaṃ raṇaṃ taritvā, tañ ca mayā kātabbaṃ ariyamaggasaṃpahāraṃ katvā. sītibhāvābhikaṅkhinī ti sabba-kilesa-daratha-pariḷāha-vūpasamena sītibhāva-saṅkhātaṃ arahattaṃ abhikaṅkhantī. sabba-saṃyojana-kkhaye ti sabbesaṃ saṃyojanānaṃ khaya-bhūte nibbāne abhiratā*.

B^e and C^e read *vihassāmi* for *vihissāmi*. See the note on **121**. K^e and S^e read *viharissāmi*, which is not metrical.

In pāda d C^e reads as P. B^e replaces *tesaṃ* by *sabba-*, and K^e and S^e replace it by *ratā*. In the lemma B^e and C^e read *sabba-*. Thī-a 228,18–19 explains: *sabbesaṃ saṃyojanānaṃ khaya-bhūte nibbāne abbhiratā*. The reading of K^e and S^e is interesting in view of the presence of *abhiratā* in the cty.

361. For *mahesino* see the note on **60**.

Here *khema* is an adjective. See EV I, p. 142 (ad Th 32) and the note on **350**.

362. Thī-a 228,23: *dhamma-ṭṭhan ti ariya-phala-dhamme ṭhitaṃ*.

Thī-a 228,23–24: *anejan ti paṭipassaddhi-tejatāya anejan ti laddha-nāmaṃ agga-phalaṃ*. Stede (p. 47) preferred to read *ānejjaṃ* as the object of *upasampajja*, presumably doubting that *aneja* could be a noun, but this seems to be unnecessary. CPD (s.v. ²*aneja*) accepts it as a noun, and quotes Spk II 282 (ad S III 83): *anejan te anuppattā ti ejā-saṃkhātāya taṇhāya pahāna-bhūtaṃ arahattaṃ*. For *aneja* as an adjective see the note on **205**.

Thī-a 228,24–25: *upasampajjā ti sampādetvā agga-maggādhigamena adhigantvā*.

363. Thī-a 228,27–28: *ajj' aṭṭhamī pabbajitā ti pabbajitā hutvā pabbajitato paṭṭhāya ajj' aṭṭhama-divaso*. The cty is therefore taking *pabbajitā* as an ablative, i.e. *pabbajita* is a past participle used as an action noun (see the note on **261**). There is, however, no need to do this, if we assume a mark of punctuation after *aṭṭhamī*, i.e. "Today is the eight day; she went forth ... ". The cty seems to recognise this alternative translation: *ito atīte aṭṭhamiyaṃ pabbajitā ti attho*.

For *maccu-hāyinī* see the note on **65**.

For *saddhamma-sobhaṇā* see the note on **331**.

There are nine syllables in pāda c (§61). We could correct this by reading *vinīt'* with B^e and C^e.

364. Thī-a 228,31–32: *bhujissā ti dāsa-bhāva-sadisānaṃ kilesānaṃ pahānena bhujissā. kāma-cchandādi-iṇāpagamena anaṇā*. PED (s.v. *aṇa*) explains *anaṇa* here as meaning "without a new birth", but I do not know the justification for this. For *sāyaṃ bhujissā anaṇā* see the note on **2**.

For *kata-kiccā* cf. Skt *kṛta-kṛtya* (MBh 7.160.36, 12.42.35).There is also Skt *kṛta-vacana* "one who has kept his word, fulfilled his promise".

365. Thī-a 229,7–8 states that this verse was added by the *saṅgīti-kārā* (§ 5).

In Skt the opening before the cadence – ⏑ ⏑ ⏓ is always ⏓ – ⏑ ⏓ (PM, § 242). We should, therefore, perhaps read *namassatî* m.c. (§ 70(e)).

366–99. This group of verses ends in *ti* (see the note on **1**). It is included in MIAR (pp. 27–31, 152–58).

366. The metre of this verse is śloka, while the rest of the group is vaitālīya (PM, § 194). This fact would support the statement at Thī-a 234,17–18 that this verse was added to the group by the *saṅgītikārā*: *theriyā vutta-gāthānaṃ sambandha-dassana-vasena saṅgīti-kārehi ayaṃ gāthā vuttā*. For the question of *br-* making position in *abravī* see § 74(a).

367–99. The metre of these verses is vaitālīya. It is analysed by Warder (PM, § 188).

367. Thī-a 234,20–21: *kin te aparādhitaṃ mayā ti kiṃ tuyhaṃ āvuso mayā aparaddhaṃ*. See the note on **417**.

368. Thī-a 234,30–34: *garuke pāsāṇa-cchattaṃ viya garu-kātabbe mayhaṃ satthu sāsane yā sikkhā bhikkhuniyo uddissa sugatena sammā-sambuddhena desitā paññattā tāhi parisuddha-padaṃ parisuddha-kusala-koṭṭhāsaṃ rāgādi aṅgaṇānaṃ sabbaso abhāvena anaṅgaṇaṃ*. MIAR, surprisingly, translates (p. 153) *anaṅgaṇa* as "a non-woman".

For *sugata* see the note on **135**.

370–71. B^e^ reads *ramāma*[*se*] and corrects the metre by reading ⟨*su-*⟩*pupphite*. K^e^ and S^e^ obtain a hyper-metric pāda by reading *ramāmase* ⟨*su-*⟩*pupphite*.

For *ramāmasĕ* or *-masi* m.c. see § 72(c). Warder (PM, § 38) reads *ramāmasi*. For the ending cf. *viharemasi* in **375**b.

371–75. Warder quotes these verses (PM, § 138, and suggests certain changes m.c.

370. Thī-a 235,7–8: *apāpikā c' asī ti rūpena alāmikā asi*.

371. Warder follows P in reading *samuddhatā*, although P suggests (p. 209) *samutthaṭā*. B^e^ C^e^ K^e^ and S^e^, however, all read *samuṭṭhitā*. Thī-a 235,14–16: *kusuma-rajena samuṭṭhitā dumā ti ime rukkhā manda-vātena samuṭṭhahamāna-kusuma-reṇu-jātena attano kusuma-rajena sayaṃ samuṭṭhitā viya hutvā samantato surabhī* (C^e^ *surabhi*) *vāyanti*. In Skt both *samuddhata* and *samutthita* can mean "raised up, towering" (MW, s.vv.), and I assume that this meaning is intended here.

372. Warder follows C^e^ in reading *va* for *ca* in pāda a (for the alternation *c/v* see the note on **12**), but I do not think that this is necessary. The *ca* possibly balances the *ca* in **371**a, "Both the trees ... and the trees ... " [IBH], or *ca* and *ca* give the idea of simultaneity (see the note on **481–82**).

For *tuyha*[*ṃ*] m.c. (with Warder) see § 68(b)(ii). For *ratî* m.c. (with Warder) see § 70(c). For *ogăhissasi* m.c. (with B^e^ and Warder) see § 72(c).

373. Thī-a 235,24–26: *kuñjara-matta-kareṇu-lolitan ti matta-kuñjarehi hatthinīhi ca migānaṃ citta-tāpanena rukkha-gacchādīnam sākhā-bhañjanena ca ālolitam*. See CPD, s.v. *āloḷita*.

For *vāḷâ-* or *v⟨iy⟩āḷa-* m.c. (with Warder) see §§ 66(b), 70(c). For *asahāyikă* m.c. (with Warder) see § 72(co.

374. Thī-a 235,29–31: *tapanīya-katā va dhītikā ti ratta-suvaṇṇena viracitā dhītalikā viya sukusalena yantācariyena yanta-yoga-vasena vissajjitā suvaṇṇa-paṭimā viya vicarasi.*

B^e^ reads *sobhasi* ⟨*su-*⟩*vasanehi* which corrects the metre of pāda d, giving the opening – ⏑ – ⏑ ⏑ ⏑ as a syncopated form of – ⏑ ⏑ – ⏑ ⏑. K^e^ and S^e^ read ⟨*ni-*⟩*vasanehi*. Warder suggests *vasan*⟨*avar*⟩*ehi*, which avoids the syncopated opening (§ 66(b)).

K^e^ and S^e^ read *vattehi* for *vagguhi*, but Dhammapāla certainly read the latter since Thī-a 235,33 glosses: *vagguhī* (B^e^ *-ubhī*) *ti siniddha-maṭṭehi* (B^e^ *-maṭṭhehi*).

Thī-a 235,32–33: *kāsika-sukhumehī ti Kāsika-raṭṭhe uppannehi ativiya sukhumehi*. MW quotes *Kāsika-sūkṣma* from lex. (s.v.), with the meaning "fine cotton from Benares". BHSD (s.v.) quotes the word as an adjective from Mvu II 116 159 III 264, translated by Jones "garments of fine Benares cotton" (II 112) and "fine clothes/garments of Benares cloth" (II 155 III 252), and as a noun from Mahāvyutpatti 9176, where the Tibetan explains: "fine cloth of Kāśi". For the meaning "cotton" or "muslin" for *kāśika*, and not "silk", see BHSD (s.v.).

For *sukhuma* in the sense of "a fine garment of ... " cf. *khoma-*, *kappāsa-*, *kambala-sukkhuma* at Mil 105, and *kambala-sūkṣma* Mvu II 116, translated by Jones (II 112) "garment of fine wool".

P states (p. 209) "*anūpame* is instr. plural". Although forms in *-e* < *-ais* are found in Pāli (see EV I, p. 149 (ad Th 49), Geiger, 2000, § 79.6, WZKSOA I. 17 and cf. *citraggala-r-u*(*g*)*ghusite*, Ja VI 483), there is no need to see one here. The ending *-e* is the vocative singular of a stem in *-ā*, as Thī-a 235,34–35 recognises: *anūpame upamā-rahite tvaṃ* ... ; "O incomparable lady". For *anūpame* m.c. see § 69(b), and cf. the note on **152**.

375. Thī-a 236,2–3: *viharemasi, vasāma ramāma.* For the optative middle form see Geiger (2000, § 129), and cf. the note on **370–71**.

M reads *viharessasi* for *viharemasi*. For the alternation *s(s)/m* see the note on **262**.

For *piya⟨t⟩taro* m.c. (with B[e]) see § 64(b) and cf. **383**. Warder suggests reading *piyâtaro*, which is equally possible (§ 79(c)) but for comparatives with *-tt-* cf. *bahuttara* Th 937. Such forms perhaps arose on the analogy of *mahattara* (cf. Sn 659).

Thī-a 236,7–8: *kinnari-manda-locane ti kinnarī viya manda-puthu-vilocane.* The shortening of *-i* is presumably m.c. (§ 71), but if we punctuate *kinnari manda-locane*, then *kinnari* is a vocative: "O kinnarī, O lady with pleasant eyes". Cf. **383**.

C[e] reads *na hi c' atthi* both here and in **383**.

376. Thī-a 236,9–13: *sukhitā ehi agāram āvasā ti ehi kāma-bhogehi sukhitā hitā agāraṃ ajjhāvasa. sukhitā hoti agāram āvasantī ti keci paṭhanti. tesaṃ sukhitā bhavissati agāraṃ ajjhavasantī ti attho.*

Thī-a 236,13–14: *pāsāda-nivāta-vāsinī ti nivātesu pāsādesu vāsinī. pāsāda-vimāna-vāsinī ti ca pāṭho. vimāna-sdisesu pāsādesu vāsinī ti attho.*

For *tĕ* m.c. see § 72(c).

377. Thī-a 236,16–18: *dhārayā ti paridaha nivāsehi c' eva uttarīyañ ca karohi. abhiropehī* (C[e] *abhirohehī*) *ti maṇḍana-vibhūsana-vasena vā sarīraṃ āropaya alaṅkarohī ti attho*. See also CPD, s.v. *abhiropeti*.

For *māla-* m.c. see § 71. It is not entirely certain that this shortening is m.c., since in both Pali and Skt *māla-* is occasionally found for *mālā* in compounds (see PED and MW, s.v. *mālā*).

For *sukhuma* see the note on **374**.

Thī-a 236,18: *māla-vaṇṇakan ti mālaṃ c' eva gandha-vilepanaṃ ca.* PED does not quote *vaṇṇaka* in this meaning, but MW gives "unguent" for Skt *varṇaka* (s.v.).

378. Thī-a 236,22–23: *sudhota-raja-pacchadan ti sudhotatāya pavāhita-rajaṃ uttara-cchadaṃ*. I presume that we should divide *sudhota-raja pacchadaṃ*, and assume that *-ṃ* has been lost m.c. (§ 68(b)(i)).

Thī-a 236,23–24: *gonaka-tūlika-santhatan ti dīgha-loma-kāḷa-kojavena c' eva haṃsa-lomādi-puṇṇāya tūlikāya ca santhataṃ.* B[e] C[e] and K[e] read *santhataṃ*, and we should adopt this reading. For *kojava* cf. BHS *kocava* (for the alternation *c/j* cf. Pāli *koja/kavaca*) and Skt *kaucapaka*, quoted from the Arthaśāstra (Burrow, 1967, p. 40).

Thī-a 236,25–27: *candana-maṇḍita-sāra-gandhikan ti gosīsakādi-sāra-candanena maṇḍitatāya surabhi-gandhikaṃ*. Although we must read *-mandita[ṃ]* (§68(b)(ii) (with Bᵉ and Cᵉ) m.c., I think we must nevertheless divide the compound as in P. PED (s.v. *sāra*) quotes only "the odour of the heart of the tree" for *sāra-gandha*, but in Skt MW quotes (from lex.) the meaning "having perfection of scent, sandalwood" [IBH]. In the context with *candana-maṇḍita* this would make excellent sense here.

For *abhirŭha* m.c. (with Bᵉ and Cᵉ) see §72(c).

379. The cadence of pāda a is irregular, and probably corrupt. It can be made to scan by assuming shortening of the final vowel of *udakatŏ* (see §72(c)) and assuming resolution of – into ⏑⏑, but this would be unique in the vaitālīya stanzas of Thī (§51(c)(iv)). Bᵉ reads *udakā samuggataṃ*, and since Cᵉ reads *uggataṃ* for *ubbhataṃ* this reading may well be correct, although we should need to read *c'* (or *v'* (see below)). P's reading may have been influenced by the alternation *g/bh* (see the note on **25**). Thī-a 237,2: *udakato uggataṃ* (M *ubbhataṃ*) *uṭṭhitaṃ accuggamma ṭhitaṃ suphullaṃ uppalaṃ*. It is possible that *udakato* was originally a gloss upon *udakā* which has come into the text. We might assume that *suphullaṃ* was merely an insertion of the cty into the explanation, were it not for the fact that in the paraphrase of the verse the cty seems to gloss the word: *taṃ suṭṭhu phullaṃ uppalaṃ*. I should therefore wish to read *suphullaṃ* (in the form *su⟨p⟩phullaṃ* m.c. (§64(b)) in place of *yathāyaṃ* (Bᵉ and Cᵉ *yathā taṃ*). I take this too to be an insertion from the cty, where it occurs as a gloss upon *va* which we must read for *ca* in pāda a (with P (v.l.) and Cᵉ (text), although the lemma has *ca*). For the alternation *c/v* see the note on **12**. The cty seems already to have had the reading *ca* since it glosses: *ca-kāro nipāta-mattaṃ*, which is repeated at Thī-a 237,24–25 (ad **381**), where the reading *va* is ruled out by the occurrence of *iva* in the same pāda.

There seems to be a pun upon the compound *amanussa-sevitaṃ*. Thī-a 237,3–5: *amanussa-sevitan ti tañ ca rakkhasa-pariggahitāya pokkharaṇiyā jātattā nimmanussehi sevitaṃ kenaci aparibhuttam eva bhaveyya*: "As a lotus rising up from a pool has been courted by non-humans (rakkhasas), i.e. has not been courted by humans, so you will not be courted by men".

Thī-a 237,6–8: *sakesu aṅgesu attano sarīrāvayavesu kenaci aparibhuttesu yeva jaraṃ gamissasi vuddhā yeva jarā-jiṇṇā bhavissasi*. I do not know this sense of "kept for oneself, not enjoyed by another, i.e. virgin", for *saka*. The metre of pāda d is defective; it could be repaired by reading *ses'* for *sakesu* (§ 67(a)), and assuming that the latter word has been inserted from the cty.

For *uppala*[*ṃ*] and *tuva*[*ṃ*] m.c. see § 68(b)(ii).

380. Thī-a 237,13–15: *kin nāma tava sāran ti sammataṃ sambhāvitam, yaṃ disvā vimano aññatarasmiṃ ārammaṇe vigata-mana-saṅkappo, etth' eva vā avimano somanassiko hutvā uddikkhasi taṃ mayhaṃ kathehi.* I translate *vimano*. PED (s.v. *vimana*) suggests "infatuated" for this context.

Thī-a 237,11: *kesādi-kuṇapa-pūre*. For *kuṇapa* see EV I, p. 223 (ad Th 453) and cf. Spk I 353 (ad S I 236): *nimuggā kuṇapesv ete ti dasa-māse mātu-kucchi-saṅkhāte kuṇapasmiṃ ete nimuggā.* The cty ad **466** is silent. Ñāṇamoli (1956, p. 868) suggests "ordure" as a translation for *kuṇapa*, but I am not convinced that he is correct. He gives this translation for Vism 259, where Kosambi reads *karīsa*, not *kuṇapa*, and also for Vism 345, where *kesa-loma-nakha-dantādīni nānā-kuṇapāni* seems to be very similar to the cty here, and refers to the (apparently dead, and therefore corpse-like) parts of the body. Cf. Vism 249 foll.

For *pūra* see the note on **253**. For *-pŭramhi* m.c. see § 72(c).

The cty makes no reference to *susāna-vaḍḍhana*, but Thī-a 264,24–25 (ad **502**) explains: *kaṭasiṃ vaḍḍhente ti kaṭasiṃ susānaṃ āḷāhanam eva vaḍḍhente.* For this phrase see EV I, p. 223 (ad Th 456), and cf. *kaṭasī-vaḍḍhaka* in Th-a II 28,24–26 ad Th 152 (see EV I, p. 174). I take *susāna-vaḍḍhana* to have the same meaning as *bhūmi-vaḍḍhana* in Ja VI 19. In Skt we find *bhūmi-vardhana* (lex.), in the meaning "earth-increasing = corpse" (MW, s.v.). See Lüders (1954, pp. 24–27), and Mehendale (p. 57).

381. Thī-a 237,24–26: *turī vuccati migī. miga-cchāpāya va te akkhīnī ti attho. koriyā-r-ivā ti vā pāḷi kuñca-kāra-kukkhuṭiyā ti vuttaṃ hoti.* I assume that it is the cty's gloss on the v.l. which led PED to translate "hen" (s.v. *turī*), although one would expect *migī* to mean "doe" and *miga-chāpā* "fawn" in any context where eyes are concerned, since the epithet "doe-eyed" is so common. See PED (s.vv. *migī* and *manda*), and cf. *miga-manda-locanā* Pv 10 Vv 60 (E[e] *mita-* Vv-a (lemma) *miga-*) (= *migī viya mandakkhi-pātā* Pv-a 57, *miga-cchāpikānaṃ viya mudu-siniddha-diṭṭhi-nipātā* Vv-a 279). Since *turī* is not attested elsewhere, and since the cty's explanation could be merely a guess in the context, it is worth-while pointing out that Skt *Turī* exists in the sense of "the wife of Vasudeva". This might not be inappropriate here, since the alternative comparison is also to a superhuman being, i.e. a *kinnarī*. PED surprisingly lists *koriyā* in that form instead of *korī* which is presumably the stem form. Nor is any etymology given s.v. *koriyā*, although s.v. *turī* a connection with Tamil *kōḷi* "hen" is postulated. DED does not list *kōḷi*, but *kori* occurs (DED 1799) with the meaning "sheep", and it is quoted from Telegu in the sense of "species of antelope, etc.".

C^e^ reads *udikkhiya* for *dakkhiya*, and reads *nayanān*[*i*] to correct the metre. Although the same pāda recurs in **382**, C^e^ there reads *nayanāni*.

Thī-a 237,24–25: *ca-saddo nipāta-mattaṃ*. See the note on **379**.

For sandhi *-r-* see the note on **3**.

For *tûriyā* (with B^e^) m.c. see § 70(c). For *-ratî* (with B^e^) or ⟨*p*⟩*pavaḍḍhati* m.c. see §§ 63(b), 70(c).

382. Thī-a 237,31–32: *uppala-sikharopamāni te ti ratt'-uppal'-agga-sadisāni pamhāni tava*. It is clear from this explanation that Dhammapāla considered that *te* is to be separated from the compound preceding it, and B^e^ follows this reading. I do not understand why the cty inserts *pamhāni*. In the context, *uppala-sikharopamāni* can only agree with *nayanāni*. I am not convinced that the cty is correct, since the presence of both *te* and *tava* in the sentence is unnecessary, although explicable. I see no objection to the reading *-opamānite*, regarding it as a locative in agreement with *mukhe*. The etymology given by PED (s.v. *upamānita*) is surprising, since it is not at all clear how the causative of *upa-mā-* could get this form. It would seem desirable to take *upamānita* as the past participle of the denominative verb from *upamāna*. I should, however, like to suggest that we have here an example of the alternation *t*/*y* (see the note on **43**), and that the correct reading is *-opamāniye*, which would represent an alternative form of the future passive participle of *upa-mā-* (cf. *upameyya*) "to be compared".

For pāda c see the note on **381**.

PED would seem to be incorrect in the statement (s.v. *kāma*) that *kāma-guṇa* is always plural, as being *pañca* in number. Cf. BHS *mā te kāma-guṇo matheta cittaṃ* (Udāna-v 31.31).

383. Thī-a 237,34: *api dūra-gatā ti dūraṃ ṭhānaṃ gatā pi*. M (v.l. and lemma) reads *asi* in both places. For the alternation *p*/*s* see the note on **6**.

Thī-a 237,34–35: *saramhase ti aññaṃ kiñci acintetvā tava nayanāni eva anussarāmi*. The cty seems to be taking the verb as an indicative, and since B^e^ and C^e^ read *-amhase* we should probably adopt this reading.

Thī-a 237,35–238,1: *āyata-pamhe ti dīgha-pakhume*. For *pamha* see Geiger (2000, § 59.1).

Thī-a 238,1: *visuddha-dassane ti nimmala-locane*. Cf. S I 181.

B^e reads *piyattaro* and C^e *piyataro*. Thī-a 238,1–3: *na hi m'* (C^e *c'*) *atthi tayā piyattaro* (C^e *piyataro*) *nayanā ti tava nayanato añño koci mayhaṃ piyataro n' atthi. tayā ti hi sāmi-atthe eva karaṇa-vacanaṃ*. The use of *tayā* as a genitive singular is quite unacceptable in this context. Dhammapāla apparently took the pāda to mean "No one is dearer to me than your eye". The pāda seems, however, to be exactly parallel to **375**c, and I should therefore prefer to follow P's reading, and translate "No eyes are dearer to me than you", with a possible implication of "even my own". For other examples of Dhammapāla being wrong in his interpretation see § 37.

For *piya⟨t⟩tarā* m.c. see § 64(b) and cf. **375**. For *-pamhĕ* m.c. see § 72(c).

For *kinnari* as a vocative see the note on **375**.

384. K^e and S^e read *patthesi* for *maggayasi*, but this is unmetrical and has probably been introduced as a gloss. P's reading, however, is also unmetrical, and we should read *ma[g]gâyasi* m.c. (see §§ 65(b), 70(c)). This raises the possibility that we are dealing here with a derivative from a denominative verb from Skt *mṛga*, i.e. **mṛgāyati* "to hunt", rather than the direct development from Skt *mārgayati*.

For *buddha-suta* see the note on *putta* in **46**.

385. Thī-a 238,19: *athā ti nipāta-mattaṃ*. *Atha* probably has the meaning "but" here and in **386**. See EV I, p. 191 (ad Th 237).

386. B^e and C^e read *iṅgāla-kuyā* for *iṅghāḷa-khuyā*, and since there is no evidence elsewhere for *-gh-* in this word (see CDIAL 125) it is probable that *iṅgāla-* is the correct reading. Thī-a 238,22 glosses: *aṅgāra-kāsuyā*. For *kāsu* see the note on **491**. CPD (s.v. *iṅgāla-kuyā*), refers to Haebler 1964, who suggests that *iṅgāla-kuyā* is a wrong formation from an original AMg **iṅgāla-kuvā*, where *-kuvā* is m.c. for *kūvā*. Cf. Sp I 220 *aṅgāra-puṇṇa-kūpa* (= *aṅgāra-kāsu* Sp-ṭ (B^e) II 23). The ending *-ā* is, therefore, an ablative.

Thī-a 238,22: *ujjhito ti vāt'-ukkhitto viya yo koci. dahaniyā indhanaṃ viyā ti attho*. PED does not list *dahanī*. The past participle *ujjhito*, translated "jumped out from" in CPD (s.v.) seems strange, and the inclusion of *ukkhitto* in the cty suggests to me that *ujjhito* is either a mistake or a bye-form of *ukkhito*, with *-jjh-* < *-kṣ-*. For Skt *ukṣ-* "scatter sparks" see MW (s.v.), although Skt *ukṣita* occurs only in the meaning "sprinkled, moistened" (see the note on **391**).

Thī-a 238,23: *visapatto-r-ivā ti visagatabhājanaṃ viya*. For sandhi *-r-* see the note on **3**.

In pāda b P and C^e read *aggato kato*, and B^e reads *aggito kato*. The explanations also differ. Thī-a 238,24–25 reads: *aggito kato ti aggito aṅgārato apagato kato* (Ce: *agghato hato ti agghato abhihato, app'-agghanako kato*). *visassa lesam pi asesetvā apanīto vināsito ti attho*. The presence of *agghanaka* in Ce persuades me that we should read *agghato* with Ce, and translate *agghato kato* as "made as regards value", i.e. "valued as". CPD (s.v. *abhihata*) prefers *abhihata* to *abhirata*. See also CPD s.v. *appagghanaka* and appendix p. 545 (s.v. [1]*aggha*). The phrase *aggato kataṃ* occurs in **394**, where Thī-a 240,11 explains *aggato* as *purato*, but *agghato* would make good sense in the context.

For *atha* see the note on **385**.

387. Pāda a is unmetrical, but the metre can be corrected by reading *yass' assa* (§ 67(a)) for *yassa siyā* (cf. CPD's suggestion (p. 557, s.v. *anupāsita*) of reading *yassāssa*). The reading in P could easily have been introduced from the cty, where both words occur in the explanation.

CPD (s.v. *apaccavekkhita*) translates "not closely examined". Can the word here possibly be a past participle used as an action noun (see the note on **261**) = *apaccavekkhanā* "not examining, non-investigation, non-attention" (see CPD, s.v.)? Perhaps we should translate "of whom there is lack of observation".

Be and Ce read *anupāsito* for *anusāsito*, and this is clearly the correct reading. Thī-a 238,27–29: *satthā vā anupāsito siyā ti satthā vā dhamma-sarīrassa adassanena yassā itthiyā anupāsito siyā*. For the alternation *p/s* see the note on **6**. See CPD, p. 557 (s.v. *anupāsita*). For *upāsati* cf. **54**.

Thī-a 238,31: *palobhaya upagaccha* (Ce *palobhaya upacchandaya*). M reads *palobhassa* for *palobhaya* in the lemma and explanation, but this reading is unmetrical, and cannot be correct. M glosses: *palobhassa upacchandassa*. M's form *palobhassa* probably arises from the alternation *y/s*(*s*) (see the note upon **84**). PED does not list *upacchandati*, but it occurs in the form *upacchādemi* as a gloss upon *chādemi* in **409** (see the note upon **409**). Skt *upacchand-* occurs, in the causative, with the meaning "entice, seduce" (MW, s.v.).

In Skt *pralubh-* means "to lust after", and the causative means "to cause to lust after, allure, entice, attempt to seduce" (MW, s.v.), which exactly fits this context. PED (s.v. *palobheti*) gives "to desire, to be greedy" which is not so suitable, although *paluddha* is defined as "seduced, enticed" (s.v.).

The structure of pāda d is somewhat defective. We must presumably understand some part of the verb *palobheti* again, perhaps the absolutive, "having tried to seduce (i.e. if you try to seduce) one who knows, you will … ". The cty understands *āgamma*.

For *so* with a second person verb see the note on **24**. For *sŏ* (or *sa*) m.c. see § 72(c).

388. Thī-a 239,1–2: *akkuṭṭha-vandite ti akkose vandanāya ca.* Cf. *akkuṭṭha-vanditaṃ* at Sn 702, explained (Pj II 492): *akkosañ ca vandanañ ca.* For past participles used as action nouns see the note on **261**.

For *a[k]kuṭṭha-* m.c. see § 65(b). For *satî* m.c. (with B^e^) see § 70(c).

389. Thī-a 239,8–9: *magg'-aṭṭhaṅgika-yāna-yāyinī ti aṭṭhaṅgika-magga-saṃkhātena ariya-yānena nibbāna-puraṃ yāyinī upagatā.* For *yāna* as an equivalent of *magga* see PED, s.v. *yāna.*

390. Thī-a 239,11–12: *sucittā ti hattha-pāda-mukhādi-ākārena suṭṭhu cittitā viracitā. sombhā ti sumbhakā.* See Lüders, 1940, pp. 426–27 and cf. BHSD s.v. *śobhika.*

B^e^ and C^e^ read *dāruka-pillakāni va* in place of *-cillakā navā.* Thī-a 239,12–13: *dāruka-pillakāni vā ti dāru-daṇḍādīhi uparacita-rūpakāni.* The ending *-āni* in the gloss, and the lack of any reference to *navā*, make it fairly certain that the reading of B^e^ and C^e^ should be adopted. PED gives for *pillaka* (s.v.) the meaning "the young of an animal, sometimes used as a term for a child". For *dāru-pillaka* in the sense "doll", cf. *dāru-dhītalikā* "doll" at Vin III 126. If this reading is correct, then the entry *cillaka* should be deleted from PED. Cf. *dāru-kaṭallako* "puppet" (= *dāru-maya-yanta-rūpakaṃ viya,* Ja V 18).

Thī-a 239,13–14: *khīlakehī ti hattha-pāda-piṭṭhi-kaṇṇakādi-atthāya ṭhapita-daṇḍehi.* PED (s.v. *khīlaka*) implies that *khīlaka* is found only in the compound *a-khīlaka*; CDIAL 3202 follows this, and lists *khīlaka* only as an adjective. Clearly *-ka* gives a diminutive sense here.

B^e^ and C^e^ read *panaccakā* for *panaccitā.* Thī-a 239,15–16: *vividhaṃ panaccakā ti yanta-suttādīnaṃ añchana-vissajjanādinā paṭṭhapita-nacakkā. panaccantā viya diṭṭhā ti yojanā.* It seems to me that this explanation better fits P's reading *panaccitā* "caused to dance". For the alternation *k/t* see the note on **43**. PED does not list *añchana* "pulling", nor *vissajjana* in the sense of "loosening", i.e. the opposite of *añchana.*

For *tantîhi* m.c. (with B^e^ C^e^ and K^e^) see § 70(c).

391. Thī-a 239,17–20: *tamh' uddhaṭe tanti-khīlake ti sannivesa-visiṭṭha-racanā-visesa-yuttaṃ upādāya rūpaka-samaññātamhi tantimhi khīlake ca ṭhānato uddhaṭe bandhato vissaṭṭhe visuṃ karaṇena aññamaññaṃ vikale tahiṃ tahiṃ khipanena parikrite* (C^e^ *paripakkhite*) *vikirite. Vikirita* is not listed in PED, where the only past participle given for *vikirati* is *vikiṇṇa.* It is possible to take *tamh'* as being for *tamhi* or *tamhā.* If locative it should be understood as going with *tanti-khīlake.* If, however, we take it as *tamhā* it means: "when the string and sticks have been removed from it".

P's *paripakkate* is not metrical. Although B[e] *parikrite* is metrical, I doubt that it can be correct. We could possible read *pari[pa]kkate* (§67(a)) or *parikkite* (see Ja V 74), or if we take note of *-kkh-* in C[e] and the vv.ll. at Ja V 74 we could read *parukkhite* < *pari* + *ukkhita*. For *ukkhita* see the note on **386** and cf. *ruhirukkhita* (so read for *ruhirakkhita*) Ja IV 331, and for *okkhita*, which is probably merely a scribal variation of *ukkhita*, cf. *candanokkhita* **145** and *okkhita* which is a v.l. for *okkita* in the lemma at Ja V 74.

Just as *vekalla* is opposed in meaning to *sākalya* at Pj I 187, so I take *vikala* to be the opposite of *sakala*. The definitions given in PED are not quite satisfactory. It means "mutilated, impaired" in Skt (see MW, s.v.).

P and C[e] read *avinde*; B[e] reads *na vindeyya*. Thī-a 239,20–22: *na vindeyya* (C[e] *avinde*) *khaṇḍaso kate ti potthaka-rūpassa avayave khaṇḍā-khaṇḍite kate potthaka-rūpaṃ na vindeyya na upalabheyya*. I would suggest that the reading of B[e] arose because the gloss had crept into the text. The metre of pāda c is defective and I suggest that we read *avind⟨iy⟩e*, which then gives the syncopated opening ⏑ – ⏑ – – (see §66(b)). The corruption of the text is certainly older than Dhammapāla (§46), whose explanation *na vindeyya na upalabheyya* is based upon the belief that *avinde* is a negative optative. For such negative verbs see EV I, pp. 215 foll. (ad Th 405), de Jong (1972), and CPD 3a- (7).

For *vi⟨s⟩saṭṭhe* (with B[e] and C[e]) m.c. see §64(b). For *uddhatĕ* m.c. see §72(c). For *kimhî* m.c. see §70(c).

392. Pāda a causes difficulties, with its mixture of singular and plural forms: similarly *vattanti* occurs in pādas bc where the metre requires *vattati*. B[e] and C[e] read *tathūpamā*, and *vattati* in pāda c, but this still leaves the problem of *maṃ* in pāda a and *vattanti* in pāda b. Dhammapāla clearly read *maṃ*, since Thī-a 239,28 explains: *man ti me paṭibaddhā upaṭṭhahanti*, but I think that he was misled (§36). Stede (p. 95) proposed reading *tathūpamāni dehakān' imāni*, but this is unmetrical. I would suggest that the original reading for pāda a was *tathūpamaṃ dehakam imaṃ*, in *which dehakam* became *dehakām* m.c. (cf. the v.l. *dehakāmi mam* quoted by P (n.)). For the sandhi change *-am* > *-ām* see Warder (PM, p. 50, n. 2), and cf. *kasām iva*, Dhp 143; *ajjatanām iva*, Dhp 227; *Sunarikām api*, M I 39; *kusalām iti*, Sn 712; *passatām iva*, Sn 763. This unusual sandhi could easily have led to the appearance of *dehakāni*, and the reading *vattanti* would have evolved as an attempt to correct the grammar.

The situation in pāda c is slightly different in that, as stated, B[e] and C[e] read *vattati*. I presume that this pāda is a locative absolute, "[the body] not existing without ... ". In support of my belief that we should read the singular form *dehakām* is the fact that the explanation replaces the word by *deho*; in support of the suggestion that pāda is a locative absolute is the phrase *evaṃ sante* in the explanation.

For *tĕhi* m.c. see § 72(c). For *vatta[n]ti* m.c. in pāda b (with P v.l.) and in pāda c (with Be and Ce) see § 68(a)(ii). For *kimhî* m.c. see § 70(c).

393. Thī-a 240,3–4: *yathā kusalena citta-kārena bhittiyaṃ haritālena makkhitaṃ littaṃ tena lepaṃ datvā kataṃ ālikhitaṃ cittikaṃ itthī-rūpena addasa passeyya.* For an aorist in the sense of the optative see BHSG §§ 32.119–24, but *addasa* makes perfectly good sense as an indicative: "you have seen a well-painted mural, and your eye has been deceived by it". For another example of trompe-l'œil painting, cf. the Jain story of the girl who painted a peacock feather on the ground so realistically that the king broke his fingernails trying to pick it up (Erz, p. 49).

Be and Ce read *saññā* for *paññā*. Thī-a 240,5–10: *tattha yā upathambhana-khepanādi-kiriyā-sampattiyā mānusikā nu kho ayaṃ bhitti apassāya ṭhitā ti saññā, sā niratthakā manussa-bhāva-saṅkhātassa atthassa tattha abhāvato, mānusī ti pana kevalaṃ tahiṃ tassa ca viparīta-dassanaṃ, yāthāvato gahaṇaṃ na hoti, dhamma-puñja-matte itthi-purisādi-gahaṇam pi evaṃ sampadam idaṃ daṭṭhabban ti adhippāyo.* I now prefer to follow the reading *saññā* and translate "perception". For the alternation *p/s* see the note on **6**.

For *yathā* and *tĕ* m.c. see § 72(c). For *cittika[ṃ]* m.c. see § 68(b)(ii).

394. Thī-a 240,11–12: *māyam viya aggato katan ti māyā-kārena purato upaṭṭhāpitaṃ māyā-sadisaṃ.* It is clear from the explanation that Dhammapāla had the reading *aggato*, but a reading *agghato kataṃ* (see the note on **386**) would make excellent sense, i.e. "you run towards something valued like (= as valuable as) illusion".

Be and Ce read *upagacchasi* for *upadhāvasi*. Thī-a 240,14–15: *rittakaṃ tucchakaṃ anto-sāra-rahitaṃ idaṃ atta-bhāvaṃ evaṃ māmā ti sara-vantaṃ viya upagacchasi abhinivisasi*, which seems to support the reading *upagacchasi*. For *abhinivisati* see the note on **466**.

Thī-a 240,16–17: *jana-majjhe-r-iva ruppa-rūpakan ti māyā-kārena mahā-jana-majjhe dassitaṃ rūpiya-rūpa-sadisam sāraṃ viya upaṭṭhahantaṃ; asāran ti attho.* Although PED (s.v. *rūpiya*²) separates this word from *rūpiya*¹ = "silver", I see no reason for doing this. The reference is presumably to confidence tricksters who try to deceive credulous bystanders and persuade them to buy what seems to be (i.e. has the form of) silver. The Arthaśāstra has a section (II.14) on the methods of producing and detecting frauds of this kind. See also Lüders, 1940, pp. 394–95.

For sandhi *-r-* see the note on **3**.

395. Thī-a 240,18–19: *vaṭṭani-r-ivā ti lākhāya guḷikā viya. koṭarohitā ti koṭare rukkha-susire ṭhapitā.* PED does not list *koṭara*. CDIAL 3496 gives a Dravidian etymology for the word. Although Burrow earlier suggested this (1955, p. 382), the suggestion is not repeated in DED, but see DED 1383.

B[e] reads *pubbuḷakā* for *bubbuḷakā*. Thī-a 240,19–20: *akkhi-dala-majjhe ṭhita-jala-bubbula-*(B[e] *pubbuḷa-*)*sadisā*. Since *budbuda* exists in Skt in the sense of "the pupil of the eye" (MW, s.v. *nayana*), I should prefer to follow P's reading.

Thī-a 240,20–21: *pīḷikoḷikā ti akkhi-gūthako. Akkhi-gūtha* is explained at Pv-a 198 as *akhi-mala*. This accords with the fact that the word is found at Sn 197 in company with *kaṇṇa-gūthaka* "earwax".

Thī-a 240,21–23: *ettha jayatī ti etasmiṃ akkhi-maṇḍale ubhosu koṭīsu visa-gandhaṃ vāyanto nibbattati. pīḷikoḷikā ti vā akkhi-dalesu nibbattanakā pīḷikā vuccati.* PED gives two explanations of the word; s.v. *koḷikā* it translates "having boils of jujube size", taking the word as an adjective referring to *itthi*, which can hardly be correct. The translation is probably a reminiscence of such phrases as (*piḷikā*) *kola-mattiyo ahesum* Sn p. 125. S.v. *pīḷikoṭikā* it translates "eye secretion". Since in the context the word must be a noun, I should favour the second of these alternatives. The reference given in PED to JPTS 1884, p. 68, is a mistake for p. 88.

Thī-a 240,23–24: *vividhā ti nīlādi-maṇḍalānann c' eva ratta-pītādīnaṃ sattannaṃ paṭalānañ ca vasena aneka-vidhā.* For the seven membranes of the eye cf. As 307.

Thī-a 240,24–25: *cakkhu-vidhā ti cakkhu-bhāvā cakkhu-ppakārā vā. tassa aneka-kalā-paggaha-bhāvato piṇḍitā ti samudhitā.*

In pāda d B[e] and C[e] read *ca* for *va*. For the alternation *c/v* see the note on **12**.

For sandhi *-r-* see the note on **3**.

For *pīḷikoḷikă* m.c see § 72(c).

396. The other editions agree with P in reading *na ca pajjittha*. Thī-a 240,33: *tasmiṃ cakkhusmiṃ saṅgaṃ nāpajji.* PED (s.v. *pajjati*) states that the simple verb occurs only in one doubtful passage, i.e. A IV 362. An examination of that passage, however, makes it clear that we should read *pacchati* (with the v.l. and Mp), and take it as a future (< *prāpsyati*, cf. *lacchati* < *lapsyati* (Geiger, 2000, § 150)). Mp IV 168 glosses: *pāpuṇissati*. The reading *pajjittha* here is clearly a mistake for *sajjittha*, and the common alternation *p/s* (see the note on **6**) has been helped by the occurrence of *āpajj-* in the explanation.

For *tĕ* m.c. see § 72(c).

Thī-a 240,29: *asaṅga-mānasā ti katthaci pi ārammaṇe anāsatta-cittā.*

397. Thī-a 241,2–3: *tatthā ti akkhimhi, tassaṃ vā theriyaṃ. athavā tatthā ti tasmiṃ yeva ṭhāne.* I follow the third of these alternatives.

For the aorist form *viramāsi* (Thī-a 241,1–2 glosses: *tassa rāgo vigacchi*) see Geiger (2000, § 165.1).

For *puno* see the note on **292**.

For *khamāpayî* m.c. see § 70(c).

Thī-a 241,4–5: *sotthi siyā brahma-cārinī ti seṭṭha-cārini mahesike tuyhaṃ ārogyam eva bhaveyya.* PED does not list *mahesikā.*

398. M (lemma) reads *āhariya* for *āhaniya*, but neither reading is metrical. We could read *āhaniyâ* (§ 70(c)), but B[e] and C[e] read *āsādiya*, which CPD (s.v. *āsādeti*) accepts. Thī-a 241,7: *āsādiyā ti ghaṭṭetvā.*

Thī-a 241,8: *liṅgiyā ti pajjalitaṃ aggim āliṅgetvā.* PED (s.v. *liṅgeti*) points out that the absolutive is formed as from the verb **liṅgati*. See also BHSD (s.v. *liṅgita*).

B[e] and C[e] read *gaṇhiya*, and I accept this reading instead of *gaṇhissaṃ*, as the absolutive matches *āsādiya* and *liṅgiya*. P *-ss-* is doubtless a development of *-s-*. For the *y/s* alternation see the note on **84**.

For *api nu* as an alternative see PED (s.v. *api*).

For *nû* m.c. see § 70(c).

399. Thī-a 241,9: *tato ti tasmā dhutta-purisā.* Although this interpretation would be possible, I see no reason for seeing any other meaning than the usual "after that, then" here.

Thī-a 241,10–11: *buddha-varassa santikan ti sammā-sambuddhassa santikaṃ.* It seems probable that the cty is here taking *buddha-vara* to mean "the choice one of the enlightened ones, i.e best of … ". In his review of EV I, however, de Jong has given reasons for not taking *buddha-vara* as a tatpuruṣa compound. We can therefore take it to mean "the Buddha, the choice one, i.e. the excellent Buddha". Cf. **454**, and see the note on *buddha-seṭṭha* in **332**.

Thī-a 241,11–12: *passiya vara-puñña-lakkhaṇan ti uttamehi puñña-sambhārehi nivvatta-mahā-purisa-lakkhaṇaṃ disvā.* The absolutive is floating, but the simplest way to take it is with an understood *tassā* "[of her] having seen … the eye was as before". It is not entirely clear what *vara-puñña-lakkhaṇa* means, since it can be a tatpuruṣa compound or a bahuvrīhi: "the mark of excellent merit" or "the one possessing the mark[s] of excellent merit". The mark of excellent merit, in the singular as the tatpuruṣa must be, could only in the context refer to her blind eye, but it seems odd to say that she was healed when she saw herself. It would seem more logical that she should be healed by the Buddha when he saw her affliction, but to assume that *passiya* goes with *Buddhassa* in pāda b is straining the syntax. If pāda d had contained a past participle, e.g. *kataṃ*, we could have understood *tena*: "[by him] having seen ... the eye was restored". If we could assume that this poem was originally composed in a dialect where ca became *ya*, we could then take *passiya* as *passi ya* = *passi ca*, and translate: "she went to the Buddha, and he saw ... ; her eye was as before". In view of my doubts about this verse I translate *vara-puñña-lakkhaṇa* as a bahuvrīhi, referring to the Buddha.

For *agamî* and *cakkhû* m.c. see § 70(c). For *să* m.c. see § 72(c).

400–47. Mrs Rhys Davids stated (Sist., p. 163 note) that she was unable to classify the metre throughout this poem. For its identification see the note on **213–23**. All the verses are gaṇacchandas except **416**a* and **444**a, which are śloka. The gaṇacchandas verses are mostly āryā, although **410**b is very corrupt. Pāda b of **441** is also very corrupt, but it is possible that the metre is upagīti. See the notes on **410** and **441**.

For *ti* at the end of the group see the note on **1**.

For the Jain references in this group of verses, especially in **428** and **431**, see the note on **87–91**, and Mrs Rhys Davids' comment (Sist., p. xxii).

There are several features in this poem which might be held to support a date for its composition which is later than that of most of Thī. While I would not deny this, I doubt whether these features can provide us with a precise dating (see also the note on **448–522**).

(a) The mention of Pāṭaliputta in **400** must clearly be later than that city's foundation and rise to pre-eminence. There is, however, no need to assume that this is later than Aśoka's time (§ 24), and moreover **400** is one of the verses which are recognised by the cty as a later addition by the *saṅgīti-kārā* (§ 5).

(b) Winternitz (p. 111) claimed that this poem seemed to belong to a later period of decay, when "Buddhism had already passed through many a crisis". We have, however, merely to refer to the earliest texts to see that from the first days of Buddhism monks were guilty of crimes far more heinous than leaving the Order to get married.

(c) Mrs Rhys Davids (Sist., p. xviii) regarded this poem and **448–522** as the products of later literary craft. Warder's analysis (PM, § 214) would support this, but any such dating is relative rather than absolute. Since the āryā metre fell into disuse among Buddhist writers, nothing in that metre is likely to be very late. See Alsdorf (1965, pp. 64 foll.).

(d) Mrs Rhys Davids also drew attention (Sist., p. xviii) to the fact that although several therīs are reputed to have remembered previous existences, only Isidāsī and Sumedhā (**448–522**) actually recount these to their contemporaries. Again, it does not seem possible to date a practice of this kind.

400–402. Thī-a 242,18 states that these three verses were added by the *saṅgīti-kārā* (§ 5).

400. B^e and C^e read *maṇḍe* at the end of pāda b, correctly (§ 57(c)). Thī-a 245,3: *pathaviyā maṇḍe ti sakalāya pathaviyā maṇḍa-bhūte*. Ja IV 234 (ad Ja IV 233) explains: *puthavi-maṇḍe ti maṇḍo sāro*. There is no connection between *puthavi-maṇḍa* and *puthavi-maṇḍala* as PED (s.v. *maṇḍa*) seems to imply. For the meaning "best part", cf. BHS *pṛthavīya maṇḍa* and *mahī-maṇḍa* (BHSD, s.v. *maṇḍa*) and see Vāk 5.158.

The reference to Pāṭaliputta in this verse is of no value for dating purposes (see the note on **400–47**).

For *guṇa-vatîyo* or ⟨*hi*⟩ *guṇa-vatiyo* (with B^e and C^e) m.c., see Alsdorf (Ap. II, p. 240) and §§ 66(c), 70(d).

Thī-a 245,4: *Sakya-kula-kulīnāyo ti Sakya-kule kula-dhītāyo. Sakya-puttassa bhagavato sāsane pabbajitatāya.*

401. Thī-a 245,6: *tatthā ti tāsu dvīsu bhikkhunīsu.*

Thī-a 245,7: *jhāna-jjhāyana-ratāyo ti lokiya-lok'-uttarassa jhānassa jhāyane abhiratā*. It is clear, therefore that Dhammapāla read as P. Alsdorf, however, points out (App. II, p. 240) that we must read *-jjhăyana-* m.c. (§ 72(d)). The question then arises whether we should understand *-jjhayana-* as being m.c. for *-jjhāyana-*, or should punctuate *jhān'-ajjhayana-* and translate "meditation and study". This latter is perhaps more likely, although the combination of *jhāna* and *jhāyana* is not impossible, cf. *jhānaṃ jhāyati* D II 237 [IBH]. PED quotes *ajjhayana* only from Mil 225, the more common form being *ajjhena*. CPD lists *jhānajjhena* (s.v. *ajjhena*), which means either that such a compound exists, which would support Alsdorf's reading and the second interpretation, or that the editors of CPD at the time proposed to make such an emendation themselves, with the second interpretation.

For *Isidāsĭ* m.c. see § 72(d).

For [*ca*] in pāda b and *bahussutā*[*yo*] in pāda d see § 67(c). The latter correction avoids Warder's objection to the form of the sixth gaṇa (PM, § 209 note 1). He was presumably reading *dhutā-kilesāyo*, which would give a gīti verse.

403. Thī-a 245,17–18: *pāsādikā 'sī ti rūpa-sampattiyā passantānaṃ pasādāvahā asi.*

Thī-a 245,19–20: *kiṃ disvāna valikan ti kīdisaṃ vyālikaṃ dosam gharāvāse ādīnaṃ disvā.* For *valîkaṃ* m.c. (with PED, following Kern (1916B, p. 113)) see §70(d). See also **417**.

Thī-a 245,20–21: *athā ti nipāta-mattaṃ.*

For *nekkhamma* see the note on **226**.

404. Thī-a 245,22: *anuyuñjamānā ti pucchiyamānā.* We therefore require a passive form. CPD (s.v. *anuyuñjati*) suggests *anuyujjamānā.* B^e and C^e read *anuyuñjiyamānā*, which is passive but does not scan.

For *Isidāsĭ* m.c. see §72(d). For [*idaṃ*] in pāda c (with B^e and C^e) m.c. see §67(c).

For -*br*- making position in *abravi* see §74(a). For *abravi* m.c. see §71.

In pāda d we should separate *yathā mhi* or read *yathămhi* with C^e. Cf. **407**.

405. For *ekă* m.c. (with B^e and C^e) see §72(d). We should punctuate *eka-dhītā* with B^e and C^e and translate "only daughter". Thī-a 245,26: *piyā ti eka-dhītu-bhāvena piyāyitabbā.*

For *mayha*[*ṃ*] m.c. see §68(b)(ii). For *manāpā* ⟨*ca*⟩ m.c. (with B^e and C^e) see §66(c).

406. There is some doubt about the reading in pāda b. B^e and C^e read *varakā āgacchuṃ uttama-kulīnā* for P's *varako āgacchi uttama-kulīno*. Thī-a 245,29–30: *mama varakā maṃ vārentā āgacchuṃ ... yena te pesitā, so seṭṭhi,* confirming that *varakā* is plural. This leaves the syntax of pāda c floating "[there was] a merchant". For *varaka* in the sense of "asking for a wife for someone else" see MW (s.v.) and VI (s.v.).

B^e and C^e read *pahūta*- for *bahuta*-, and since the metre demands -*ū*-, Alsdorf adopts this reading (App. II, p. 240). There is, however, no need to depart so far from P's reading, for if we read *bahu*[*t*]*ta*- (§64(b)), this is perfectly satisfactory. See also **435**. PED quotes *bahutta* only as a noun "multiplicity, manifoldness", but for its use as an adjective see CDIAL 9190.

For *Sāketâto* (cf. the Pkt ablative ending -*āo* (Pischel, 1900, §363) and *tâto* in **420 436** and *seṭṭhî* m.c. (with B^e C^e K^e and S^e) see §70(d). For *adā*[*si*] m.c. see §67(c). For *ta*[*s*]*sa* m.c. see §65(b).

Thī-a 245,31–32: *suṇhaṃ, suṇisaṃ puttassa bhariyaṃ.*

407. For *sassûyā* m.c. (with C^e^) see § 70(d). For *sa[s]surassa* (with B^e^ and C^e^) m.c. see § 65(b). Since the form expected historically is *sasura*, it is by no means clear why the reading *sassura* arose, although PED is probably correct (s.v. *sasura*) in assuming contamination by *sassu*. Cf. **417**.

Thī-a 245,35–36: *yath' amhi anusiṭṭhā ti tehi yathā anusiṭṭhā amhi tathā karomi, tesaṃ anusiṭṭhiṃ na atikkamāmi*. PED does not list *atikkamati* in the sense of "to transgress [an order]", although this meaning is given in CPD.

For *yathā mhi* see the note on **404**. C^e^ reads *yathămhi*.

408. For *parijano* ⟨*vā*⟩ (with B^e^ and C^e^) m.c. see § 66(c). For [*tam*] m.c. see § 67(c). For *mayha*[*ṃ*] m.c. see § 68(b)(ii). For *sāmikassâ* and *bhaginîyo* m.c. see § 70(d).

Alsdorf (App. II, p. 240) suggests reading *ĕka-vārakaṃ* m.c. (§ 72(d)). PED does not quote *vāraka* in the sense of *vāra* "turn". B^e^ and C^e^, however, read *eka-varakaṃ* which is metrical. It would seem that Dhammapāla had this reading, for Thī-a 246,1 explains: *eka-varakam pī ti eka-valabham pi*.

Thī-a 246,1: *ubbiggā ti tasantā*.

Mrs Rhys Davids (Sist., p. 158) and PED (s.v. *bhātar-*) take *bhātuno* as nominative plural "sisters, brothers, and retinue". This certainly makes good sense, but the plural ending *-uno* is not quoted from an *r*-declension word elsewhere (see Geiger, 2000, § 91), and it would be more usual as a genitive singular form, cf. *jeṭṭhassa bhātuno* Ap 581 (quoted Thī-a 70,10). A comparable form is quoted for Pkt (from the grammarians) by Pischel (1900, § 391), i.e. *piuṇo* from *piu* < *piṭr-*.

409. Thī-a 246,4: *chādemī ti upacchādemi*. It would appear that *upacchādemi* is a variant of *upacchandemi*. The latter form occurs in Thī-a 238,31 (ad **387**), where C^e^ *palobhaya* is glossed: *upacchandaya*. PED (s.v. *chādeti*²) gives only the simplex meaning "to delight in, approve". It does not list the causative sense we have here "to cause to approve, to gratify". Cf. Skt *chandayati* "to gratify anyone (accusative) with something (instrumental)" (MW, s.v. ³*chad-*) and *upacchandayati* "to conciliate, coax, entice" (MW, s.v. *upacchand-*). I do not understand why PED (s.v. *chādeti*²) says "to *khyā*?". The derivation is < *chand-*. See also the note on **387**.

For *annena* ⟨*ca*⟩ (with B^e^ and C^e^) m.c. see § 66(c).

410. B^e^ and C^e^ read *ummāre* at the end of pāda b, correctly (§ 57(c)). The fact that Dhammapāla read this is clear from Thī-a 246,6: *ummāre ti dvāre*.

Thī-a 246,6–7: *dhovantī hattha-pāde ti hattha-pāde dhovinī āsiṃ. dhovitvā gharaṃ samupagamāmī ti yojanā*. For *dhovantĭ* m.c. see § 72(d). I am, however, not convinced that this reading is correct. A present participle seems strange: "in the very act of washing my hands and feet I approached my husband". I should prefer to read *dhovitvā* (*dhovitvă* m.c., see § 72(d)), which the cty might be held to support. I should then assume that P's reading is in fact a gloss upon *dhovitvā hattha-pāde* which has crept into the text, i.e. *dhota-hattha-pādā* "possessing washed hands and feet".

In pāda a Alsdorf prefers to read *kāle*[*na*] *u*⟨*pa*⟩*ṭṭhahitvā* (with B^e and C^e) (§§ 66(c), 67(c)), although P's reading is perfectly metrical. In view of the fact that in **413** Isidāsī states that she was *uṭṭhāyikā*, I should prefer to see a reference to her early rising here, and read as P.

Alsdorf points out the difficulties in pāda b. B^e and C^e read *samupagamāmi* for *samupagamiṃ*. K^e and S^e read ⟨*pati-*⟩*gharaṃ*. Alsdorf suggests (App. II, p. 240, n.) reading *āgamemi* "I await", although the pāda is then three morae short. A metrical āryā pāda can be obtained if we combine the reading of B^e and C^e with that of K^e and S^e, and make some minor changes m.c.: ⟨*pati-*⟩*ghara*[*ṃ*] *samupâgamāmi, ummāre* (§§ 66(c), 68(b)(ii), 70(d)).

411. Thī-a 246,8: *kocchan ti massūnaṃ kesānañ ca ullikhana-kocchaṃ*. Cf. *kocchan ti usira-mayaṃ vā puñja-mayaṃ vā pabbaja-mayaṃ vā* (Sp 1217). For *koccha* see the note on **254**.

Thī-a 246,8–10: *pasādan ti kaṇha-cuṇṇādi-mukha-vilepanaṃ. pasādhanan ti pi pāṭho pasādhana-bhaṇḍaṃ*. For *pasād*⟨*han*⟩*aṃ* m.c. see § 66(c). For the alternation *d*/*dh* cf. *sadā*/*'saddhā* in **452**. As Alsdorf points out, the suggestion of reading *pāsaka*, made by Morris (1891–93, pp. 45 foll.), cannot be correct, although adopted by PED (s.v. *pasāda*).

Pādas ab are *vipulā* (§ 57(a)).

Thī-a 246,10–11: *parikamma-kārikā viyā ti agga-kulikā vibhava-sampannā pi patiparicārikā ceṭikā viya*.

412. Thī-a 246,12: *sādhayāmī ti pacāmi*.

For *tathă* m.c. see § 72(d). For *putta*[*ka*]*ṃ* m.c. see § 67(c).

Pādas ab are *vipulā* (§ 57(a)).

B^e and C^e read *dhovantī* for *dhoviṃ*, against the metre. This would seem to be a reading which has been introduced in error from the cty, where *dhovantī paricarāmī ti yojanā* has been interpreted as a gloss upon *dhovantī*.

413. Thī-a 246,14: *bhatti-*(C^e *bhati-*)*katan ti kata-sāmi-bhattikaṃ* (B^e and C^e *-bhatikaṃ*, but cf. *sāmi-bhattino* "devoted to their lord" at Mhv 7.50). I assume that *bhatti-kata* is a bahuvrīhi compound with *kata* as a past participle used as an action noun, cf. *nāga-hata* "possessing the destruction of an elephant" =

"destroyer of an elephant", and therefore translate "possessing the doing of reverence" = "revering". For such a use of past participles see the note on **261**. It would also be possible to see the use of *kata* in the sense of *gata* "gone to devotion". See the notes on **219** and **450**.

B^e^ and C^e^ read *anurattaṃ* for *anuttaraṃ*. Thī-a 246,14: *anurattan ti anuratta-vantiṃ*. The word *anuratta* occurs in **446** where Thī-a 249,7 explains: *anurattā bhattāran ti bhattāraṃ anurāgavatī* (M *anubhavati* B^e^ *anuvattikā*). Since M reads forms from *anubhavati* on both occasions (the second is probably a mistake for *anubh⟨āv⟩avatī*), it seems likely that this is the correct reading. Since *bhāva* occurs in Pkt (e.g. Utt 22.44) with the meaning "affection", *anubhāva* would stand in the same relationship to it as *anurāga* to *rāga*. For metathesis see the note on **271**.

Thī-a 246,16: *uṭṭhāyikan ti uṭṭhāna-viriya-sampannaṃ*. See the note on **410**.

Thī-a 246,17–18: *dussate ti dussati kujjhitvā bhaṇati*.

For [*taṃ*] m.c. see § 67(c).

414. Alsdorf points out (App. II, p. 241, n.) that his C^e^ reads *icchaṃ* as a v.l. for *vacchaṃ*, and he therefore suggests adopting this reading. First person singular present indicatives in *-aṃ* are very rare in Pāli (see Alsdorf, 1936, p. 322, where, however, *gacchaṃ* is the only present indicative quoted for Pāli, and this is probably a future (see the note on **130**)), and it is therefore doubtful whether this reading should be adopted. Thī-a 246,22 (B^e^ and C^e^) explains: *vacchan ti vasissaṃ*, but this leaves the infinitive (*ā-*)*vatthuṃ* floating. M, however, has *saccaṃ* as a v.l. for *vacchaṃ* in the lemma and glosses: *na cemhiyaṃ* (?). P also quotes *saccaṃ* as a v.l. A similar pāda-yuga occurs in **425**, where Thī-a 247,24 (B^e^ and C^e^) again glosses: *vasissaṃ*, but M explains: *na pakkhiyaṃ*, with the same v.l. *saccaṃ* in the lemma. P lists the vv.ll. *paccaṃ* and *pacchaṃ* for **425**. The alternation *p*/*s* (see the note on **6**) in the vv.ll. leads me to see the same alternation in *pakkhiyaṃ*, and to assume it is a mistake for *sakkhiyaṃ*, which in turn is a mistake for *sakkhi*(*s*)*saṃ* (for the alternation *y*/*s*(*s*) see the note on **84**). I would then suggest that the cty originally read *sacchaṃ*: *sakkhissaṃ*, i.e. the correct reading is *sacchaṃ* which the cty explained as the future of *sakkoti*. Although theoretically the group *-kṣy-* in Skt *śakṣyati* could develop to either *-cch-* or *-kkh-*, (cf. Pāli *dakkhaṃ*, Pkt *dacchaṃ* < *drakṣyāmi*) I do not know any other example of *-cch-* in this root, which would explain why the reading became corrupt.

For *āpucch-* "take leave, say goodbye", cf. **416** **426** and see Erz, p. 54 line 21, where the word is used of a king, and hence probably does not mean literally "ask permission".

Pādas ab are *vipulā* (§57(a)). For [*saha*] m.c. in pāda c (with Cᵉ and **425**) see §67(c). For *ăhaṃ* m.c. (with Bᵉ) see §72(d). For *eka-ghare* for *ekāgāre* m.c. (with Bᵉ v.l. and **425**) see §72(d). For *sahâ* m.c. (or for *sahāvatthuṃ* < *saha* + *āvatthuṃ*) see §70(d) and Alsdorf (App. II, p. 241, n.), and cf. **416** and **425**.

415. For *eva*[*ṃ*] and *tuyha*[*ṃ*] m.c. see §68(b)(ii). For *avacâ* m.c. see §70(d). For -*vy*- making position in *parivyatta* see §74(d).

416. Pāda a is śloka according to Alsdorf (App. II, p. 241, n.), who reads *hiṃsatî* (§70(e)) to give the cadence ⏑ – – ⏓ (*pathyā*). If, however, we read *kiñcî*, we have an āryā pāda.

For *c' ăhaṃ* m.c. see §72(d). For *sahâ* m.c. (or for *sahāvacchaṃ* < *saha* + *āvacchaṃ*) see §70(d) and Alsdorf (App. II, p. 241, n.), and cf. **414** and **425**. For *ca* = *tu* see the note on **55**.

For *āpucch*- see the note on **414**. With *alaṃ me* cf. *alaṃ mayhaṃ* in **425**. Thī-a 246,23–24: *alam me ti payojanaṃ me tāya n' atthī ti attho*. The cty ad **425** gives the same explanation.

Thī-a 246,24–25: *gamissāmī ti videsaṃ pakkamissāmi*.

417. Thī-a 246,26: *ki 'ssa, kiṃ assa*. I doubt the possibility of the elision of -*ṃ* before *ssa* (see the discussion of *evaṃ sa* and *yaṃ sa* in EV I, p. 189 (ad Th 225)), and would rather assume that *kissa* is for *kiṃ sa* = *kiṃ su*, i.e. (*s*)*sa* is not the third person singular pronoun, but < *svid* (for *sa*/*su*/*ssu* < *svid* see EV I, p. 144 (ad Th 37)). Cf. *kissābhilepanaṃ brūsi* Sn 1032, where Pj II 586 glosses: *kiṃ assa lokassa abhilepanaṃ brūsi*. There the equivalence of *ssa* with *svid* is guaranteed by the presence of *su* or *ssu* in the other pādas of the verse, and by the absence of anything parallel to *assa* in the corresponding pāda of Sn 1033, although *tassa* in 1032d is so paralleled. For the development of -*ṃs*- < -*ss*- see the note on **12**. Alternatively, *kissa* here could be "why". See the note on **467**.

Bᵉ Cᵉ Kᵉ and Sᵉ read *maṃ* for *me*, and this reading should be adopted.

Thī-a 246,26–27: *tava sāmikassa tassā aparaddhaṃ vyālikaṃ kataṃ*. For *vyālika* see the note on **403**, and cf. **367**.

Bᵉ Kᵉ and Sᵉ read *vissaṭṭhā* for *vissatthā*. For such non-historic developments of -*st*- > -*ṭṭh*-, cf. Pkt *anusaṭṭhi* < *anuśāsti*.

For *sa*[*s*]*suro* m.c. (with Bᵉ and Cᵉ) see §65(b) and the note on **407**.

418. Bᵉ and Cᵉ read *hiṃsemi* for *hiṃs' eva*, and Bᵉ Cᵉ and Kᵉ read *bhaṇāmi* for *gaṇāmi*, and these readings should be adopted. For the alternation *g*/*bh* see the note on **25**.

Bᵉ (with CPD, s.v. *aparajjhati*) correctly reads *dubbacanaṃ* at the end of pāda b (§ 57(c)). Pādas ab are *vipulā*, but the fourth gaṇa is not – ⏑⏑ – (§ 57(b)). CPD (s.v. *aparajjhati*) suggests reading *aparajjhāmi* (better *-āmī*) [*kiñcī*], but Alsdorf corrects the metre of pāda b by reading [*pi*] (§ 67(c)). For *vi⟨d⟩dessate* m.c. (with Bᵉ and Cᵉ) see § 63(b), and cf. *viddesanam* in **446**.

Thī-a 246,28: *aparajjhan ti aparajjhiṃ*. This is the first person singular of a past tense derived from the old imperfect, without an augment.

Bᵉ and Cᵉ read *kātu⟨ye⟩*, and Alsdorf accepts this reading, comparing Pkt *kāuṃje* (App. II, p. 234). It seems most unlikely to me that an infinitive in *-tuye* or *-tuyye* existed in Pāli. Although the former is called an archaic infinitive by Warder (PM, p. 10, n. 2), and a Vedic infinitive by Miss Horner (BD VI, p. xvii), no such infinitive is listed in the Skt or Vedic grammars, and all the examples quoted for Pāli are capable of being explained otherwise. It is also found in: *marituye* **426** (where Alsdorf similarly reads *marituyye*, although no edition has this reading), *dātuye* Ap 398, *hetuye* Bv 7 *gaṇetuye* Bv 22. The last three examples are in the cadence of śloka posterior pādas, so it would be possible to assume that *-u-* arises m.c. Thī-a 246,30 explains: *kiṃ sakkā kātuye ti kiṃ mayā kātuṃ ayye sakkā*, clearly taking *ye* as a vocative particle, explaining it as an abbreviation of *ayye*. Alsdorf's reference to Pkt *kāuṃje* (a type of infinitive found in AMg as early as Utt 19.39–40) prompts me to suggest that we are dealing with ordinary infinitives in *-tuṃ* followed by the emphatic particle *ye*. The examples from Ap 398 Bv 7 22 show the change *-tu*[*ṃ*] m.c. (§ 68(b)(i)), cf. *chettu* Th 1121 *daṭṭhu* A III 75. PED does not list the particle *ye*, but it is found in *nirodhe ye vimuccanti*, It 45, 62; It-a II 42 glosses: *ye ti nipātamattaṃ*. It is also attested for the Aśokan inscriptions (see Norman, 1967, pp. 162–63). Aśokan *yo* is also paralleled in Pāli, although not listed in PED, e.g. *aladdhā yo taṃ* S I 126 (Spk I 187: *yo ti nipāta-mattaṃ*; *alabhitvā va*); *evaṃ yo* (v.l. *ye*) Ja III 402. For an exact parallel of an infinitive without anusvāra followed by an emphatic particle, cf. *kartu vai* Udāna-v 30.12 Mvu II 236 (although *kartuṃ vai* occurs in Mvu II 417). For the use of Pkt *je* as a vocative and an emphatic particle, and its use after infinitives, see Schwarzschild (pp. 211–13) and Norman (1994B, pp. 221–25). For *kātu⟨ṃ⟩ ye* see § 70(d).

419. Bᵉ reads *adhibhūtā* for *avibhūtā*, and this reading should be adopted. Alsdorf (App. II, p. 241, n.) states that the reading *abhibhūtā* is more probable, but the error in P is most easily explained as an example of the alternation *v*/*dh* (see the note on **7**).

Pādas ab are *vipulā* (§ 57(a)). We should punctuate *paṭi-nayiṃsu* (with Sᵉ). For *pitû* m.c. (with CPD, s.v. *abhibhūta*) see § 70(d). For *du*[*k*]*khena* m.c. (with

B^e and CPD) see § 65(b). Alsdorf's spelling *puttaṃ* is presumably merely a misprint for *puttam*.

We should read *adhibhūtā* at the end of pāda b (§ 57(c)).

B^e reads *jitā 'mhase* and C^e *jita mhase*. It is clear that we should read *jita* rather than *jina*. As Alsdorf points out (App. II, p. 241, n.) *ji-* takes a double accusative in Skt (see also EV I, p. 262 (ad Th 743)), and therefore retains one accusative when used in the passive, cf. *sahassaṃ parājito viya dukkhī* Ja II 160 "like one who has lost a thousand pieces".

Thī-a 246,34–247,2: *rūpiniṃ Lacchin* (B^e *Lakkhin*) *ti rūpavatiṃ Siriṃ. manussa-vesena carantiyā Siri-devatāya parihīnā vatā ti attho*. The meaning is then: "By persuading our son not to leave home, we have lost someone who is the goddess of beauty incarnate".

420. Thī-a 247,3–7: *aḍḍhassa gharamhi dutiya-kulikassā ti paṭhama-sāmikaṃ upādāya dutiyassa aḍḍhassa jula-puttassa gharamhi maṃ adāsi. dento ca tato paṭhama-suṅkato upaḍḍha-suṅkena adāsi. yena maṃ vindatha seṭṭh ti yena suṅkena maṃ paṭhamam seṭṭhi vindatha paṭilabhi tato upaḍḍha-suṅkenā ti yojanā.*

For the translation "kinsman" for *dutiya-kulika* see BHSD s.v. *dvitīyā*, where Edgerton suggests "a second (= another) or fellow (second) kinsman", and Mvu trsl III 405, where Jones translates so (see ibid. note 8).

For *suṅka* "dowry" see the note on **25** and Mil pp. 47 foll.

Pādas cd are *vipulā* (§ 57(a)). For *tâto* (in pāda c) and *vindathâ* m.c. see § 70(d). It would, however, be equally metrical to read *ta⟨t⟩to* (§ 64(b)), cf. Pkt *tatto* (PSM s.v.) and see the note on **243**. Cf. **436**c.

Alsdorf reads *seṭṭhī* in pāda d, but not m.c. He does not do so in **405**b.

421. Alsdorf follows B^e in reading *paṭiccharati* (Thī-a B^e has *paṭiccharayi*) in pāda b. P includes a reading *-ccharāti* among the vv.ll. The cty glosses: *maṃ nīhari so gehato nikkaḍḍhi*. Perhaps we should read *paṭicchurati*. There is a v.l. *nicchurati* for *nicchubhati* in *sā maṃ gharā nicchubhati* at Ja III 512–13 (glosed: *nīharati*). This would enable us to see some connection with Skt *chor-* "to abandon, throw away". For *paṭiccha⟨ra⟩ti* m.c. see § 66(c).

Alsdorf reads *dāsĭ* m.c. (§ 72(d)) following P v.l. both here and in **447**, but it is not at all clear to me what this is intended to mean. Thī-a 247,9 here and at 249,10 (ad **447**) explains *dāsī viya*, i.e. taking it as a nominative. It seems clear to me that we should read *dāsi⟨ṃ⟩ va* = *dāsiṃ iva*, with the elision of *-ṃ* m.c. (§ 68(b)(i)) or *dāsĭva* < *dāsīva*, contracted from *dāsiṃ iva* (cf. aggiṃ + *iva* >

aggīva, Ja I 122) with -ĭ- m.c. (§72(d)), and translate "he threw me out as though I were a slave-girl [and not his wife]".

422. C^e K^e and S^e agree with P in reading *so hi si*, but B^e and N^e introduce *hohisi* against the mss. If it is thought desirable to make a change, the presence of an imperative in pāda d might suggest an imperative in pāda c. We could read *hohi pi* (for the alternation *p*/*s* see the note on **6**).

For ⟨*ca*⟩ m.c. in pāda b see §66(c).

C^e agrees with P in reading *pontiṃ* (*pontiñ*) but B^e and Thī-a B^e read *poṭṭhiñ*.

Thī-a 247,14–15 (Ce) explains *ponti* as *pilotikā-khaṇḍa*. PED (s.v. *ponti*) is doubtful about the word, but Edgerton (BHSD, s.v. *pontī*) accepts it, although he explains it as "a garment worn by a Buddhist nun". See CDIAL 8400. If Kuiper is correct (1948, p. 98), *ponti* is not connected with *pottha*^I, despite the similarity of explanation given (see PED s.v.).

423. B^e correctly reads *pontiṃ* (in the form *poṭṭhiṃ*) in pāda b (§57(c)). For *punâ* m.c. (or *puno* (see the note on **26**)) see §70(d). The metre also requires the second *ca* in pāda c to be read as *câ* (§70(d)).

424. In pāda c B^e reads *kīrati*, which is followed by Alsdorf. C^e reads *kirati*. Thī-a 247,20: *na kīrati, na sādhīyati*. In pāda d no edition reads *kīrihiti*, but it seems reasonable to follow Alsdorf in this, in view of the reading *kīr-* in pāda c. Cf. *abhikīritūna* in **447**.

For [*me*] m.c. see §67(c). For *bhaṇatî* m.c. (with B^e) see §70(d). For *tĕ* m.c. see §72(d). For *idhâ* or *idha*⟨*ṃ*⟩ m.c. see §70(d), and cf. EV I, p. 270 (ad Th 784) and p. 292 (ad Th 1222).

For *kîrati* in pāda c and *kîrihiti* in pāda d see §70(d). For the use of the future in a potential sense see Sen (§127).

Thī-a 247,18: *naṃ, taṃ bhikkhakaṃ*.

425. Thī-a 247,22–23: *yadi me attā sakkotī ti yadi mayhaṃ attā attādhīno bhujisso ca* (C^e *ce*) *hoti*. Alsdorf conjectures *sakkato* for *sakkoti*, but a reading *sakkito* would be easier to explain, as being a simple metathesis of vowels. For metathesis see the note on **271**.

The inclusion of *mayhaṃ* in the explanation makes it clear that Dhammapāla was reading *me*, but we must read [*me*] m.c. (§67(c)). For *bhanatî* and *sahâ* m.c. see §70(d). For *sahā* see the note on **414**.

For the suggestion that we read *sacchaṃ* instead of P's *vacchaṃ* and Alsdorf's *icchaṃ*, see the note on **414**.

For *alaṃ mayhaṃ* cf. *alaṃ me* in **416**.

426. For the suggestion that we read *maritu⟨ṃ⟩ ye* (§70(d)) instead of P's *marituye* and Alsdorf's *marituyye*, see the note on **418**.

Thī-a 247,26–27: *āpucchitūna gacchan ti mayhaṃ pitaraṃ vissajjetvā gacchāmi.* We must presumably understand *vissajj-* in a causative sense, which is not given in PED, i.e. "having made my father let me go".

For *gacchaṃ* as a future see the note on **130**.

For *vi⟨s⟩sajjito* (with Bᵉ and Cᵉ) m.c. see §64(b) and cf. **516**.

Thī-a 247,27: *vā ti vikappatthe nipāto.*

427. For *āgacchî* m.c. see §70(d).

428. The name Jinadattā suggests that the nun was a Jain (cf. the note on **431**).

Alsdorf suggests reading *amha kule* for *amhākaṃ*, although the latter does make sense: "rising up from our seat". He also reverses the order of *paññā-payiṃ* and *tassā*, m.c.

For *disvān[a]* (with Cᵉ) m.c. see §67(c). For *āsana[ṃ]* m.c. see §68(b)(ii). For *pa[ñ]ñāpayiṃ* m.c. see §65(b).

Alsdorf points out (App. II, p. 242, n.) that the first gaṇa of pāda c lacks one mora. This can be remedied by reading *ni⟨si⟩sinnāya* (see the note on **243** and §64(b)).

429. For *santappayitvă* m.c. see §72(d).

Cᵉ adds ⟨*ti*⟩ to pāda d, but this is unmetrical. It is noteworthy that in this group of verses *ti* is often omitted at the end of utterances, cf. the ends of **430 431 432**.

430. Thī-a 247,31–32: *puttakā ti sāmañña-vohārena dhītaraṃ anukampento ālapati.* The masculine form is, however, odd, and we should perhaps read *puttike* with Kᵉ and Sᵉ, i.e. *puttikĕ* m.c. The word *puttaka* used of a girl occurs also in **462–63**, but there the metre shows that it is an error for *putti*, as is very likely *putta* in **464** too.

In pāda b *taṃ* can be taken with *dhammaṃ*, or it may be the second person pronoun, to be taken with *carāhi*. Bᵉ reads *tvaṃ*, and the explanation in the cty seems to favour the interpretation as a pronoun: *carāhi taṃ pabbajitvā caritabbaṃ brahmacariyādi-dhammaṃ cara.*

For *bhaṇatî* m.c. see §70(d).

431. Thī-a 247,35: *nijjaressāmī ti jīrāpessāmi vināsessāmi* (Cᵉ omits, M *vināpessāmi*; for the alternation *p/s* see the note on 6). *Nijjara* is a technical term in Jainism "the gradual destruction of all actions" (see MW s.v. ²*nirjara* (p. 554) and SBE XLV, p. xv). PED is wrong in stating (s.v. *nijjara*) that Skt *nirjara* has a different meaning; the author of this statement must have been referring to ¹*nirjara* (see MW, p. 541).

For other references to Jainism see the note on **87–91**.

For *ath' ăhaṃ* (with Bᵉ) m.c. see § 72(d).

432. For *bhaṇatî, labhassû*, and *sacchikarî* m.c. (with Bᵉ) see § 70(d).

433. For *-pitaro* in place of *-pitū* in pāda a see Alsdorf (App. II, p. 243).

Pādas ab are *vipulā* (§ 57(a)).

For *abhivādayitvă* m.c. see § 72(d). For *aphassayi⟨sa⟩ṃ* or *aphassayi ⟨'ha⟩ṃ* m.c. see § 66(c) and the notes on **436 438**. For *phass-* see the note on **6**.

434. Thī-a 248,8–10: *yassāyaṃ phala-vipāko ti yassa pāpa-kammassa ayaṃ sāmikassa amanāpa-bhāva-saṅkhāto nissanda-phala-bhūto vipāko. taṃ tava ācikkhissan ti taṃ kammaṃ tava kathessāmi.*

For the remembering of the last seven births, cf. Ja VI 236–37.

For *yass' ăyaṃ* (with Bᵉ) m.c. see § 72(d). For p*hala*[*ṃ*]-*vipāko* (with Bᵉ) m.c. see § 68(b)(ii).

Pādas ab are *vipulā* (§ 57(a)).

435. For the v.l. *āsevitaṃ* listed by P see the note on *nikūjitaṃ* in **261**.

For *so 'haṃ* see the note on **24**.

For *Era*[*ka*]*kacche* (with Bᵉ and Cᵉ) m.c. see § 67(c). For dittography see the note on **474**.

For *ăsevî* m.c. see §§ 70(d), 72(d). Bᵉ and Cᵉ read *asev*i.

For *bahu⟨t⟩ta-* m.c. see § 64(b) and the note on **406**. Bᵉ and Cᵉ read *pahūta-*.

436. No edition reads *pakko* at the end of pāda b, although the metre shows that this is necessary (§ 57(c)). For *tâto* or *ta⟨t⟩to* m.c. see §§ 64(b), 70(d) and the note on **420**. For *akkami⟨sa⟩ṃ* or *okkami ⟨'ha⟩ṃ* m.c. see § 66(c) and the note on **433**. It would also be possible to read *okkāmiṃ*, cf. *pakkāmi* S I 92 120, etc. (see PED, s.v. *pakkamati*).

For *so 'haṃ* see the note on **24**.

437. Thī-a 248,18: *yūtha-po ti yūtha-pati.* I do not understand why PED says that the word refers to elephants here.

Thī-a 248,19–20: *tassa*, *tassa mayhaṃ*. If the cty is correct in seeing the *sā aham* type of expression here (see the note on **24**), we should assume that *tass'* is for *tassā*. Cf. **447**.

For *sattāha[ṃ]-jātakaṃ maṃ* (with Bᵉ and Cᵉ) m.c. see § 68(b)(ii). For *-kapî* m.c. see § 70(d). For *ni[l]lacchesi* m.c. see § 65(b) and cf. **439–40**.

For *yathāpi* see BHSD (s.v.), where Edgerton points out its use to give a reason, "because of course ... ". Cf. **210**.

Thī-a 248,20–21 glosses *gantvāna* by *atikkamitvā*. PED euphemistically translates the former "approach", and does not mention this use of *atikkam-* at all. In Skt *gam-* can mean "to have sexual intercourse with", *ati-kram-* "to transgress, sin", and *abhi-kram-*, "to attack, assault". For the alternation *ati-/abhi-* see EV I, p. 221 (ad Th 447).

438. All editions read *karitvā* in pāda b, but Alsdorf (App. II, p. 243) suggests reading *katvāna* m.c. For this change of forms, cf. the note on **311**.

For *okkami⟨sa⟩ṃ* or *okkami ⟨'ha⟩ṃ* m.c. see § 66(c) and the note on **433**. It would also be possible to read *okkāmiṃ* (cf. the note on **436**).

For *so 'haṃ* see the note on **24**.

439. Thī-a 248,24: *dārake parivahitvā ti piṭṭhiṃ āruya kumārake vahitvā.*

Thī-a 248,25: *kiminā v' aṭṭo ti abhijāta-ṭṭhāne kimi-paraṃgato va* (M *ca*; for the alternation *v/c* see the note on **12**) *hutvā. aṭṭo aṭṭito.* Thī-a 248,30 (ad **441**) states: *andho v' aṭṭo ti kāṇo va hutvā. aṭṭo pīḷito.* The inclusion of *va* in the explanation, and the glosses on *aṭṭo* make it clear that Dhammapāla thought *vaṭṭo* should be taken as standing for *va* + *aṭṭo*. P, however, states (p. 213) that this explanation is hardly correct, and suggests the meanings "crooked, crippled" for *vaṭṭa*. PED does not list *vaṭṭa* in this sense, although *vatta* at Ja V 443 is said (s.v. *vatta*[4]) to be corrupt for *vaṇṭha* "cripple". This word is not listed by PED either. For this whole group of words meaning "defective" see CDIAL 11236. Of this group the most likely in this context is *vaṇṭa* (cf. Pāli *a-vaṇṭa*, wrongly defined in PED) meaning "tailless", which would be very appropriate as a defect for an animal.

For *kimino* "full of worms" instead of *kiminā* (with Alsdorf, App. II, p. 243 n.) cf. *kiminaṃ jivhaṃ* Ja V 270 (explained: *kimīhi bharitaṃ* Ja V 275), and cf. Skt *kṛmiṇa*.

For *aka[l]lo* (cf. **441**) and *ni[l]lacchito* m.c. see § 65(b) and cf. **437 440**.

For *yathāpi* see the note on **437**.

440. For *ni[l]lacchito* m.c. see § 65(b) and cf. **437 439**.

For *so 'haṃ* see the note on **24**.

441. Thī-a 248,29: *voḍhūnā ti vahitvā*. P's reading doubtless arose because at some stage *te* replaced *vo* (cf. EV I, p. 209 (ad Th 359) and the note on **474**). Pāda b is, as Alsdorf states (App. II, p. 243, n.) truncated. I take *dhārayati* to mean "to pull a cart", a meaning which is not quoted for Skt or Pāli. If we read *vā dhārayāmī* ⟨*'haṃ*⟩, we have an upagīti verse. We might then assume that the final *'haṃ* was lost because pāda a already seemed to contain *ahaṃ*. If, however, we divide *naṅgala mahaṃ*, and assume that *naṅgala* is for *naṅgala⟨ṃ⟩* (§ 68(b)(i)), and that *mahaṃ* is neuter singular (= *mahantaṃ*), as in AMg, e.g. *tiṇṇo hu si aṇṇavaṃ mahaṃ* Utt 10.34, *suhāvahaṃ dhammadhuraṃ anuttaraṃ dhārejja nivvāṇa-guṇāvahaṃ mahaṃ* Utt 19.98, then this apparent tautology disappears.

For *câ dhārayāmî* m.c. see § 70(d). For *aka[l]lo* m.c. see § 65(b) and cf. **439**. For *vaṇṭo* in place of *vaṭṭo* see the note on **439**. For *yathāpi* see the note on **437**. For ⟨*'haṃ*⟩ see § 66(c).

Thī-a 248,29: *naṅgalan ti sīraṃ*.

442. The inclusion of two locatives, *vīthiyā* and *ghare*, in pāda b presents difficulties. Thī-a 248,31 glosses: *vīthiyā ti nagara-vīthiyaṃ*, which confirms that Dhammapāla was reading either *vīthiyā* or *vīthiyaṃ*. The cty continues: *dāsiyā ghare jāto ti ghara-dāsiyā kucchimhi jāto*. The absence of any word which might be glossed *kucchimhi* in the text is not conclusive, cf. *gāviyā jāto* in **440**, but we may not be entirely wrong if we assume that the original version had a word for "womb", which was replaced by *ghare*, extracted from the gloss *ghara-dāsī*. That some change has occurred in the pāda is shown by the fact that the cty quotes a v.l. Unfortunately it is not clear what the v.l. is, since C^e reads *vaṇṇa-jātiyā* and B^e reads *vaṇṇa-dāsiyā*. Possibly the reading intended was *vaṇṇa-dāsiyā jāto*, and we should translate "I was born of a prostitute in a street".

For *vīthîyā* m.c. see § 70(d). For *yathāpi* see the note on **437**.

For *so 'haṃ* see the note on **24**.

443. Thī-a 248,35: *sākaṭika-kulamhī ti senaka-kule*. I know of no evidence to support this gloss.

Thī-a 248,35–37: *dhanika-purisa-pāta-bahulamhī ti. iṇāyikānaṃ purisānaṃ adhipatana-bahule bahūhi iṇāyikehi abhibhavitabbe*. C^e reads *aṇika-* for *dhanika-*. PED does not list this word.

444. Pāda a is śloka; pādas bcd are āryā. For *vaḍḍhîyă* m.c. see §§ 70(d), 72(d).

Thī-a 249,1: *ussannāyā ti upacitāya*.

Thī-a 249,2–3: *kula-gharassā ti mama jāta-kula-gehato*. Be reads *-gharasmā* which Alsdorf adopts in place of *-gharassa*. For an ablative in *-assa* see the note on **23**.

For *taṃ maṃ* see the note on **24**.

445. Be reads *kaññaṃ* at the end of pāda b, correctly (§57(c)). Be and Ce read *orundhat' assa* in place of *oruddha tassa*. It is clear that this is correct, since Thī-a 249,4–5 explains: *assa sattha-vāhassa putto mayi paṭi-baddha-citto nāmena Giridāso nāma avarundhati attano pariggaha-bhāvena gehe karoti*. See PED, s.vv. *avarundhati* and *orundhati*.

For disvā[na] m.c. see §67(c).

446. For *anurattā* see the note on **413**.

For *tassā[haṃ]* m.c. see §67(c).

447. Thī-a 249,12–13: *etaṃ tassa mayhaṃ tadā katassa paradārika-kammassa patividdesana-kammassa ca nissanda-phalaṃ*. For *tassa mayhaṃ* see the notes on **24** and **437**.

Ce read *apakiritūna* (see PED s.v.). For *apakîritūna* (with Be) m.c. see §70(d). Warder (PM p. 10, n. 2) suggests that absolutives in *-ūna* (cf. *voḍhūna* **441**, *chaḍḍūna* **469**) are examples of "archaism". They are more likely to be examples of borrowing from other dialects (§25).

For *dāsiva* m.c. see §§68(b)(i), 72(d) and the note on **421**.

In pāda d we must read *me* for *mayā* with Alsdorf (App. p. 244) m.c.

448–522. Mrs Rhys Davids noted that she was unable to identify the metre of this poem (Sist., p. xl, n. 1). For its identification see the note on **213–23**. All the verses are āryā except **472**a **487**c **488–92** **495**abc*, which are śloka, and **505** which is gīti. Pāda b of **461** is very corrupt, but it is possible that the metre is upagīti. See the note on **461**.

For *ti* at the end of the group see the note on **1**.

There are several features in this group of verses which might be held to support a date for its composition which is later than that of most of Thī. As in the case of **400–47** I would not deny this, but I would doubt whether these features can provide us with a precise dating.

(a) Winternitz (p. 111) wrote "Thī **448–521** is either a later addition or else a poem much distorted by later additions and overburdened with quotations". Mrs Rhys Davids stated that Sumedhā's harangues are quotations from a Bible (Sist., p. xxii). Some of the quotations (**448–92**) are shown by their metre (śloka) to be insertions in the poem. Those in **496** foll. are in āryā metre. All we are justified in assuming is that Sumedhā's verses are later than the sermons of which they are a summary. If we assume that the sermons were preached by the Buddha (see the note on **488–92**), we can postulate any date from the fifth century onwards.

(b) Mrs Rhys Davids (Sist., p. xviii) regarded this poem and **400–47** as the products of later literary craft. Although Warder's analysis (PM, §214) would support this, there seems to me to be no evidence for dating these poems later than Aśoka's time. See also Alsdorf (1965, pp. 64 foll.).

(c) Mrs Rhys Davids also drew attention to the fact that only Isidāsī and Sumedhā actually recount their former births to their contemporaries. The reference to hundreds of thousands of rebirths in **519** is clearly not a primitive idea, but must be the product of a time when the doctrine of transmigration had been fully developed. Since, however, the whole idea of the endlessness of *saṃsāra*, which may well be a pre-Buddhist idea, since it is found in Jainism too, has an innumerable number of rebirths as its essential concomitant, it does not seem possible to give a date to this idea.

(d) The reference to Koṇāgamana in **518** proves that Sumedhā spoke after the time when the cult of former Buddhas had been established. Since, however, we know that Aśoka enlarged a stūpa to Konākamana, we know that the cult must have been established some time before his date.

(e) In **456** and **475** there are references to six *gatis*. PED quotes these from Pv 66 and D III 264, and implies that the idea of six instead of five *gatis* must be late because these texts are late. I do not think that this necessarily follows.

448. B^e^ and C^e^ read *păsāditā* for *pāsādikā* (§72(d)). Thī-a 257,1–2: *satthu sāsana-kārehi ariyehi dhamma-desanāya sāsane pasāditā sañjāta-ratana-ttaya-pasādā katā*, which shows clearly that Dhammapāla was reading a past participle. For the alternation *k/t* see the note on **43**.

For *mahisîyă* in place of *mahesiyā* m.c. see §§70(d), 72(d). Alsdorf claims (App. II, p. 234) that this is a change of vocabulary, not merely a matter of scansion (§62). It would, however, be possible to read *mahĕsīya*. A comparable change is also necessary in **463 520**. For the various forms of the word for "queen" see Bailey (1952, pp. 432–33). See also PED (s.v. *mahā*).

449. Thī-a 257,7–8: *ubhayo nisāmethā ti tumhe dve pi mama vacanaṃ nisāmetha*. PED (s.v. *ubhaya* and *ubho*) quotes *ubhayo* from Pv 15 (glossed as *duve* at Pv-a 86) as a feminine nominative plural. Cf. **457**.

Pādas cd are *vipulā* (§57(a)). For *-kath*[*ik*]*ā* (with B^e^ and C^e^) m.c. §67(c). For *-sāsanĕ* m.c. see §72(d).

450. Thī-a 257,10: *dibban ti deva-loke pariyāpannam*. In *bhava-gata*, *-gata* seems to mean "connected with". The word *bhava-gata* recurs in **454–55 458 465 492 522**. Thī-a 257,27 (ad **455**) explains: *bhava-gate aniccamhī ti sabbasmiṃ bhave anicce*. I therefore translate as "existence". For other uses of *-gata* cf. *saṅkhāra-gata* **514**, *kāya-gata* Th 6 468 1225, *diṭṭhi-gata* Th 933, *rūpa-gata* Th 1215. See also BHSD, s.v. *gata*.

For [*a*]*haṃ* (with Bᵉ and Cᵉ) m.c. see § 67(c). For [*aṅga*] m.c. see § 67(c).

451. Thī-a 257,16–17: *samappitā ti sakammunā sabbaso appitā khittā upapannā ti attho. haññante ti bādhīyanti*.

Pādas ab are *vipulā* (§ 57(a)). For *-ratta*[*ṃ*] m.c. see § 68(b)(ii). For *du*[*k*]*khitā* m.c. see § 65(b). Alsdorf reads *haññare* for *haññante* m.c., but the same scansion can be obtained by reading *hañña*[*n*]*te* (§ 68(a)ii)).

452. Thī-a 257,18: *vinipāte ti apāye*. See the note on **456**.

Bᵉ reads *sadā* at the end of pāda b, and this line division is correct (§ 57(c)). We should, however, follow Alsdorf in reading '*sad*⟨*dh*⟩*ā* (with P v.l.) (§ 64(b)). For the alternation *d*/*dh* cf. *pasād*⟨*han*⟩*aṃ* in **411**.

For *kāyena* ⟨*ca*⟩ (with Bᵉ) m.c. see § 66(c). Cᵉ omits *bālā*, but the metre shows that this is incorrect.

453. Thī-a 257,20–21: *desente ti catu-sacca-dhamme desiyamāne*. The cty cannot be correct in taking *desente* as the passive participle; it is the active particle, used absolutely: "while [someone] is teaching".

For *desentĕ* m.c. see § 72(d).

454. For *bhava-gata* see the note on **450**. For *Buddha-vara* see the note on **399**.

Pādas ab are *vipulā* (§ 57(a)).

For [*amma*] m.c. see § 67(c), and cf. **51**. Dhammapāla must have had *amma* in the text before him, since Thī-a 257,23 glosses: *ammā ti mātaraṃ pamukhaṃ katvā ālapati*.

For [*ye*] m.c. see § 67(c).

Bᵉ and Cᵉ read *pihenti*, and since this is more correct historically, this reading should be adopted.

455. For *ca* = *tu* see the note on **55**. For *bhava-gata* see the note on **450**.

Thī-a 257,28–30: *na ca santasantī ti bālā na uttasanti na saṃvegaṃ āpajjanti. punappunam jāyatabbassā ti aparāparam upapajjamānassa*. I take *jayitabba* as a future passive participle being used as an action noun "being reborn". See Norman, 1989, pp. 220–21.

For *upapattî* m.c. see § 70(d).

456. Thī-a 257,31–34: *cattāro vinipātā ti niraya-tiracchāna- asītiyā -peta-visaya-asura-yonī ti ime cattāro 'sukha-samussayato vinipāta-gatiyo. manussa-devūpapatti-saññitā pana dve ca gatiyo*, i.e. *vinipāta* = *duggati*, and *gati* = *sugati*. See PED, s.v. *asura*. See also **475**. At M I 73 only five *gatis* are given [IBH]. PED states that the list of six *gatis* is found "in later sources".

For *d⟨u⟩ve* (with Be) m.c. see § 66(c).

For *ca* = *tu* see the note on **55**.

457. Thī-a 258,1: *appossukā ti añña-kiccesu nirussukkā*. PED lists *ussuka* in the senses "eager" and "greedy", but gives only "eagerness" for the noun *ussukka*.

For *ubhayo* see the note on **449**.

Thī-a 258,1–2: *ghaṭissan ti vāyamissaṃ bhāvanaṃ anuyuñjissāmi*.

For *anujānătha* m.c. see § 72(d). For *jātî-* m.c. see § 70(d). For *appossu*[*k*]*kā* m.c. see § 65(b) and cf. **477**.

458–59. PED does not give the meaning "compared [in number]" for *upanīta*, but it is found in this sense in Sn 677.

458. For *abhinandita*, i.e. a past participle used as an action noun, see the note on **261**.

The cty makes no comment on *kāya-kali* here. The word recurs at **501**, where Thī-a 264,17 states: a*nekānattha-sannipātato kāya-saṅkhātassa kalino*. PED (s.v. *kāya*) translates "the misfortune of having a body = this miserable body", but also (s.v. *kali*) follows Mrs Rhys Davids (Sist., p. 167, n. 2) in equating *kali* and *kheḷa*. At best, this would seem to be a pun. For the correct translation see MW (s.v. *kali*): "the worst of a class or number of objects". It has been pointed out to me [LSC] that in Th 321 the parallelism between *kalī va siyā* in pāda b and *andho va siyā* in pāda d makes it very likely that *kalī* refers to a person, as Th-a states. We could therefore adopt the translation "sinful, a sinner", which PED gives for Sn 664, following the gloss *pāpaka* in Pj II. For the pun on two meanings of *kali* in Sn 658 foll. (not stressed in PED) see BHSD, s.v. *kali*.

Pādas ab are *vipulā* (§ 57(a)). For *anujānătha* m.c. see § 72(d).

For *bhava-gata* see the note on **450**.

Thī-a 258,4–5: *bhava-taṇhāya nirodhā ti bhava-gatāya taṇhāya noridha-hetu nirodhanatthaṃ*.

459. Alsdorf reads *uppādā* for *uppādo*, but I am not convinced that this is necessary. Cf. *buddhuppādo* in the note on **4**. Thī-a 258,6–7: *buddhānaṃ uppādo laddho, vivajjito niray'-uppatti-ādiko aṭṭha-vidho akkhaṇo. khaṇo navamo khaṇo laddho ti yojanā. saddhāya paṭiladdhakkhaṇo*. For *akkhaṇa* and *khaṇa* see the note on **5**. For the use of the past participle *paṭiladdha* as an action noun see the note on **261**.

For *br-* not making position in *brahma* see § 74(a).

For *yāva⟨j⟩jīvaṃ* m.c. see § 63(b).

460. Be reads *āharissaṃ* (glossed *āharissāmi*), but in a footnote suggests *āhārisaṃ*. M reads *āhariyaṃ* (glossed *āhariyāmi*). Ce reads *āhariyāmi* (glossed *āharissāmi*). Alsdorf (App. II, p. 245, n.) quotes Ce (1930) *āharisāmi*, which he adopts (§ 65(a)). For the alternation *y/s(s)* see the note on **84**. Since the combination of *āhāra* with *āhāreti* is very likely (see PED, s.v. *āhāreti*), we should probably follow Be (n.) and read *āhārisaṃ*, particularly as this gives ⏑ — ⏑ as the second gaṇa.

For *-vasa[ṃ]-gatā* m.c. see § 68(b)(ii). for *āharisâ⟨mi⟩* m.c. see §§ 66(c), 70(d).

461. Pāda b is badly corrupted, and scans in none of the editions. Thī-a 258,14: *assā ti Sumedhāya*. This shows that Dhammapāla read as P as far as the fifth gaṇa. The end of the pāda is not clear. Be and Ce read *samabhihato* in place of P *samabhisāto*, although we should expect *samabhihāto* to give ⏑ ⏑ — in the seventh gaṇa. Ke and Se include *soka-samabhibhūto* in the pāda. Thī-a 258,14–15: *sabbaso samabhihato ti assūhi sabbaso abhihata-mukho*. The occurrence of *assūhi* in the gloss might lead us to believe that *assā* was a mistake for *assūhi*, were it not for the fact that the cty has just commented upon *assā*. M reads: *sabbaso samabhisāto ti assā pitā sabbaso abhisāta-sukho*. PED translates *samabhisāta* "joyful", but this must be wrong in the context. In Skt *sāta* exists in the sense "destroyed" (see MW, p. 1196 column 3), and in Pāli *sāta-bhakkha* occurs at Pug 55 as a v.l. for *hata-bhakkha*. There is therefore no reason to doubt that *samabhisāto* (glossed *abhihata-*) was the original reading, and has been replaced in some editions by the gloss. I would assume that *sabbaso* has also come into the text from the cty, where it was intended to explain the prefix *sam-*, and then produced the lemma *sabbaso samabhisāto* from the gloss *sabbaso abhihatamukho*. Perhaps we should read *pitā ca assā samabhisāto*, which would give an upagīti stanza. For [*sabbaso*] see § 67(c).

P quotes *paññāpetuṃ* as a v.l. for *saññāpetuṃ* (cf. the note on **514**). For the alternation *p/s* see the note on **6**.

Thī-a 258,16–17: *ghaṭenti saññāpetun ti gihī-bhavāya saññāpetuṃ ghatenti vāyamanti. ghaṭenti vāyamantī ti pi pāṭho. so eva attho.* P, following a ms which omitted *vāyamanti* from the v.l. (p. 213), suggested that *ghaṭenti* was the v.l. intended. Despite the reading of B^e^ and C^e^, I believe that P was partly correct. The reading *ghaṭenti* cannot be correct because this gives ⏑ — ⏑ as the first gaṇa. Moreover, if PED is correct, *ghaṭati* means "strive" and *ghaṭeti* means "join" (cf. the meanings of *ghaṭate* and *ghaṭayati* in Skt (MW, s.v. *ghaṭ-*)). We should therefore read *ghaṭanti* (> *ghaṭa[n]tî* m.c. with Alsdorf (§§68(a)(ii), 70(d)). Since, however, the sense of the pāda is better with a singular verb: "the mother weeps and the father strives", it is arguable that we should read *ghaṭati* in any case, not merely m.c. The root *ghaṭ-* is also found in **176 457 461 477 493 513**, and we should read *ghaṭanti* for *ghaṭenti* in **477**.

For *du[k]khitā* m.c. see §65(b). For *chamā* see the note on **17**.

462. B^e^ reads *Anîkaratta* here and throughout, and this reading should be adopted m.c. (§70(d)). C^e^ reads *Anīkadatta* throughout. P (p. 213) stated that he read *Anikaratta* m.c.!

Thī-a 258,18: *kiṃ socitenā ti kiṃ socanena.* For the use of the past participle as an action noun see the note on **261**. See also BHSD, s.v. *socita*.

Pādas ab are *vipulā* (§57(a)). Alsdorf suggests reading *putti* for *puttaka* here and in **463** m.c. (§67(c)). K^e^ and S^e^ read *puttike* in both verses. This solves the problem about gender, but the reading is still unmetrical.

For *tv-* not making position in *tvaṃ* see §74(b). We should perhaps read *taṃ* with Alsdorf (App. II, p. 245).

463. For *Anîkaratta* m.c. see §70(d) and the note on **462**. For *-mahisi* or *-mahĕsi* m.c. see §72(d) and the note on **448**. For *putti* for *puttaka* see §67(c) and the note on **462**.

For *br-* not making position in *brahma-* see §74(a).

464. B^e^ and C^e^ read *si* for *pi*, which seems to make better sense and should be adopted (cf. **483**). For the alternation *p/s* see the note on **6**.

Alsdorf suggests reading *putti* for *putta*, and this reading should be adopted. See the note on **430**.

Pādas ab are *vipulā*, but the fourth gaṇa is not ⏑ ⏓ ⏓ ⏑ (§57(b)).

K^e^ and S^e^ read ⟨*tasmā*⟩ *bhuñjāhi,* but this reading is not metrical, and seems to have been introduced from the cty.

P lists a v.l. *dhāreyyaṃ* as a v.l. and in the lemma. Similarly *dhāreyyaṃ*, glossed *vivāhaṃ*, occurs in the lemma for **472**. *Dhāreyyaṃ* is also given as a v.l. in M (text) in **465 479**. The other editions read *vāreyyaṃ* in all places. It would seem, therefore, that we are dealing with an alternation *v/dh* (see the note on **7**), and the entry for *dhāreyya* should be deleted from PED.

465. Thī-a 258,26: *ne ti mātā-pitaro.*

For *bhava-gata* see the note on **450**.

B^e^ and C^e^ read *me na* for *tena*, and this reading should be adopted.

For [*c' eva*] m.c. see § 67(c).

For the v.l. *dhāreyyaṃ* in P see the note on **464**.

466. Thī-a 258,28: *kimi vā ti kimi viya.* This makes it clear that P *kim iva* is a mistake for *kimi va*, and I now translate accordingly.

P (v.l.) B^e^ and C^e^ read *bhastaṃ* for *gattaṃ*. Thī-a 258,30–31: *kuṇapaṃ abhisaṃviseyyaṃ bhastan ti kuṇapa-bharitaṃ camma-pasibbakaṃ*. It looks as though the cty is taking *kuṇapaṃ bhastaṃ* as a split compound (see the note on **147**). Although split compounds are found with another word intervening between the components of the compound (see EV I, p. 146 (ad Th 42)), I cannot quote another example where the component parts are in different pāda-yugas. For *kuṇapa* see the note on **380**.

For the alternation *g/bh* see the note on **25**. For the alternation *bhasta/bhatta* see the vv.ll. for *bhasta* at Ja III 346–48. For the alternation *gatta/bhatta* see the note on **469**.

Thī-a 258,30–33 explains *abhisaṃviseyyaṃ* by *abhiniveseyyaṃ*. PED (s.v. *abhisaṃvisati*) takes the word as a compound with *bhastaṃ*, wrongly. PED does not list *abhiniveseti*; CPD does, with the meaning "to aspire to, apply oneself to (acc.); to affect". Perhaps we should read *abhiniviseyyaṃ* (see the note on **394**), which would make good sense in the explanation (see PED, s.v. *abhinivisati* "to cling to, adhere to, be attached to"). The meaning given in CPD for *abhisaṃvisati* (s.v.) "to lie down together with (acc.), cohabit" seems slightly off the point. PED gives the correct meaning for *saṃvisati* (s.v.), and also gives a reference to *abhisaṃvisati* there.

Thī-a 258,29: *savana-gandhan ti visaṭṭha-vissa-gandhaṃ*. C^e^ reads *savaṇa-* for *savana-*, and Alsdorf points out that we must read *sâvaṇa-* m.c. (§ 79(d)). He draws attention to Skt *srāvaṇa*, but as in other cases (§ 62), it is not essential that changes made m.c. should also imply lexical changes. In this case the meanings of Skt *sravaṇa* "sweat, urine" would suit very well.

In pāda d B^e^ reads ⟨*a*⟩*saki*⟨*ṃ*⟩ *paggharitaṃ*, and C^e^ reads ⟨*a*⟩*saki*⟨*ṃ*⟩ *paggharaṇaṃ*. Thī-a 258,32–33: *asakiṃ, sabba-kālaṃ adhippaggharantaṃ*. Although MW (s.v. *sakṛt*) gives the meaning "once for all, for ever", and PED (s.v. *saki*) translates "once and for all, always", I am not convinced that this meaning is appropriate in this context. I should prefer to read *bhastam asakipaggharitaṃ* and translate "flowing not once only, but always". Pādas cd would then be *vipulā*, but the fourth gaṇa would not be ⏑ ⏕ ⏑ (§ 57). We could produce such a gaṇa by reading *bhastaṃ asakiṃ pa[g]gharitaṃ*.

B[e] reads *kuṇapaṃ* at the end of pāda b, correctly (§ 57(c)).

For [*iva*] m.c. see § 67(c). For *abhisaṃviseyya*[*ṃ*] m.c. see § 68(b)(ii).

467. Alsdorf states that he is unable to provide a satisfactory explanation for *t' āhaṃ* in pāda a (to be read *t' ăham* m.c. with B[e] [(§ 72(d)]). Thī-a 258,37 foll. explains: *taṃ ahaṃ kaḷevaraṃ jānantī*, so it is clear that Dhammapāla took *t' āhaṃ* as standing for *taṃ ahaṃ*.

B[e] C[e] K[e] and S[e] read *-upalittaṃ* for *-palittaṃ*. The cty explains: *asucīhi mamsa-pesīhi soṇitehi ca upalittaṃ*.

Thī-a 258,35–37: *anekesaṃ kimi-kulānaṃ ālayaṃ sakuṇānaṃ bhatta-bhūtaṃ. kimi-kulāna* (B[e] *-kulāla-*)*sakuṇa-bhattan ti pi pāṭho. kimīnaṃ avasiṭṭha-sakuṇānañ ca bhatta-bhūtan ti attho*. The v.l. as given in B[e] suggests that Alsdorf is correct in suggesting *-kulăla*[*yaṃ*]*-sakuṇa-* m.c. (§§ 67(c), 72(d)), although it is clear that Dhammapāla read as P, despite his knowledge of the v.l. The reading in P may well have arisen because of the common idea of the body being a home for families of worms, cf. *kaḷebaraṃ nānā-kimi-kulākiṇṇaṃ* Pj I 47 Pj II 247, *ayaṃ kāyo asītiyā tāva kimi-kulānaṃ sādhāraṇo* Vism 235, *dvattiṃsa-kula-ppabhedā kimayo nivasanti* Vism 358. For the suggestion that *para* in the compound *para-bhatta* means "worm" see the note on **469**.

Thī-a 259,1–2: *kissa, kena nāma kāraṇena*. The same explanation is given in Thī-a 259,26 (ad **472**). For *kissa* "why" see Brown (p. 122, s.v. *kisā*) and Norman (1964, p. 67). See also Geiger (2000, § 111.1) and BHSG (§ 21.16). The same explanation could also be given for *kissa* in **417** (see the notes on **122** and **417**).

For *di*[*y*]*yatī* m.c. see § 65(b). B[e] reads *diyyati* [*ti*], which would have to be read as *diyyāti* m.c. (for the dittography see the note on **474**). This raises the possibility that we should read *deyyā ti* and translate "knowing this, to whom (or why) am I to be given [in marriage]?". This solves the problem of the lack of a finite verb in pāda a, although the cty understands *ṭhitā*. Thī-a 258,37 foll.: *taṃ ahaṃ kaḷevaraṃ jānantī ṭhitā. taṃ maṃ* (C[e] omits) *idāni vāreyya-*(for M's reading *dhāreyya-* see the note on **464**) *-vasena kissa kena nāma kāraṇena diyyatī ti dasseti. tassa tañ ca dānaṃ kim iva kiṃ viya hotī ti yojanā*.

468. B[e] reads *chuddho* for *chuṭṭho*; K[e] and S[e] read *chaḍḍito*. The latter reading is unmetrical and has probably been introduced from Thī-a 259,6, where it is the gloss. Alsdorf prefers *chuddho* because it is the reading of Dhp 41. On this see Brough (GDhp, p. 225).

Thī-a 259,5: *nibbuyhati, upanīyati*. The meaning seems to be "carried out" rather than "led out" as PED states (s.v.).

For *nibbuyhatî* m.c. see § 70(d).

469. Thī-a 259,8: *chaḍḍūna naṃ susāne ti naṃ kaḷevaraṃ susāne chaḍḍetvā*. Alsdorf quotes the reading *chuḍḍhūna taṃ* from C[e] 1930 (see App. II, p. 234). B[e] reads *chuddhūna*, presumably on the analogy of *chuddha* in **468.** For absolutives in *-ūna* see § 25 and the note on **447**.

Thī-a 259,9: *para-bhattan ti paresaṃ soṇa-sigālādīnaṃ anna-bhūtaṃ*. Cf. *sakuṇa-bhatta* in **467**, and *para-gatta* (read *para-bhatta* ?) in Th 1150 (glossed: *para-gatte, aññasmiṃ padese soṇa-sigāla-kimi-kulādīnaṃ gatta-bhūte kaḷebare*, Th-a III 167,18–21). See also *kimīnaṃ ālayam etaṃ nānā-kuṇapena pūritam* Spk I 274 Pj II 397. But note Spk II 323 (ad S III 243): *parabhattan ti nānā-vidhānaṃ kimi-ādīnaṃ bhattaṃ hutvā*, and cf. the reference to worms in the portion of Thī-a quoted in the note to **467**. Since some commentators explain that in the compound *para-bhatta* (used of corpses and usually translated "food for others") the "others" are worms (*kimi*), etc., the fact that Saka *pära* "worm" (see Bailey, 1979, p. 239) is the equivalent of Sanskrit *kṛmi* "id." suggests that there was a root *par-* "to pierce" and *para* means "piercer, borer, i.e. worm" and *para-bhatta* therefore means "food for worms".

Thī-a 259,9–11: *nhāyanti* (C[e] *nahāyanti*) *jigucchantā* (C[e] *-tī*) *ti imassa pacchato āgatā ti ettakena pi jigucchamānā sasīsaṃ nimujjanti bhāyanti, pag eva phuṭṭhavanto*. PED (s.v. *puṭṭhavant*) compares AMg *puṭṭhavaṃ*, but does not note that the AMg form is passive, not active as here: "they wash themselves before ever touching it", i.e. without touching it. The mere fact of walking behind the corpse makes them feel defiled. Clearly we require a middle form; they wash themselves, not the corpse, and so Mrs Rhys Davids' translation (Sist., p. 168) adopts this reading, but see the note on **265**. We could get the same result by reading *nhāya*[*n*]*te* (or *nhāya*[*n*]*tî*) §§ 68(a)(ii), 70(d)).

Thī-a 259,11–12: *niyakā mātā-pitaro ti attano mātā-pitaro pi*.

Thī-a 259,12–13: *kim pana sādhāraṇā janatā ti itaro pana samūho jigucchatī ti kim eva vattabbaṃ*. Cf. Pkt *sāmaṇṇa-jaṇa* "common people" (Ratnāvalī, ed. Lehot, p. 61 line 28).

470. The editions vary in their readings for pāda c. Alsdorf quotes a C^e reading *kheḷ'-ass'-uccāra-passava-paripuṇṇe*, which seems to be the most satisfactory.

Pādas cd are therefore *vipulā*, but the fourth gaṇa is not ⏑ ⏑⏑ ⏑ (§ 57(b)). For *u[c]cāra* m.c. see § 65(b). For *passăva* m.c. see § 72(d). For *nh-* not making position in *nhāru* see § 74(e).

For *saṃghāta* in place of the usual *saṃghāṭa* see PED (s.v. *saṅghāta*).

Thī-a 259,14: *ajjhositā ti taṇhā-vasena abhiniviṭṭhā.*

471. Alsdorf (App. II, p. 246, n.) asks whether we should take *gandhassa* as a gneitive after *jigucchheyya*. The cty explains: *gandhaṃ assa kāyassa asahantī.* We should therefore punctuate *gandh' assa* with B^e.

We should probably take *yo* in the sense of *si quis*. See the note on **282**.

472. Pāda a is śloka; pādas bcd are āryā. B^e and C^e read *dukkhaṃ* in pāda b, correctly (§ 57(c)).

For *dhāreyyaṃ* as a v.l. for *vāreyyaṃ* see the note on **464**. For *kissa* = *kena kāraṇena* see the note on **467**.

B^e and C^e read *anuvicinantī* for *aruciṃ bhaṇanti*. PED does not list *anuvicinā̆ti*, although the verb is quoted s.v. *anuvicinaka*. See CPD (p. 558, s.v. *anuvicinā̆ti*). The cty explains: *cintayantī* (*M vinayanti*).

Thī-a 259,20–26: *khandha-dhātu-āyatanan ti rūpa-kkhandhāyo ime pañca khandhā cakkhu-dhātu-ādayo imā aṭṭhārasa dhātuyo cakkhāyatanādīni imāni dvādasāsayatanāni ti evaṃ khandha-dhātuyo āyatanāni cā ti sabbaṃ idaṃ rūpārūpa-dhamma-jāta-sacca-sambhuyya-paccayehi katattā saṃkhataṃ na-y-idaṃ tasmiṃ bhave pavattamānaṃ dukkhaṃ, jāti-paccayattā jātimūlakan ti. evaṃ yoniso upāyena anuvicinantī cintayantī, vāreyyaṃ vivāhaṃ, kissa kena kāraṇena icchissāmi.*

For *yonisŏ* m.c. see § 72(d). We must also read *saṃkhâtaṃ* m.c. (§ 70(d)).

473. Thī-a 258,29–30 explains *tisattisatāni navanavā* as *tāvad-eva pīta-nisitabhāvena abhinavā*, where the meaning of *pīta* is not clear (see PED s.v.). IBH (MLS I p. 335) translates "whetted sharp".

Thī-a 259,31–33: *vassa-satam pi ca ghāto seyyo ti nirantaraṃ vassa-satam pi patamāno yathā-vutto satti-ghāto seyyo. dukkhassa c' evaṃ khayo ti evaṃ ce vaṭṭa-dukkhassa parikkhayo bhaveyya.* B^e and C^e read *c' eva⟨ṃ⟩*, and although we must read *c' eva* m.c. (§ 68(b)(i)), clearly this stands for *ce evaṃ*. This would seem to be a reference to the same statement that appears in M III 166, that the *dukkha* of being stabbed by 300 *satti* is as nothing when compared with the *dukkha* of remaining in *niraya* [IBH].

Thī-a 260,4–7 (ad **474**) gives a paraphrase: *yo puggalo anamataggaṃ saṃsāraṃ aparimānaṃ ca vaṭṭa-dukkhaṃ dīpentaṃ satthuno vacanaṃ viññāya ṭhito yathā-vuttaṃ satti-ghāta-dukkhaṃ sampaṭiccheyya, tena c' eva vaṭṭa-dukkhassa parikkhayo siyā ti.*

For *divasĕ* m.c. see § 72(d). For *pateyyu[ṃ]* m.c. see § 68(b)(iii). For *tĭ-* (with Bᵉ Cᵉ Kᵉ and Sᵉ) m.c. see § 72(d). For *satā[ni]* m.c. see § 67(c). For *-sattî-* m.c. see § 70(d).

474. Pāda c as read by P is unmetrical. P gives the v.l. *dīgho te saṃsāro* which is metrical but makes no sense. Bᵉ quotes the v.l. *vo* for *tesaṃ*, which makes excellent sense. For the alternation *vo/te* see the note on **441**. For the dittography in *saṃ saṃsāro* cf. the notes on **435** and **467**.

For *eva[ṃ]* m.c. see § 68(b)(ii).

475–76. For *deva* "deity" see the note on **31–32**.

475. Thī-a 260,10: *asura-kāye ti kāla-kañjakādi-petāsura-nikāye.* For the six *gatis* see the note on **456**. For *kāla-kañjaka* see DPPN s.v. *Kāḷakañjakā.* For *asurakāya* "world of asuras" cf. *devakāya* **31–32**.

For *tira[c]chāna⟨ṃ⟩* (= genitive plural of *tiraccha*) m.c. see § 65(b) and § 70(d). For *tiraccha* (not quoted as a noun in PED) see EV I, p. 194 (ad Th 258). For *dīya[n]te* m.c. see § 68(a)(ii). Bᵉ reads *dissare* for *dīyante*, and Cᵉ and Kᵉ read *dissante.* Alsdorf reads *dissare*, but see the note on **265**.

476. Bᵉ and Cᵉ restore *ghātā* at the beginning of pāda a (§ 66(c)). It had dropped out after *ghātā* in **475** by haplography (see also the note on **511**). Alsdorf (App. II, p. 246, n.) suggests reading *klissamānassa*, assuming that *kl-* does not make position (§ 74(f)). It is more likely that we should read *kili[s]samānassa* m.c. (§ 65(b)).

Thī-a 260,16–19: *nibbāna-sukhā paraṃ n' atthī ti nibbāna-sukhato paraṃ aññaṃ uttamaṃ sukhaṃ nāma n' atthi. lokiya-sukhassa vipariṇāma-saṅkhāra-dukkha-sabhāvattā. ten' āha bhagavā: nibbānaṃ paramaṃ sukhan ti* (= Dhp 204).

For *deva* = "deity", see the note on **31–32**

477. For *appossu[k]kā* m.c. see § 65(b) and cf. **457**. For *ghaṭantî* and *jātî-* m.c. see § 70(d). For *ghaṭati* in place of *ghaṭeti* see the note on **461**.

478. Pādas ab are *vipulā* (§ 57(a)). For *abhinikkhamissa[ṃ]* m.c. see § 68(b)(ii).

Thī-a 260,23: *nibbiṇṇā ti virattā*. PED does not list either *nibbiṇṇa* or *viratta* as passive. Cf. the *bahuvrīhi* compound *nivviṇṇakāma* at Utt 14.2 and 19.10.

Thī-a 260,23–24: *vanta-samā ti suvāna-vamathu-*(M *sunava-madhu-*)*sadisā*. See § 35.

Bᵉ Kᵉ and Sᵉ read *tālă-*; Sᵉ reads *-gatā* (for the alternation *k*/*g* see the note on **101**). For *tălā* m.c. see § 72(d). PED (s.v. *tāla*) suggests that *tālāvatthu-kata* is the correct reading: "a palm rendered groundless, i.e. uprooted". Such a translation seems improbable, since the compound would presumably mean "made into the non-site of a palm-tree, i.e. resembling the place where a palm-tree used to be". Nowhere, however, does any cty support the idea of *avatthu* occurring in the compound.

Thī-a 260,24: *tāla-vatthu-katā* (Cᵉ *tālā-*) *ti tālassa patiṭṭhāna-*(M *chindita-ṭṭhāna-* Cᵉ *ṭhita-ṭṭhāna-*)*sadisā*. *Tālāvatthu*, without *kata*, occurs at S I 69 Ja V 267. Spk I 134 explains: *tālāvatthu bhavanti te ti te bhikkhu-tejasā daḍḍhā vatthu-mattāvasiṭṭho matthaka-chinna-tālo viya bhavissanti,* i.e. like a palm-tree with its tuft of leaves (see MW, s.v. *mastaka*) cut off, having merely its *vatthu* (trunk, base?) left. The reference to the *matthaka* being cut off presumably precludes the actual uprooting, but implies that the tree cannot continue to grow, cf. *seyyathā pi tālo matthaka-cchinno abhabbo puna virūḷhiyā, evam eva kho ye āsavā ... ucchinna-mūlā tālāvatthu-katā āyatiṃ anuppāda-dhammā ti* (M I 250). Spk-pṭ (Bᵉ) I 173, however, seems to take *vatthu* as "site": *vatthu-mattāvasiṭṭho ti ṭhānam eva nesaṃ avasissati*: *sayaṃ pana sabbaso saha dhanena vinassantī ti* [LSC]. Ja V 273 explains: *tālavatthū ti diṭṭha-dhamme pi chinna-mūla-tālo viya mahā-vināsaṃ patvā niraye nibbattanti*. Ps II 115 (ad M I 139) gives both explanations: *tālāvatthu-katā ti sīsa-cchinna-tālo viya katā. samūlaṃ vā tālaṃ uddharitvā tālassa vatthu viya katā. yathā tasmiṃ vatthusmiṃ puna so tālo na paññāyati, evam puna apaññatti-bhāvaṃ nītā ti attho*. Spk II 69 (ad S II 62) is very similar: *tāla-vatthu viya katāni, puna avirūhanaṭṭhena matthaka-chinna-tālo viya. samūlaṃ tālaṃ uddharitvā tassa patiṭṭhita-ṭṭhānaṃ viya ca katānī ti attho*. Sp 132–33 (ad Vin III 2) (= Mp IV 78 (ad A IV 173) = Nidd-a I 170 (ad Nidd I 53)) similarly gives two explanations: *tāla-vatthu viya nesaṃ vatthu katan ti tālāvatthu-katā. yathā hi tāla-rukkhaṃ samūlaṃ uddharitvā tassa vatthu-matte tasmiṃ padese kate na puna tassa tālassa upatti paññāyati, evaṃ ariya-magga-satthena samūle rūpādi-rase uddharitvā tesaṃ pubbe uppanna-pubba-bhāvena vatthu-matte citta-santāne kate, sabbe pi te tālāvatthu-katā ti vuccanti. avirūḷhi-dhammattā vā matthaka-cchinna-tālo viya katā ti tālāvatthu-katā, yasmā pana evaṃ tālāvatthu-katā anabhāva-katā* (v.l. *-gatā* (for the alternation *k*/*g* see the note on **101** and CPD, s.v. anabhāva)) *honti, yathā nesaṃ pacchā-bhāvo na hoti tathā katā honti,* *tasmā āha anabhāva-katā ti.* Mp II 223 (ad A I 135) gives only one explanation: *tāla-vatthuṃ viya kataṃ, matthaka-cchinna-tālo viya puna avirūḷhi-sabhāvaṃ katan ti attho.*

The cties are accordingly giving two explanations: one that the tree has been torn up by the roots, so that only its site is left; the other that its top has been cut off, so that only its base is left. The inclusion of the word *matthaka* in the explanation leads me to suggest that *vatthu* is in fact a corruption of **matthu* < *mastu*. In Skt *mastu* has the same meaning as *mastaka* only in *mastu-luṅga(ka)* "brain" (MW, s.vv.), but in BHS we find *tāla-mastur iv' ūhataḥ* as a variant for pāda b in Udāna-v 10.13; *yasya tv ete samucchinnās tāla-mastakavad dhatāḥ*, cf. *yasya doṣāḥ samucchinnās tāla-mastakavad dhatāḥ* (with no v.l.) Udāna-v 29.9. I should therefore translate *tāla-vatthu-kata* "made into the top of a palm-tree, i.e. treated like the top, i.e. cut off".

There is some evidence that the phrase was not entirely understood in BHS. At Mvu III 360 occurs: *uddaliyatu imaṃ nagaraṃ, kālavastuṃ karīyatu.* Edgerton (BHSD, s.v. *kāla-vastu*) translates "abode of death, i.e. place of destruction", and is inclined to accept PED's suggestion that *kāla-* is here a corruption of *tāla-*. If this is so, then it probably arises from a graphic confusion of *t* and *k*, since there is no likelihood of phonetic confusion as in the examples given in the note on **43**. The change could, however, have resulted from an interpretation of *tāla-* as being < *tāḷa-* < *tāḍa-*, i.e. *tāla-vatthu* = "in place of beating, punishment, death".

479. I take *ca* ... *ca* here and in **481–82** to mean that the two actions occurred simultaneously. For this usage in Skt see MW (s.v. *ca*).

For *eva[ṃ]* m.c. see § 68(b)(ii). For *yassa* ⟨*sā*⟩ (with B[e] and C[e]) m.c. see § 66(c). For *Anîkaratta* (with B[e]) m.c. see § 70(d) and the note on **462**.

K[e] and S[e] read *pĭ taruṇāvuto* for *pītaruṇāvuto*. For the readings of the other editions see Alsdorf (App. I, p. 247, n.). We should read *pĭ taruṇă-vuto* m.c. (§ 72(d)). The entry in PED (s.v. *pīta*[2]) should be deleted.

For the v.l. *dhāreyya* in P see the note on **464**.

480. B[e] reads *Sumedhā* in pāda b, correctly (§ 57(c)).

In pāda c we must either read ⟨*ca*⟩ *pidhatvā* or *pid⟨a⟩hitvā* (with B[e]) m.c. (§ 66(c)).

Thī-a 260,25–26: *athā ti pacchā mātā-pitūnam attano ajjhāsayaṃ pavedetvā Anīkarattassa ca āgata-bhāvaṃ sutvā.* For the past participle *āgata* as an action noun in the compound *āgata-bhāva* "state of arrival" see the note on **261**.

481. I take *ca* ... *ca* in pādas ab to express the contemporaneity of the two actions. See the note on **479**. In pāda c B^e reads *va* for *ca*, and this reading should be adopted. For the alternation *c/v* see the note on **12**.

Thī-a 261,2–5: *anicca-saññā su bhāvetī ti jhānato vuṭṭahitvā jhānaṃ pādakaṃ katvā vipassanaṃ paṭṭhapetvā yaṃ kiñci rūpan ti ādinā aniccānupassanaṃ suṭṭhu bhāveti. anicca-saññā-gahaṇen' evam ettha dukkha-saññādīnam pi gahaṇaṃ katan ti veditabbaṃ.* B^e reads *-saññaṃ*, with a note "*-saññā sabbattha*". The singular would certainly be more usual in such a context.

It is unlikely that *su* could = *suṭṭhu* in this context. I would suggest that it is to be derived < Skt *sma*, and that it gives the force of a past tense to the present tense *bhāveti*. See the notes on **204 255**.

For *tahi*[*ṃ*] m.c. see § 68(b)(ii). For *Anîkaratto* m.c. (with B^e) see § 70(d).

482. I take *ca* ... *ca* in pādas ab to express the contemporaneity of the two actions. See the note on **479**.

For *manasī-karotî, āruhî, katañjalî* m.c. see § 70(d). For *Anîkaratto* (with B^e) m.c. see § 70(d) and the note on **462**.

For *āruhi* m.c. see § 71. **???**

483. For pādas abc cf. **464**abc. Pādas ab are *vipulā*, but the fourth gaṇa is not ⏑ ⏓ ⏓ ⏑ (§ 57(b)). B^e and C^e read *si* for *pi*, which seems to make better sense and should be adopted. For the alternation *p/s* see the note on **6**. For [*su-*]*dullabhā* (with B^e K^e and S^e) m.c. see § 67(c).

484. For *ni*⟨*s*⟩*saṭṭhaṃ* (with C^e) m.c. see § 64(b). For *ahosî* m.c. see § 70(d). For *du*[*k*]*khitā* m.c. see § 65(b).

485. Thī-a 261,18: *mā kāme abhinandī ti vatthu-kāme* (M *-kāmehi*) *kilesakāme mā abhinandi*. The reading *-kāmehi* in M might possibly be an attempt to explain *kāme* as an instrumental plural in *-e* < *-ais* (see EV I, p. 149 (ad Th 49) and p. 163 (ad Th 102)), but it is more likely to be a mistake, since *abhinandati* seems to be constructed with the accusative elsewhere in both Skt and Pāli (see MW and PED s.v.).

For *abhinandî* (with C^e) m.c. see § 70(d). For *-u* > *-v* in *kāmesv* see the note on **226**.

486. Thī-a 261,22: *Mandhātā ti evaṃnāmo rājā kāmabhogīnaṃ aggo aggabhūto āsi*. For the story of Mandhātar see Ja II 311 foll.

For *-bhoginaṃ* m.c. see § 71. For *a⟨t⟩titto* m.c. see § 64(b) and the note on **243**, and cf. **487**d. For [*āsi*] m.c. see § 67(c). For *kāla*[*ṅ*]*-kato* (with K^e and S^e) m.c. see § 68(a)(ii).

487. Pādas abd are āryā; pāda c is śloka. Pādas ab are *vipulā* (§ 57(a)).

Thī-a 261,30: *vuṭṭhimā ti devo*. See EV I, p. 129 (ad Th 1).

For the ten directions cf.

> *disā catasso vidisā catasso,*
> *uddhaṃ adho, dasa disatā imāyo* (Sn 1122)

In pāda c *ca* seems to be used in its disjunctive sense. See the note on **55**.

Thī-a 261,32–34: *yathā tvaṃ Mandhātu mahā-rājassa evaṃ sante pi na vijjati titti kāmānaṃ; kāmānam atittā va maranti narā. ten' āha bhagavā: na kahāpaṇa-vassena titti kāmesu vijjatī ti* (= Dhp 186). The idea seems to be that individuals are not satisfied even if a rain of gold coins occurs. King Mandhātar was not satisfied even by a rain of the seven jewels. For the seven jewels see PED (s.v. *ratana*).

For *a⟨t⟩tittā* m.c. see § 64(b) and cf. **486**c. For *vâ* (= *eva*) m.c. see § 70(d) and Alsdorf's note (App. II, p. 247, n.).

488–92. These verses are in śloka metre, but see the note on **492**. They represent a versified version of the ideas expressed in M I 130 144 364 foll. Cf. also S I 128 A III 97.

488. For the similes in this verse see the list of ten similes at M I 130; the first seven are given in detail at M I 364–67.

B^e reads *asi-sūnūpamā* for *asi-sūlūpamā*, and this reading should be adopted. Thī-a 262,1: *asi-sūnūpamā kāmā adhikuṭṭan'-aṭṭhena*. See CPD (s.v. *adhikuṭṭana*).

C^e reads *-ūpamā* for *-opamā* in pādas bc, and Alsdorf adopts these readings.

In pāda c there is resolution of the sixth syllable (§ 60).

PED does not list *kaṅkāla* (read by P and K^e), or *kaṅkhala* (read by C^e), and CPD (s.v. *aṭṭhi-kaṅkala*) reads *-ă-* but Skt has *kaṅkāla* (MW, s.v.).

489. Thī-a 262,4–5: *aghamūlā ti aghassa dukkhassa mūlā kāraṇabhūtā*. Since *dukhapphalā* is a *bahuvrīhi* compound "having pain as the fruit", I take *aghamūlā* here and in **491** as "having evil (misery) as the root", although the cty explanation does not support this.

For *du*[*k*]*kha-* m.c. in pāda d see §§ 59(a), 65(b). For *-pphalā* m.c. see § 64(a).

490. For *rukkha-pphal'* m.c. to avoid the opening ⏓ ⏑ ⏑ – see § 64(a) and the note on **10**.

For *du[k]khā* m.c. see § 65(b). For the scansion of *sup^{i}n'* see § 75. K^{e} and S^{e} read *vañcanīyā* (§ 70(e)), and Alsdorf adopts this reading, although metrically *vañcaniyā* is satisfactory.

491. Thī-a 262,10–11: *rujjan'-aṭṭhena* (M *rujaṭṭhe* C^{e} *rujan'-aṭṭhena*) *rogo dukkhatā-sulabhattā* (M *-sulayo*). *gaṇḍo kilesāsuci-*(M *-āsuvi-* (for the alternation *c/v* see the note on **12**))*paggharaṇato*.

Thī-a 262,11–12: *dukkh'-uppādan'-aṭṭhena aghaṃ*. See EV I, p. 166 (ad Th 116).

Thī-a 262,12: *maraṇa-sampāpanena nighaṃ*. See PED (s.v. *nigha*[2]) and CPD (s.v. *anigha*).

Thī-a 262,12–13: *aṅgāra-kāsu-sadisā, mahābhitāpan'-aṭṭhena*. The word *aṅgāra* is used as a gloss upon *iṅgāḷa-kuvā* in **386**. Th-a II 178,25–27 (ad Th 420) explains: *bhavaṃ aṅgāra-kāsuṃ vā ti kāma-bhavādīnava-vidham pi bhavaṃ ekādasahi aggīhi āditta-bhāvato sādhika-porisaṃ aṅgāra-kāsuṃ viya*. At Mvu III 149 the same simile is used of women.

Thī-a 262,13–14: *bhaya-hetutāya ceva vadhaka-pahūtatāya ca bhayaṃ vadho nāma*.

As in **489**, I take *aghamūlaṃ* as a *bahuvrīhi* compound, in this case in agreement with *bhayaṃ* "fear which has evil (misery) as its root", although the cty gives no support for such an interpretation.

492. For *-du[k]khā* m.c. (with C^{e}) to give the cadence ⏑ – – ⏓ (*pathyā*) see § 65(b) and the note on **37**. For *bhava-gata* see the note on **450**.

For *gacchâātha* m.c. to avoid the opening ⏓ ⏑ ⏑ ⏑ see § 70(e) and the note on **44**. In pāda c there is resolution of the sixth syllable (§ 60). On the other hand both these metrical changes can be avoided if we read *attāno*, since pādas cd are then regular āryā pādas.

493. Thī-a 262,20–21: *ten' āha*: *anubhandhe jarā-maraṇe ti tassa jarā-maraṇassa sīsa-ḍāhassa ghātāya samugghātāya ghaṭitabbaṃ vāyamitabbaṃ*. It seems essential to read *anubaddhe* with Alsdorf. For *ghaṭ-* "to strive" see the note on **461**.

Mrs Rhys Davids must be wrong in translating (Sist., p. 172) "for me whose head is wrapped in flames". The reference is surely to the helper; "what can another do for me, when his own head is on fire?".

For *a[t]tano* m.c. see § 65(b). For *anubaddhĕ* m.c. see § 72(d). For *tassâ* (with P v.l.) m.c. see § 70(d). Although the cty takes *tassa* as referring to *jarā-*

maraṇa (see above), the need for such a (seemingly) feminine form could be avoided if we read *tesaṃ* for *tassa*.

494. Alsdorf suggests reading *chamā* for *chamaṃ* (with P (v.ll.)). Thī-a 262,22: *chaman ti chamāyaṃ*. See the note on **17**.

Be and Ce read *avoca⟨ṃ⟩* for *avoca*, but a first person verb (referring back to the teller of the story) would be out of keeping with the rest of the story, where the third person is used.

Ce reads *avāpuritvāham*. For the alternation *v/p* see the note on **84**.

For *apāpuritvā[na] 'yaṃ* and *disvā[na]* m.c. see § 67(c). For *Anîkarattañ* (with Be) m.c. see § 70(d) and the note on **462**. For ⟨*sā*⟩ *idam* m.c. see § 66(c) and Alsdorf's note (App. II, p. 248, n.). In view of the frequency of the occurrence of *sā* with a first person verb in this text (see the note on **24**), the reason suggested for the loss of *sā* must be suspect.

495. Alsdorf states (App. II, p. 248, n.) that pādas abc are śloka, and pāda d is āryā. If, however, we read *anamata[g]ge*, as in **498**, and do not lengthen *pitu* > *pitū*, then pāda c is āryā.

The cty does not comment on *anamatagga* here, but Thī-a 262,33–35 (ad **496**) explains: *anamataggato, saṃsārassa anamataggattā aviditaggattā*. The gloss *anamata* = *avidita* seems to indicate that Dhammapāla was taking *ana-* as the double negative prefix (= *a-*). See CPD (s.v. [1]*an-a-*) and EV I, p. 310 (ad Th 1089). For *anamatagga* see PED and CPD (s.v.), BHSD (s.v. *anavarāgra*), Brough (GDhp, p. 256), and Burrow, 1979, pp. 42–43.

For *agga* in the sense of "end" cf. Mhv IV 45 *anaggāni bhassāni* "endless talk".

For *bālāna[ṃ]* m.c. (with Ke) see § 68(b)(ii) and the note on **28**. For *anamata[g]ge* m.c. see § 65(b). For *pitû* m.c. see § 70(e).

For *punappuna[ṃ]* m.c. to avoid the opening ⏓ – ⏑ – see § 68(b)(ii) and the note on **74**.

496–99. The references in these verses are, as Mrs Rhys Davids pointed out (Sist., p. 172, n. 2), to the Anamatagga-saṃyutta (= S II 178 foll.).

496. Mrs Rhys Davids drew attention (Sist., p. 172, n. 2) to the fact that the perennial blood-flow is lacking in the Anamatagga-saṃyutta. It is, in fact, there, as she noted later (KS II p. 120, n. 2).

P's reading *samsaritaṃ* would make perfectly good sense if we took it as a past participle used as an action noun (see the note on **261**, and cf. *dukkhe ciraṃ saṃsaritaṃ* Th 1126). But since Be and Ce read *saṃsaratam*, and the cty explains: *saṃsarataṃ, aparāparaṃ saṃsarantānaṃ samsaritaṃ*, it is probable that we should read *samsarataṃ* and take it as the genitive plural of the present participle. The reading *saṃsaritaṃ* doubtless arose because the word occurs at the end of the gloss. A similar alternation *-itaṃ*/*-ataṃ* can be seen in *paññā-jīviṃ jīvitaṃ āhu seṭṭhaṃ* S I 42 214 Sn 181, where Pj II quotes a v.l. *jīvataṃ* which is explained: *jīvantānaṃ*; at Spk I 355 where the lemma includes *kujjhitaṃ* (although *kujjhataṃ* occurs at S I 240) glossed: *kujjhantānaṃ*; and in *vo palāyitaṃ* (B^e *-ataṃ*) Pv 21, glossed: *gacchantānaṃ* (Pv-a 103).

For *aṭṭhīna*[*ṃ*] m.c. see § 68(b)(ii). For [*ca*] m.c. see § 67(c).

For *anamattagga* see the note on **495**.

For *assû* m.c. see § 70(d).

497. Pāda a is unmetrical and we should read *cattāro udadhī* with Alsdorf. For *cattāro* as accusative see Geiger (2000, § 115) and BHSG § 19.16. Pādas cd are *vipulā* (§ 57(a)).

For *aṭṭhīna*[*ṃ*] m.c. see § 68(b)(ii). For *Vîpulena* or *Vepul*[*l*]*ena* m.c. see § 70(d) and Alsdorf's note (App. II p. 248, n.). The same alternation is found elsewhere, e.g. the gloss in Spk-pṭ (B^e) I 168 (ad S I 67): *Vipulo*, *Vepulla-pabbato* [LSC].

498. B^e and C^e read *mātā-mātusv* for *mātā-pitusv*, and it is certain that we must accept this reading (in the form *-mātūsu* [*eva*] m.c. (§ 67(c)), for Thī-a 263,16–19 explains: *Jambudīpo ti saṅkhātam mahā-paṭhaviṃ kolaṭṭhi-mattā badaraṭṭhi-mattā guḷikā katvā tatth' ekekā ayaṃ me mātu, ayaṃ me mātu-mātū ti evam vibhājiyamāne tā guḷikā mātā-mātūsv eva na ppahontī ti.* The inclusion of *mahā-paṭhaviṃ* in the cty's explanation supports Alsdorf's suggestion of reading ⟨*mahā-*⟩*mahiṃ* m.c. (see § 66(c)).

For *anamata*[*g*]*ge* and [*p*]*pahonti* see § 65(b).

For *anamatagga* see the note on **495**.

499. No edition reads *pitusu* at the end of pāda b (with Alsdorf) as the metre demands (§ 57(c)).

Mrs Rhys Davids' translation "squares of straw" (also found at KS II 118) is presumably poetic licence, since *caturaṅgulika* can only mean "four aṅgulas long", as Thī-a 263,25–26 makes clear: *caturaṅgula-ppamāṇāni khaṇḍāni.*

For *tiṇa-kaṭṭha*[*ṃ sākhā*]*-palāsaṃ* m.c. see § 67(c). For *pitû-* m.c. see § 70(d). For [*p*]*pahonti* m.c. see § 65(b).

For *-u* > *-v* in *-pitusv* see § 73(a) and the note on **226**.

500. This simile is from M III 169, as Mrs Rhys Davids pointed out (Sist., p. 173, n. 2). Cf. S V 455 Mil 204 As 60. The cty in fact quotes from M III 169: *vuttaṃ hi etaṃ: seyyathā pi bhikkhave puriso mahā-samudde eka-cchiggaḷaṃ* (C^e *-chiddaṃ*) *yugaṃ khipeyyā ti ādi.* Cf. Skt *mahārṇava-yuga-cchidra-kurma-grīvārpaṇopamā*, quoted by Harināth De, JPTS 1906–1907, p. 174.

C^e reads *sara* for *siraṃ* in pāda c. It is debatable whether this is the correct reading and *siraṃ* has come into the other editions from the cty, or whether *siraṃ* is correct but has been displaced in C^e because of *sara* in pāda a.

Thī-a 264,6–10: *pubba-samudde aparato ca yuga-cchiddan ti puratthima-samudde aparato ca pacchimuttara-dakkhiṇa-samudde vāta-vegena pari-bbhamantassa yugassa eka-cchiddaṃ. siraṃ* (C^e *sara*) *tassa ca paṭimukkan ti kāṇa-kacchapassa sīsaṃ tassa ca vassa-satassa vassa-satassa accayena gīvaṃ ukkhipantassa sīsassa yuga-cchidde pavesanañ ca sara.* B^e and C^e read *pubba-samudde*, which is more metrical (§ 72(d)), and seems to be the reading which Dhammapāla had.

PED does not give the meaning "eastern" for *pubba*, but see MW, s.v. *pūrva*. For *aparato* "to the west" cf. *aparena* (see NPED, s.v.) and Skt *apareṇa*.

For Jain references to this simile see AR s.v. *jugacchiḍḍa*. They show that *pubbasamudde* means "in the eastern sea" and *aparato* means "in the other direction". For a discussion of the Jain parallels and of Bollée's comments on this verse in his review of EV II (Bollée, 1973), see Norman, 1972, pp. 331–35.

In pāda c I follow C^e's reading *sara*, and assume that *paṭimukka* is a past participle passive used as an action noun (see the note on **261**) and the equivalent of Skt *pratimoka* "putting or hanging around" (MW, s.v. *prati-muc-*). The meaning of the pāda is therefore: "and remember the putting around (the neck) of it (= the yoke)".

Pādas ab are *vipulā*, but the fourth gaṇa is not ⏑ ⏕ ⏑ (57(b)). For *sira*[*ṃ*] m.c. (which perhaps supports the reading *sara*) see § 68(b)(ii). For -[*c*]*chiddaṃ* m.c. (with Be) see § 65(b).

501. Pādas ab are *vipulā* (§ 57(a)).

For *rūpa*[*ṃ*] m.c. see § 68(b)(ii). For *kāya-kali* see the note on **458**.

Thī-a 264,16–17: *phena-piṇḍopamassā ti vimaddāsahanato phena-piṇḍa-sadisassa.*

502. Thī-a 264,23–26: *sara kaṭasiṃ vaḍḍhente ti punappunaṃ tāsu tāsu jātīsu aparāparaṃ uppattiyā punappunaṃ kaṭasiṃ susānaṃ āḷāhanam eva vaḍḍhente satte anussara. vaḍḍhanto ti vā pāḷi. tvaṃ vaḍḍhanto ti yojanā.* See the note on *susāna-vaḍḍhana* in **380**.

Thī-a 264,26–28: *kumbhīla-bhayānī ti udara-posanatthaṃ akicca-kāritā-vasena odarikatta-bhayāni. vuttaṃ hi kumbhīla-bhayan ti kho bhikkhave odarikattass' etaṃ adhivacanan ti.* The reference is, as Mrs Rhys Davids states (Sist., p. 174, n. 1), to the similes at M I 459–61 and A II 124. For *kumbhîla-* m.c. (with Bᵉ and Cᵉ) see § 70(d).

503. Thī-a 265,5–8: *kiṃ tava pañca-kaṭukena pītenā ti apariyesanā ārakā pari-bhogo vipāko cā ti pañcasu pi ṭhānesu tikhiṇatara-dukkhānubandhatāya sa-vighāṭattā sa-upāyāsattā kiṃ tuyhaṃ pañca-kaṭukena pañca-kāma-guṇa-rasena pītena.*

For *amata* see the note on **149**.

504. Thī-a 265,12–14: *jalitā kuthitā kampitā* (M *kupitā*) *santāpitā ti ekādasahi aggīhi pajjalitā pakkuthitā ca hutvā taṃ-samaṅginaṃ* (M *-īnaṃ*) *kampanakā* (M *kampanattā*) *santappanakā* (M *santappanattā*) *ca.* It is clear from this explanation that Dhammapāla must have had the same reading as Bᵉ and Cᵉ with *kampitā* for *kupitā*. The pāda is, however, unmetrical, as Alsdorf points out (App. II, p. 249, n.), and he suggests reading *jalitā santāpitā* [*kupitā*] *kuthitā* (§ 67(c)). M (v.l.) omits *kupitā*.

For *parîḷāhā* m.c. see § 70(d).

For *amata* see the note on **149**.

505. Thī-a 265,15–16: *asapattamhī ti sapatta-rahite nekkhamme. samāne ti sante vijjamāne.* Thī-a 266,26 (ad **512**) explains: *sapatta-kara-dhammābhāvato asapattaṃ.*

Thī-a 265,17–19: *rājūhi ca agginā ca corehi ca udakena ca appiyehi ca rājaggi-cora-udakappiyehi sādhāraṇato te sattūpamā vuttā.* Because of the occurrence of *sādhāraṇato* in the cty Alsdorf suggested (App. II, p. 249, n.) the inclusion of this in the text in place of *sādhāraṇā*. This cannot be correct because the line then has one gaṇa too many. If P's reading is retained we have the first and second pādayugas identical, i.e. gīti, cf. **216**. Although PED does not list *sādhāraṇa* in the sense of "like, similar" it exists in Skt in this sense (see MW, s.v.).

Pādas cd are *vipulā* (§ 57(a)). For [*kāmā*] in pāda d m.c. see § 67(c).

506. Bᵉ and Cᵉ read *a-sakāmā* (cf. M (v.l.) *asā-*) *vadha-bandha-dukhāni* (Cᵉ *-dukkhāni*) in place of *vadha-bandho kāma-kāmā dukkhāni*, and Alsdorf accepts this reading. Thī-a 265,24–26: *asa-kāmā* (M *kāma-kāmā* Cᵉ *asatā-kāmā*) *nām' ete asanto hīnā lāmakā ti attho. aha-kāmā* ti *vā pāṭho. so ev' attho. ahā ti lāmaka-pariyāyo. aha-lokitthiyo nāmā ti* (= Ja I 288 (Eᵉ *āsā lokitthiyo nāma*;

cty: *āsā ti asatiyo lāmakā)) ādisu viya*. For *asa* and *aha* see CPD, s.vv. ²*a-sa* and *aha*. Although the cty takes *asa* in the sense of *asat* "not good", I should prefer to take *a-sakāma* as the negative of *sa-kāma* which occurs in Skt, Pāli, and Pkt with the meaning "willing, contented, etc.". I therefore translate "unwilling, discontented": Alsdorf (App. II, p. 249, n.) suggests "involuntarily, against their will".

For *-du[k]khāni* (wth Bᵉ) m.c. see § 65(b).

Thī-a 265,20–21: *yesu vadha-bandho ti yesu kāmesu kāma-nimittaṃ maraṇa-pothanādi-parikkileso. andu-bandhanādi-bandho ca hotī ti attho.*

507. For *daha[n]ti* m.c. in pāda b see (§ 68(a)(ii)). The plural verb doubtless arose because of *dahanti* in pāda d.

508. Thī-a 265,33–34: *puthulomo ti laddha-nāmo maccho*. At Ja IV 466 the word is explained: *puthula-pattehi nānā-macchehi*; Vv-a 191 (ad Vv 40) explains: *pokkharañño puthuloma-nisevitā ti dibba-macchena upasevitā*. Cf. Skt *pṛthu-roman* "having broad hairs or scales, a fish" (MW, s.v.). The references to ornamental ponds and broad scales make it very likely that the fish is the carp. PED does not give the meaning "fish-scale" for *patta*.

For *hetû*, *jahî* (with Bᵉ), and *vihaññâsi* m.c. see § 70(d). For *su⟨k⟩khaṃ* m.c. see § 64(b). For *puthu-lomŏ* and *gilitvă* m.c. see § 72(d).

The fact that *hetu* is to be read as *hetū* lends weight to Senart's suggestion (quoted by Edgerton (BHSD, s.v. *hetu*)) that this usage of *hetu* is to be derived < Skt *hetoḥ*, i.e. an ablative of origin. See Geiger, 2000, § 22. Cf. Th 934c 1123c and 1128a where *hetū* is to be read. Cf. *taṃ kissa hetu*, e.g. A III 303, and Skt *tat kasya hetoḥ* Suv. 80′ 86′.

A similar development of *-u* < *-ū* < *-o* is probably to be seen in *Rāhu* in S I 50–51. Although this makes perfectly good sense as a vocative, the corresponding Skt version, quoted by Waldschmidt (p. 181), probably had *Rāhoś*, i.e. an ablative. For the comparable development of *-u* < *-ū* < *-o* as a genitive see GD, p. 247 (ad *Rāhu gahanā* "from the grasp of Rāhu", Sn 465).

509. Thī-a 266,5 explains *kāmaṃ* as *yadi pi*. For the adverbial use of *kāmaṃ* "rather", usually with an imperative, see NPED (s.v. *kāma*).

M reads *saṅkhāna-* in the lemma in place of *saṅkhalā-*, but this must be a gloss which has crept in, since it is unmetrical.

The other editions (except M (text)) read *kāhinti*, and it is clear from the gloss *karissanti* at Thī-a 265,7 that Dhammapāla had this reading too. I therefore think that P was wrong to introduce *khāhinti* into the text (see § 40 and P, p. 216).

Pādas ab are *vipulā* (§ 57(a)).

510. Alsdorf points out (App. II, p. 249, n.) that the first gaṇa lacks one mora. For such gaṇas see the note on **243**. We could correct the metre by reading *a⟨p⟩pari-* (§ 64(b)), *aparî-* (§ 70(d)), or *apari-⟨m⟩mitan* (§ 64(b)). For *aparî-* cf. the suggestion of *parîlāha* in **504**.

For ⟨*su-*⟩*bahum* m.c. see § 66(c). B^e K^e and S^e read *kāma-yutto*, but we should read *kāma-yu*[*t*]*to* m.c. (§ 65(b)).

PED does not list *paṭinissajati*, but *-sajati* would be the expected form < *-sr̥jati*.

For *kāma-* < *kāme*[*su*] see § 67(c).

511. B^e C^e and K^e read *yesu jarā* and this word division seems preferable. We should certainly accept Alsdorf's suggestion (App. II, p. 249, n.) of reading *jara-⟨maraṇaṃ⟩* m.c. (§ 66(c)), and assuming that *-maraṇaṃ* was lost by haplography (see also the note on **476**). For *jarǎ-* m.c. see § 72(d). For *vyādhî-* and *jātîyo* m.c. see § 70(d).

For *ajara* see the note on **149**.

For *vy-* making position in *-vyādhi-* see § 74(d).

512. For *ajaraṃ* and *-padaṃ* m.c. see § 70(d). For *-mara*[*ṇa*]*-* m.c. (with C^e) see § 67(c). For *asokaṃ* ⟨*ca*⟩ m.c. see § 66(c).

In Alsdorf's text *akalitaṃ* and *nirupapātaṃ* are presumably merely misprints for *akhalitaṃ* and *nirupatāpaṃ*.

For *asapatta* see the note on **505**.

For *amara*, *amaraṇa* and *ajara* see the note on **149**.

513. Thī-a 267,2 includes *pana* in the explanation of *na ca sakkā aghaṭamānena*. For *ca* in the sense of "but" see the note on **55**. For *ghaṭ-* in the sense of "strive" see the note on **461**.

For *bahūhî* m.c. see § 70(d).

For *amata* see the note on **149**.

514. For *-gata* in *saṅkhāra-gata* see the note on **450**.

B^e reads *ca* for *va*, and Alsdorf follows this reading. Thī-a 267,9–10: *kese va* (B^e and C^e *ca*) *chamaṃ chupī* (B^e and C^e *khipi*) ti *attano khaggena chindetvā* (B^e and C^e *chinne*) *kese va* (B^e and C^e *ca*) *bhūmiyaṃ khipi chaḍḍesi*. In this context *va* would seem to make better sense than *ca*. For the alternation *c*/*v* see the note on **12**.

For *anunenty* m.c. see §73(b) and cf. *pamuty* in **248**. Bᵉ and Cᵉ gloss: *saññāpentī*; M glosses *paññāpentī* (cf. the note on **461**). For the alternation *p/s* see the note on **6**.

For *Anîkaratto* (with Bᵉ) m.s. see §70(d) and the note on **462**.

515. For *uṭṭhāy[a]* m.c. see §67(c). For *pabbajitu[ṃ]* see §68(b)(ii). For *-da[s]sā* m.c. see §65(b). Alsdorf prefers to follow Cᵉ 1926 (see App. II, p. 234) in reading an accusative, but a nominative makes perfectly good sense, and seems to have been read by Dhammapāla: *sā ca pabbajitvā vimokkha-sacca-dassā aviparīta-nibbāna-dassāvinī hotū ti attho* (Thī-a 267,14–15).

Bᵉ and Cᵉ read *yācat' assā* for *yāci tassā*. Cf. M's v.l. *yāva tassā* (with the alternation *c/v* (see the note on **12**)). Thī-a 267,11–12 glosses: *assā Sumedhāya pitaraṃ yācati*, which seems to confirm this reading. For *assă* m.c. see §72(d). For *Anîkaratto* m.c. (with Bᵉ) see §70(d).

For *pabbajituṃ* as an infinitive of purpose see Hendriksen, pp. 95–96.

516. Thī-a 267,16–17: *soka-bhaya-bhītā ti ñāti-viyogādi-hetuto sabbasmā pi saṃsāra-bhayato bhītā ñāṇuttara-vasena utrāsitā*.

For *sikkhamānā* see the note on **2**.

Thī-a 267,18–19: *agga-phalaṃ, arahattaṃ*.

Pādas ab are *vipulā* (§57(a)). For *vissajjitā ⟨ca⟩* m.c. see §66(c). For *pabbâji* or *pabba⟨j⟩ji* m.c. see §§64(b), 70(d) and Alsdorf's note (App. II, p. 250, n.).

517. For *abbhuta* see the note on **316**. The cty does not comment on the word here.

Thī-a 267,23: *pacchime kāle ti pacchime khandha-parinibbāna-kāle*. See EV I, p. 291 (ad Th 947) and de Jong's review of EV I.

For *vy-* not making position in *vyākari* see §74(d).

For *pubbe-nivāsa* see the note on **63**.

For *yathă* m.c. see §72(d).

518. All editions except P read *tisso* for *tīṇi*, but Ap (Eᵉ) reads *tīṇi*, and this is also given as a v.l. in the Ap portion of Cᵉ. Although Alsdorf adopts *tisso*, we should really retain the lectio difficilior *tīṇi*. It is not easy to fit a neuter plural into the verse. It would be possible to take *-dānaṃ* as a plural form with *-aṃ* < *-āni* (see EV I, p. 131 (ad Th 2)), but in the context "three gifts of vihāras" is not very likely. I would therefore suggest that *tīṇi* is a feminine plural form. In Pkt *tiṇṇi* is found for all three genders (Pischel, 1900, §438), and in BHS *trīṇi* is found in the masculine and feminine as well as the neuter (BHSG, §§6.14, 6.16, 10.160). For feminine plural forms in *-ni*, cf. *sabhāni* (= *sabhāyo*) Ja IV 223 and

Aśokan *anusathini* in Pillar Edict VII(K). For other examples of the *-ni* ending see Lüders, 1940, pp. 288–91.

For *tīṇî* m.c. see § 70(d) and BHSG § 10.161.

The cty does not comment on *janiyo*, nor is the word found in PED. I presume it is the equivalent of Skt *jani* "woman", which is also found in the Aśokan inscriptions at Kalsi in Rock Edict IX.

Although the mention of the former Buddha Koṇāgamana in this verse may well be taken as implying a late date of composition (see the note on **448–522**), it is worth pointing out that his cult was certainly established earlier than the date of Aśoka, who recorded in an inscription (Hultzsch, p. 165) the fact that he had enlarged a stūpa of Konākamana to twice its previous size. Cf. Th 490 where a list of seven Buddhas is given.

519. For -[*k*]*khattuṃ* (four times) m.c. see § 65(b). For [*ca*] m.c. see § 67(c). For *upapa*[*j*]*jimhā* m.c. see § 65(b).

520. For *-iddhîkā*, *mânussakamhi*, and *itthî-* (with K^e^) m.c. see § 70(d). For *ahumhă* m.c. (with B^e^ and C^e^) see § 72(d). For *mahĕsī* or *mahisī* m.c. see § 72(d) and the note on **448**. For the seven jewels see PED (s.v. *ratana*).

521. Thī-a 268,12–16: *sā va sāsane khantī ti sā eva idha satthu sāsana-dhamme nijjhāna-kkhanti. taṃ pathama-samodhānan ti tad eva satthu sāsana-dhammena paṭhamaṃ samodhānaṃ paṭhamo samāgamo, tad eva satthu sāsana-dhamme abhiratāya pariyosāne nibbānan ti phalūpacārena kāraṇaṃ vadati.* For *samodhāna* cf. Skt *samavadhāna* "the being brought together, meeting" (MW, s.v.). For *khanti* see EV I, p. 303 (ad Th 1029).

B^e^ and C^e^ read *sā va* for *satthu* in pāda b, and the cty's explanation seems to support this reading. It would seem that *satthu* has crept into the text from the cty, but stylistically *sā va* is far superior, since the form of the verse demands a third singular pronoun with each noun.

Thī-a 268,11–12: *so yathā-vuttāya dibba-sampattiyā va hetu, so pabhavo, taṃ mūlan ti tass' eva pariyāya-vacanaṃ.* For *pariyāya-vacana*, cf. Skt *paryāya-vācaka* "expressing corresponding notion" (MW, s.v.). Ñāṇamoli (1994, s.v.) gives the meaning "metaphor, figure of speech" for *pariyāya*. This meaning is not given in PED.

For *hetû* m.c. see § 70(d).

522. Pādas ab are *vipulā* (§ 57(a)).

For *bhava-gata* see the note on **450**.

B^e^ and C^e^ read *karonti* for *kathenti*.

Thī-a 268,21–22: *anoma-paññassā ti ñeyya-pariyantika-ñāṇatāya paripuṇṇa-paññassa sammā-sambuddhassa.*

For *nibbind-* followed by *virajj-* see the note on **26**.

INDEX OF PARALLEL PASSAGES

This index, which does not aim at completeness, includes only parallel passages in Skt, Pkt, and non-canonical Pāli. For identical passages in Th and Thī Stede 1924–27 should be consulted. References for canonical texts can be found by consulting any of the CD-ROM versions of the Pāli canon which are now available.

3 *b*) cf. Mvu III 366
5 *bcd*) GDhp 131 Udāna-v 3.14, 5.17
6 *d*) GDhp 156–59 Udāna-v 1.37, 4.3
8 *cd*) GDhp 127 Udāna-v 31.44
9 *c*) GDhp 127 Udāna-v 31.44
d) GDhp 156–59 Udāna-v 1.37, 4.3
12 Udāna-v 2.9
14 Dhp-a III 117
15 Ud-a 3
c) cf. Udāna-v 33.59 (v.l.)
d) Udāna-v 21.4 (v.l.)
16 *d*) Udāna-v 21.4 (v.l.)
18 *c*) Udāna-v 26.12
e) cf. Udāna-v 33.59 (v.l.)
19 *a*) Nett 35 Dhp-a III 117
b) Dhp-a III 117
20 *d*) Dhp-a III 117
21 *d*) Ps III 137 Udāna-v 15.1
22 *b*) cf. Udāna-v 26.28
cd) Udāna-v 32.41
26 *d*) cf. Udāna-v 31.6
31 *ab*) Dhp-a IV 21 Mvu III 1–2
cd) Dhp-a IV 21
34 *d*) Udāna-v 21.4 (v.l)
35 *d*) cf. Udāna-v 6.9 Mvu II 359
45 *d*) Ps III 137 Udāna-v 15.1
47 *b*) Udāna-v 29.39
c) Udāna-v 32.40–47
d) Udāna-v 32.41
55 *b*) cf. GDhp 72 Udāna-v 32.20 Mvu III 421
61 *d*) GDhp 57 Udāna-v 31.46
63 *cd*) GDhp 5 Udāna-v 33.47
64 *ab*) GDhp 5 Udāna-v 33.47
66 *a*) Udāna-v 28.4
d) Udāna-v 21.4 (v.l.)
76 *b*) Udāna-v 29.39
d) Udāna-v 21.4 (v.l.)
82 *a*) Nett 35 Dhp-a III 117
b) Dhp-a III 117
83 *ab*) Dhp-a III 117
d) Nett 35 Dhp-a III 117
84 *b*) cf. Udāna-v 6.7
95 *b*) cf. Udāna-v 1.41
96 *b*) GDhp 56 Udāna-v 32.10
101 *d*) Udāna-v 21.4 (v.l.)
105 *d*) cf. Udāna-v 33.41
106 *d*) Udāna-v 32.41
109 Thī-a 297
118 *b*) Udāna-v 9.15
139 *c*) GDhp 57 Udāna-v 31.46
140 *ab*) GDhp 156–59 Udāna-v 1.37
143 *b*) cf. Udāna-v 24.16
160 *b*) Udāna-v 26.28
c) Udāna-v 32.40–47
d) Udāna-v 32.41
161 *b*) Udāna-v 4.3
164 *c*) Udāna-v 31.6

171 *a*) Udāna-v 27.33 cf. Divy 164.12
176 *b*) Udāna-v 9.15
182 *c*) GDhp 70 Udāna-v 4.31
d) GDhp 70 Udāna-v 4.31, 26.23, 32.21
186 Udāna-v 27.34 Divy 164.13
d) GDhp 247
189 *c*) GDhp 70 Udāna-v 4.31
d) GDhp 71 Udāna-v 32.32
193 Udāna-v 27.34 Divy 164.13
d) GDhp 247
196 *b*) Udāna-v 29.16
c) GDhp 71–72 Udāna-v 32.20–21 cf. Mvu III 421–22
d) GDhp 71–72 Mvu III 421 cf. Udāna-v 32.20
206 *c*) cf. Udāna-v 8.15
211 *d*) GDhp 127 Udāna-v 31.44
212 *b*) cf. Udāna-v 6.7
215 *d*) Udāna-v 27.33
239 *a*) Udāna-v 1.10
241 cf. Sūyag I.7.15
243 cf. Sūyag I.7.16
246 *cd*) Nett 131 Udāna-v 9.3
247 *ab*) Net 131 Dhp-a IV 21 Udāna-v 9.3
cd) Nett 131 Dhp-a IV 21 Udāna-v 9.4
248 *ab*) Nett 131 Dhp-a IV 21 Udāna-v 9.4
cd) Nett 131 Udāna-v 9.3
262 *ab*) cf. Mvu II 297
277 cf. Dhp-a III 467
278 cf. Dhp-a III 468
279 *a*) cf. Udāna-v 22.11
b) cf. Udāna-v 8.7
c) cf. Udāna-v 8.10
280 *a*) cf. Udāna-v 22.11
b) cf. Udāna-v 8.7
281 *b*) GDhp 24–25 Udāna-v 8.10, 28.8
c) Udāna-v 33.47
282 *ac*) cf. Mvu III 452
283 *ab*) cf. Mvu III 453 Manu 4.7
c) cf. Mvu III 453 Utt 2.30
285 *abc*) cf. Mvu III 453
288 *ab*) Udāna-v 9.3
301 *d*) cf. Mil 369 Mvu II 406
306 *c*) Udāna-v 33.56
309 *d*) GDhp 247
310 Udāna-v 27.34 Divy 163.13
d) GDhp 247
317 *c*) Udāna-v 33.56
319 *d*) cf. Udāna-v 7.11
321 Udāna-v 27.34 Divy 164.13
d) GDhp 247
334 *c*) Udāna-v 33.27
d) GDhp 48 Udāna-v 33.32
336 *d*) cf. GDhp 48 Udāna-v 33.32
337 *c*) cf. Udāna-v 33.27
d) cf. Udāna-v 33.32
341 *b*) GDhp 126 132
343 *d*) cf. Udāna-v 27.20, 24A, 26AC
350 *b*) Udāna-v 29.39
353 *d*) cf. Udāna-v 18.13
364 *d*) cf. GDhp 48 Udāna-v 33.32
468 *bc*) cf. GDhp 153 Udāna-v 1.35
495 *a*) cf. Udāna-v 1.19
507 *cd*) cf. Udāna-v 2.4

INDEX OF NAMES

This index includes the names of persons and places which occur in the Therīgāthā, and also the names of the therīs to whom verses are ascribed and to whom verses were uttered. When a therī's name occurs in her own verses (indicated by an asterisk prefixed to the verse number(s)) in the same form as in the rubric, the reference is not included.

Index of Words Discussed or Quoted in the Notes

An asterisk (*) signifies that the word, or the precise meaning assigned to it, is not given in PED.

bhāvita 222
bhikkhunī 43
bhidura 35
bhujissa 364
bhūmi-vaḍḍhana 380
*bhoga 267

-m- 48
makaci 252
makkhita 268
*magāyati 384
maggayati 384
maccu-jāyin 65
matt(h)a 268
maṇḍa 400
maṇḍita 268
*-matin 107
*matthaka 478
*matthu 478
madhu 54
manta-bhāṇin 281
marituye 418
*mahaṃ 441
mahisī 448
mahesi 60
*mahesikā 397
mahesī 448
māgavika 242
māṇava 112
mānava 112
*-mānin 305
māpakā 259
māmikā 207
māyā 74, 394
Māra 7
maccassu 2
muñcassu 2
mudī 262
muni 53, 205
musalassa 23
mūlaka-kanda 264
mūla-mūlikā 264
medhaga 344

*ya (= si quis) 282, 471
yattaka 25
yattha 35, 225
*yathāpi 437
yathā-bhucca 143
yathāyaṃ 379
yad-atthaṃ 163
yava-pītaka 260
Yāma 197
yāva 25, 31
yuga-chidda 500
yujjassu 5
yuñjassu 5
*yuñjatha 346
yūtha-pa 437
*ye 418
*yo 418
yoga 2, 4
yoga-kkhema 6

-r- 3
raja 371
raṭṭha-piṇḍa 2
raṇa 358
raṇa-kara 358
rāja-rukkha 255
Rāhu-ggaha 2
rittī 265
rindī 265
*rutti 265
*ruppa 394
*ruhati 87
rūpa 26, 294
*rūpinī 419
rūpiya 394
reṇu 371

Index of Grammatical Terms Used in the Cty

ablative: in *-aṃ* 93, 245; in *-assa* 23; in *-āto* 406 420
absolutives: in *-aṃ* (see *ṇamul*); in *-(t)ūna* 447
accusative singular feminine in *-iyaṃ* 283
action nouns: future passive participles as 455; past participles as 261
adverbial accusative 1
adverbial phrases, reduplicated 92
-a + *iva* 116
-am > *-ām* 392
-aṃ < *-ān* 183
-aṃ < *-āni* 518
-āni, accusative plural masculine in 13
aorist, optative used as 393
Aśokan inscriptions, parallels with 12, 13, 128, 271, 418, 447, 518
aspiration 452

bh/g 25

c/dh 7
c/j 378
c/v 12
cadence (*Rathoddhatā*) 252–70
(*Śloka*) —, ⏑ ⏑ ⏓ 28
— — — ⏓ 37
changes of case 2
changes of gender 13, 209
compounds, split 147

dh/c 7
dh/v 7
dittography 435, 467, 474
double negatives 495

-e < *-aiḥ* 374
-e > *-ya* 66
-e, nominative singular masculine in 2, 3
Eastern forms 2, 3, 51, 128
external sandhi 66

feminine accusative singular in *-iyaṃ* 83
feminine locative singular in *-iṃ* 283
first person pronoun with third person pronoun 24
future in sense of potential 424
future in *-s-* 84
future passive participles used as action nouns 455

g/bh 25
g/k 101
gender, change of 13, 209
grammatical terminology (see separate index)

haplography 476
haplography (m.c.) 54
h/t 222

-i > *-y* 248
-iṃ, feminine locative singular in 283
infinitives in *-uṃ ye* 418
-iyaṃ, feminine accusative singular in 283

k/g 101
k/t/y 43

locative singular feminine in *-iṃ* 283

-m- (see *sandhi* consonants)

Some Alternative Readings for Therīgāthā

These alternatives do not include the frequent confusion of *ca* and *va*, the shortening or lengthening of vowels, the writing of a single consonant as double or vice versa, or the addition or omission of *anusvāra*, except where this makes some difference to the syntax, e.g. in compounds. All these points are mentioned in the notes.

2b	*read* Rāhuggahā *for* -ggaho
6a	*read* phassehi *for* phusehi
12a	*read* avasāyī *for* avasāye
c	kāmesu ⟨cā⟩
23a	*read* sumuttikā *for* sumuttike
d	deḍḍubhaṃ vāti *for* daḷidda-bhāvā ti
24b	*read* cicciṭi cicciṭī *for* vicchindantī
25c	*read* negamo *for* nigamo
31a	*read* cātuddasiṃ pañcadasiṃ *for* -ddasī -dasī
51a	[amma]
54a	*read* k' ime *or* kim ime *for* kiṃ me
58b	*read* khandhā 'saṃ *for* khandhānaṃ
67c	⟨n'⟩ acchara-
90c	*read* yathābhūtaṃ *for* tathābhūtaṃ
92b	*read* agārasmānagāriyaṃ
93d	*read* na bujjhi *for* nirajji
95c	*punctuate* purā 'yaṃ
96a	*read* avekkhantī *for* apekkhantī
98a	*read* puttaṃ *for* putta-
99a	*read* santī *for* santiṃ
109c	⟨maṃ⟩ avaca
111a	*read* vata *for* ca
114f	*punctuate* v' ajāniyaṃ
124d	*read* pabbājeh' *for* pabbajiṃ
127c	*read* sattaṃ *for* puttaṃ
129a	*read* tat' āgacchi *for* tato 'gacchi
134a	*read* vasiṃ *for* vīthi-
141b	*read* khandhā 'saṃ *for* khandhānaṃ
149d	*read* phassayiṃ *for* phusayiṃ
155d	*read* phassayiṃ *for* phusayiṃ
158c	*read* bhāvit' *for* ariy'
161c	*read* passe *for* passa
163b	*read* vasuṃ piyaṃ *for* samussayaṃ
171c	*punctuate* bojjhaṅg' aṭṭhaṅgikaṃ
183a	*read* kaṃ *for* kiṃ
186c	ariy⟨aṃ c'⟩ aṭṭhaṅgikaṃ
193c	ariy⟨aṃ c'⟩ aṭṭhaṅgikaṃ
200b	pa[ri]dīpito
201a	*read* akampiyaṃ *for* akampitaṃ
210c	*read* -saṃhitā *for* -saññitā
214b	[pa]vaḍḍhati
d	[pi]
215b	*transfer* nirodhañ ca *from* c
c	⟨ca⟩ maggaṃ
d	⟨pi⟩ ariya-saccāni
217a	gal⟨ak⟩e
	read api kantanti *for* apa-

b *read* sukhumālīyo *for* sukhumāliniyo

218c *transfer* panthe *from* b, *but read* panthamhi vijāyitvā[na]

219c [ca]

221a *read* vasitā *for* passi taṃ

c -kul[ik]a

222a ⟨saṃ⟩bhāvito

d *read* avekkhī *for* apekkhi

223c [su]vimutta-

d ⟨a⟩bhaṇī

225d *read* saha-bhariyā *for* sabhariyā

226b *read* daṭṭhu *for* daḷha-

d *read* agārasmānagāriyaṃ

231a *read* sahassāni *for* -ānaṃ

234b *read* khandhā 'saṃ *for* khandhānaṃ

238a *read* vata maṃ *for* ca tuvaṃ

239a vuḍḍho [vā]

240b *read* ajānantass' *for* -assa

241c *read* nakkā *for* nāgā

243ab *move* te *to end of* b

d [tvaṃ]

253a *punctuate* surabhī karaṇḍako

b *punctuate* uttamaṅg' abhu

c *read* jarāy' atha sa-loma- *for* jarāya sasa-loma-

255a *read* -kaṇḍaka- *for* -gandhaka-

c *read* khalitaṃ *for* khalati

256a *read* lekhiyā *for* lekhitā

257b *punctuate* nett' ahesuṃ

259b [pure]

read -pāliyo *for* -pāḷiyo

260a *read* sattalī- *for* pattali-

c *read* khaṇḍiyā va pītakā *for* khaṇḍā yavapītakā

261a *read* kānanamhi *for* kānanasmiṃ

262a *read* -kambu-r-iva *for* -kampurī va

c *read* vināmitā *for* vināsitā

263c *read* jarāy' abalikā va pāṭalī *for* jarāya yathā pāṭalī dubbalikā

266a *read* saṃmaṭṭhaṃ *for* sumaṭṭhaṃ

269c *read* phuṭitā *for* phuṭikā

270c *read* palepa- *for* 'palepa-

271a [maṃ]

read vissapi *for* vipassi

282b *read* nāvalokenti *for* na vilokenti

293ab *read* kujjhi *for* kujjha

294c *punctuate* itthī rūpena

310c ariy⟨aṃ c'⟩ aṭṭhaṅgikaṃ

311b *read* karitvā *for* katvāna

312b *read* khādemānā *for* khādamānā

313a *read* khādetvā *for* khāditvā

314a -satā[ni]

318a *read* brāhmaṇ' *for* brāhmaṇa

321c ariy⟨aṃ c'⟩ aṭṭhaṅgikaṃ

327a *punctuate* hatthī gavassaṃ

b *read* gaha- *or* ghara- *for* geha-

328a *punctuate* hatthī gavassaṃ

b *read* gaha- *or* ghara- *for* geha-

337d *read* pādāna *for* pādāni

339b *read* bhusaṃ *for* bhūsaṃ

341f *read* āvame *for* āgame

342b *read* santiyā *for* santaye

344d *punctuate* puthu kubbantī

350a *read* mahesīhi *for* mahesinā

363c *read* vinīt' *for* vinītā

371b *read* samuṭṭhitā *for* samuddhatā

374d vasan⟨avar⟩ehi
378b *read* -santhataṃ *for* -santataṃ
379a *read* v' udakā samuggataṃ *for* ca udakato ubbhataṃ
b *read* supphullam *for* yathā yaṃ
d *read* ses' *for* sakesu
383a *read* saramhase *for* saremhase
386a *read* ukkhito *for* ujjhito
b agg⟨h⟩ato
387a *read* yass' assa *for* yassā siyā
390b *read* -pillakāni vā *for* -cillakā navā
391b *read* parukkhite *for* paripakkate
c avind⟨iy⟩e
392a *read* dehakām imaṃ *for* dehakāni maṃ
393d *read* saññā *for* paññā
394c *read* upagacchasi *for* upadhāvasi
398a *read* āsādiya *for* āhaniya
c *read* gaṇhiya *for* gaṇhissaṃ
400b *transfer* maṇḍe *from* c
401b [ca]
d bahussutā[yo]
404a *read* anuyujamānā *for* anuyuñjamāna
c [idaṃ]
d *separate* yathā mhi
405d manāpā ⟨ca⟩
406d adā[si]
407d *separate* yathā mhi
408b parijano ⟨vā⟩
c [taṃ]
409a annena ⟨ca⟩
410b *transfer* ummāra- *from* c, *but read* ummāre
read ⟨pati-⟩ghara(ṃ) samupāgamāmi *for* gharaṃ samupagamiṃ
c *read* dhovitva hattha-pāde *for* -dhota-hattha-pādā
411a pasād⟨han⟩aṃ
412c ekaputta[ka]ṃ
413b *read* anurattaṃ *for* anuttaraṃ [taṃ]
414c [saha]
read sacchaṃ *for* vacchaṃ
d *read* ekaghare *for* ekāgāre
read sahāvatthuṃ *for* saha vatthuṃ
416b *read* sahāvacchaṃ *for* saha vacchaṃ
417b *read* maṃ *for* me
418b *transfer* dubbacanaṃ *from* c [pi]
read hiṃsemi *for* hiṃs' eva
read bhaṇāmi *for* gaṇāmi
c *read* kātuṃ ye *for* kātuye
419ab *punctuate* paṭi-nayiṃsu
b *transfer* avibhūtā *from* c, *but read* adhibhūtā
d *read* jitā 'mhase *for* jināmhase
421b paṭicch⟨ur⟩ati
c *read* dās' iva *for* dāsī va
422b dantaṃ ⟨ca⟩
423b *transfer* pontiṃ *from* c
424b [me]
c *read* kīrati *for* karati
read kīrihiti *for* karihiti
425b [me]
read sakkito *for* sakkoti
c *read* sacchaṃ *for* vacchaṃ
d *read* sahāvatthuṃ *for* saha vatthuṃ

428a *read* disvān' amha kule *for* disvāna amhākaṃ
b *read* paññāpayiṃ tassā *for* tassā paññāpayiṃ
433a *read* -pitaro *for* -pitū
d *read* aphassayi⟨sa⟩ṃ *or* okkami ⟨'ha⟩ṃ *for* okkamiṃ
434b *read* yass' ayaṃ *for* yassā yaṃ
read phala-vipāko *for* phalaṃ vipāko
435a Era[ka]kacche
436b *transfer* pakko *from* c
d *read* okkami⟨sa⟩ṃ *or* okkami ⟨'haṃ⟩ *for* okkamiṃ
437a *read* sattāha-jātakaṃ maṃ *for* sattāhaṃ jātakammaṃ
438b *read* katvāna *for* karitvā
d *read* okkami⟨saṃ⟩ *or* okkami ⟨'ha⟩ṃ *for* okkamiṃ
439c *read* kimino vaṇṭo *for* kiminā vaṭṭo
441a *read* voḍhūna *for* te puna
punctuate naṅgala mahaṃ
b dhārayāmī ⟨'haṃ⟩
c *read* vaṇṭo *for* vaṭṭo
445b *transfer* kaññaṃ *from* c
disvā[na]
c *read* orundhat' assa *for* oruddha tassa
446d [haṃ]
447b *read* apakīritūna *for* apa-karitūna
c *read* dās' iva *for* dāsī va
d *read* me *for* mayā
448b *read* -mahisīya *for* -mahesiyā
d *read* pasāditā *for* pāsādikā
449a -kath[ik]ā
450a *read* nibbānābhiratâhaṃ *for* nibbānābhiratā ahaṃ
c [aṅga]
452b *transfer* sadā *from* c, *but read* 'sad⟨dh⟩ā
c kāyena ⟨ca⟩
454a [amma]
c [ye]
d *read* pihenti *for* pihanti
456b d⟨u⟩ve
460c *read* āharisāmi *for* āhariyaṃ
461b [sabbaso]
c *read* ghaṭatī *for* ghaṭenti
462a *read* putti *for* puttaka
463a *read* mahisī *for* mahesī
d *read* putti *for* puttaka
464b *read* si *for* pi
d *read* putti *for* puttaka
465d *read* me na *for* tena
[c' eva]
466a *read* kimi va *for* kim iva
b *read* sāvaṇa- *for* savana-
transfer kuṇapaṃ *from* c
c *read* bhastaṃ *for* gattaṃ
467b *read* -soṇit'-upalittaṃ *for* -soṇita-palittaṃ
c *read* kimi-kulala-sakuṇa- *for* kimikulālayaṃ sakuna-
468c *read* chuddho *for* chuṭṭho
470c *read* kheḷ'-ass'-uccāra-passava- *for* kheḷass'-umucchāssava-
471c *punctuate* gandh' assa
472b *transfer* dukkhaṃ *from* c
c *read* anuvicinantī *for* arucim bhaṇanti
473ab *read* ti-satti-satā[ni]
474c *read* vo *for* tesaṃ
475b *read* tiracchāna⟨ṃ⟩ yoniyā *for* tiracchānayoniyā
d *read* dissante *for* dīyante

476a ⟨ghātā⟩ nirayesu
477c *read* ghaṭantī *for* ghaṭenti
479b yassa ⟨sā⟩
c *read* pi taruṇa-vuto *for* pītar-uṇāvuto
480b *transfer* Sumedhā *from* c
c pāsādaṃ ⟨ca⟩
481d *read* -saññaṃ *for* -saññā
483b *read* si *for* pi
d [su-]dullabhā
488a *read* asisūnūpamā *for* asisūlūpamā
493c *read* anubaddhe *for* anubandhe
494a *read* apāpuritvā[na 'yaṃ] *for* apāpuṇitvāna 'yaṃ
c disvā [na]
read chamā *for* chamaṃ
d rodante ⟨sā⟩
496c *read* saṃsarataṃ *for* saṃsaritaṃ
d [ca]
497a *read* cattāro udadhī *for* caturo 'dadhī
d *read* Vepulena *for* Vipulena
498b ⟨mahā⟩mahiṃ
d *read* mātā-mātūsu *for* mātā-pitusv
[eva]
499a *read* tiṇa-kaṭṭha-palāsaṃ *for* tiṇa-kaṭṭhaṃ sākhā-palāsaṃ
b *transfer* pitusu *from* c
500b *read* pubba-samudde *for* pubbe samudde
504d [kupitā]
read santāpitā kuthitā *for* kuthitā santāpitā
505d [kāmā]
506c *read* asakāma *for* kāmakāmā
d *read* vadha-bandha-dukhāni *for* vadha-bandho dukkhāni
509c *read* kāhinti *for* khāhinti
510b ⟨su⟩bahūni
c *read* kāma-yuto *for* kāmesu yutto
511b *read* yesu jara-⟨maraṇaṃ⟩ *for* ye sujarā
512b -mara[ṇa]-
asokaṃ ⟨ca⟩
514c *read* anunenty *for* anunentī
515a *read* uṭṭhāy' *for* uṭṭhāya
b *read* yācat' assā *for* yāci tassā
d *read* -dasaṃ *for* -dassā
516a vissajjitā ⟨ca⟩
519b [ca]
520c *read* mahisī *for* mahesī
521b *read* sā va *for* satthu